The
Non Sequitur
Legal Lampoon

The *Non Sequitur* Legal Lampoon

A Biased, Unfair, and Completely Accurate Law Review from Non Sequitur

By Wiley

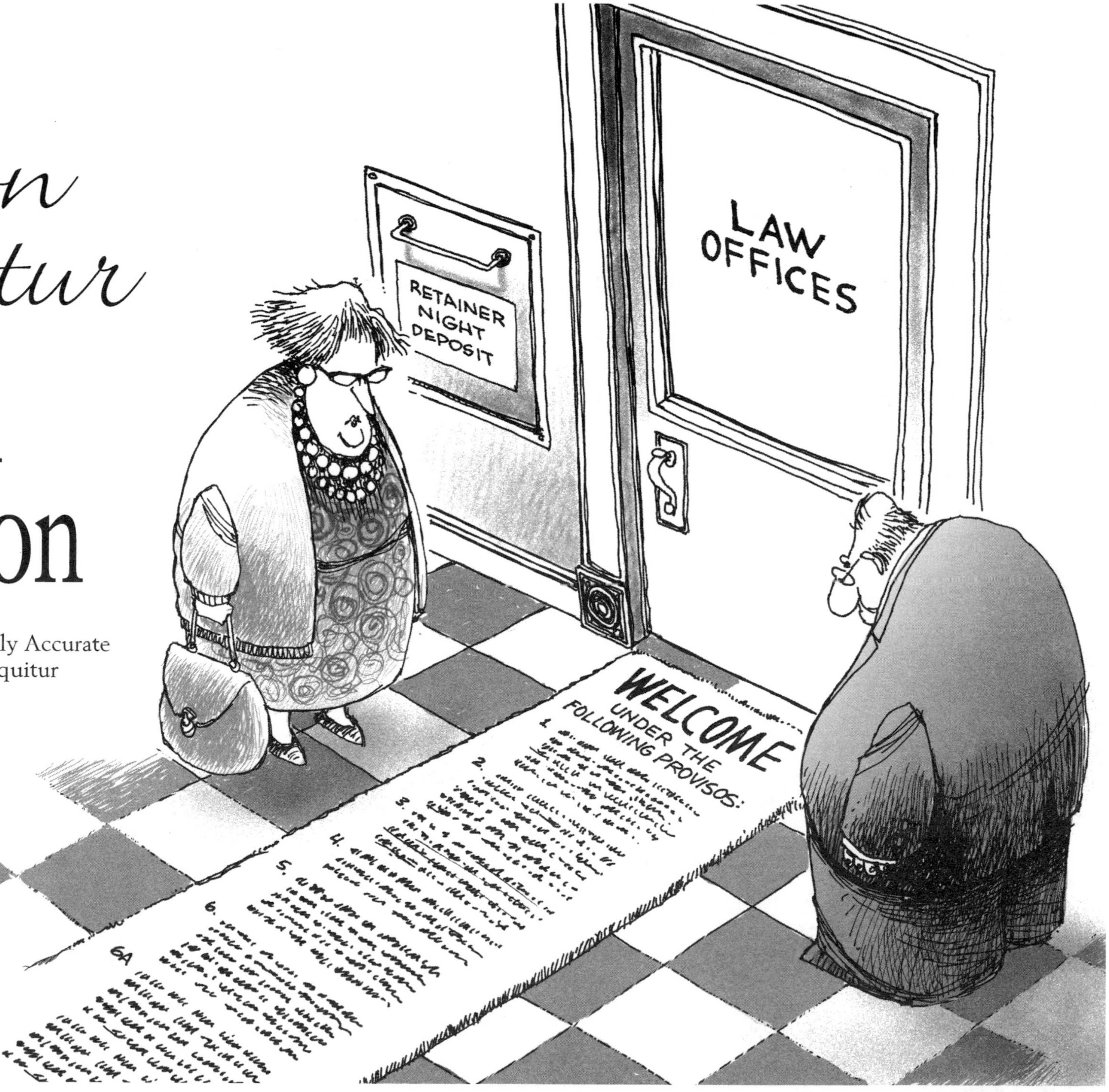

LAW OFFICES
RETAINER NIGHT DEPOSIT
WELCOME
UNDER THE FOLLOWING PROVISOS:

Andrews McMeel Publishing

Kansas City

Non Sequitur is distributed internationally by Universal Press Syndicate.

02 03 04 05 06 QUD 10 9 8 7 6 5 4 3 2 1

ISBN: 0-7407-2673-0

Library of Congress Catalog Control Number: 2002103764

www.uComics.com

Introduction

I was just wondering . . . what does non-sequitur mean? I've attempted
its denotation in at least five dictionaries, and still . . . NOTHING.
Thanks.
—Kat

This, sadly, is an actual e-mail I received yesterday. Even more frightening, I get this same question almost on a daily basis. I kept wondering how can people not find it in the dictionary? Has this term, which I always thought was a rather common one, become so obscure in our dumbed-down society that it's not even in the dictionary anymore? Then it suddenly occured to me what the problem is. They're looking under "s" instead of "n." I try not to think that these people vote, although it does explain how we've ended up with the individuals who are in office today.

But at least some of these people made an attempt to educate themselves. The majority of these inquiries come from people who don't even try to look in the dictionary first. They would rather wait to get an e-mail back from me. I guess this is how dependent we've become on the Internet, where normal brain functions freeze up and and we wait passively for some electronic input while munching on a bag of Doritos. Looking something up in a dictionary is now prehistoric and far too labor intensive. I suspect that someday we'll have a USB port installed in our skulls so we can just plug ourselves directly into our computers.

So for all of you who slept through high school English, here's the definition:

non se·qui·tur n.

1. An inference or conclusion that does not follow from the premises or evidence.

2. A statement that does not follow logically from what preceded it.

Now when someone asks that question, I won't get angry or frustrated about the demise of education in this country. I'll just turn the lemons into lemonade by telling them they have to buy my book for the answer! I figure if they're too stupid to look it up in a dictionary, they'll be dumb enough to run out to the bookstore to buy this book. The sheer volume of the vocabulary-challenged out there should guarantee the book's getting on the best-seller list. If you can't beat 'em, profit from them, I always say.

Which brings us to lawyers.

The second most frequently asked question I've gotten over the years is "What do you have against lawyers?" This usually comes from lawyers who don't like seeing themselves in the cartoons and want me to stop. This, of course, only encourages a smart-ass satirist such as myself to do more of them. And the more they squeal, the easier it is to tell if the material is on target.

But it may surprise many that I don't have anything against lawyers, per se. Like any other profession, most lawyers are decent, hard-working people. These lawyers, however, are not the focus of my cartoons, nor that of society's ire on a whole. Nor should they be. Conducting themselves in an honest, decent manner to serve justice is what lawyers are supposed to do. That's the minimum requirement. You shouldn't expect praise for doing the bare minimum of your job.

Besides, decent, hard-working people just aren't funny. They're ordinary, and ordinary isn't very entertaining. Humor and satire are solely dependent on the oddities of the human condition.

Sociopaths, on the other hand, are ideal for entertainment and satire as their complete lack of a moral conscience tends to make you stare at them in stunned bewilderment . . . like a car wreck on the highway. We only notice the bad lawyers and their outrageous courtroom behavior instead of the decent ones for the same reason we don't hear anything about the priests who aren't molesting children or the drivers who make it home without getting into a pileup on the highway.

Our legal system is tailor-made for the ethically deficient, as lawyers are given free reign to say and do things that would land the rest of us in jail. Behavior that would bring charges of extortion against you and me is just standard practice in the legal profession. This is what makes my job so much easier.

For most of us, the only exposure we get to a court hearing is some high-profile case on TV. This is when we see the high-priced defense attorneys weave their magic of half-truths and innuendo, doing everything they can to direct attention away from the issue they're supposed to be dealing with. The last thing a sharp defense attorney wants to deal with is the actual issue. Confusion and obfuscation is the order of the day to confound a jury and attain the goal of "reasonable doubt". . . and pile up the billable hours.

This strategy, of course, is made easier by making sure they have a jury made up of people who can't spell DNA.

And prosecuting attorneys aren't any better when they ignore or hide evidence that they know will help the defense. If you're poor and have to rely on a public defender, your chances of survival are just barely above nonexistent.

Such bad news for the public is good news for satirists. It has been that way since Eve dared Adam to eat the apple. Her serpent attorney said it was okay.

There are many who believe that the bad image lawyers have today was created by the media. This theory, it should be pointed out, is put forth in the most part by the legal profession. Everyone loves playing the victim these days, and the legal community is no different. At first this sounds like a valid point . . . until you think about it for more than a nanosecond.

The truth is, media creates nothing. Never has, never will. Media dorks (like cartoonists and columnists) aren't bright enough to create an image. Media only reflects. If someone doesn't like the image they see, they shouldn't blame the mirror.

This point was emphasized, ironically enough, by the legal profession itself. The ABA Journal conducted an extensive national survey in an effort to find out why lawyers are held in such low esteem. They discovered what most of us already knew: The people who had the lowest regard for lawyers were the ones who had the most contact with them.

So much for being a victim of bad press.

This finding by the *ABA Journal* has been reflected in my mail over the past decade from readers on a regular basis. The people I hear from with the worst image of lawyers are the ones who have more contact with lawyers than anyone else—judges.

Oh, their stories make you wonder how they keep their sanity. And they're all former lawyers!

But don't get me wrong—I don't rail against the legal system with the hope of getting things changed. Quite the contrary. If it weren't for idiocy, there wouldn't be much to satirize and I might have to get a real job.

So I say, let's keep the legal profession just the way it is! Sociopaths are people, too, and should have the opportunity to make a living.

As long as we have semiliterate, ambitionless kids going to college whose only passion in life is to make money, our law schools will always be filled. This will guarantee we'll always have more practicing attorneys than postal employees (yes, it's true). The sheer volume of people in a profession that attracts sociopaths by rewarding anti-social behavior guarantees there will always be work for satirists and screenwriters.

All hail the legal profession! Without it working just the way it is, you wouldn't be reading this book. And for that, I am eternally grateful.

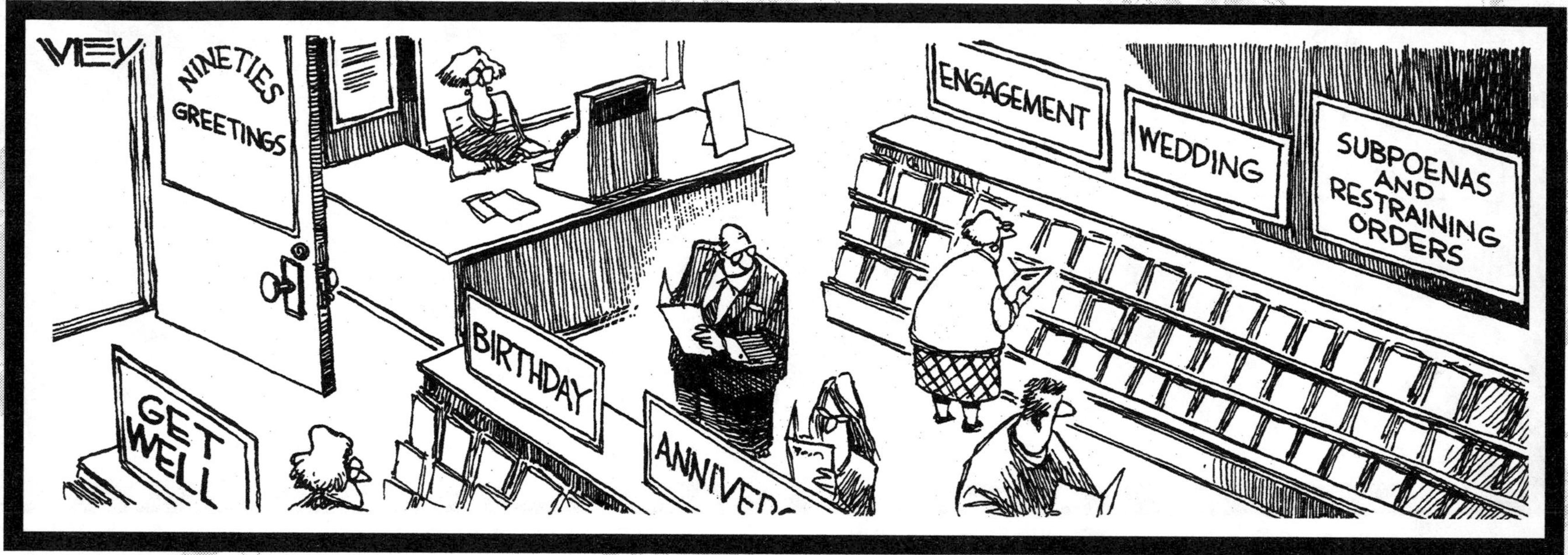
VEY
NINETIES GREETINGS
ENGAGEMENT
WEDDING
SUBPOENAS AND RESTRAINING ORDERS
BIRTHDAY
GET WELL

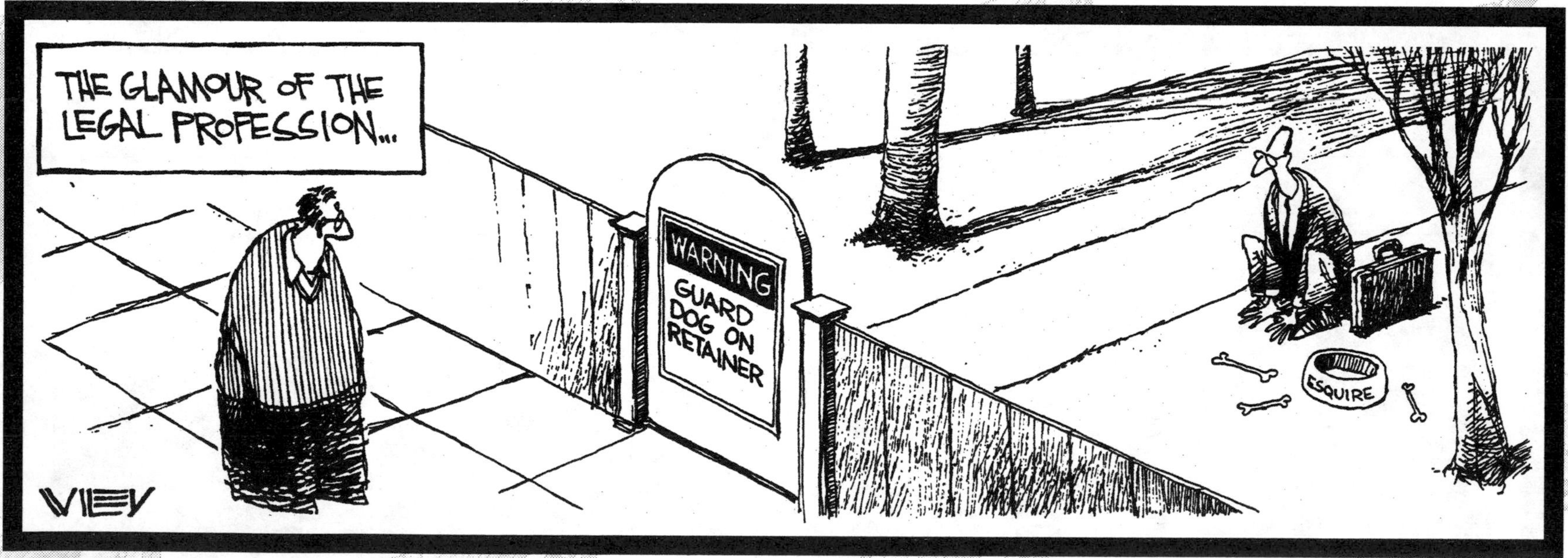
THE GLAMOUR OF THE LEGAL PROFESSION...
WARNING
GUARD DOG ON RETAINER
ESQUIRE
VEY

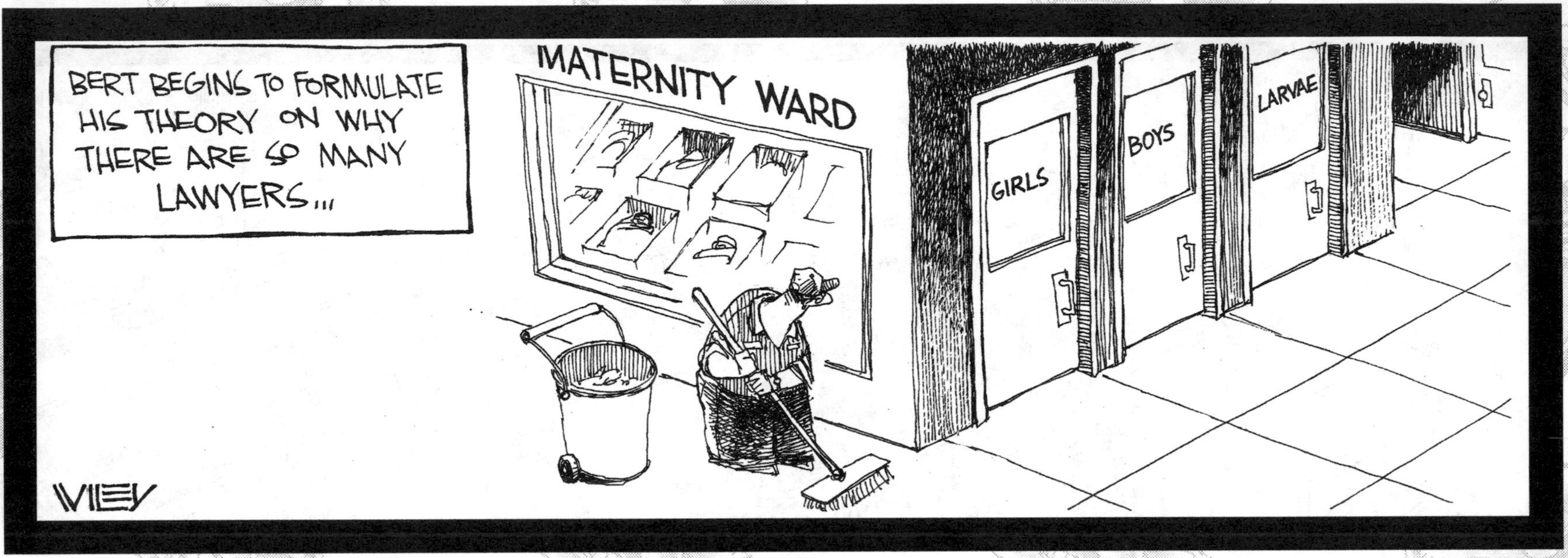
BERT BEGINS TO FORMULATE HIS THEORY ON WHY THERE ARE SO MANY LAWYERS...
MATERNITY WARD
GIRLS
BOYS
LARVAE
WILEY

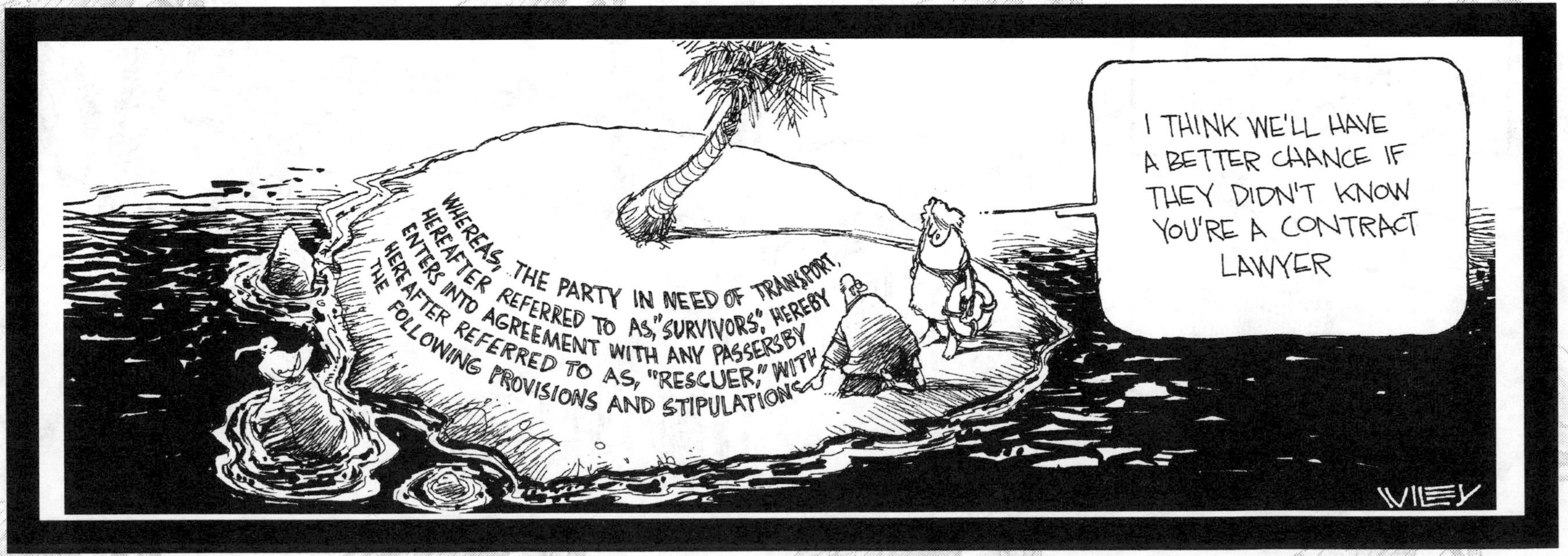
WHEREAS, THE PARTY IN NEED OF TRANSPORT, HEREAFTER REFERRED TO AS, "SURVIVORS", HEREBY ENTERS INTO AGREEMENT WITH ANY PASSERSBY HEREAFTER REFERRED TO AS, "RESCUER," WITH THE FOLLOWING PROVISIONS AND STIPULATION
I THINK WE'LL HAVE A BETTER CHANCE IF THEY DIDN'T KNOW YOU'RE A CONTRACT LAWYER
WILEY

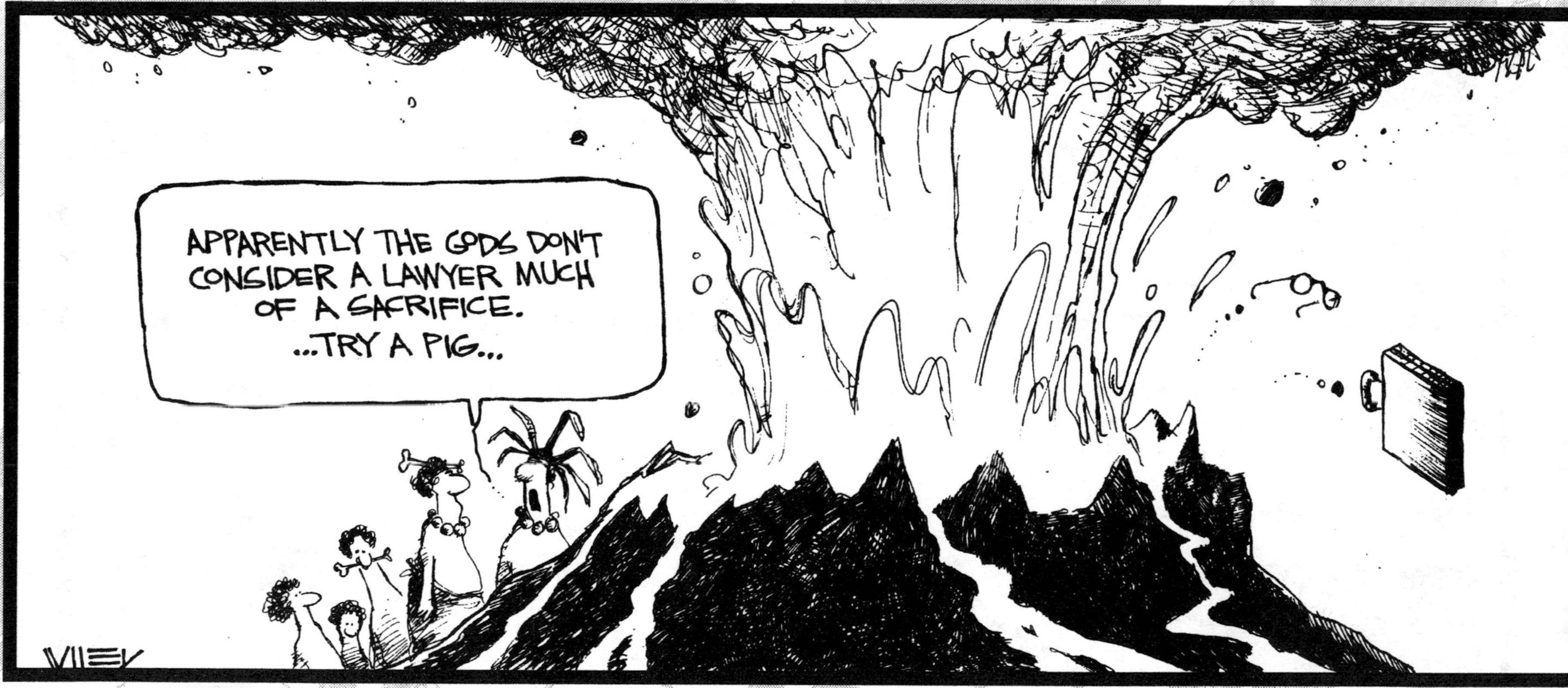
APPARENTLY THE GODS DON'T CONSIDER A LAWYER MUCH OF A SACRIFICE. ...TRY A PIG...
WILEY

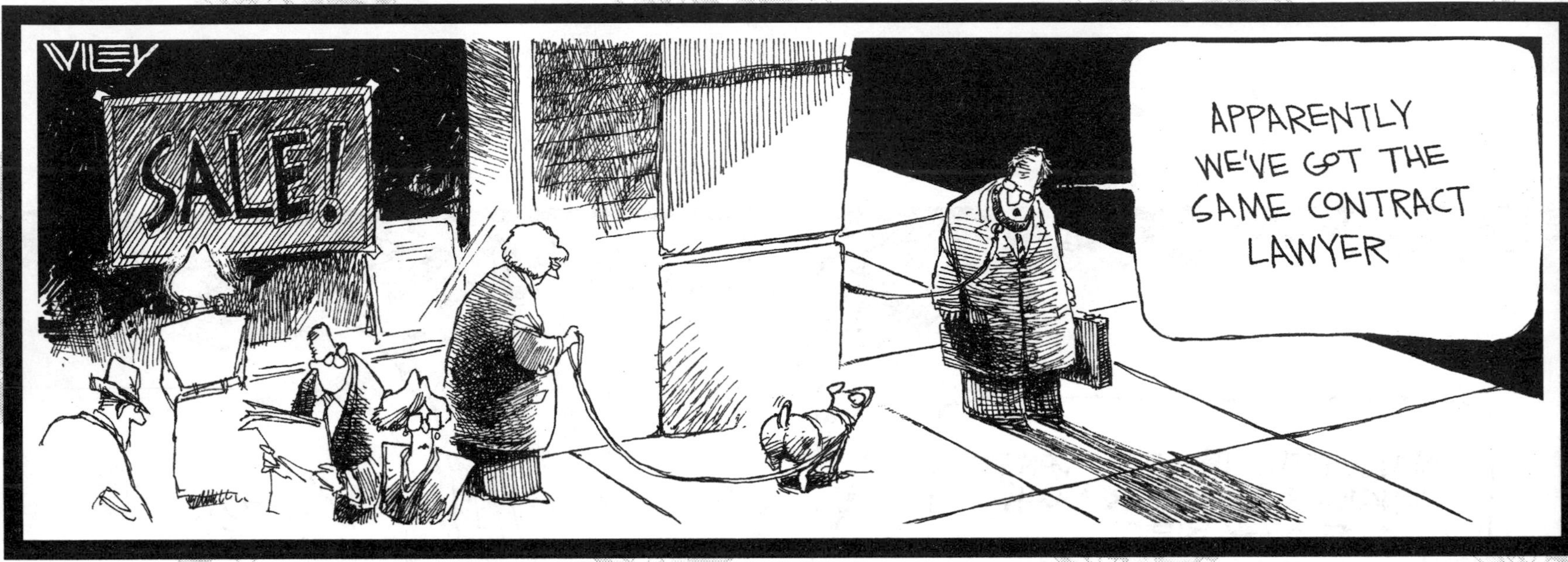
WILEY
SALE!
APPARENTLY WE'VE GOT THE SAME CONTRACT LAWYER

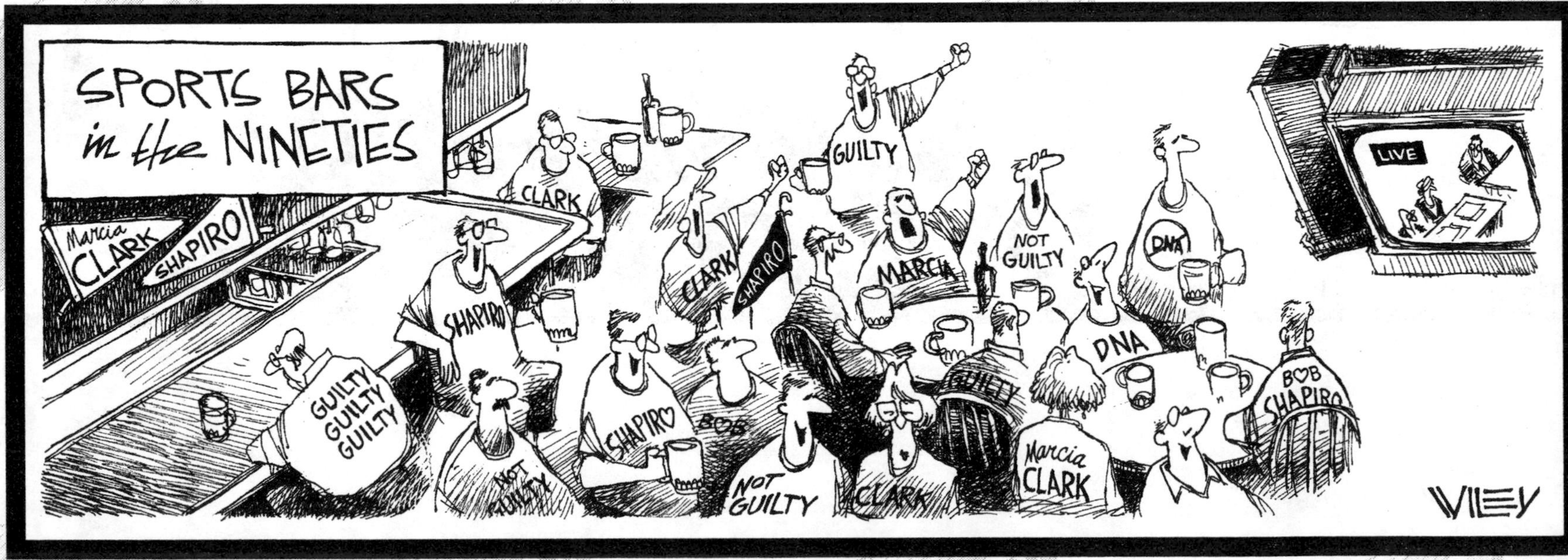
SPORTS BARS in the NINETIES
Marcia CLARK
SHAPIRO
CLARK
GUILTY
LIVE
CLARK
SHAPIRO
MARCIA
NOT GUILTY
DNA
SHAPIRO
DNA
GUILTY GUILTY GUILTY
NOT GUILTY
SHAPIRO
BOB
NOT GUILTY
CLARK
GUILTY
Marcia CLARK
BOB SHAPIRO
WILEY

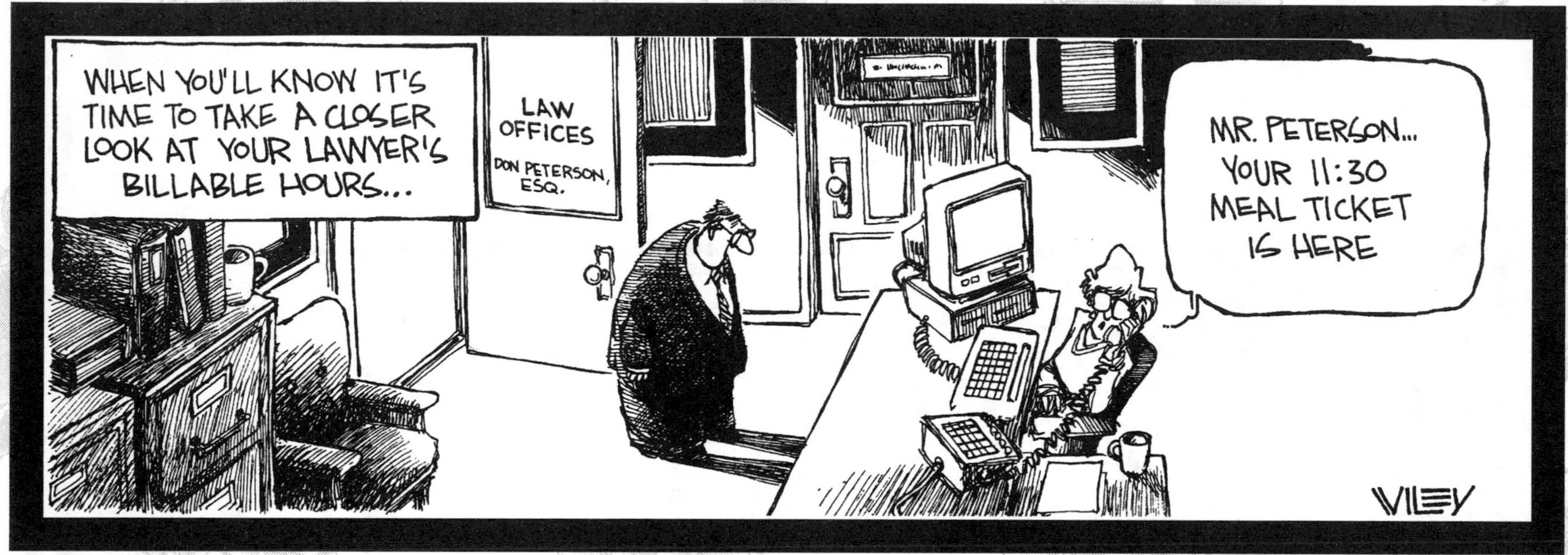
WHEN YOU'LL KNOW IT'S TIME TO TAKE A CLOSER LOOK AT YOUR LAWYER'S BILLABLE HOURS...
LAW OFFICES
DON PETERSON, ESQ.
MR. PETERSON... YOUR 11:30 MEAL TICKET IS HERE
WILEY

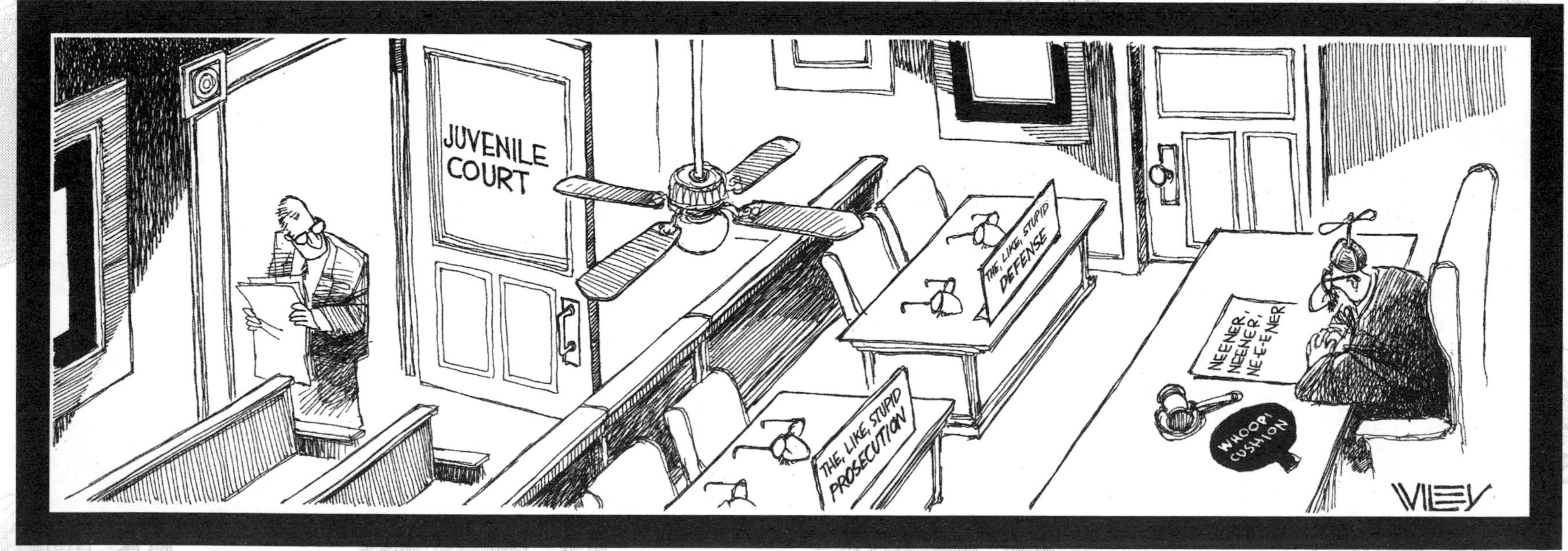
JUVENILE COURT
THE, LIKE, STUPID DEFENSE
THE, LIKE, STUPID PROSECUTION
NEENER, NEENER, NE-E-ENER
WHOOPI CUSHION
WILEY

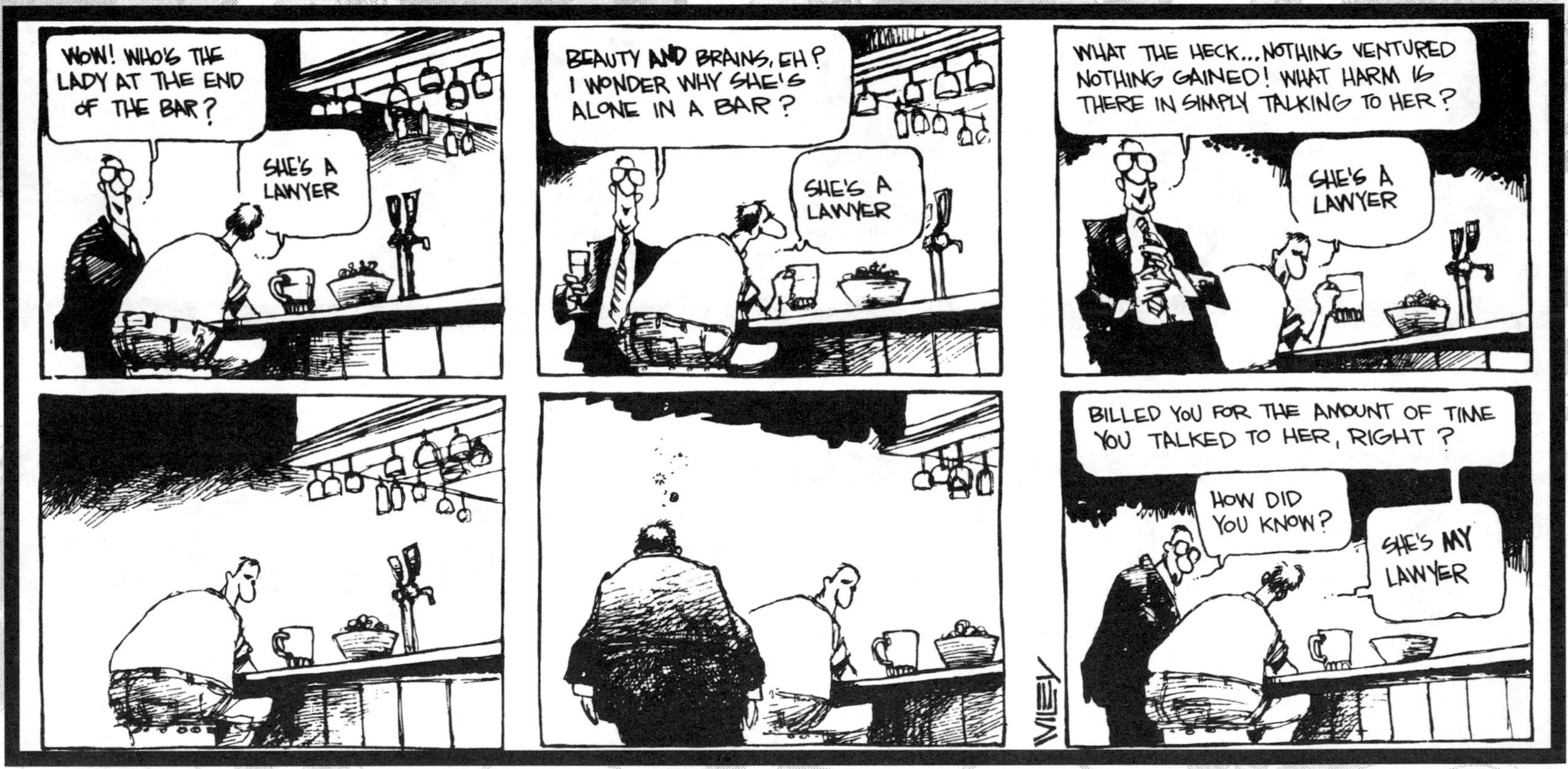
WOW! WHO'S THE LADY AT THE END OF THE BAR?
SHE'S A LAWYER
BEAUTY AND BRAINS, EH? I WONDER WHY SHE'S ALONE IN A BAR?
SHE'S A LAWYER
WHAT THE HECK... NOTHING VENTURED NOTHING GAINED! WHAT HARM IS THERE IN SIMPLY TALKING TO HER?
SHE'S A LAWYER
BILLED YOU FOR THE AMOUNT OF TIME YOU TALKED TO HER, RIGHT?
HOW DID YOU KNOW?
SHE'S MY LAWYER
WILEY

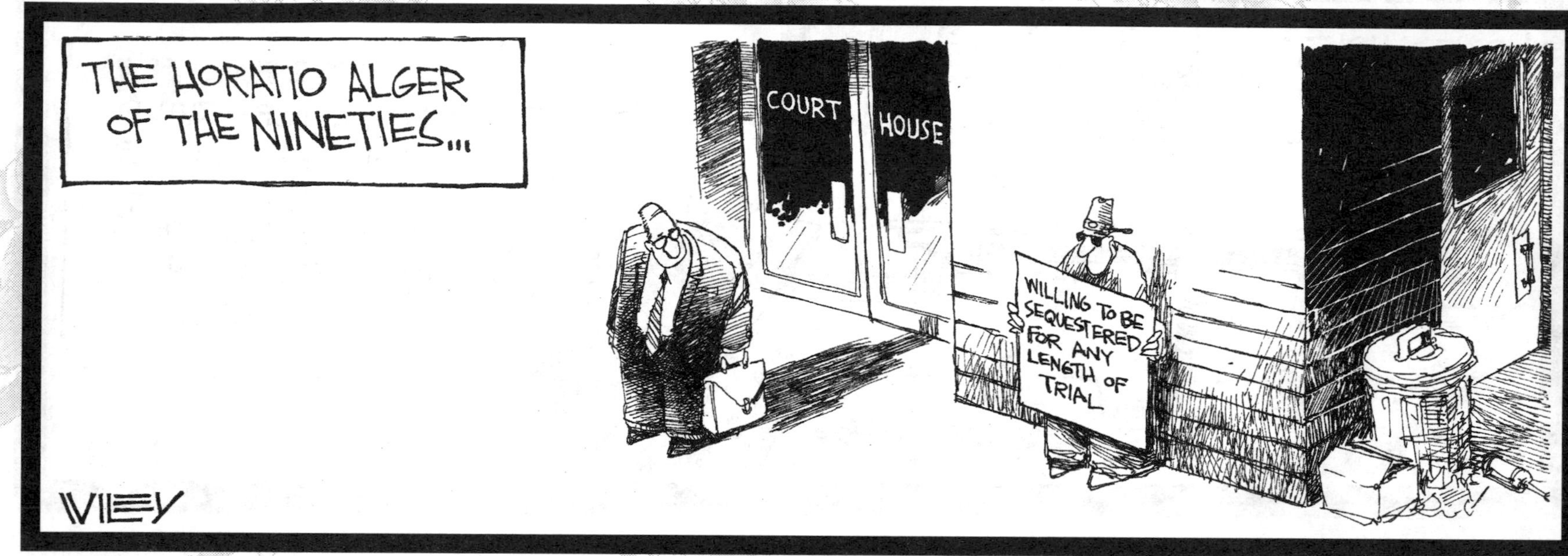
THE HORATIO ALGER OF THE NINETIES...
COURT HOUSE
WILLING TO BE SEQUESTERED FOR ANY LENGTH OF TRIAL
WILEY

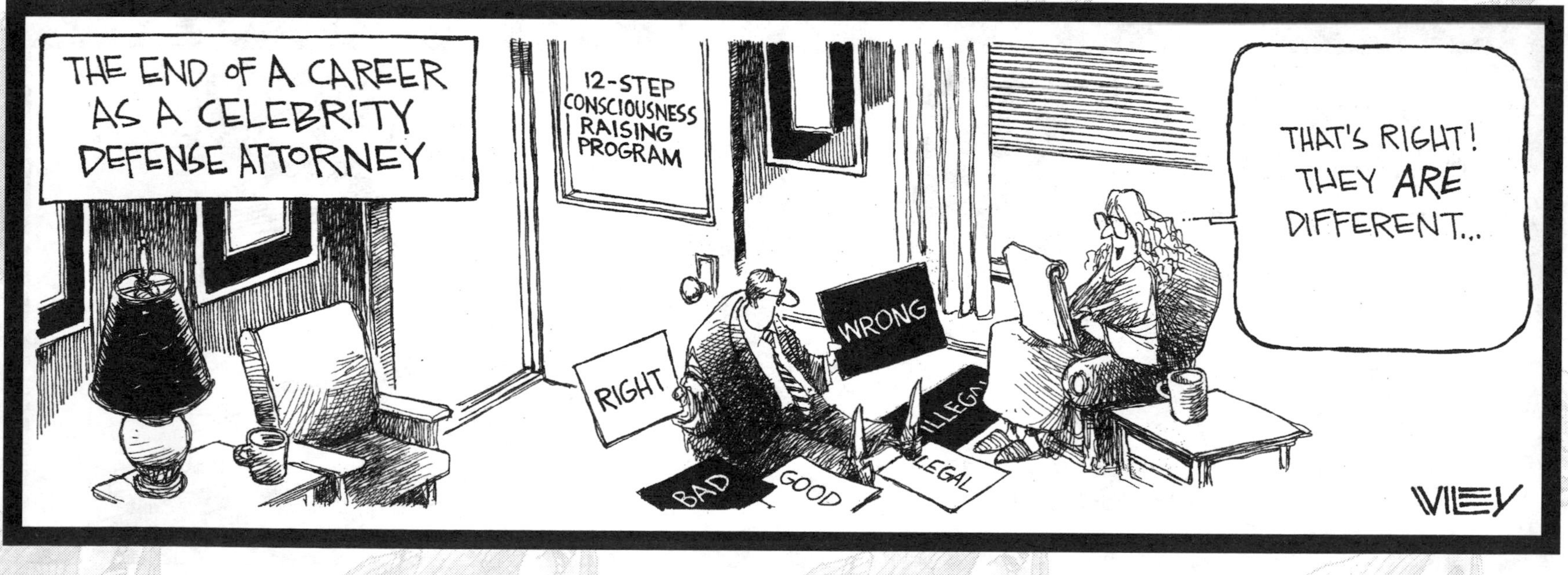
THE END OF A CAREER AS A CELEBRITY DEFENSE ATTORNEY
12-STEP CONSCIOUSNESS RAISING PROGRAM
THAT'S RIGHT! THEY ARE DIFFERENT...
RIGHT
WRONG
ILLEGAL
LEGAL
GOOD
BAD
WILEY

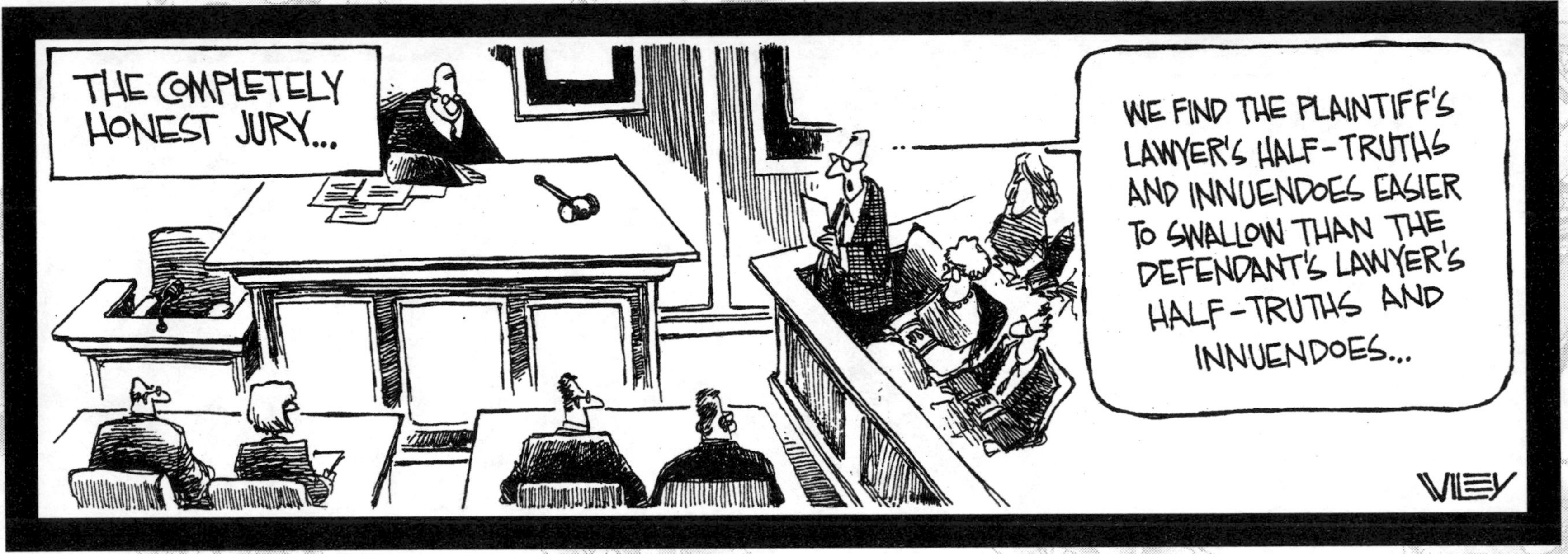
THE COMPLETELY HONEST JURY...
WE FIND THE PLAINTIFF'S LAWYER'S HALF-TRUTHS AND INNUENDOES EASIER TO SWALLOW THAN THE DEFENDANT'S LAWYER'S HALF-TRUTHS AND INNUENDOES...
WILEY

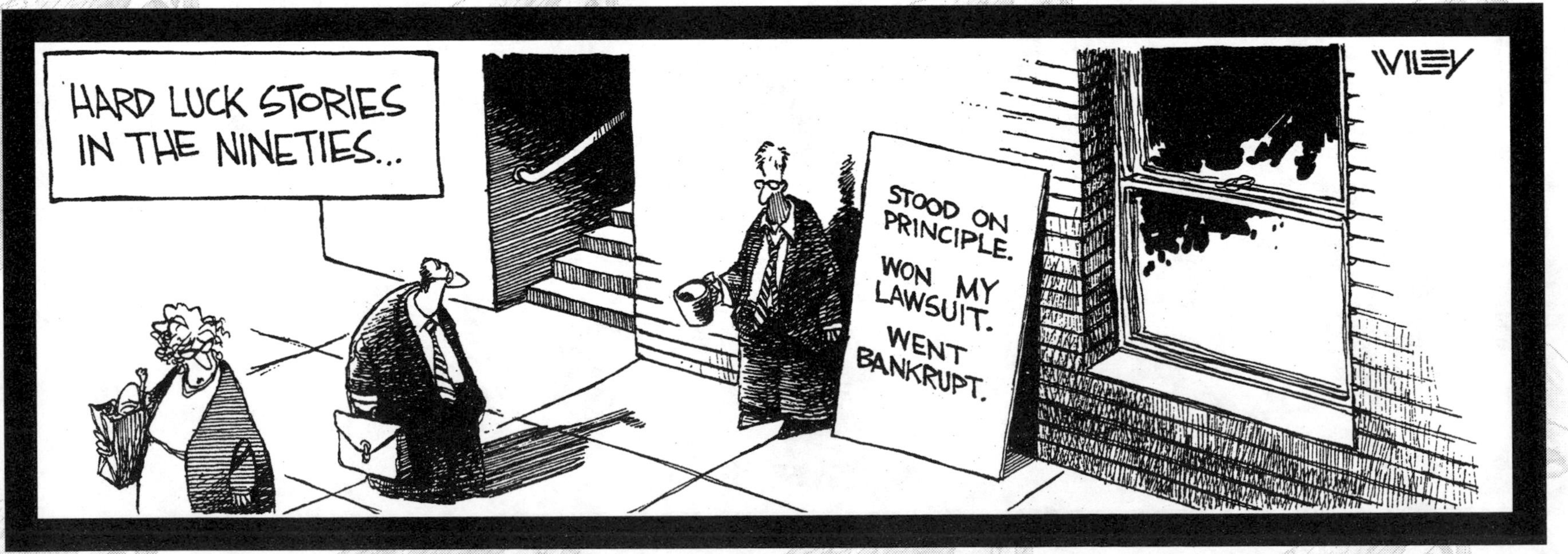
HARD LUCK STORIES IN THE NINETIES...
STOOD ON PRINCIPLE.
WON MY LAWSUIT.
WENT BANKRUPT.
WILEY

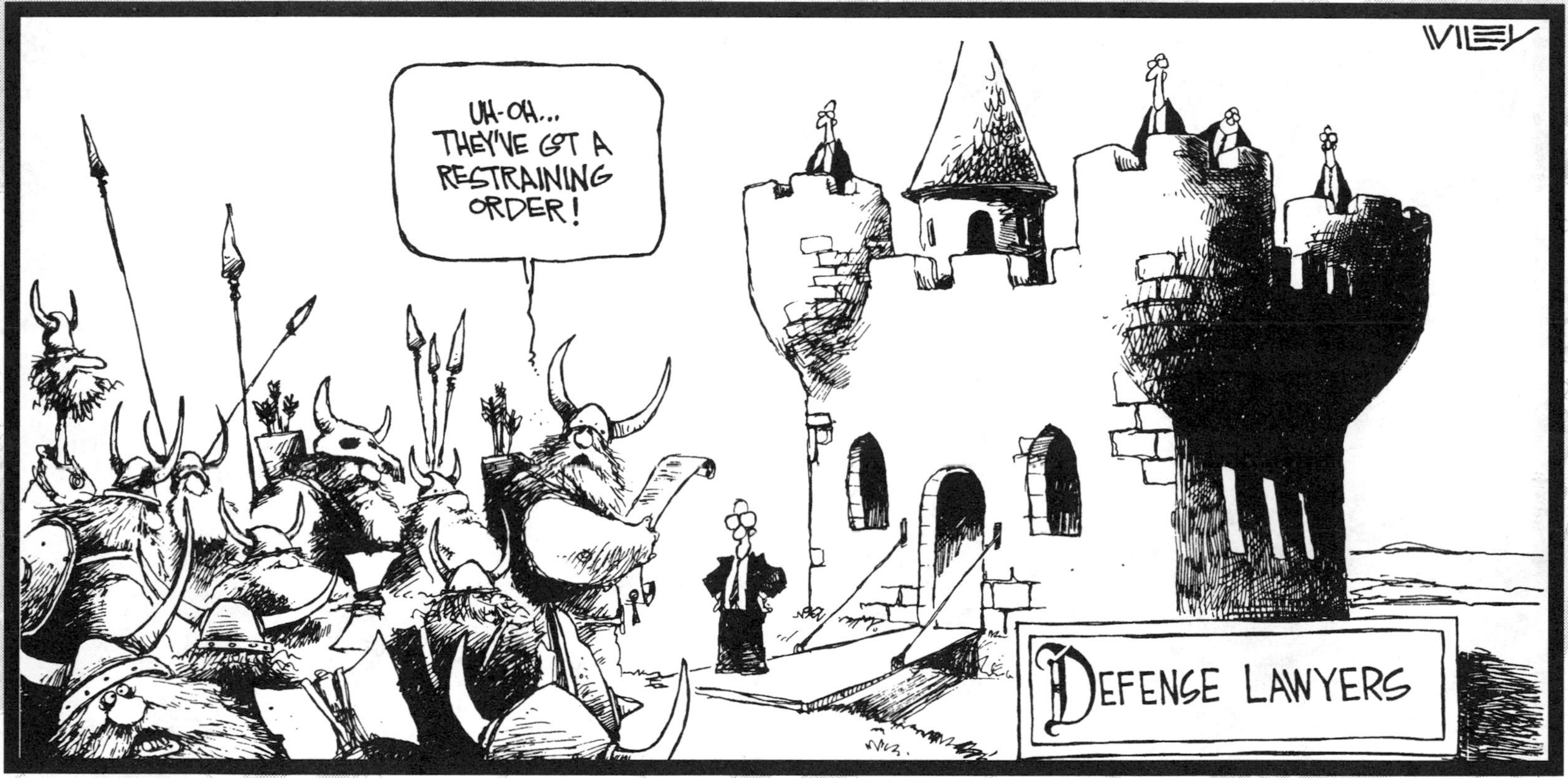
WILEY
UH-OH... THEY'VE GOT A RESTRAINING ORDER!
DEFENSE LAWYERS

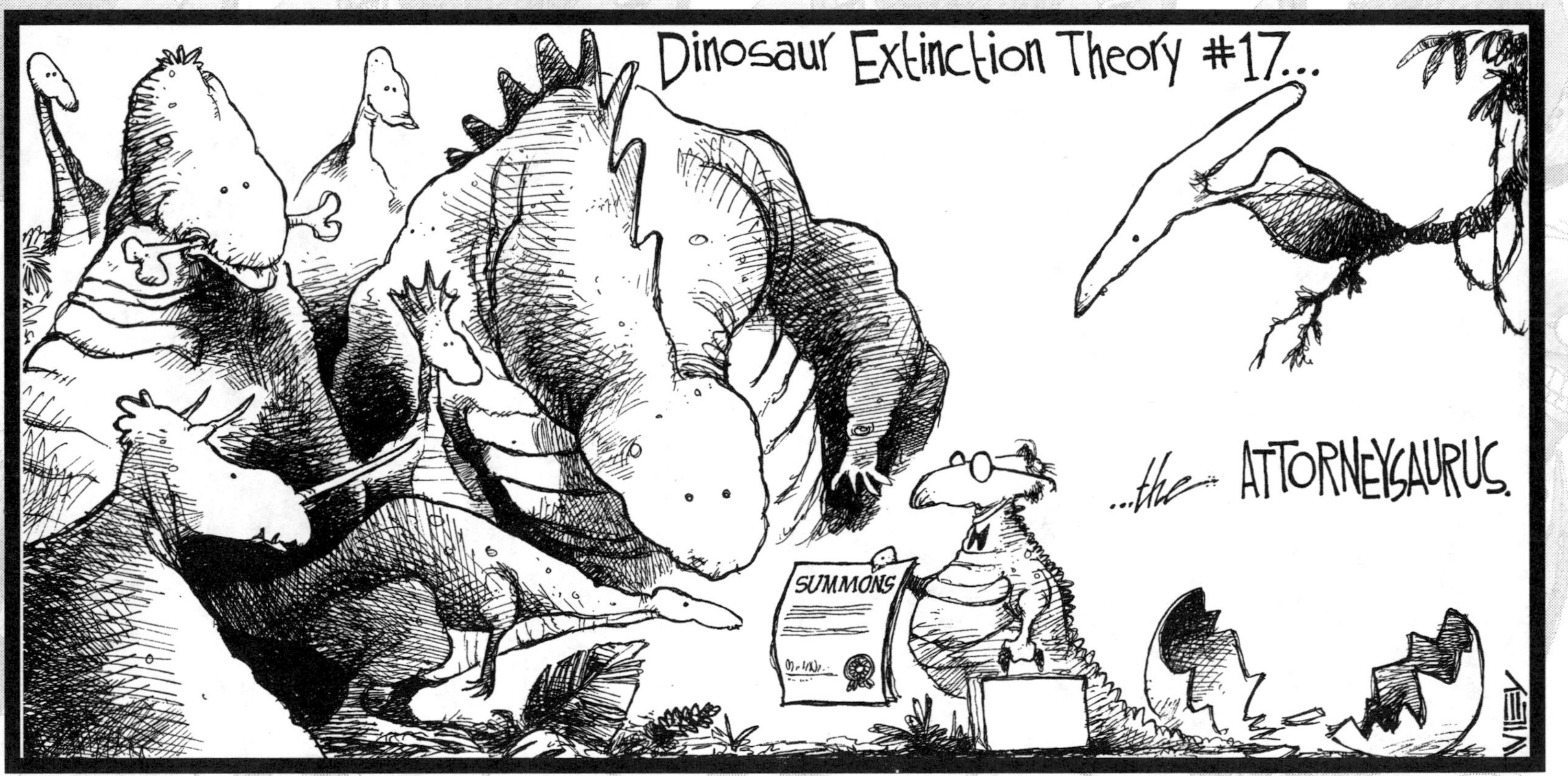
Dinosaur Extinction Theory #17...
SUMMONS
...the ATTORNEYSAURUS.
WILEY

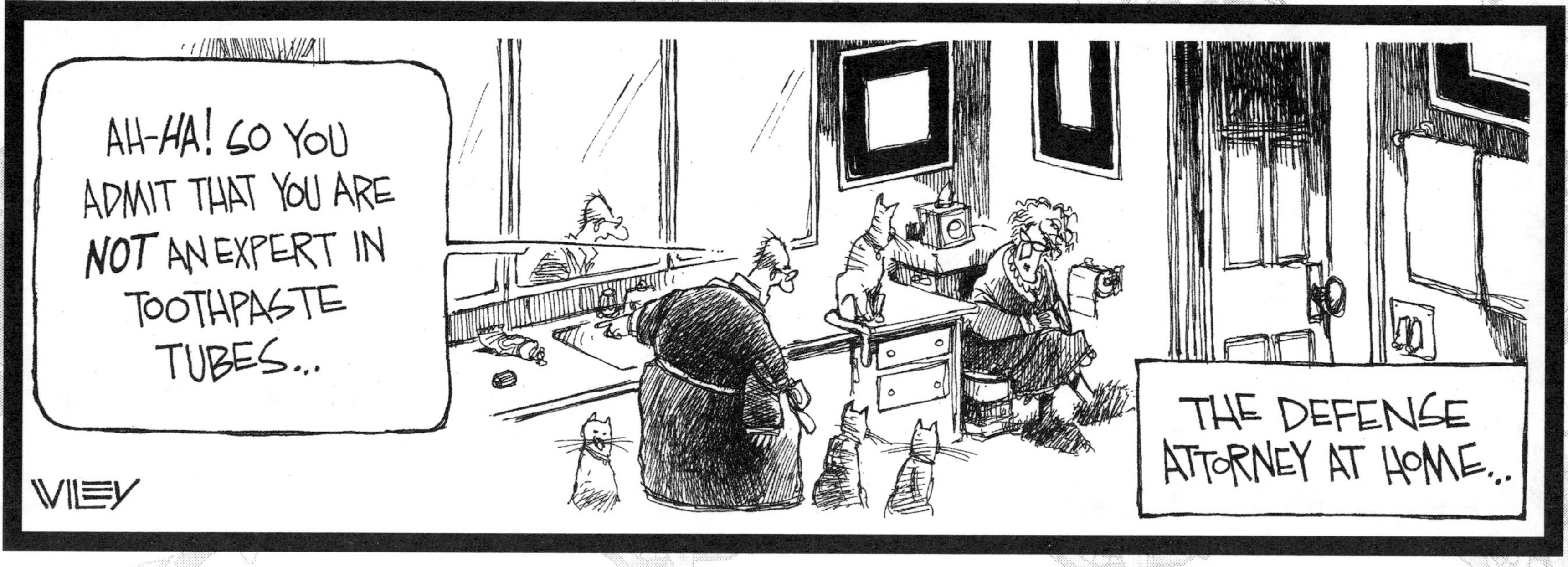
AH-HA! SO YOU ADMIT THAT YOU ARE NOT AN EXPERT IN TOOTHPASTE TUBES...
THE DEFENSE ATTORNEY AT HOME...
WILEY

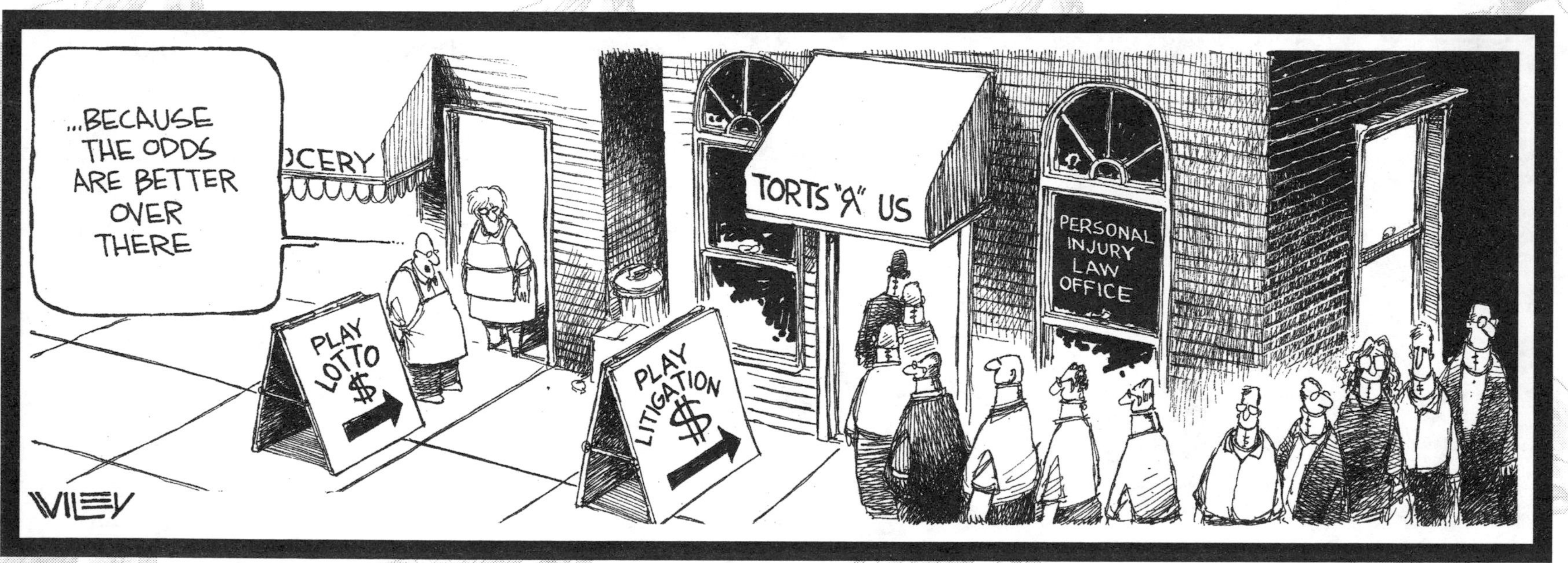
...BECAUSE THE ODDS ARE BETTER OVER THERE
OCERY
TORTS "Я" US
PERSONAL INJURY LAW OFFICE
PLAY LOTTO $
PLAY LITIGATION $
WILEY

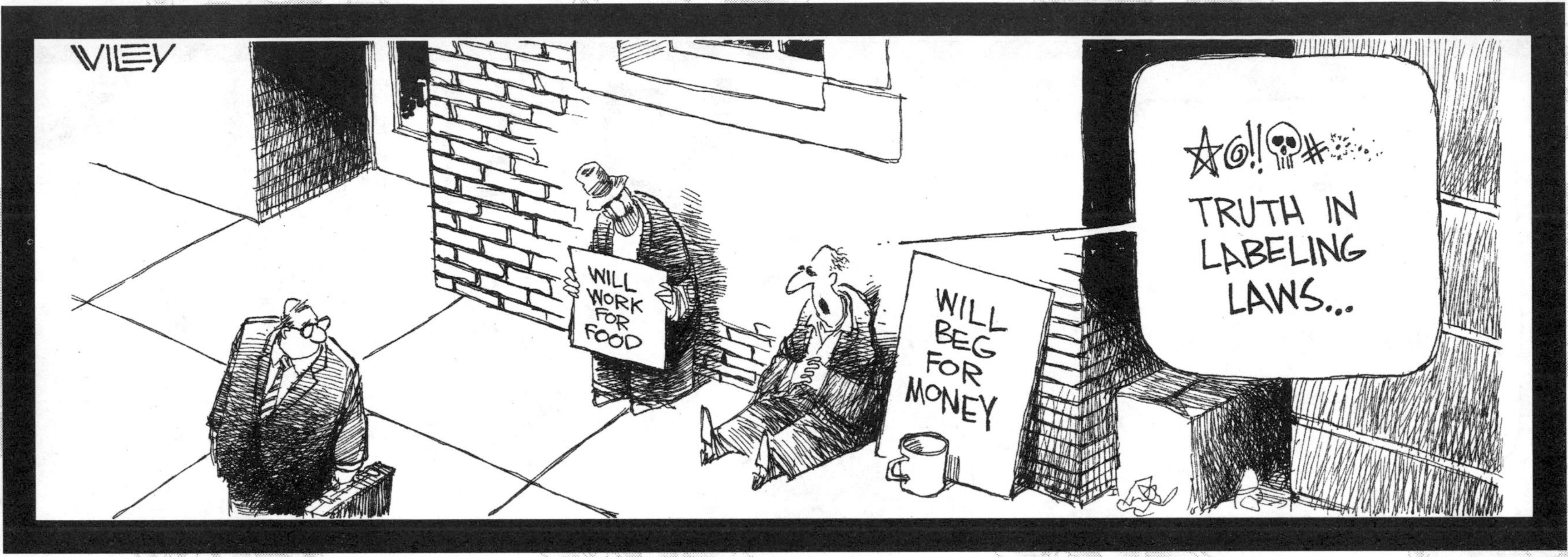
WILEY
WILL WORK FOR FOOD
WILL BEG FOR MONEY
TRUTH IN LABELING LAWS...

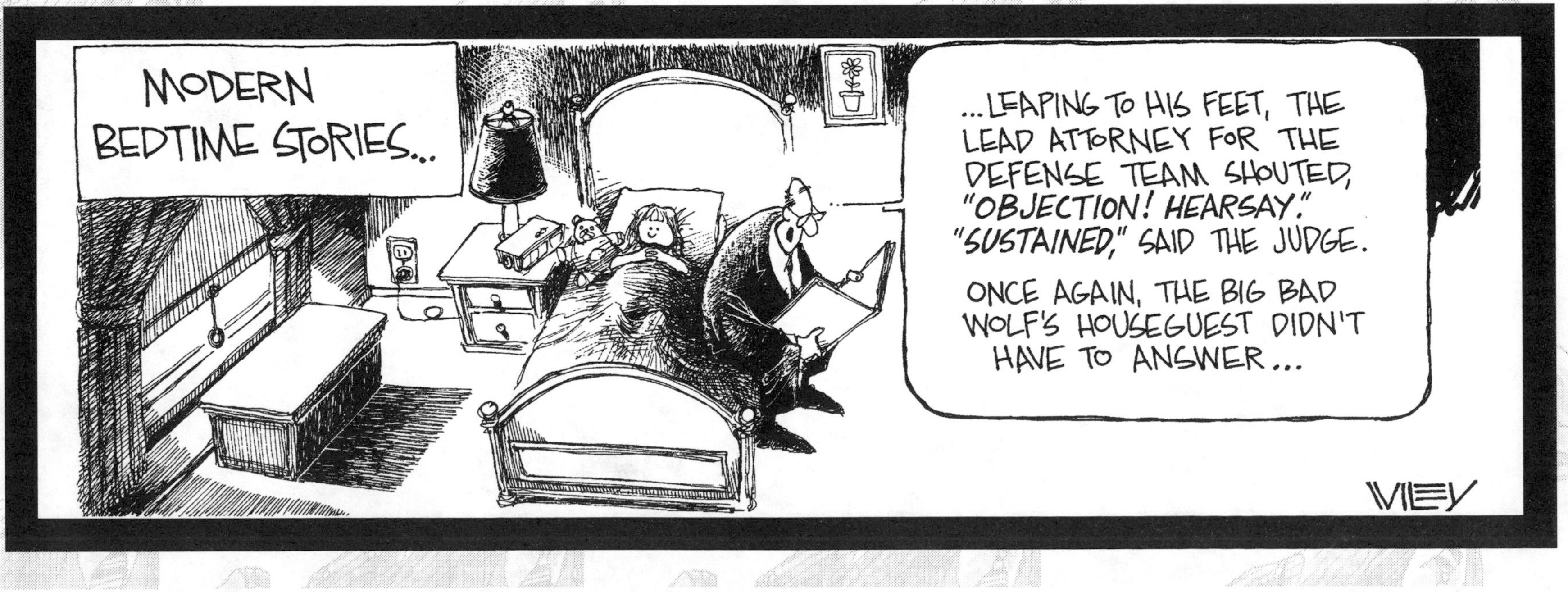
MODERN BEDTIME STORIES...
...LEAPING TO HIS FEET, THE LEAD ATTORNEY FOR THE DEFENSE TEAM SHOUTED, "OBJECTION! HEARSAY." "SUSTAINED," SAID THE JUDGE.
ONCE AGAIN, THE BIG BAD WOLF'S HOUSEGUEST DIDN'T HAVE TO ANSWER...
WILEY

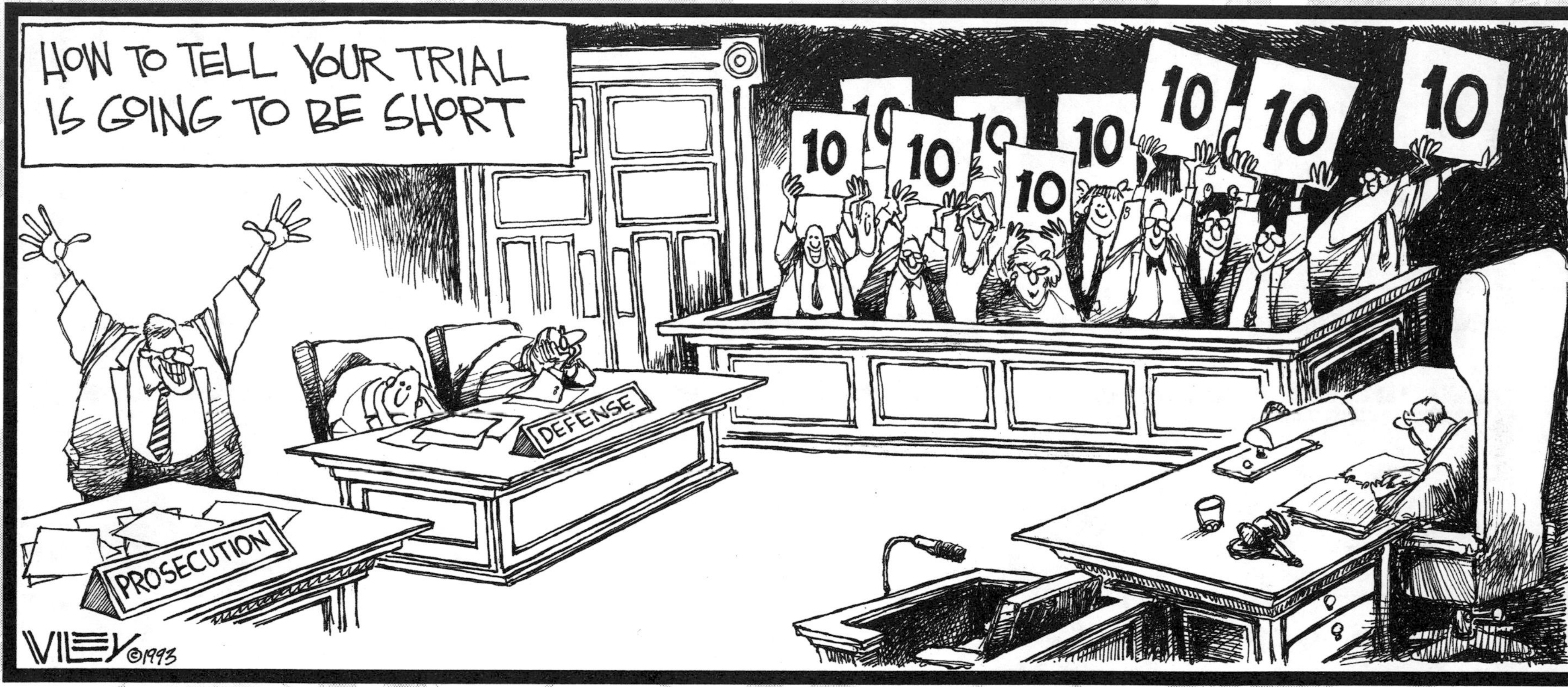
HOW TO TELL YOUR TRIAL IS GOING TO BE SHORT
10
10
10
10
10
10
10
10
DEFENSE
PROSECUTION
WILEY ©1993

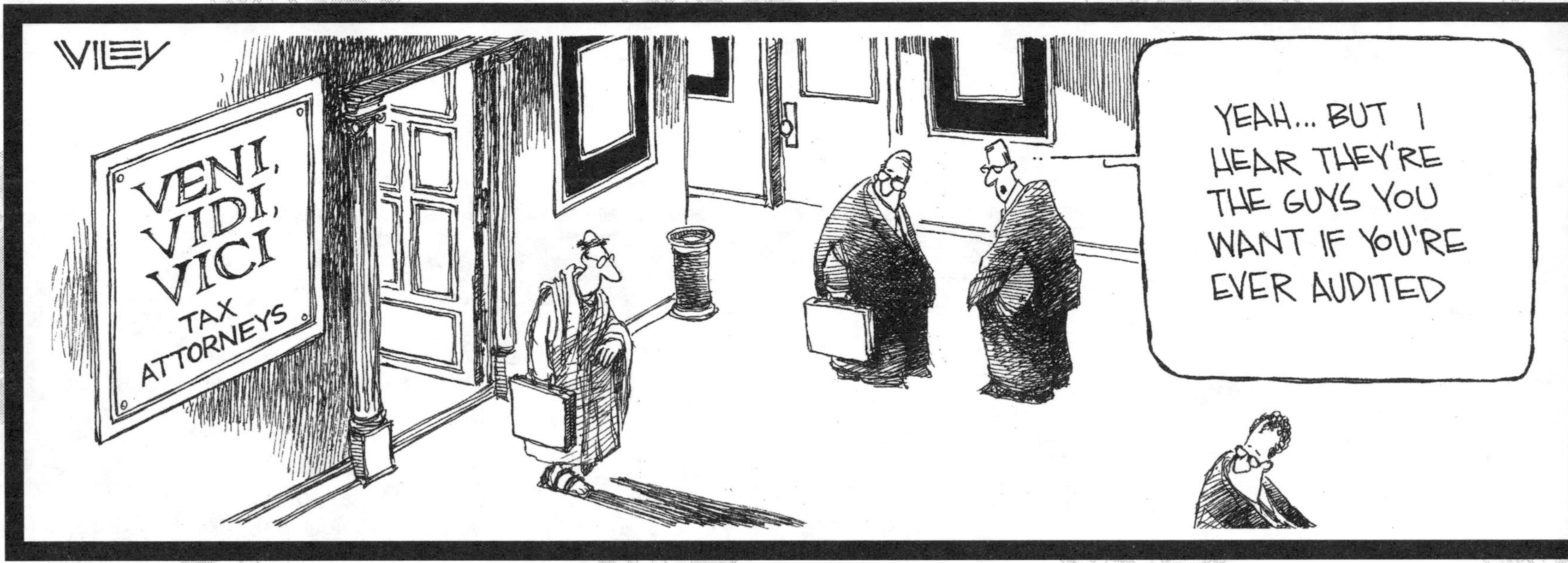
VILEY
VENI, VIDI, VICI TAX ATTORNEYS
YEAH... BUT I HEAR THEY'RE THE GUYS YOU WANT IF YOU'RE EVER AUDITED

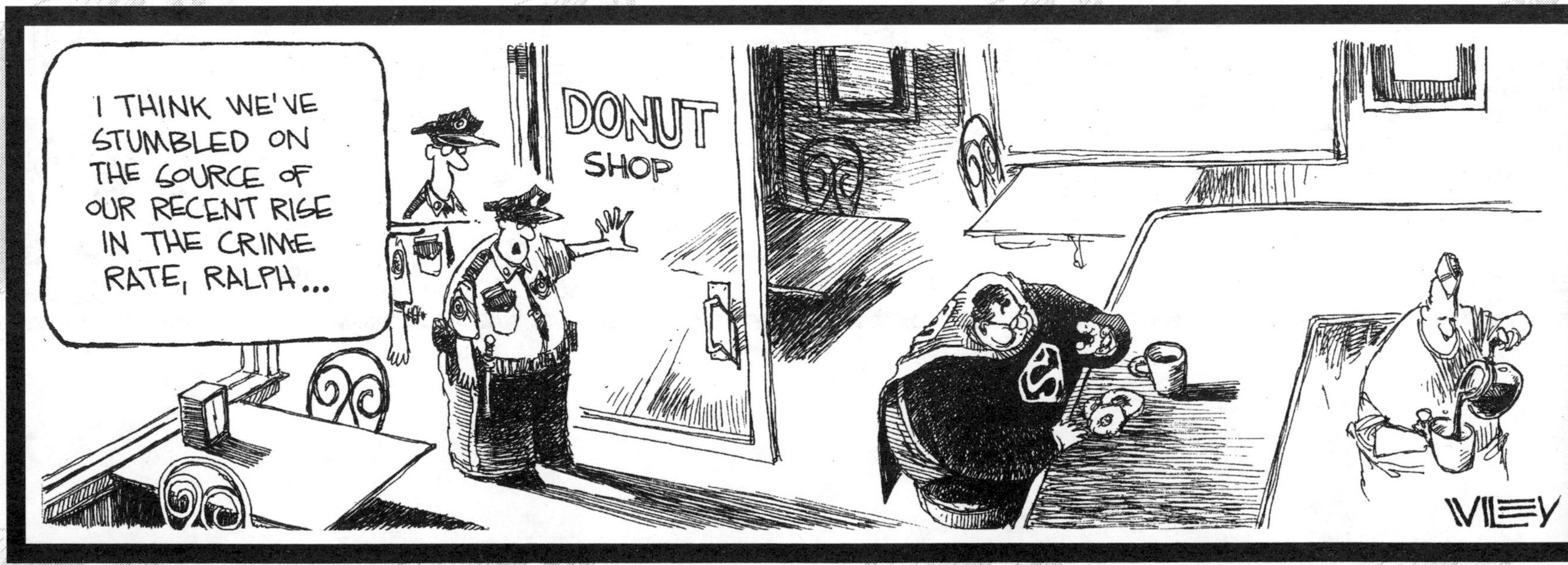
I THINK WE'VE STUMBLED ON THE SOURCE OF OUR RECENT RISE IN THE CRIME RATE, RALPH...
DONUT SHOP
VILEY

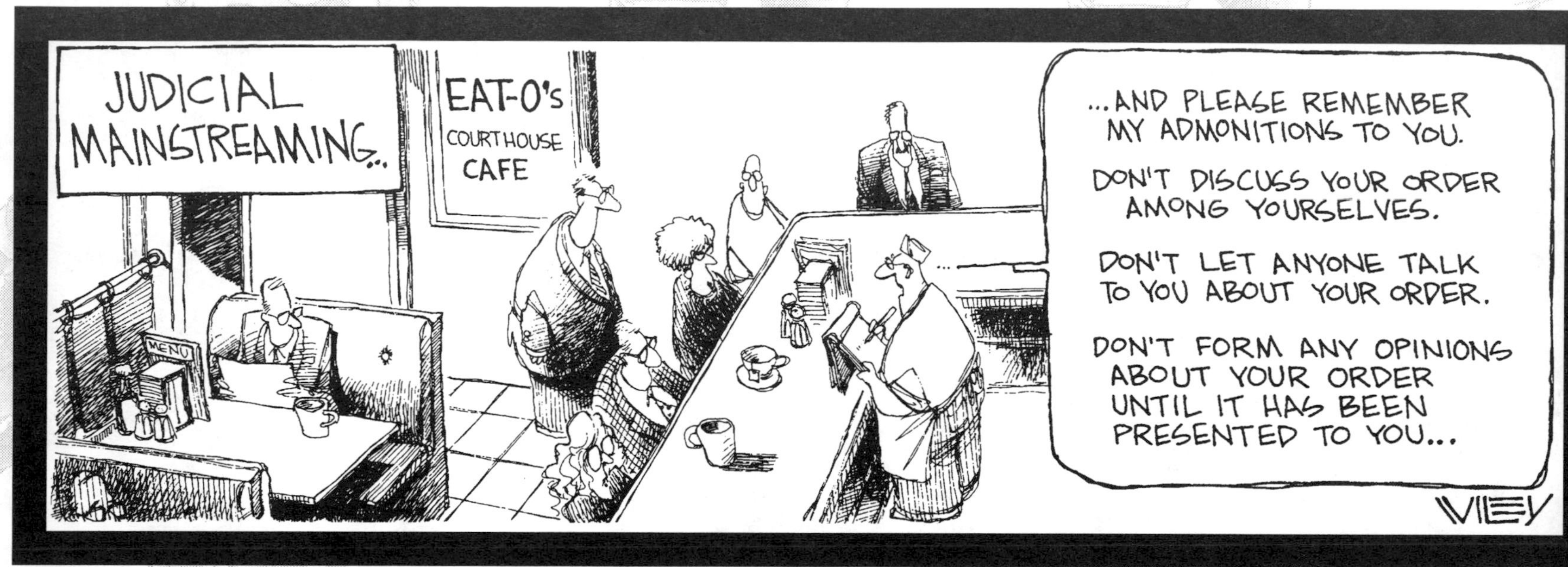

JUDICIAL MAINSTREAMING...
EAT-O's COURTHOUSE CAFE
MENU
...AND PLEASE REMEMBER MY ADMONITIONS TO YOU.
DON'T DISCUSS YOUR ORDER AMONG YOURSELVES.
DON'T LET ANYONE TALK TO YOU ABOUT YOUR ORDER.
DON'T FORM ANY OPINIONS ABOUT YOUR ORDER UNTIL IT HAS BEEN PRESENTED TO YOU...

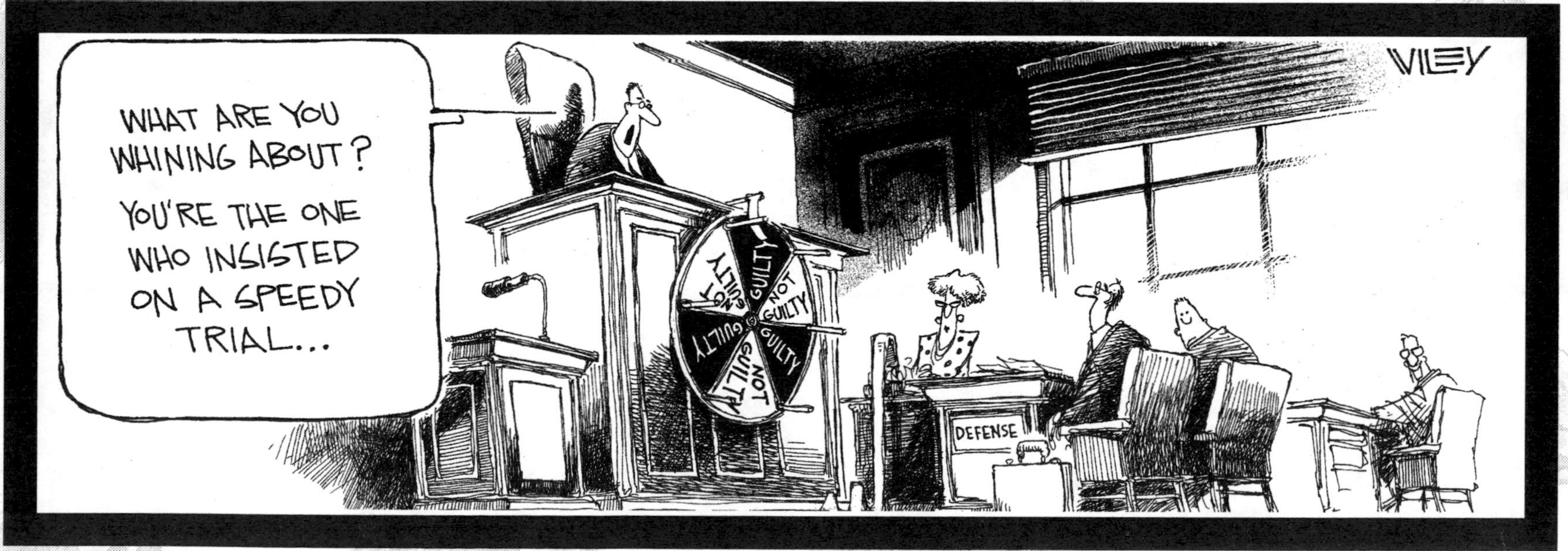

WHAT ARE YOU WHINING ABOUT?
YOU'RE THE ONE WHO INSISTED ON A SPEEDY TRIAL...
GUILTY
NOT GUILTY
DEFENSE

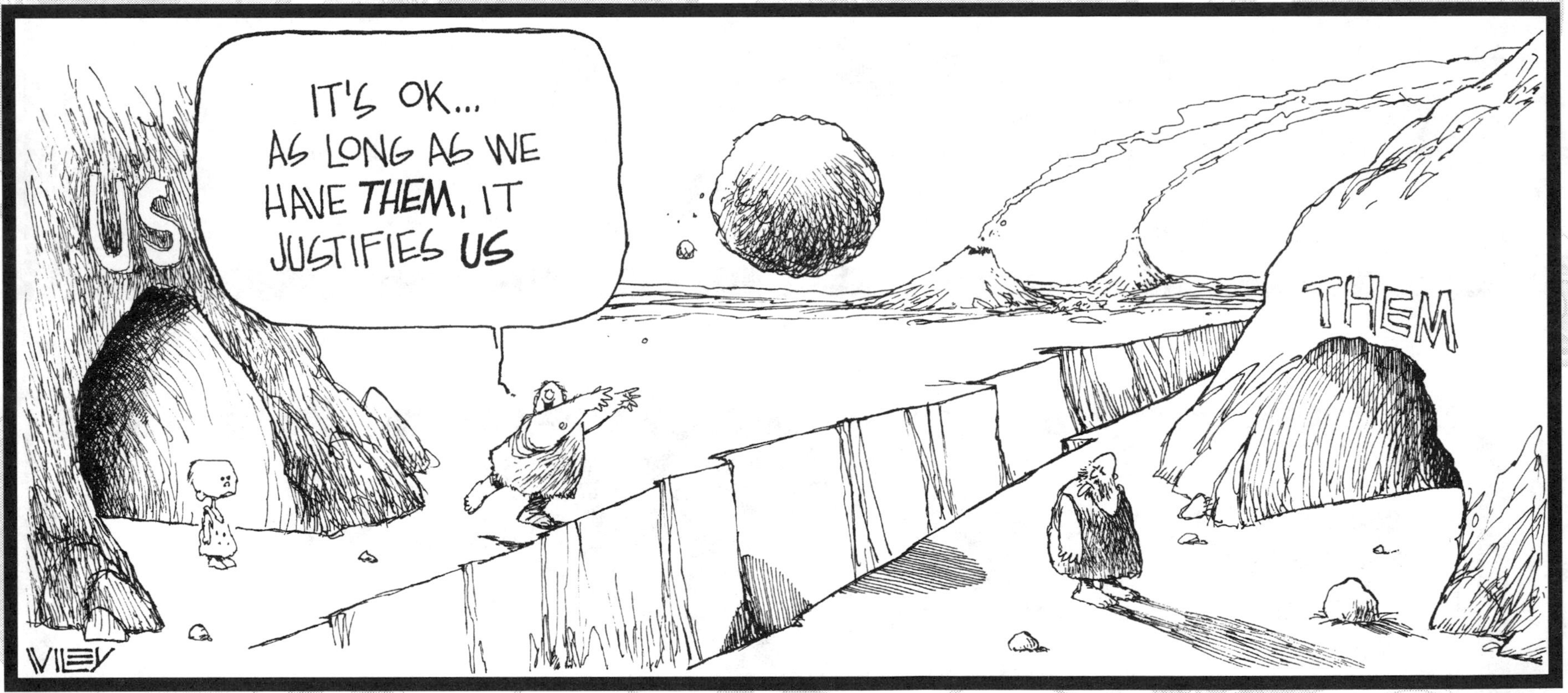
US
IT'S OK... AS LONG AS WE HAVE **THEM**, IT JUSTIFIES **US**
THEM
WILEY

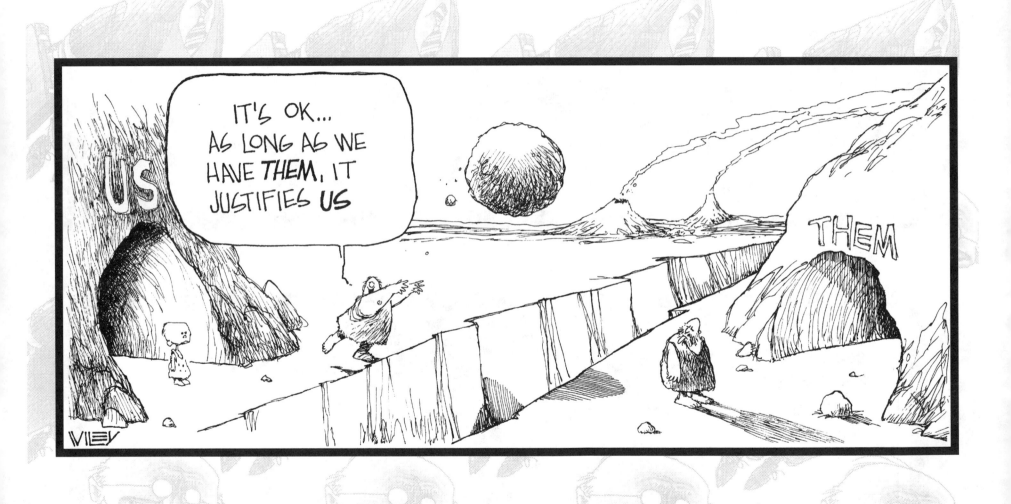

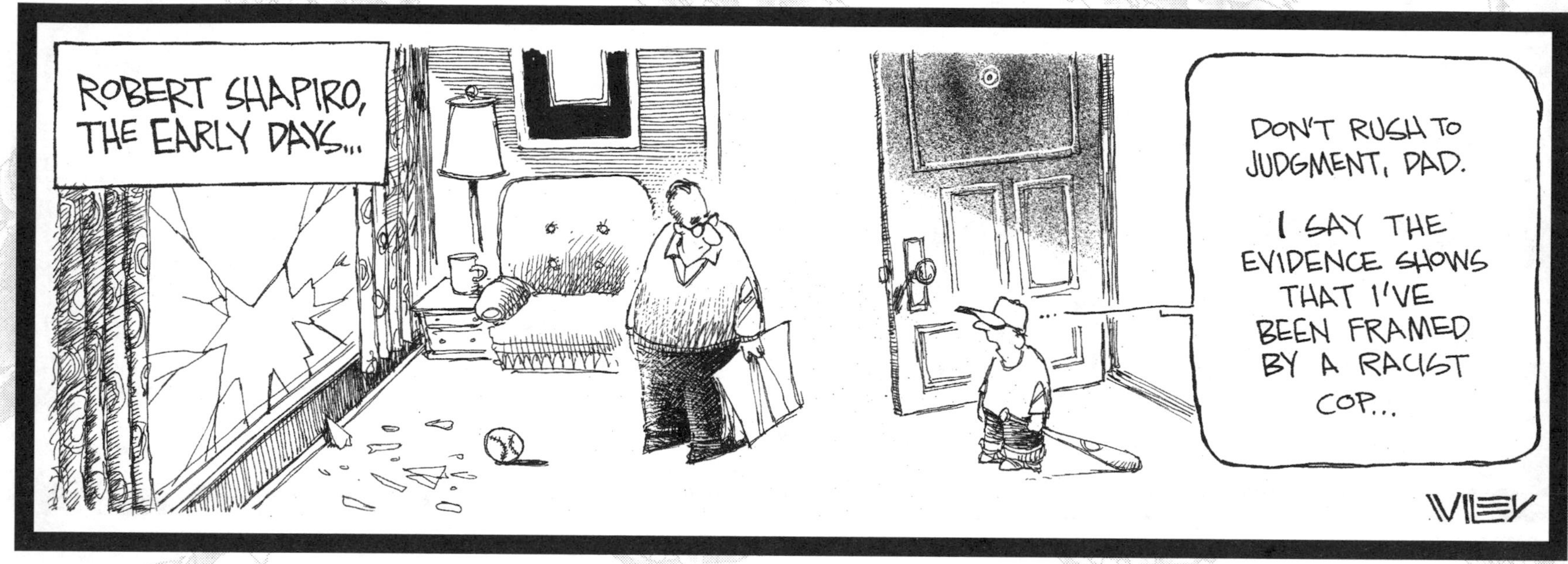
ROBERT SHAPIRO, THE EARLY DAYS...
DON'T RUSH TO JUDGMENT, DAD.
I SAY THE EVIDENCE SHOWS THAT I'VE BEEN FRAMED BY A RACIST COP...

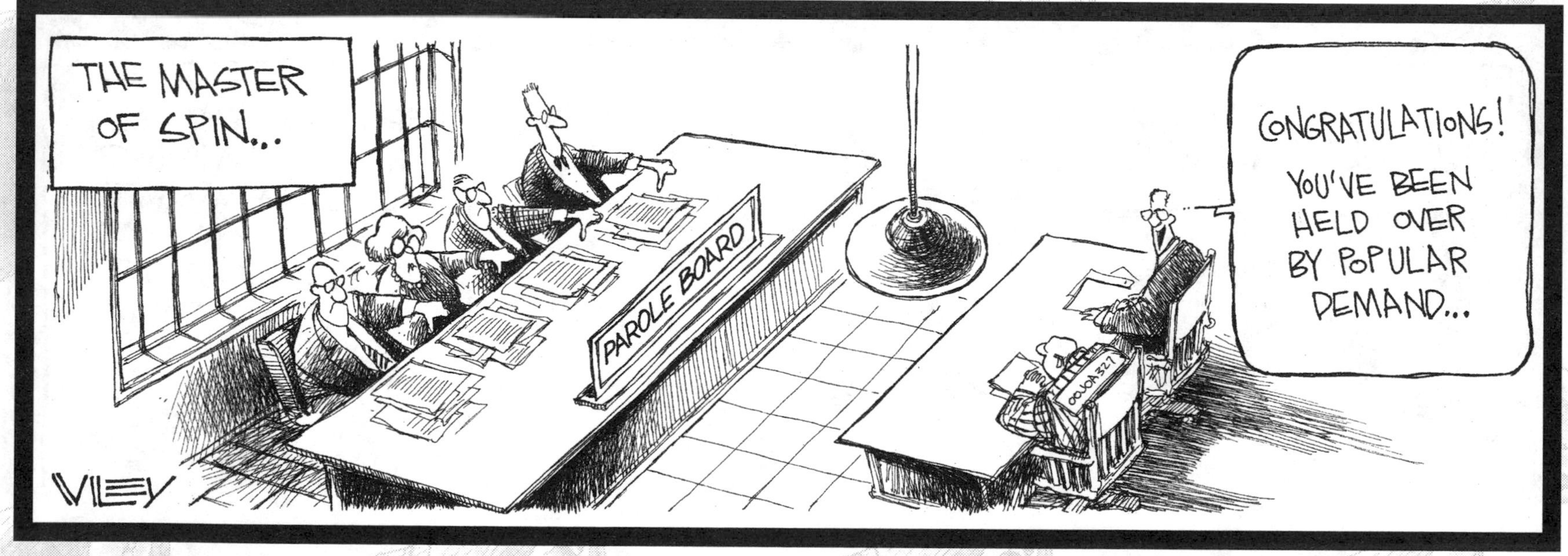
THE MASTER OF SPIN...
PAROLE BOARD
CONGRATULATIONS!
YOU'VE BEEN HELD OVER BY POPULAR DEMAND...

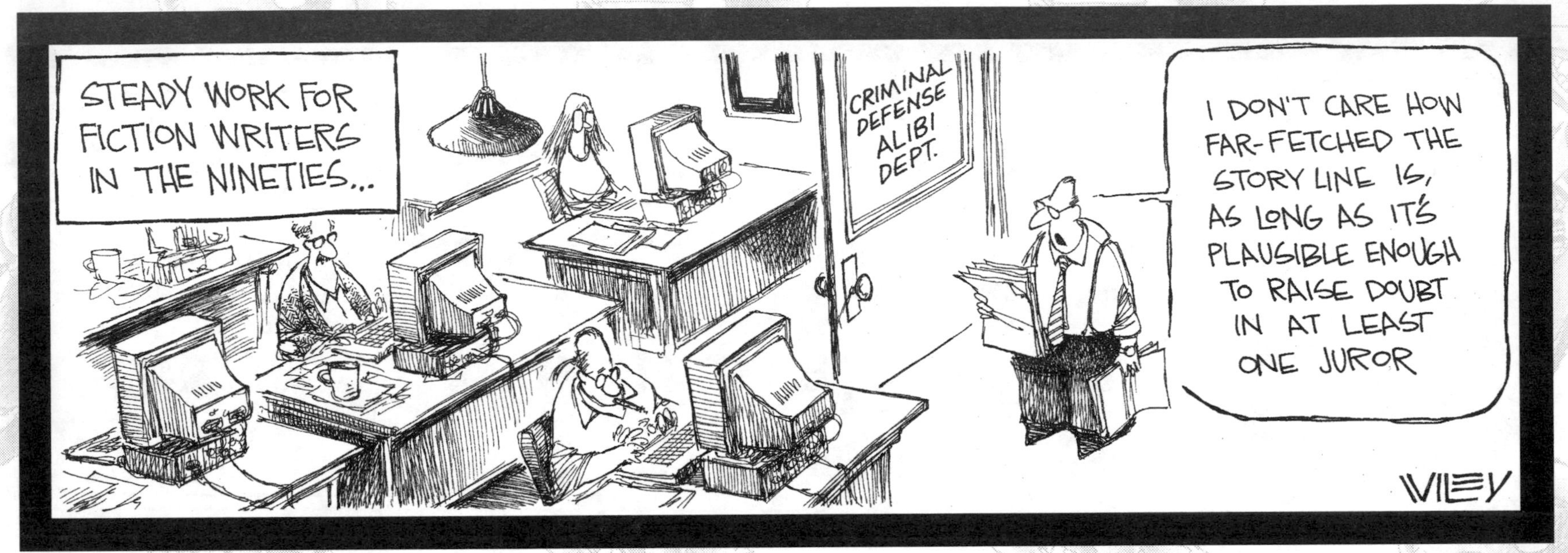
STEADY WORK FOR FICTION WRITERS IN THE NINETIES...
CRIMINAL DEFENSE ALIBI DEPT.
I DON'T CARE HOW FAR-FETCHED THE STORY LINE IS, AS LONG AS IT'S PLAUSIBLE ENOUGH TO RAISE DOUBT IN AT LEAST ONE JUROR
WILEY

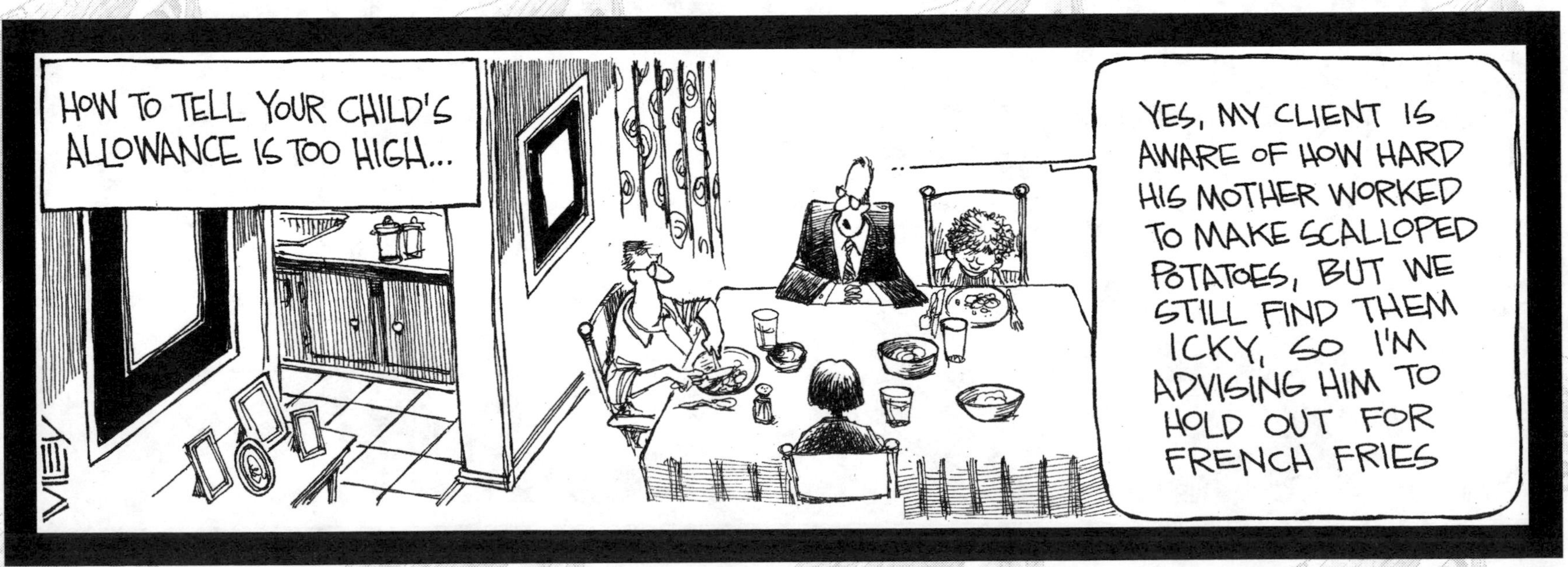
HOW TO TELL YOUR CHILD'S ALLOWANCE IS TOO HIGH...
YES, MY CLIENT IS AWARE OF HOW HARD HIS MOTHER WORKED TO MAKE SCALLOPED POTATOES, BUT WE STILL FIND THEM ICKY, SO I'M ADVISING HIM TO HOLD OUT FOR FRENCH FRIES
WILEY

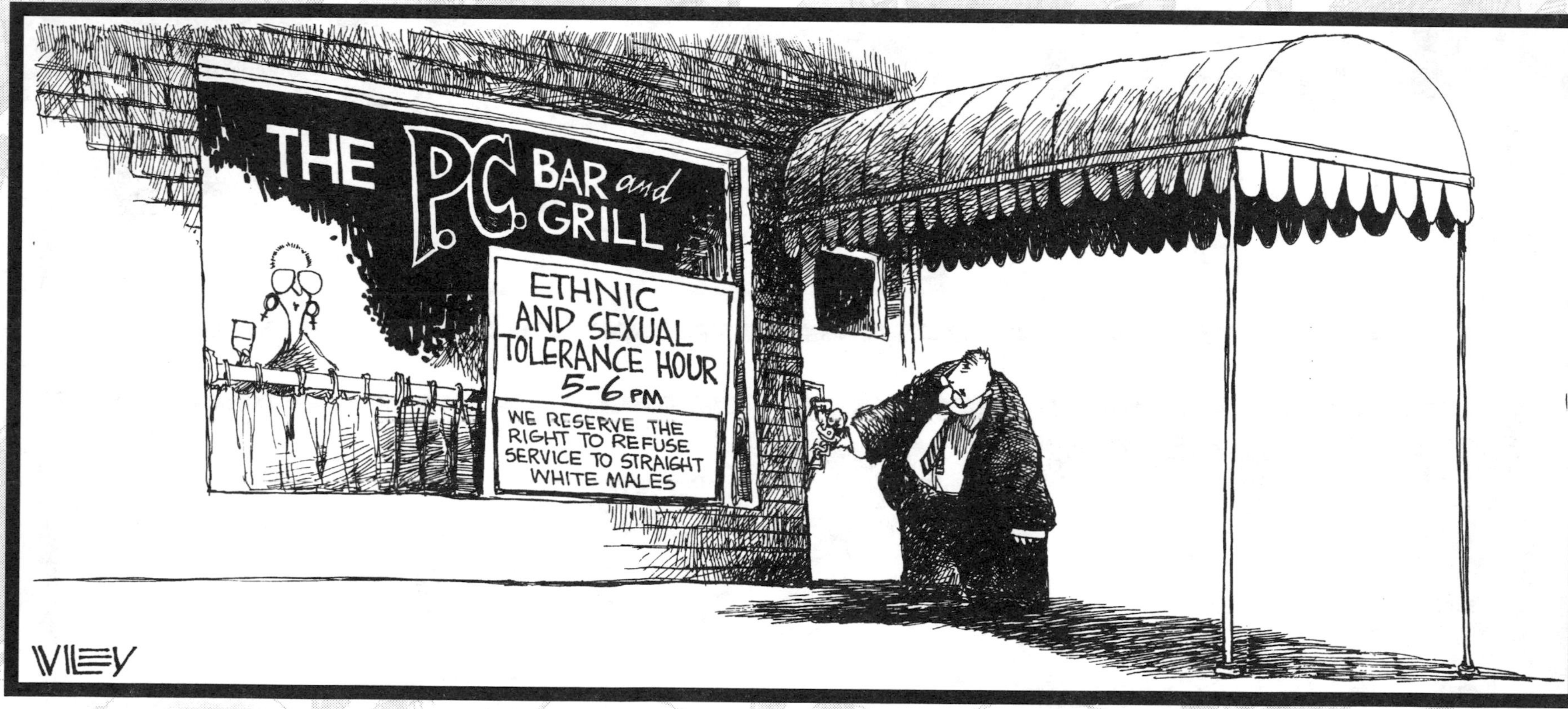
THE P.C. BAR and GRILL
ETHNIC AND SEXUAL TOLERANCE HOUR 5-6 PM
WE RESERVE THE RIGHT TO REFUSE SERVICE TO STRAIGHT WHITE MALES
WILEY

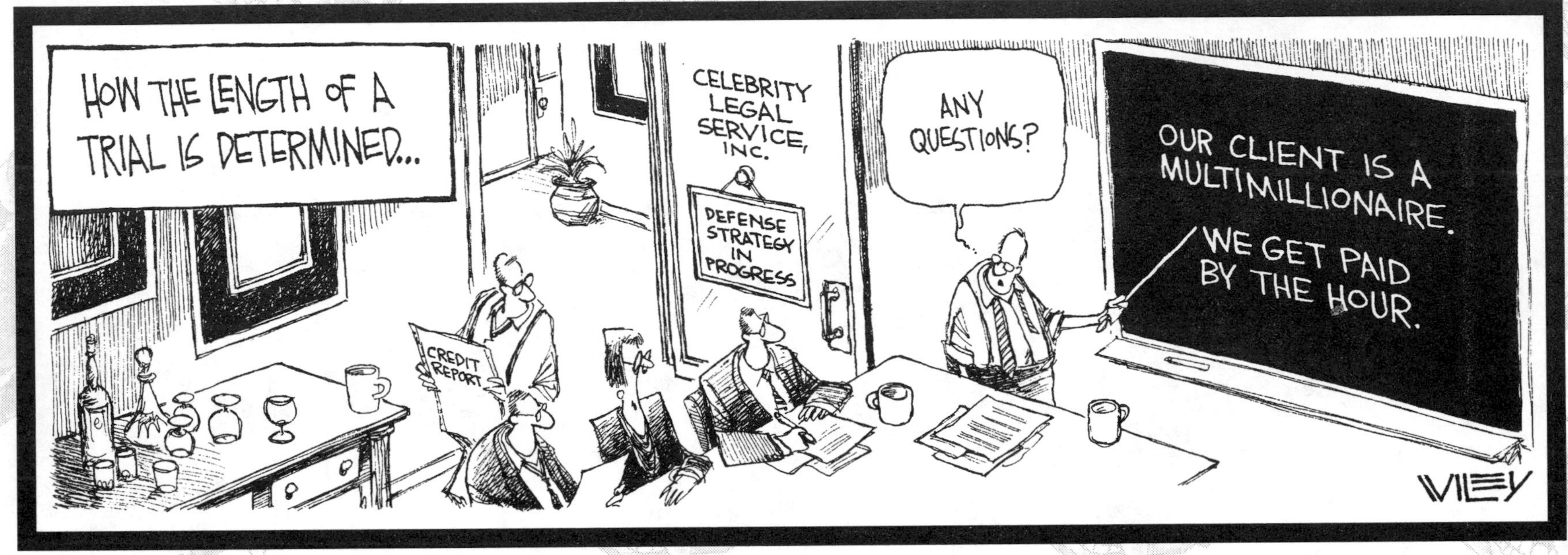
HOW THE LENGTH OF A TRIAL IS DETERMINED...
CELEBRITY LEGAL SERVICE, INC.
DEFENSE STRATEGY IN PROGRESS
CREDIT REPORT
ANY QUESTIONS?
OUR CLIENT IS A MULTIMILLIONAIRE.
WE GET PAID BY THE HOUR.
WILEY

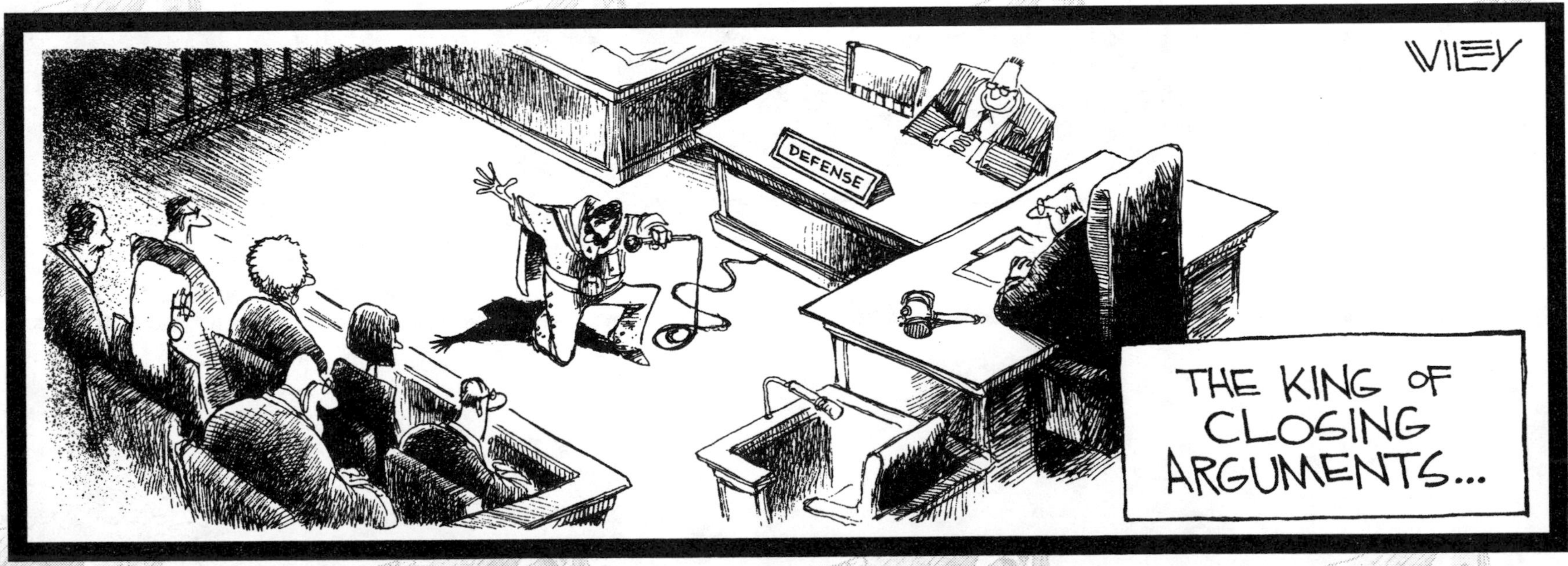
WILEY
DEFENSE
THE KING OF CLOSING ARGUMENTS...

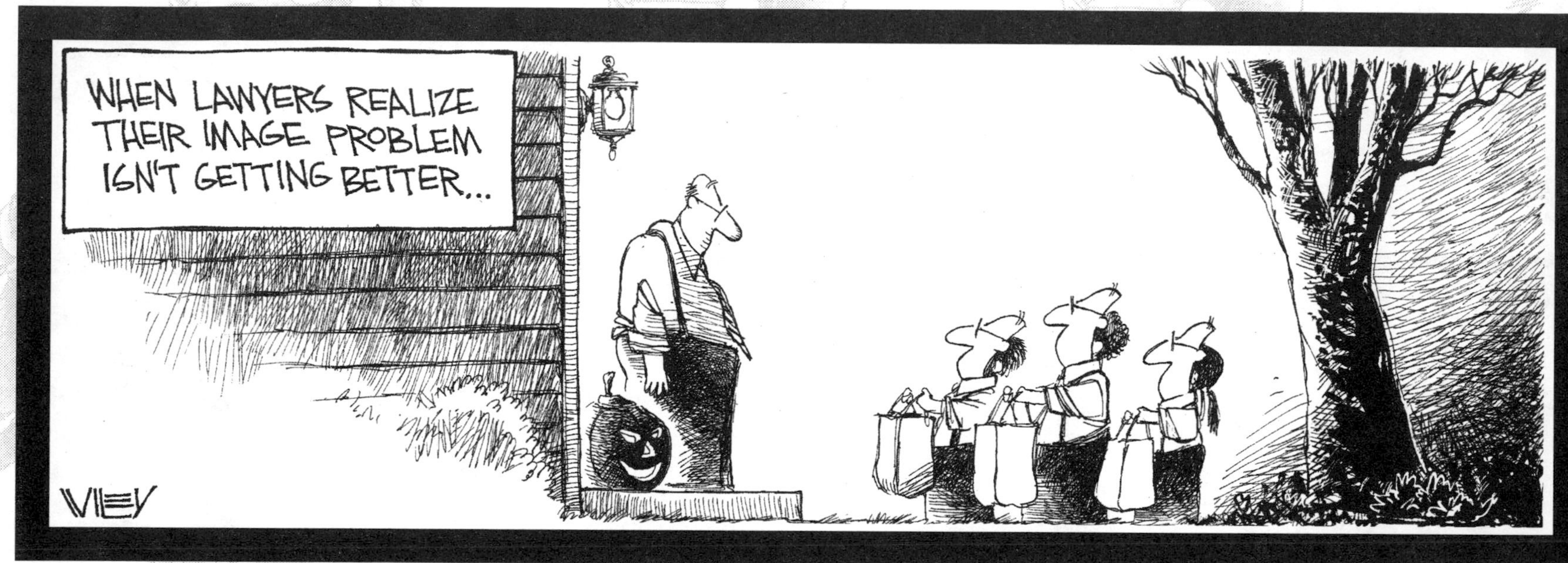
WHEN LAWYERS REALIZE THEIR IMAGE PROBLEM ISN'T GETTING BETTER...
WILEY

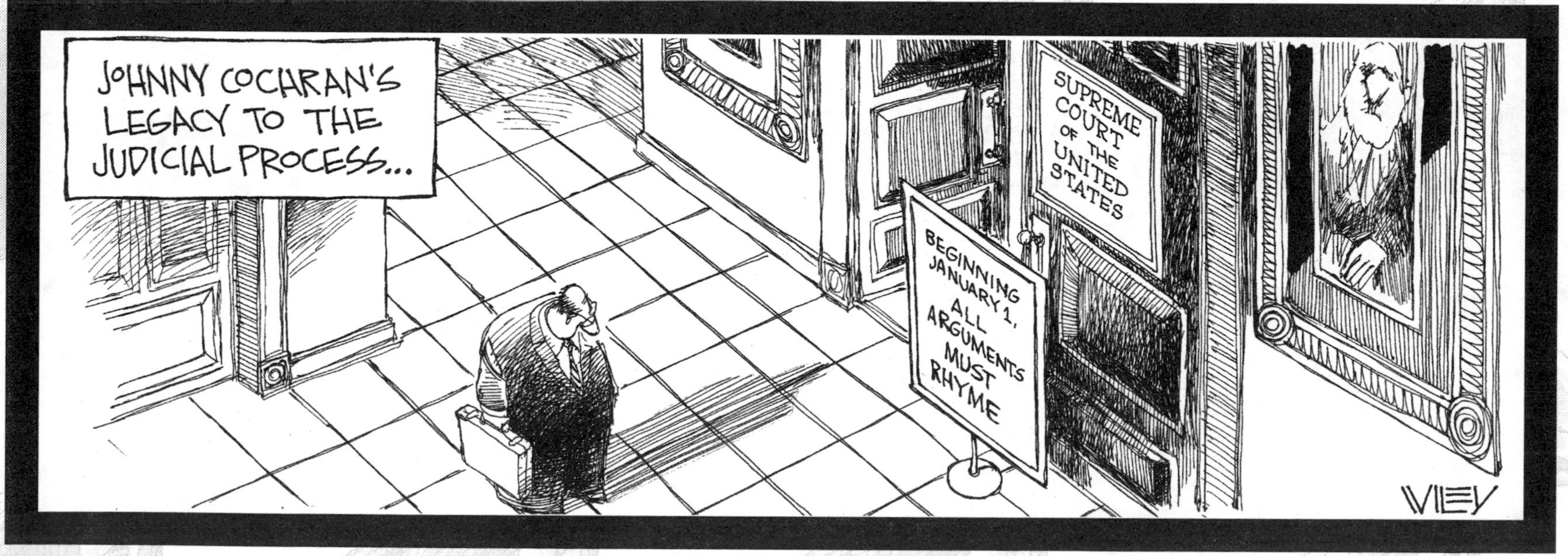
JOHNNY COCHRAN'S LEGACY TO THE JUDICIAL PROCESS...
SUPREME COURT OF THE UNITED STATES
BEGINNING JANUARY 1, ALL ARGUMENTS MUST RHYME
WILEY

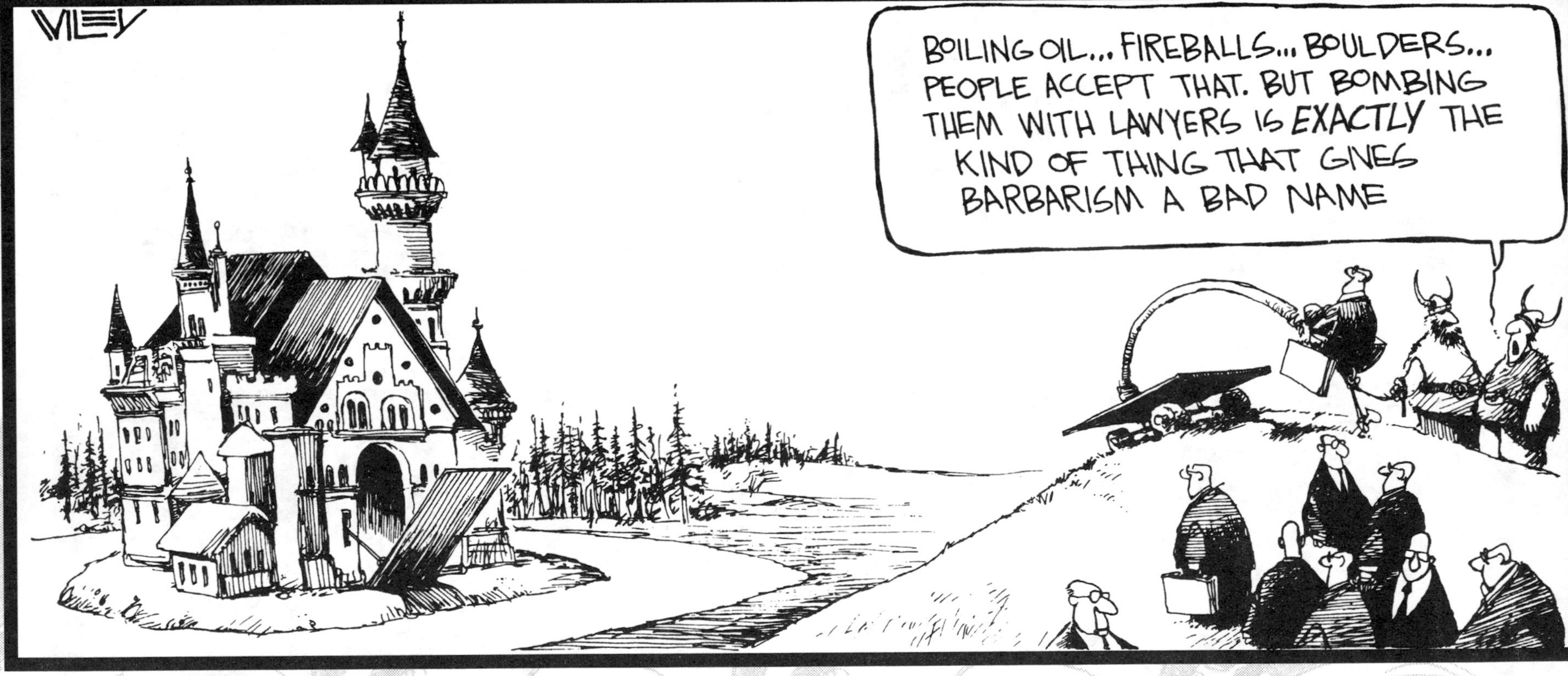
BOILING OIL... FIREBALLS... BOULDERS... PEOPLE ACCEPT THAT. BUT BOMBING THEM WITH LAWYERS IS *EXACTLY* THE KIND OF THING THAT GIVES BARBARISM A BAD NAME

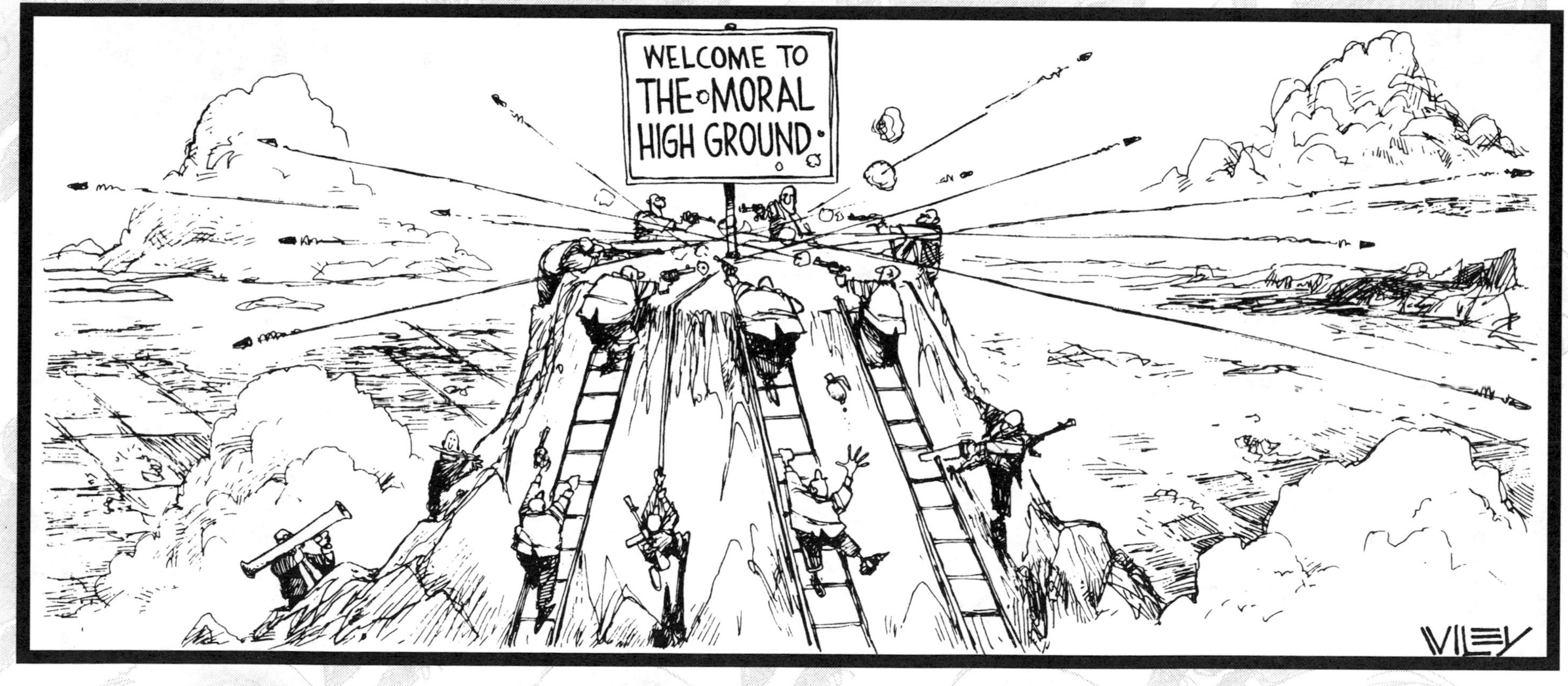
WELCOME TO
THE MORAL
HIGH GROUND
WILEY

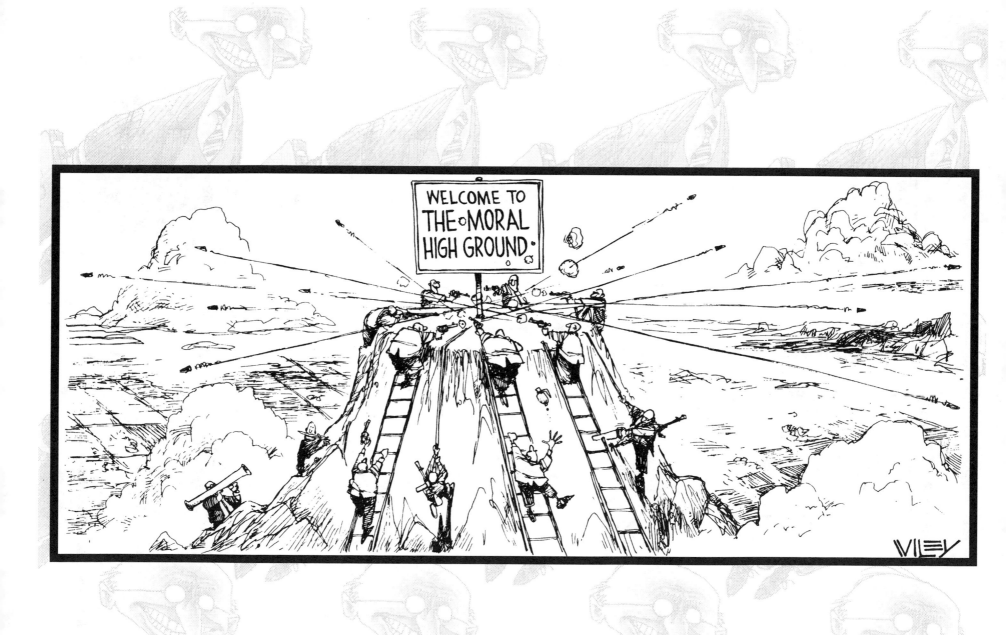

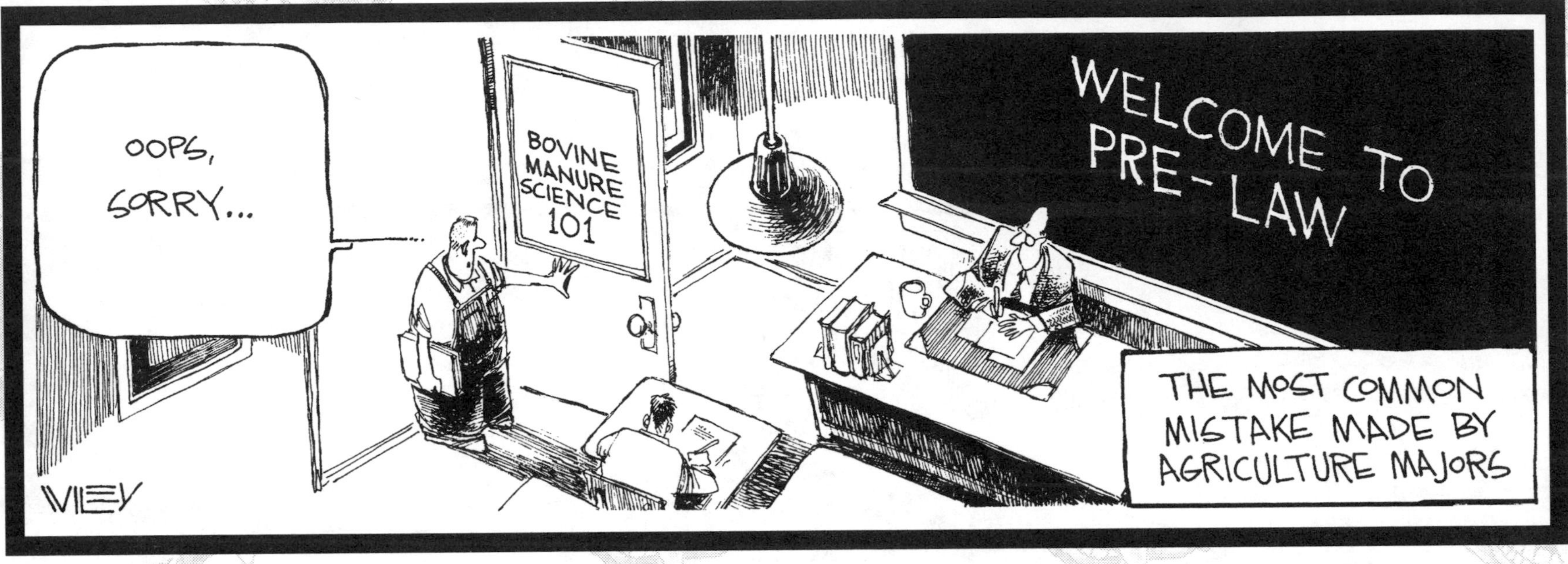
OOPS, SORRY...
BOVINE MANURE SCIENCE 101
WELCOME TO PRE-LAW
THE MOST COMMON MISTAKE MADE BY AGRICULTURE MAJORS
WILEY

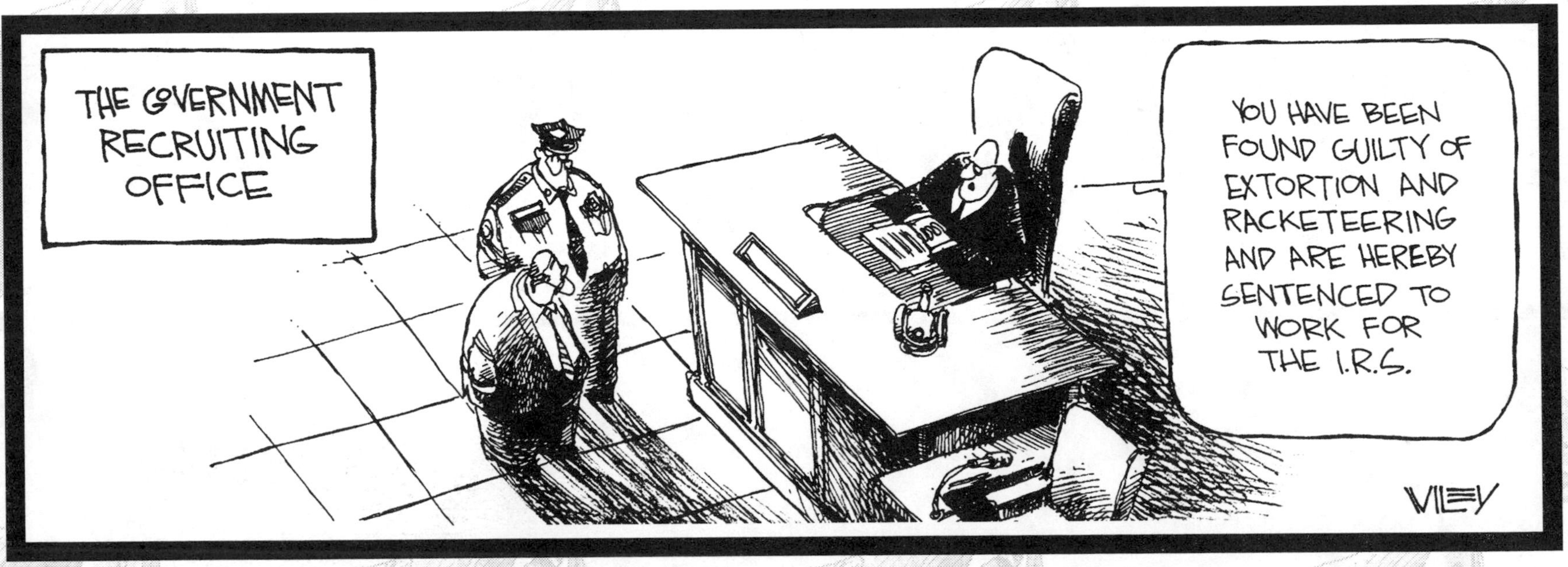
THE GOVERNMENT RECRUITING OFFICE
YOU HAVE BEEN FOUND GUILTY OF EXTORTION AND RACKETEERING AND ARE HEREBY SENTENCED TO WORK FOR THE I.R.S.
WILEY

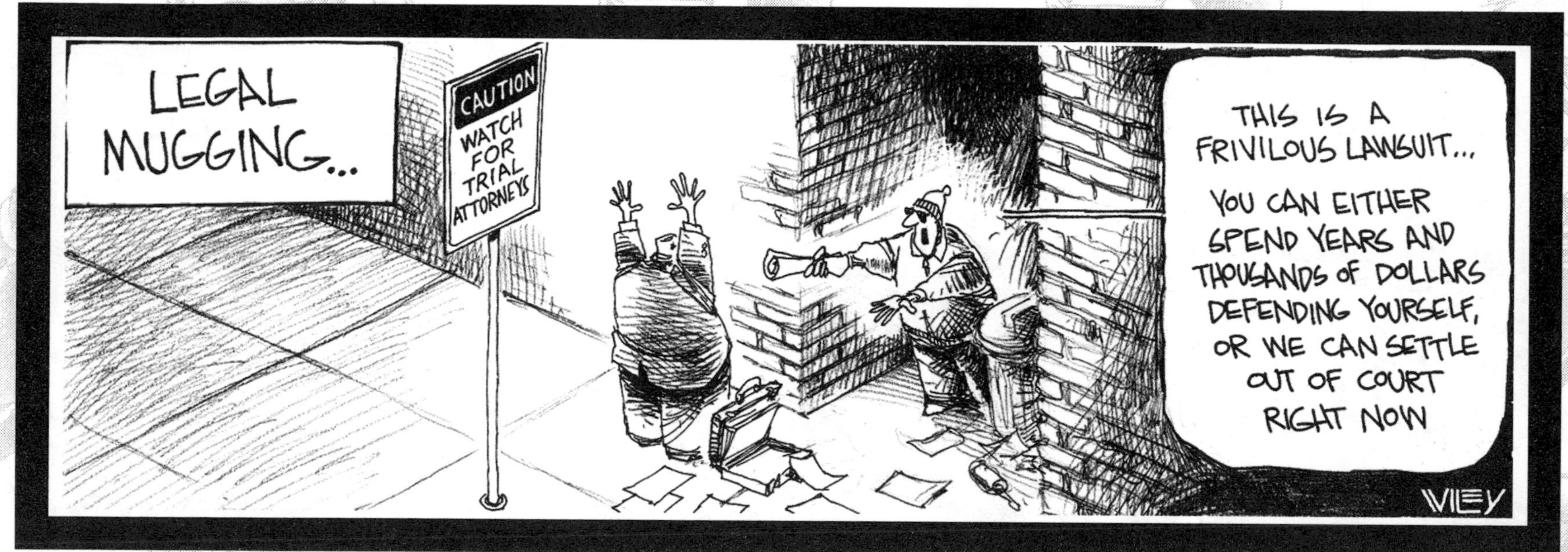
LEGAL MUGGING...
CAUTION WATCH FOR TRIAL ATTORNEYS
THIS IS A FRIVILOUS LAWSUIT...
YOU CAN EITHER SPEND YEARS AND THOUSANDS OF DOLLARS DEFENDING YOURSELF, OR WE CAN SETTLE OUT OF COURT RIGHT NOW
WILEY

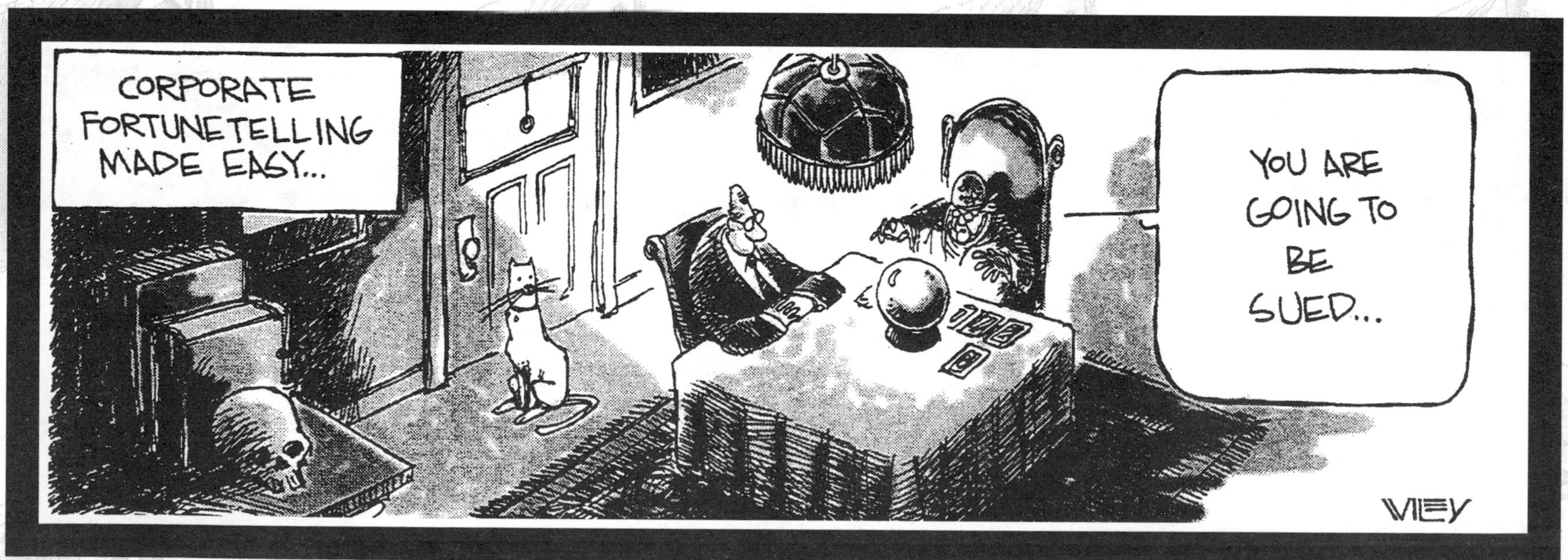
CORPORATE FORTUNETELLING MADE EASY...
YOU ARE GOING TO BE SUED...
WILEY

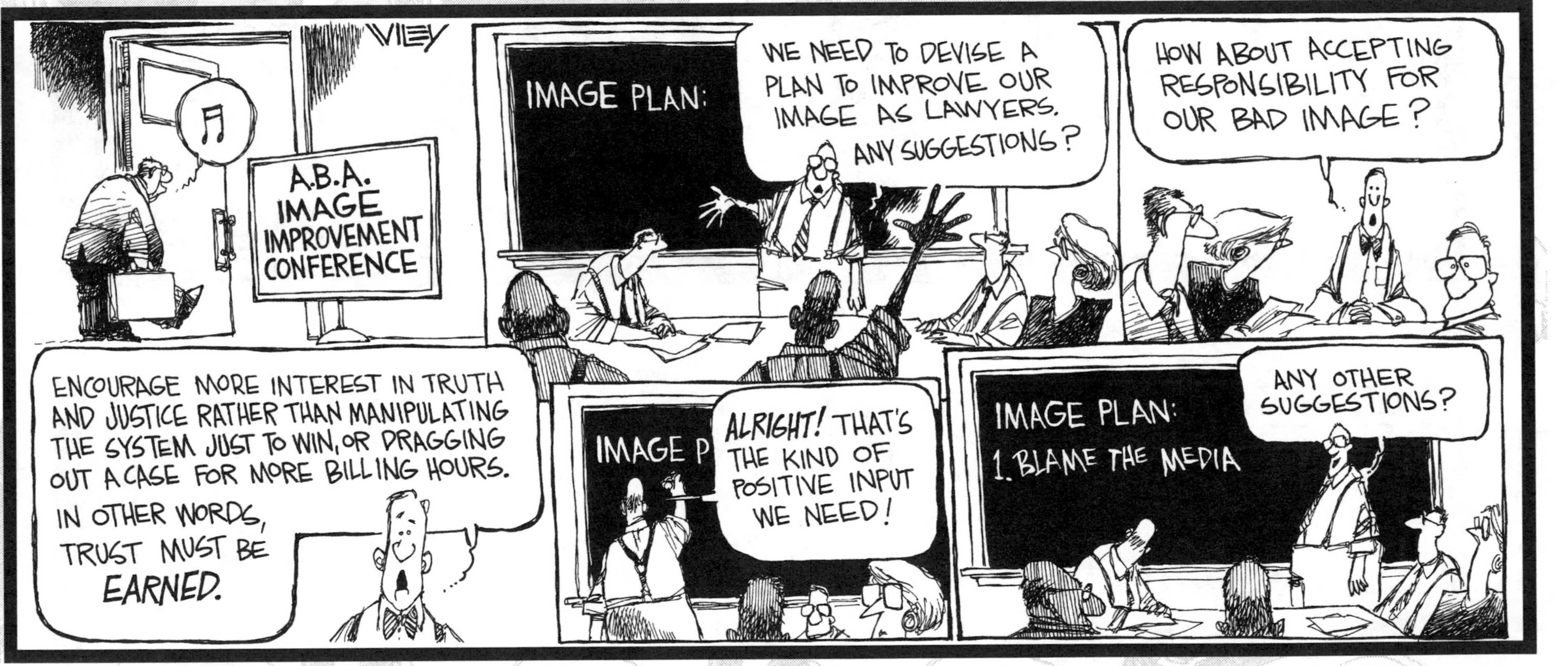
WILEY
A.B.A. IMAGE IMPROVEMENT CONFERENCE
IMAGE PLAN:
WE NEED TO DEVISE A PLAN TO IMPROVE OUR IMAGE AS LAWYERS.
ANY SUGGESTIONS?
HOW ABOUT ACCEPTING RESPONSIBILITY FOR OUR BAD IMAGE?
ENCOURAGE MORE INTEREST IN TRUTH AND JUSTICE RATHER THAN MANIPULATING THE SYSTEM JUST TO WIN, OR DRAGGING OUT A CASE FOR MORE BILLING HOURS.
IN OTHER WORDS, TRUST MUST BE EARNED.
IMAGE P
ALRIGHT! THAT'S THE KIND OF POSITIVE INPUT WE NEED!
IMAGE PLAN:
1. BLAME THE MEDIA
ANY OTHER SUGGESTIONS?

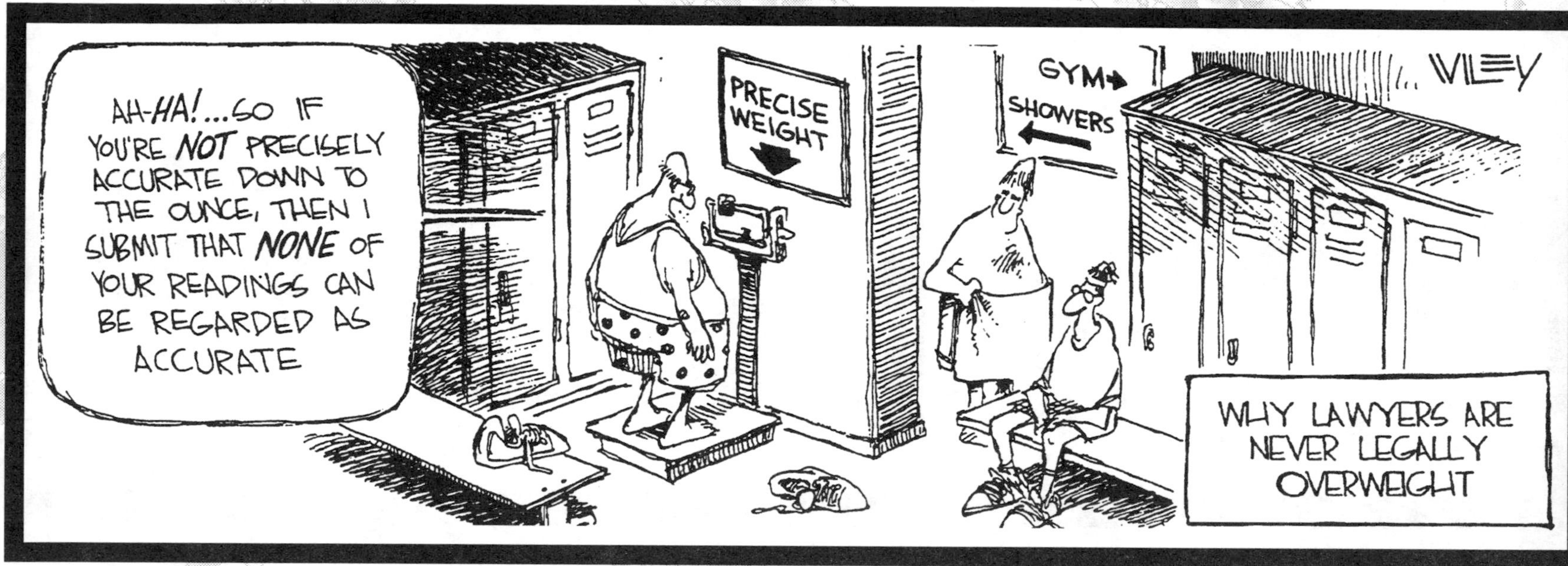
AH-HA!...SO IF YOU'RE NOT PRECISELY ACCURATE DOWN TO THE OUNCE, THEN I SUBMIT THAT NONE OF YOUR READINGS CAN BE REGARDED AS ACCURATE
PRECISE WEIGHT
GYM
SHOWERS
WILEY
WHY LAWYERS ARE NEVER LEGALLY OVERWEIGHT

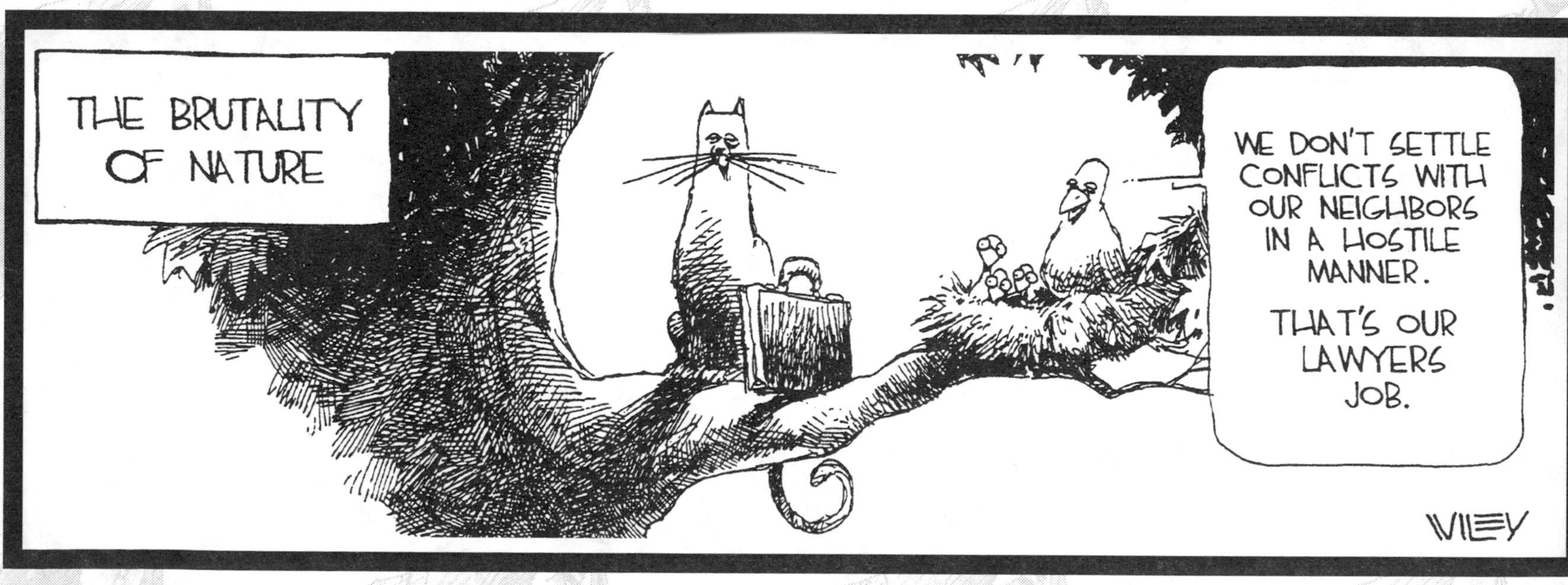
THE BRUTALITY OF NATURE
WE DON'T SETTLE CONFLICTS WITH OUR NEIGHBORS IN A HOSTILE MANNER.
THAT'S OUR LAWYERS JOB.
WILEY

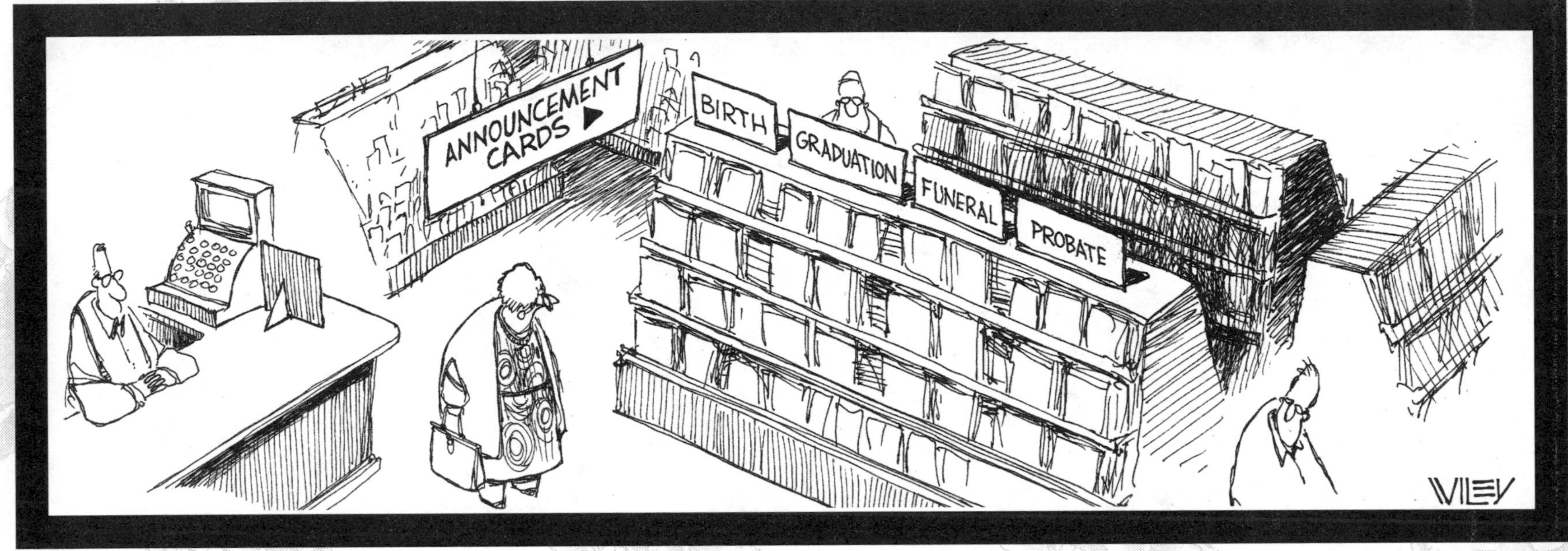
ANNOUNCEMENT CARDS
BIRTH
GRADUATION
FUNERAL
PROBATE
WILEY

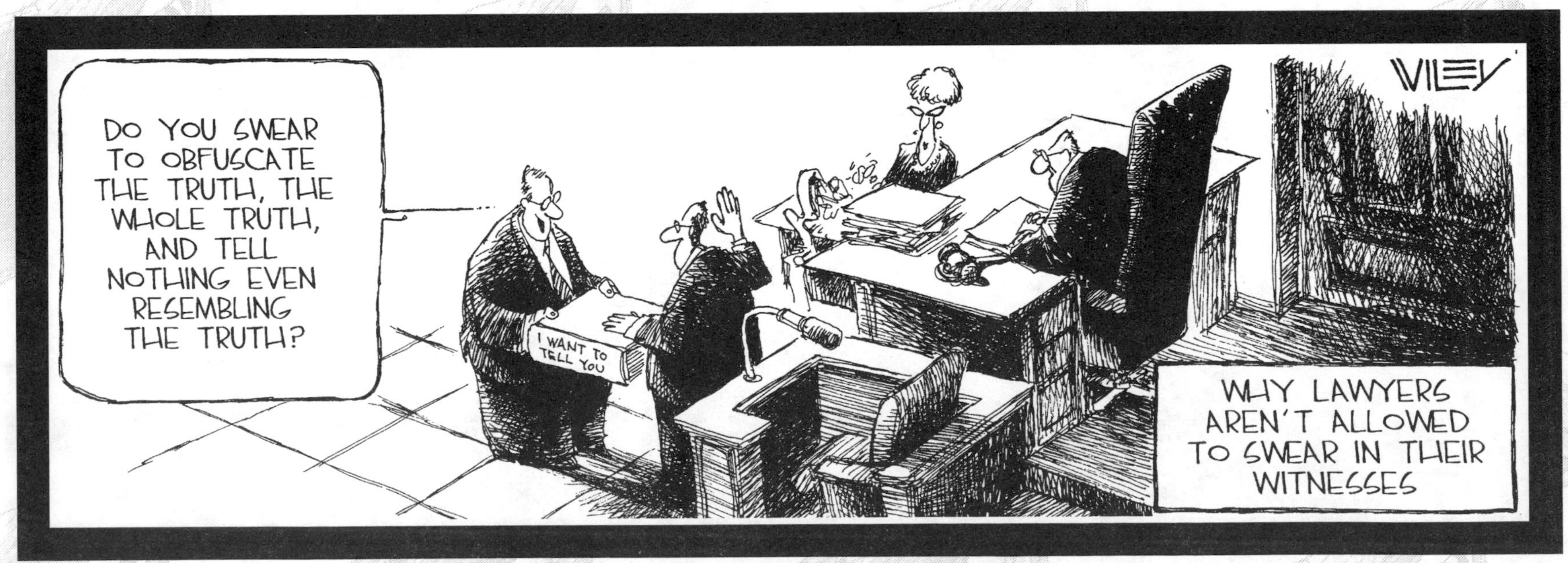
WILEY
DO YOU SWEAR TO OBFUSCATE THE TRUTH, THE WHOLE TRUTH, AND TELL NOTHING EVEN RESEMBLING THE TRUTH?
I WANT TO TELL YOU
WHY LAWYERS AREN'T ALLOWED TO SWEAR IN THEIR WITNESSES

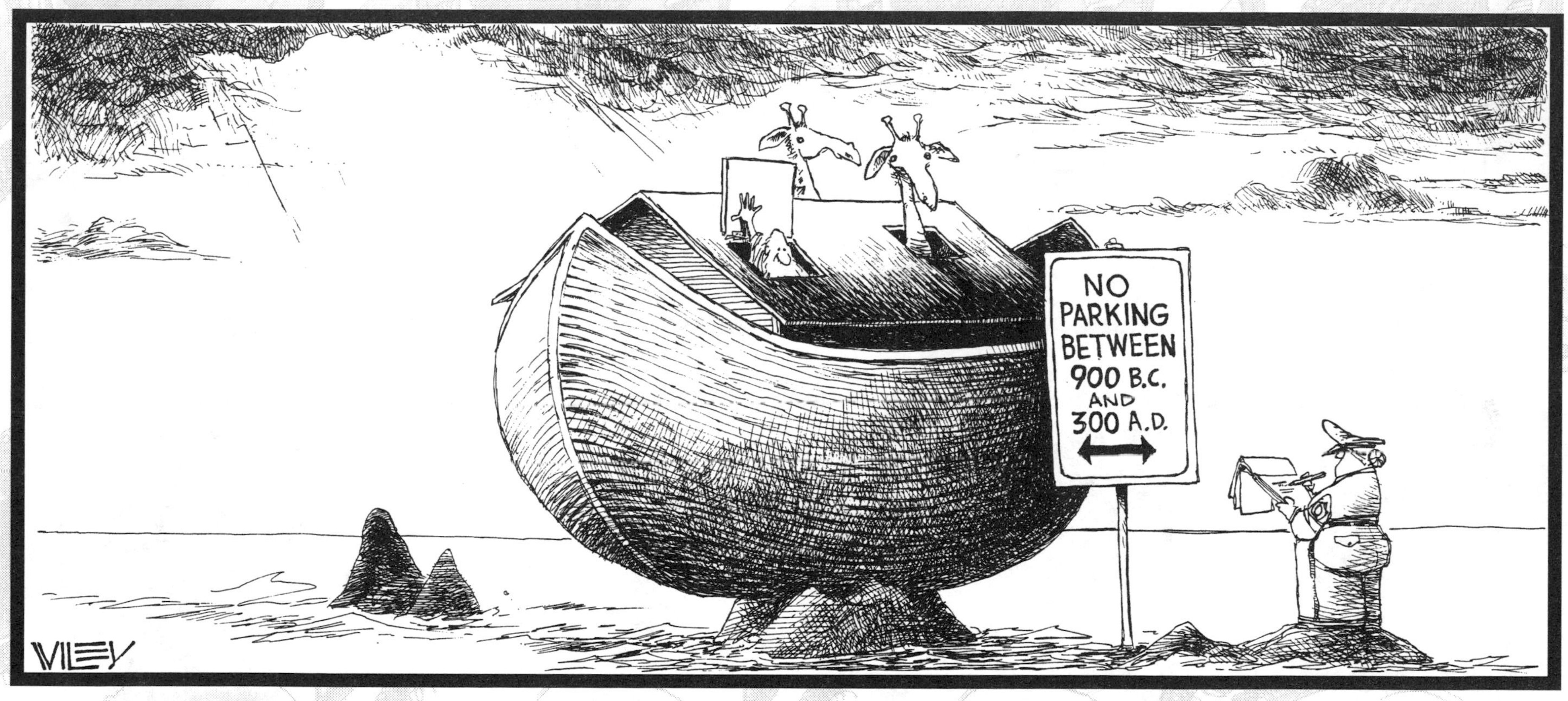
NO PARKING BETWEEN 900 B.C. AND 300 A.D.
WILEY

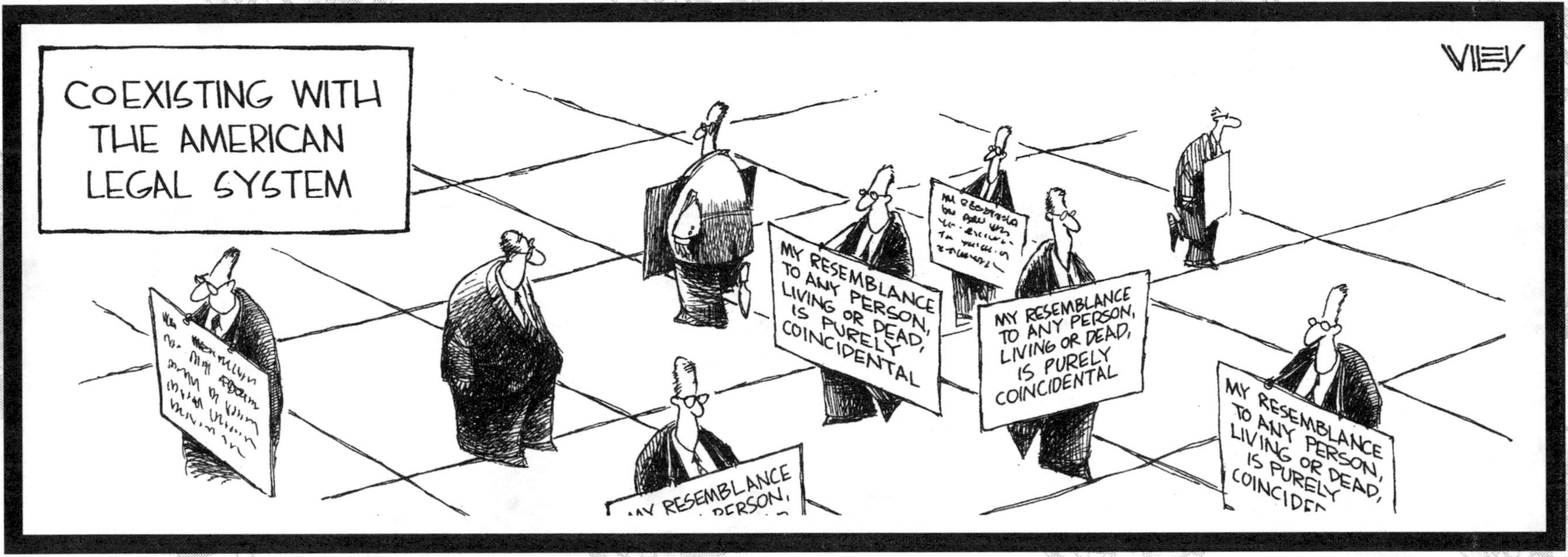

COEXISTING WITH THE AMERICAN LEGAL SYSTEM
WILEY
MY RESEMBLANCE TO ANY PERSON, LIVING OR DEAD, IS PURELY COINCIDENTAL
MY RESEMBLANCE TO ANY PERSON, LIVING OR DEAD, IS PURELY COINCIDENTAL

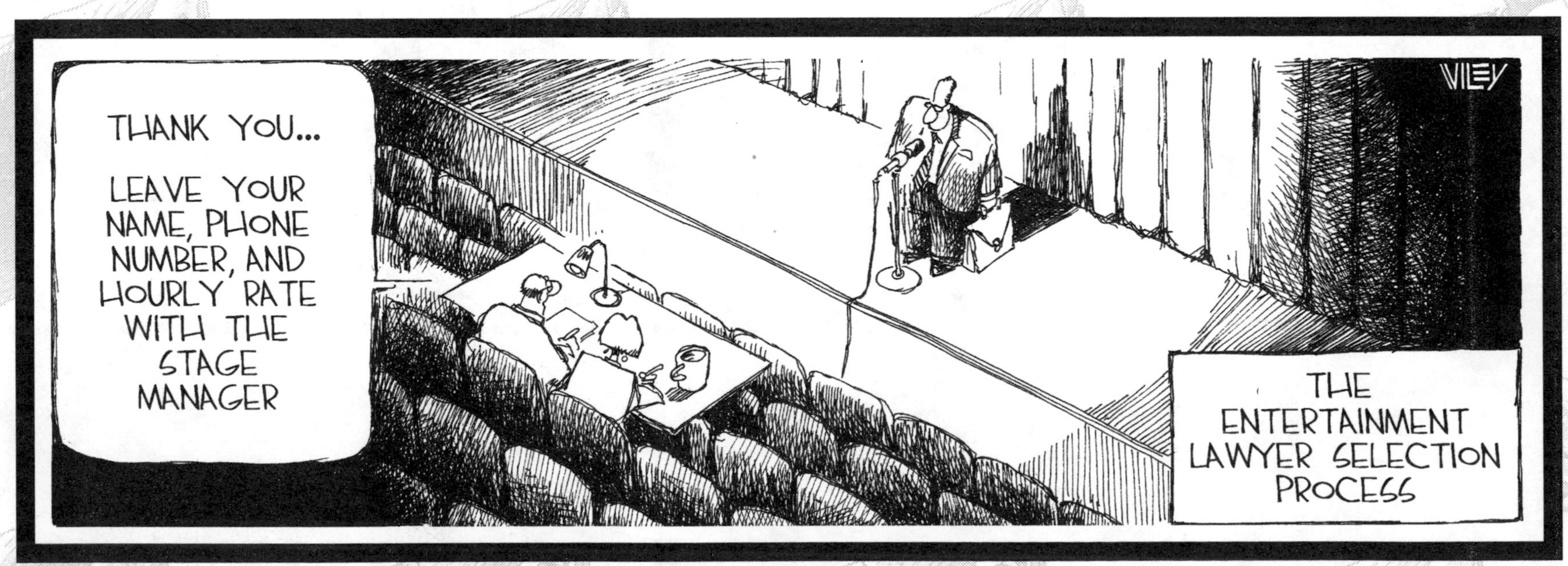

THANK YOU...
LEAVE YOUR NAME, PHONE NUMBER, AND HOURLY RATE WITH THE STAGE MANAGER
WILEY
THE ENTERTAINMENT LAWYER SELECTION PROCESS

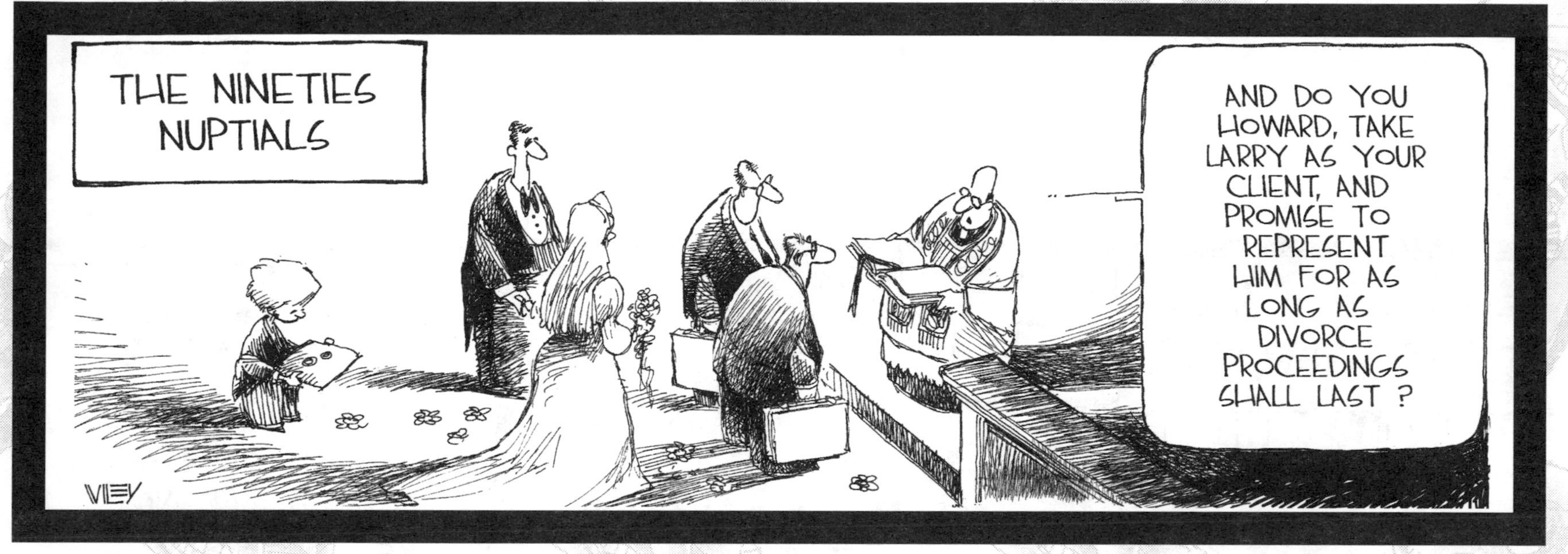
THE NINETIES NUPTIALS
AND DO YOU HOWARD, TAKE LARRY AS YOUR CLIENT, AND PROMISE TO REPRESENT HIM FOR AS LONG AS DIVORCE PROCEEDINGS SHALL LAST ?
WILEY

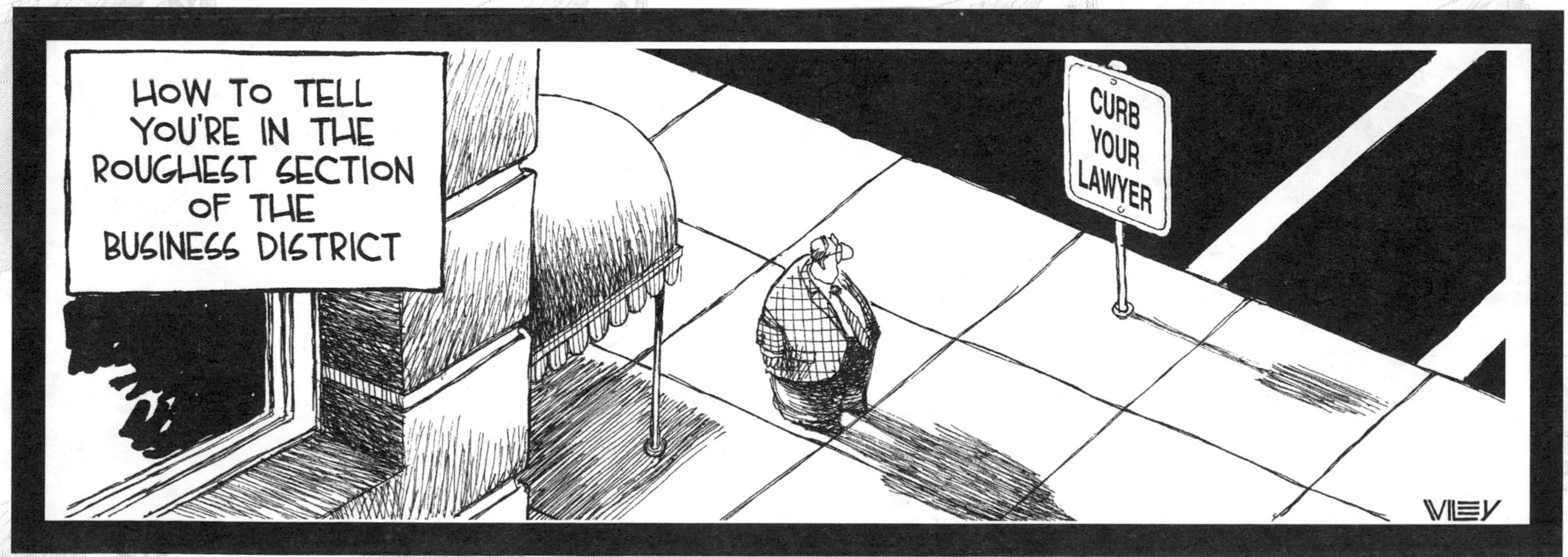
HOW TO TELL YOU'RE IN THE ROUGHEST SECTION OF THE BUSINESS DISTRICT
CURB YOUR LAWYER
WILEY

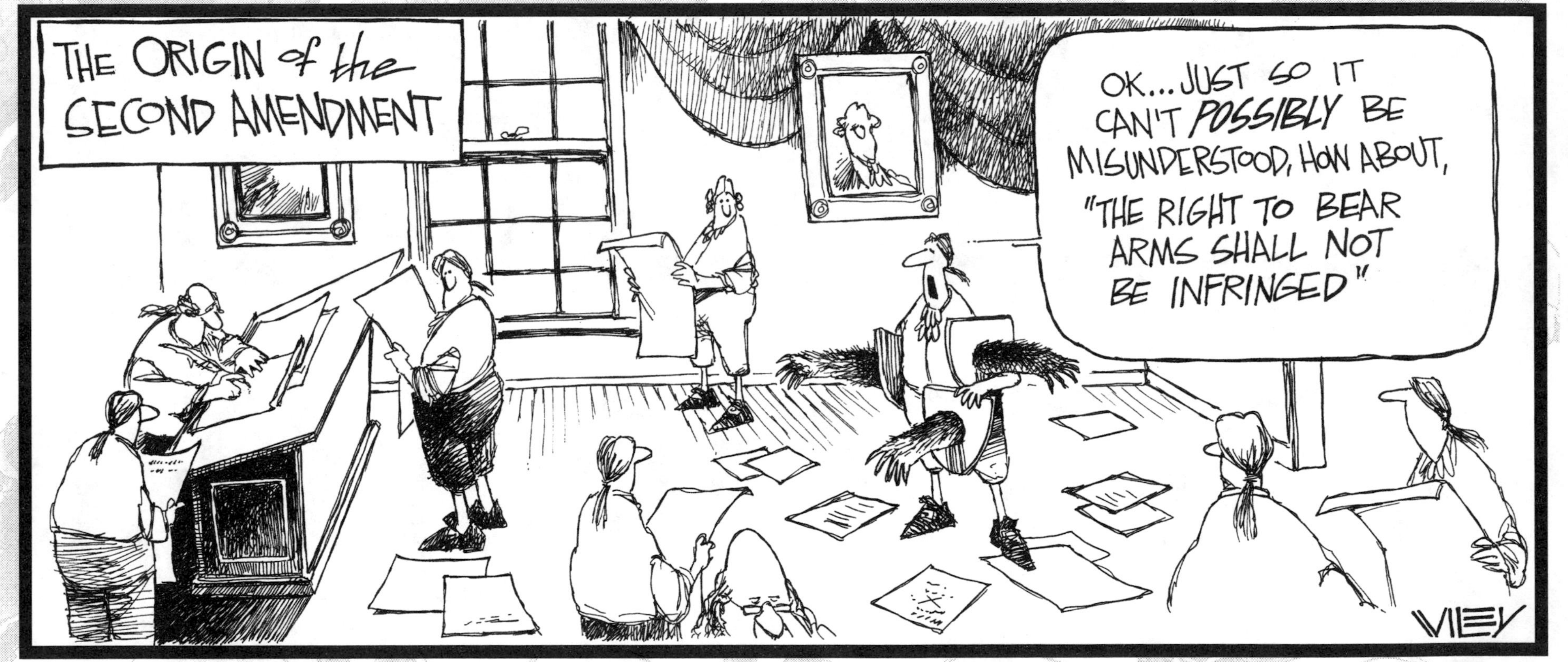
THE ORIGIN of the SECOND AMENDMENT
OK... JUST SO IT CAN'T POSSIBLY BE MISUNDERSTOOD, HOW ABOUT, "THE RIGHT TO BEAR ARMS SHALL NOT BE INFRINGED"

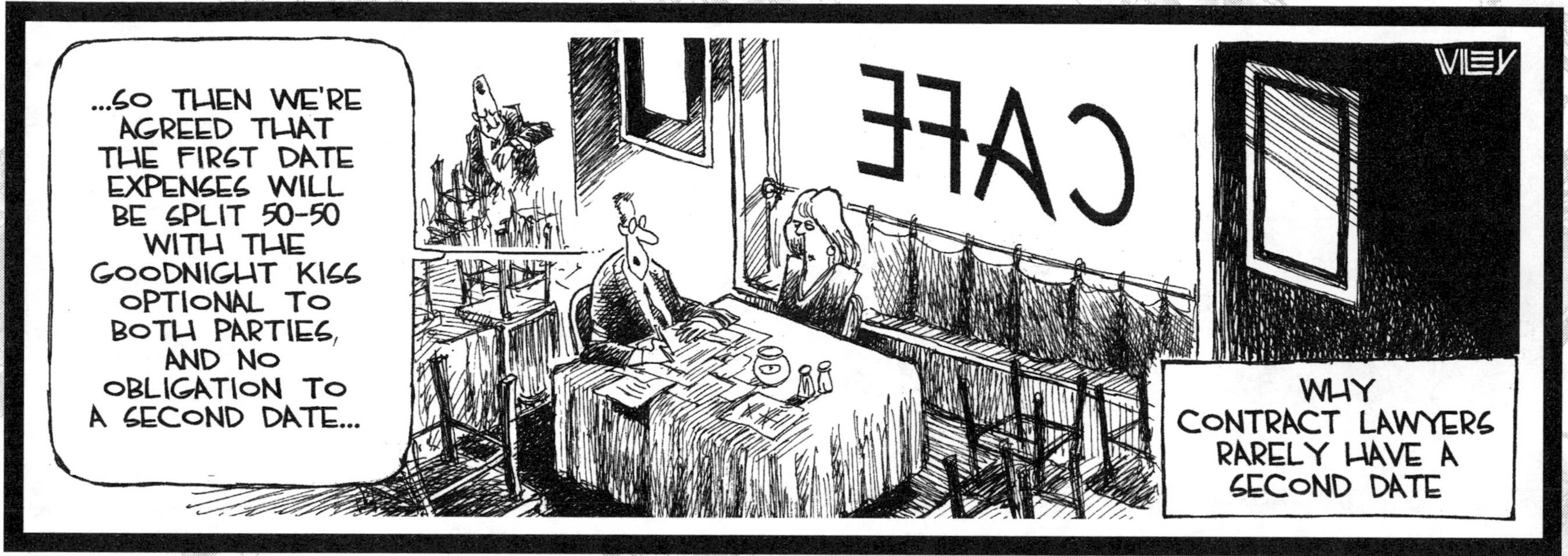

...SO THEN WE'RE AGREED THAT THE FIRST DATE EXPENSES WILL BE SPLIT 50-50 WITH THE GOODNIGHT KISS OPTIONAL TO BOTH PARTIES, AND NO OBLIGATION TO A SECOND DATE...
CAFE
WHY CONTRACT LAWYERS RARELY HAVE A SECOND DATE

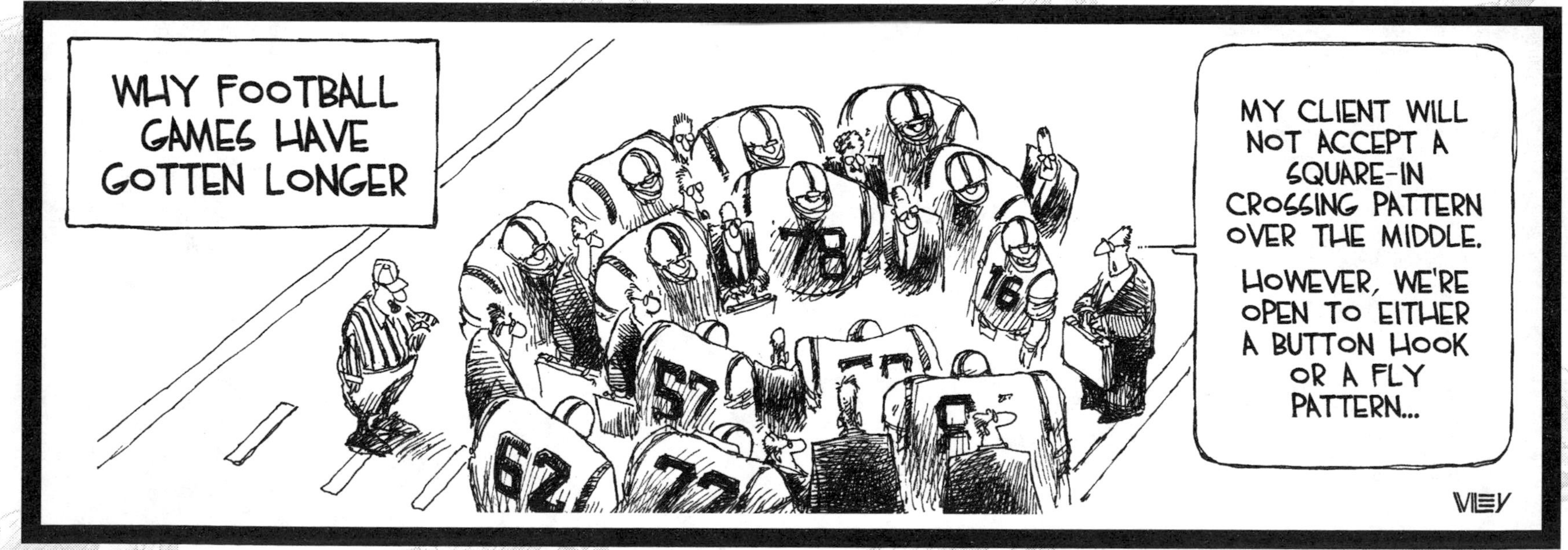

WHY FOOTBALL GAMES HAVE GOTTEN LONGER
MY CLIENT WILL NOT ACCEPT A SQUARE-IN CROSSING PATTERN OVER THE MIDDLE.
HOWEVER, WE'RE OPEN TO EITHER A BUTTON HOOK OR A FLY PATTERN...

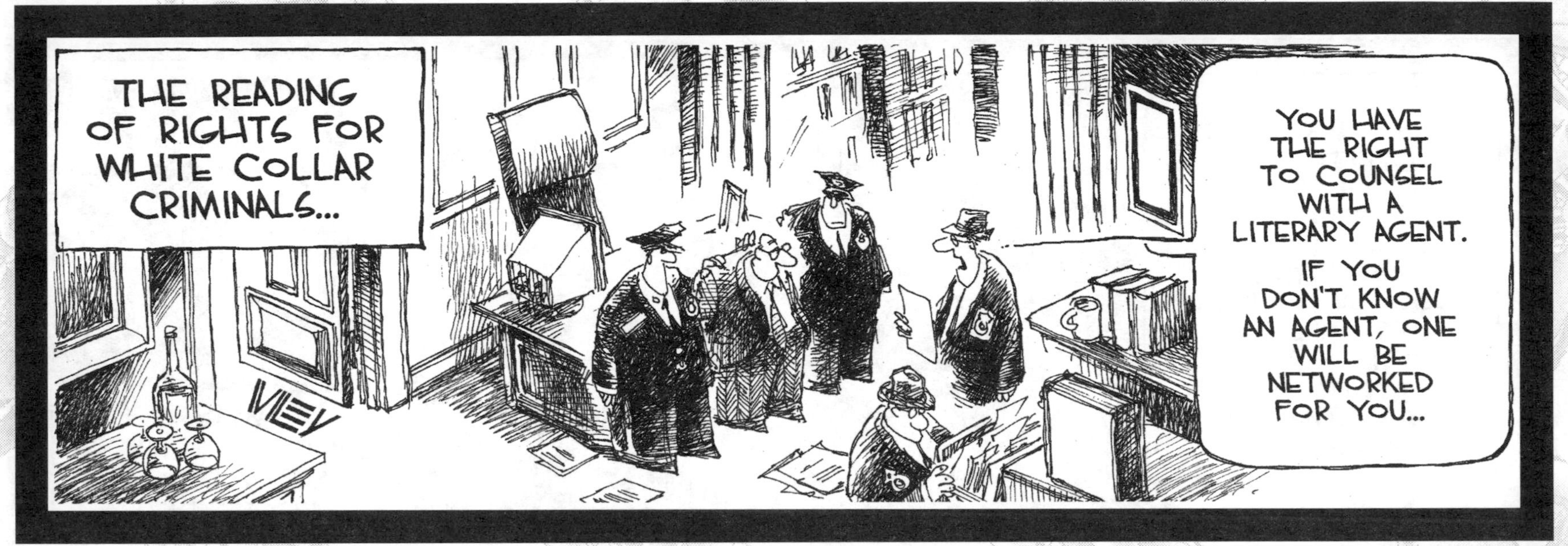
THE READING OF RIGHTS FOR WHITE COLLAR CRIMINALS...
YOU HAVE THE RIGHT TO COUNSEL WITH A LITERARY AGENT.
IF YOU DON'T KNOW AN AGENT, ONE WILL BE NETWORKED FOR YOU...
WILEY

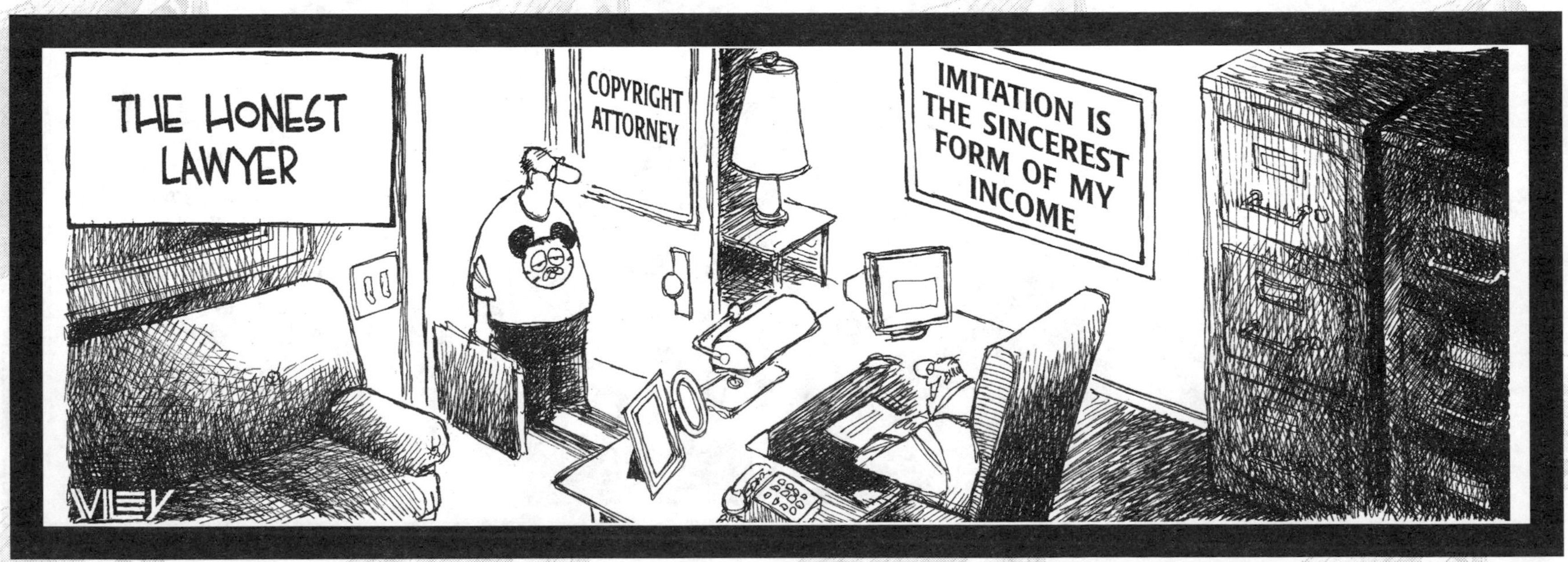
THE HONEST LAWYER
COPYRIGHT ATTORNEY
IMITATION IS THE SINCEREST FORM OF MY INCOME
WILEY

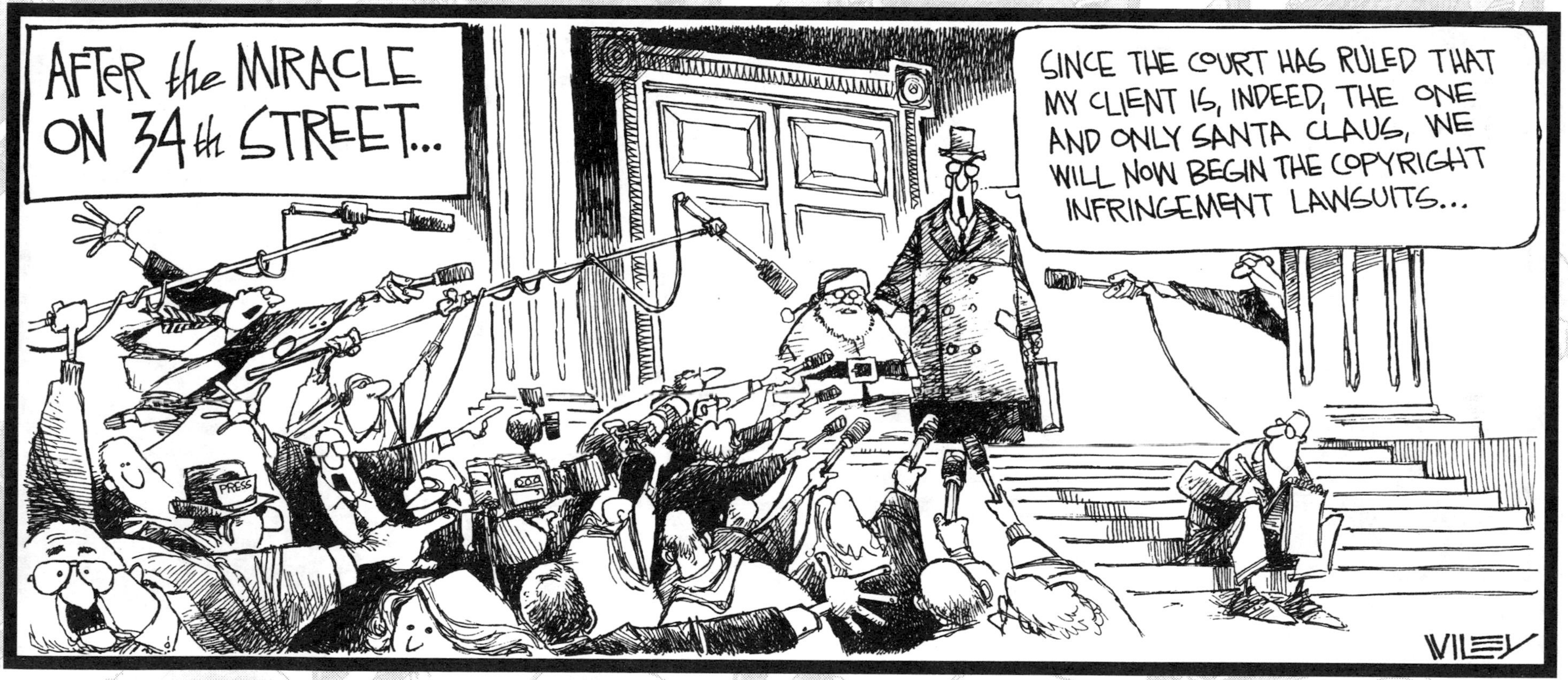
AFTER the MIRACLE ON 34th STREET...
SINCE THE COURT HAS RULED THAT MY CLIENT IS, INDEED, THE ONE AND ONLY SANTA CLAUS, WE WILL NOW BEGIN THE COPYRIGHT INFRINGEMENT LAWSUITS...
PRESS
WILEY

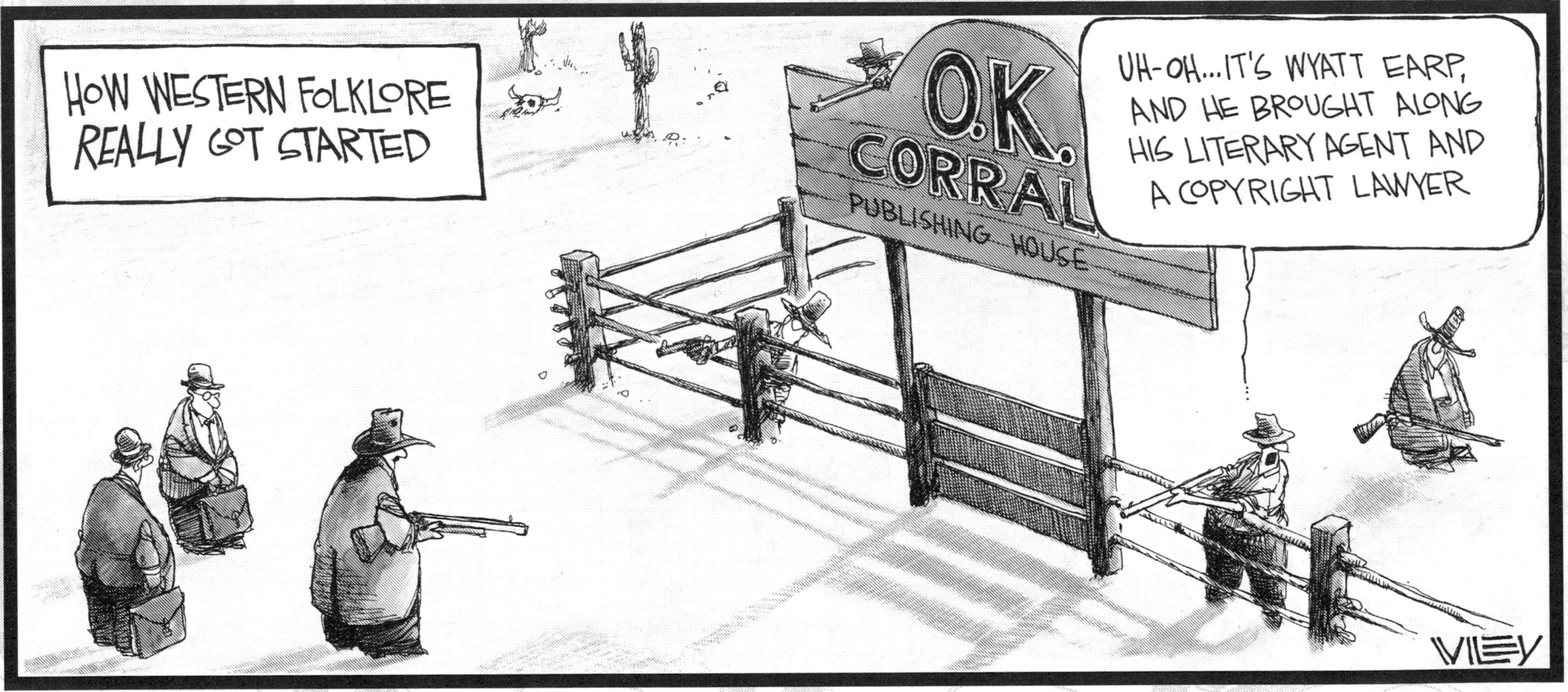
HOW WESTERN FOLKLORE REALLY GOT STARTED
O.K. CORRAL
PUBLISHING HOUSE
UH-OH...IT'S WYATT EARP, AND HE BROUGHT ALONG HIS LITERARY AGENT AND A COPYRIGHT LAWYER
WILEY

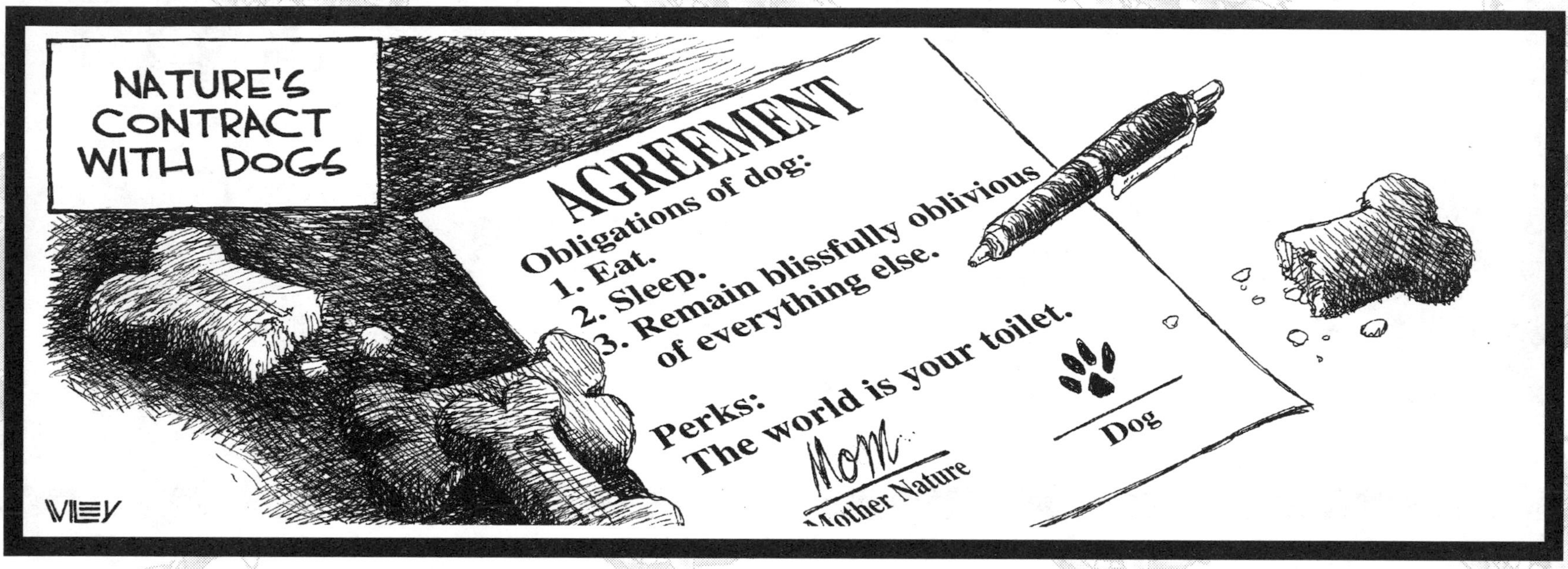
NATURE'S CONTRACT WITH DOGS
AGREEMENT
Obligations of dog:
1. Eat.
2. Sleep.
3. Remain blissfully oblivious of everything else.
Perks:
The world is your toilet.
Mom
Mother Nature
Dog
VILEY

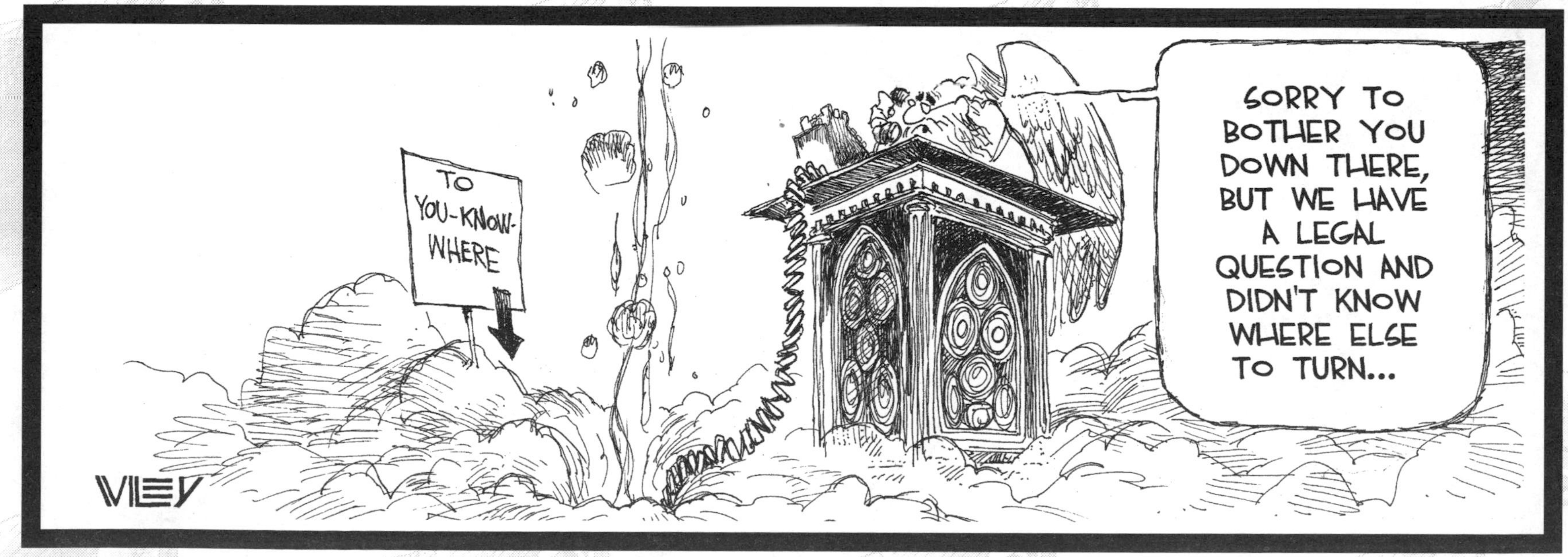
TO YOU-KNOW-WHERE
SORRY TO BOTHER YOU DOWN THERE, BUT WE HAVE A LEGAL QUESTION AND DIDN'T KNOW WHERE ELSE TO TURN...
VILEY

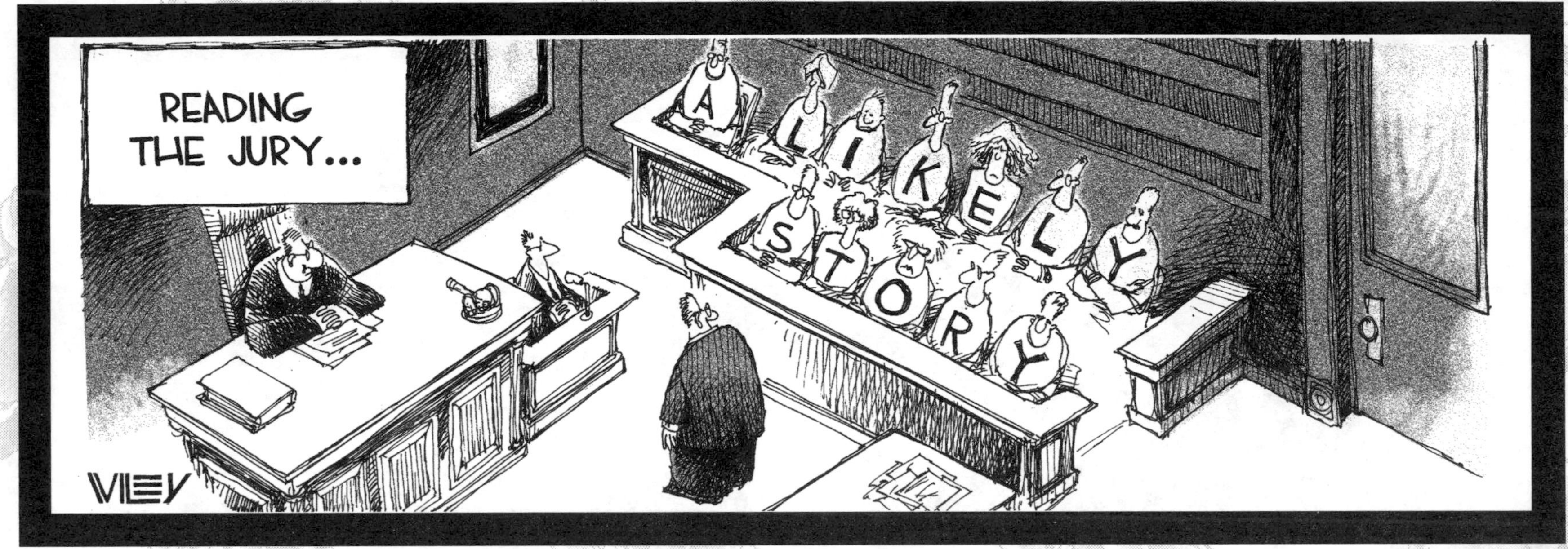
READING THE JURY...
A LIKELY STORY
A LIKELY STORY
VLEY

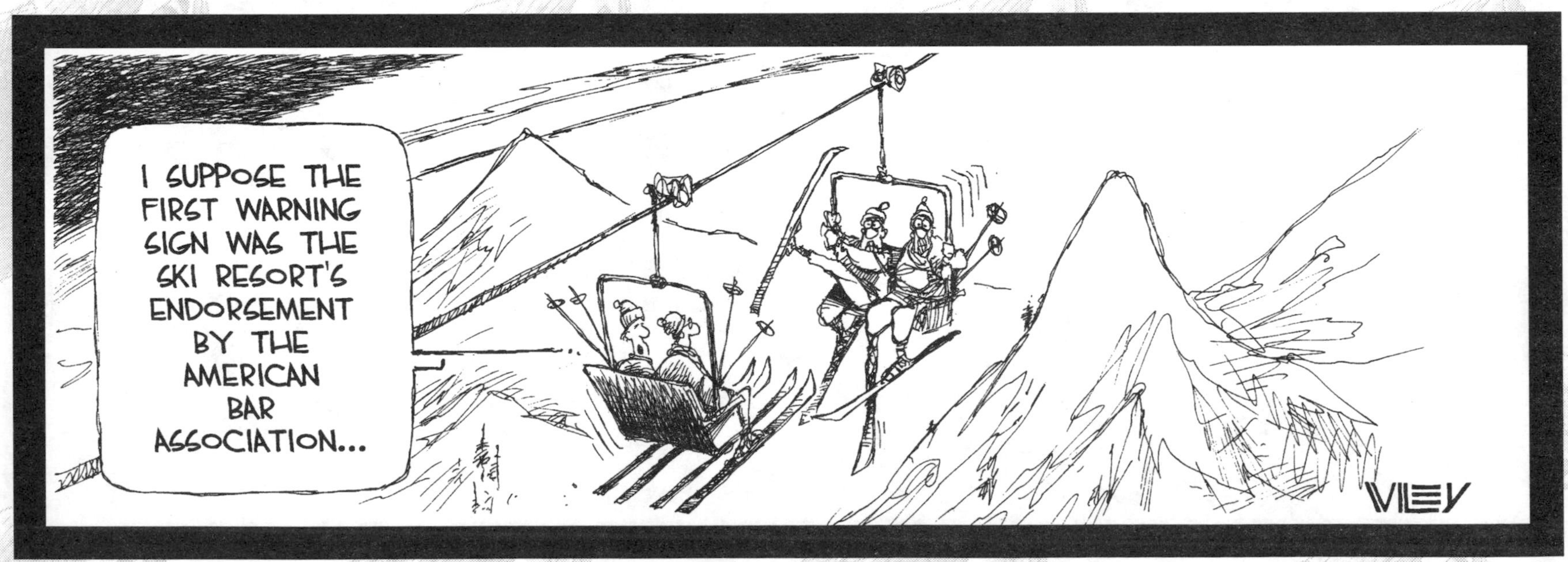
I SUPPOSE THE FIRST WARNING SIGN WAS THE SKI RESORT'S ENDORSEMENT BY THE AMERICAN BAR ASSOCIATION...
VLEY

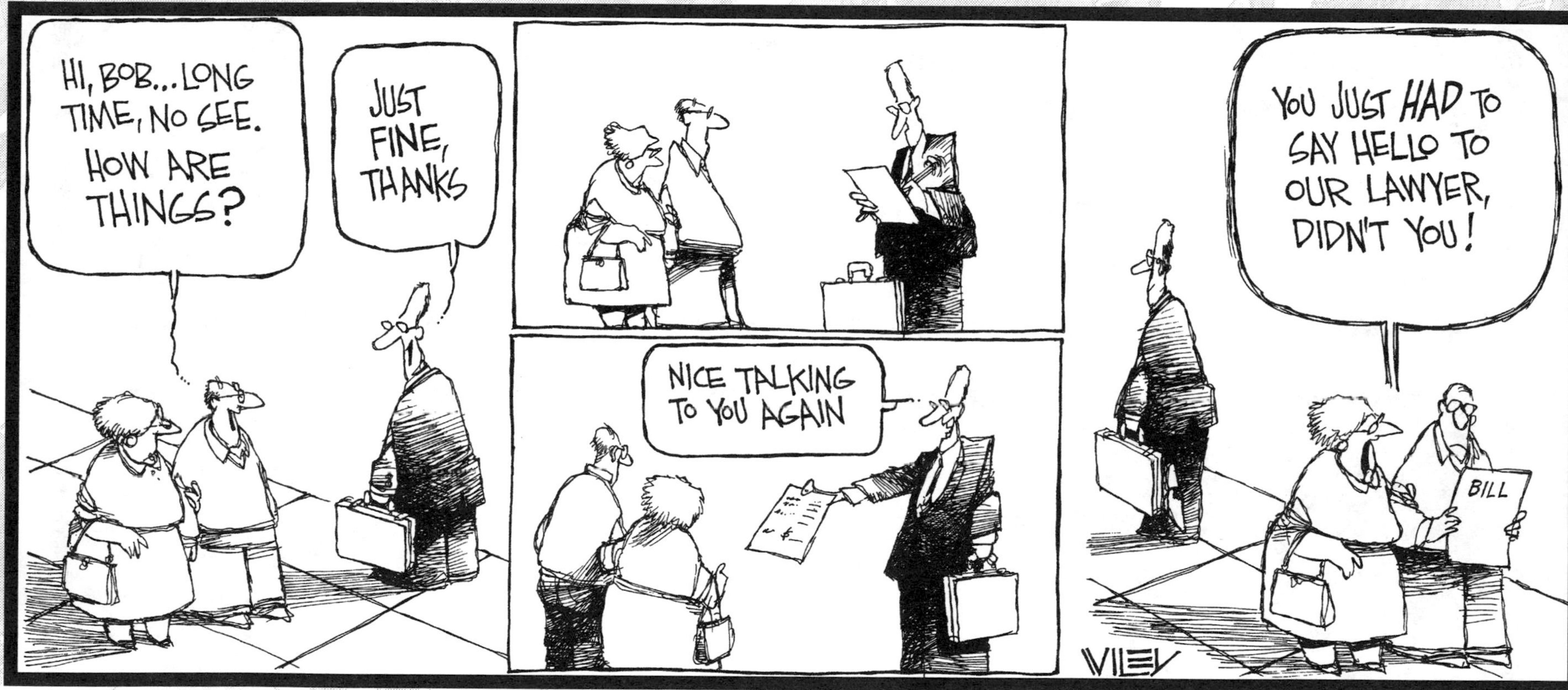
HI, BOB...LONG TIME, NO SEE. HOW ARE THINGS?
JUST FINE, THANKS
NICE TALKING TO YOU AGAIN
YOU JUST HAD TO SAY HELLO TO OUR LAWYER, DIDN'T YOU!
BILL
WILEY

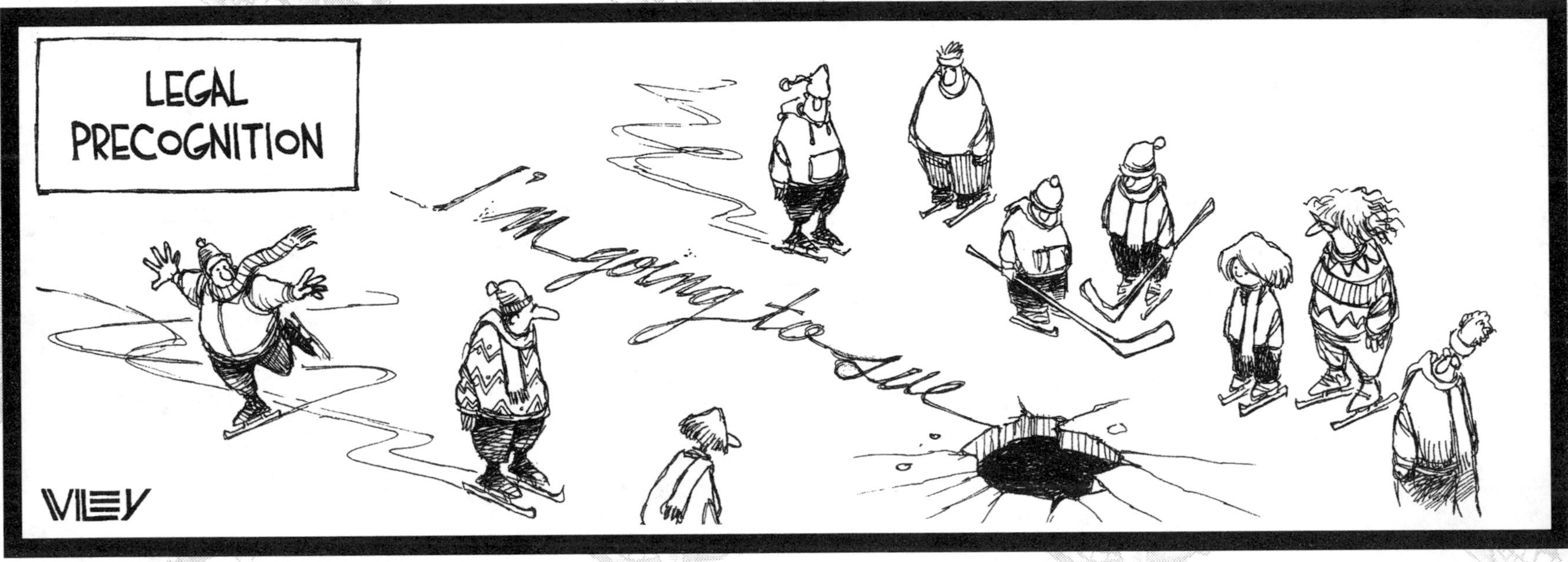
LEGAL PRECOGNITION
I'm going to sue
VILEY

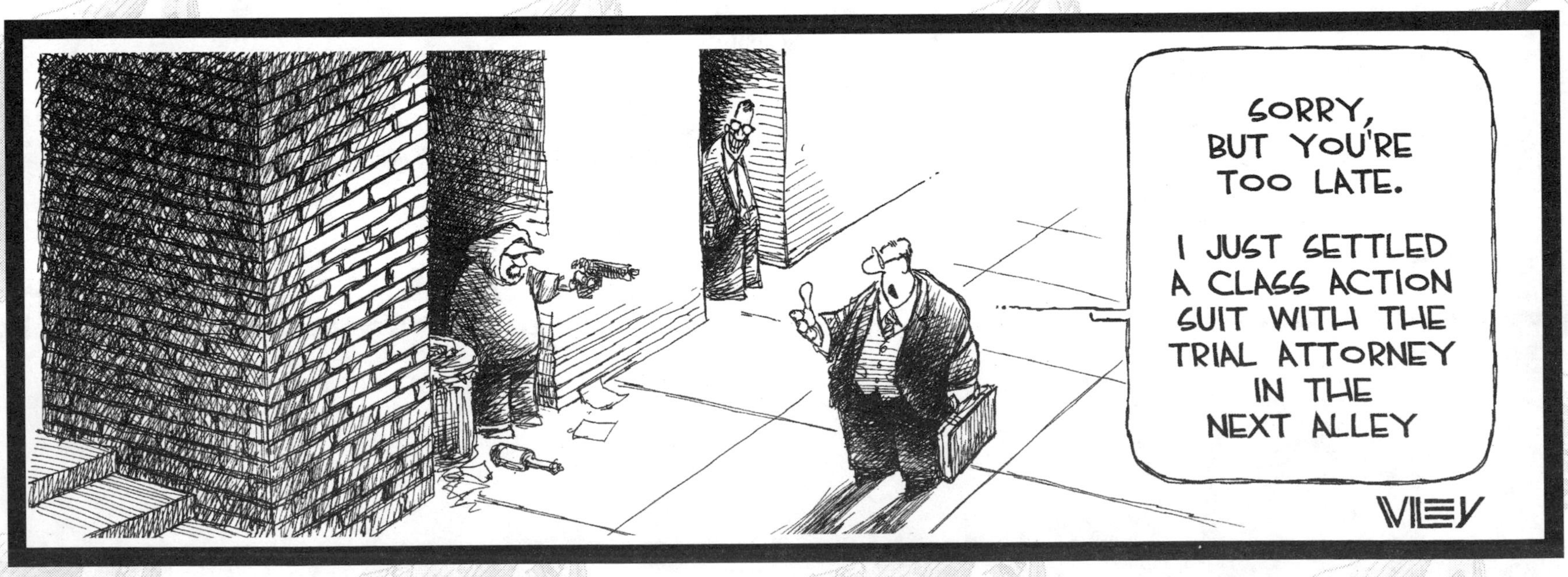
SORRY, BUT YOU'RE TOO LATE.
I JUST SETTLED A CLASS ACTION SUIT WITH THE TRIAL ATTORNEY IN THE NEXT ALLEY
VILEY

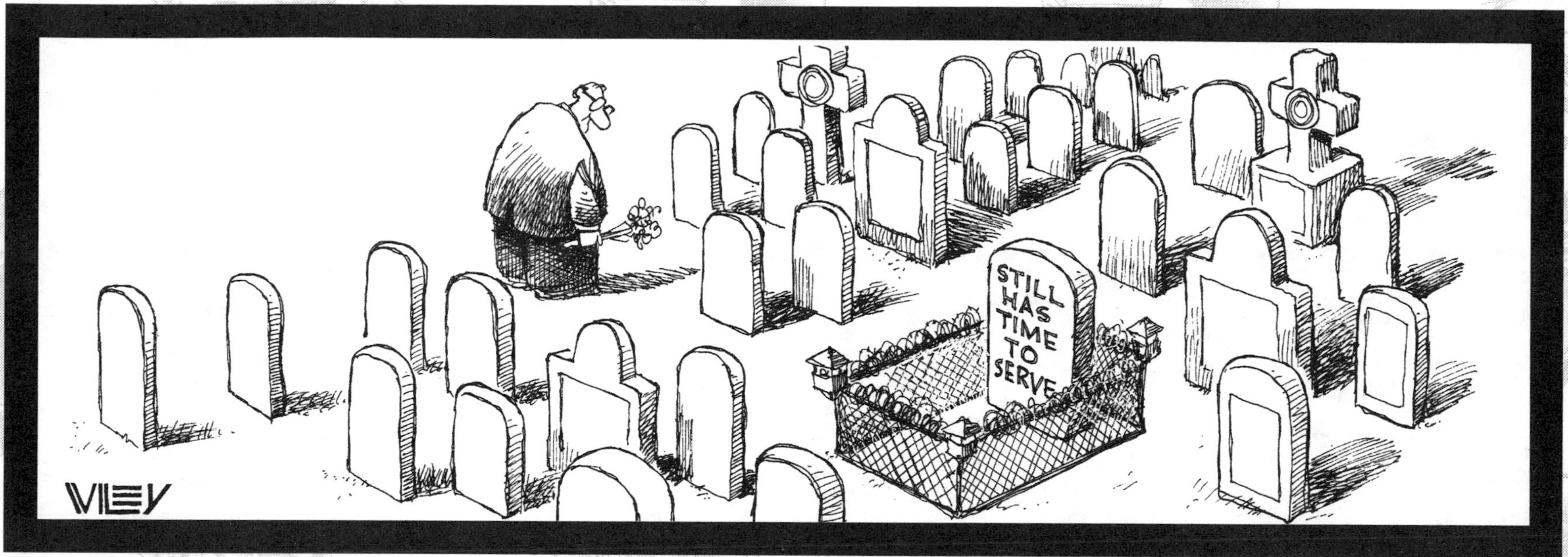
STILL HAS TIME TO SERVE
VILEY

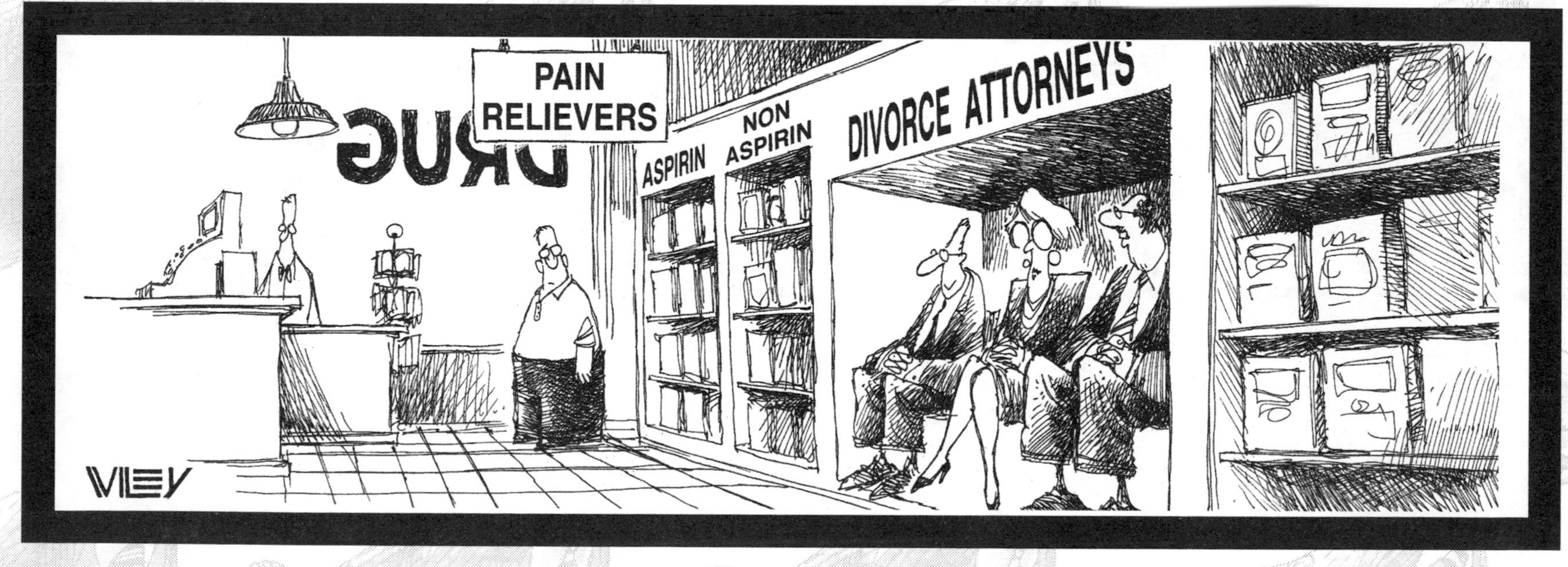
DRUG
PAIN RELIEVERS
ASPIRIN
NON ASPIRIN
DIVORCE ATTORNEYS
VILEY

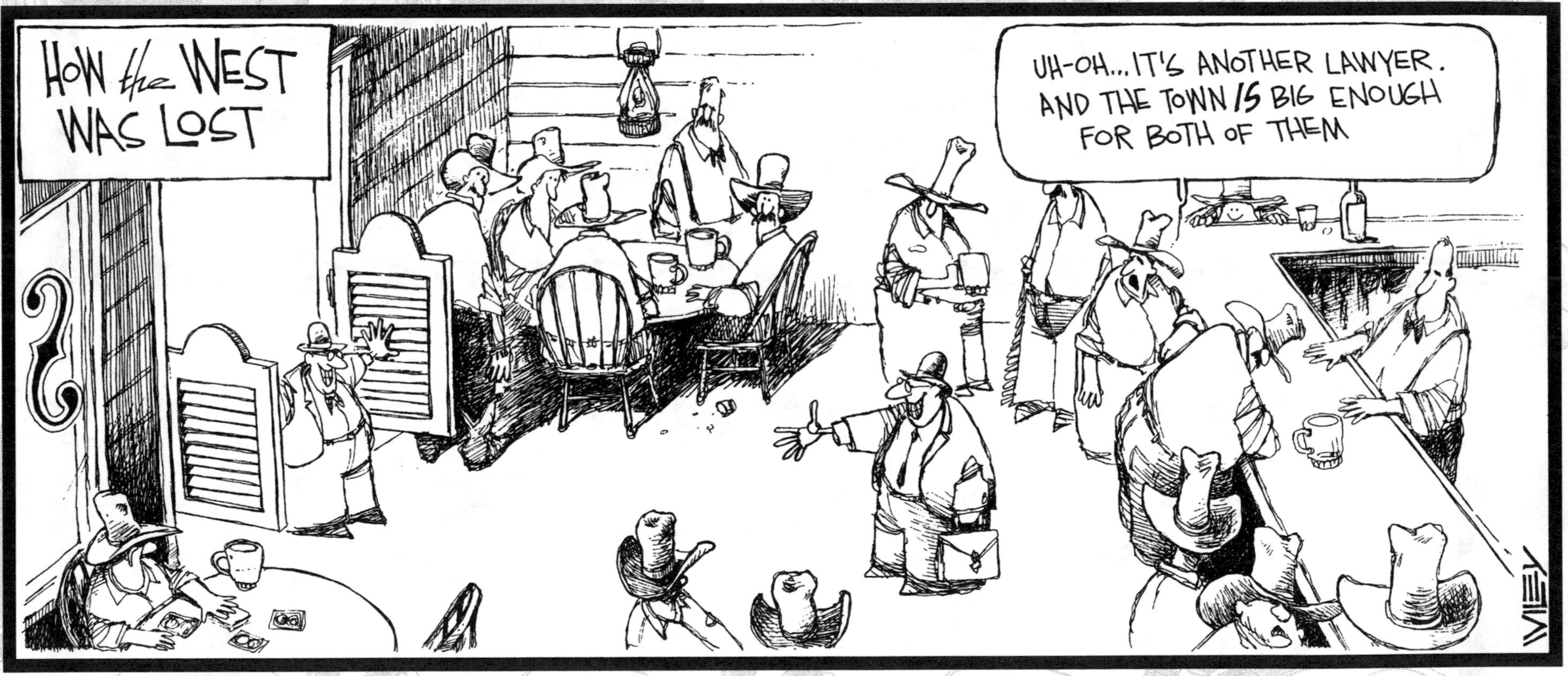
HOW the WEST WAS LOST
UH-OH... IT'S ANOTHER LAWYER. AND THE TOWN IS BIG ENOUGH FOR BOTH OF THEM
WILEY

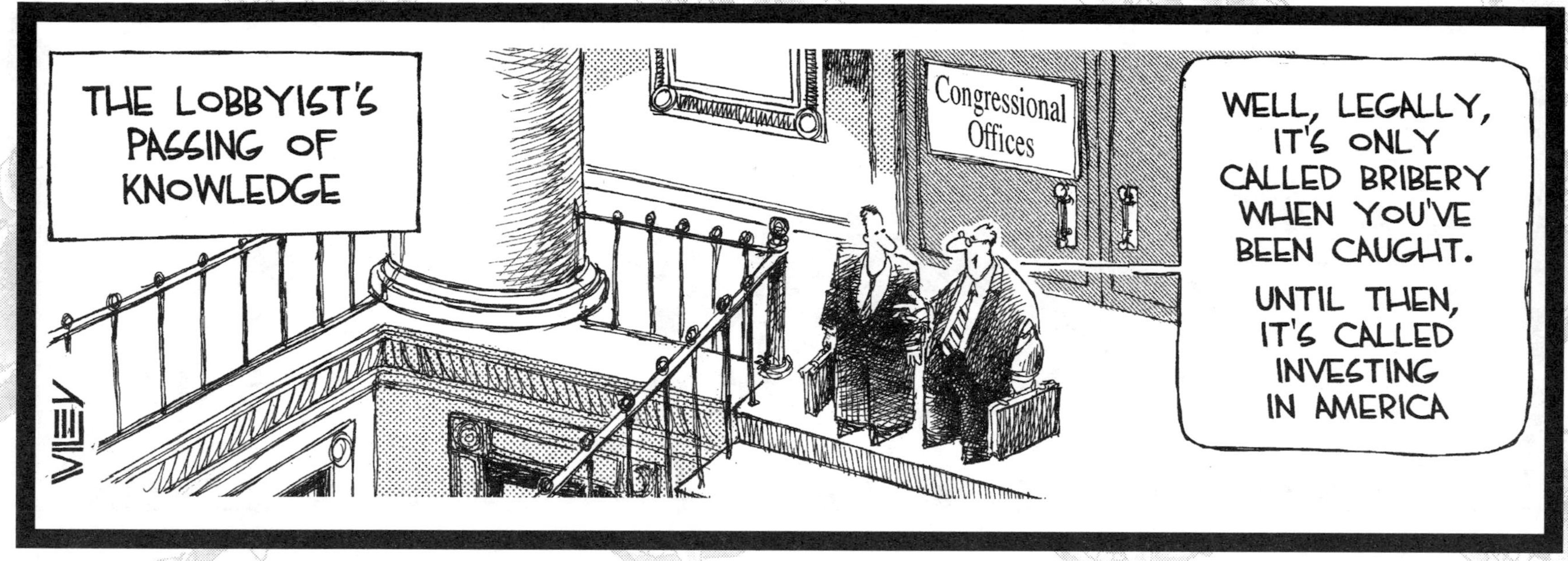
THE LOBBYIST'S PASSING OF KNOWLEDGE
Congressional Offices
WELL, LEGALLY, IT'S ONLY CALLED BRIBERY WHEN YOU'VE BEEN CAUGHT.
UNTIL THEN, IT'S CALLED INVESTING IN AMERICA
VILEY

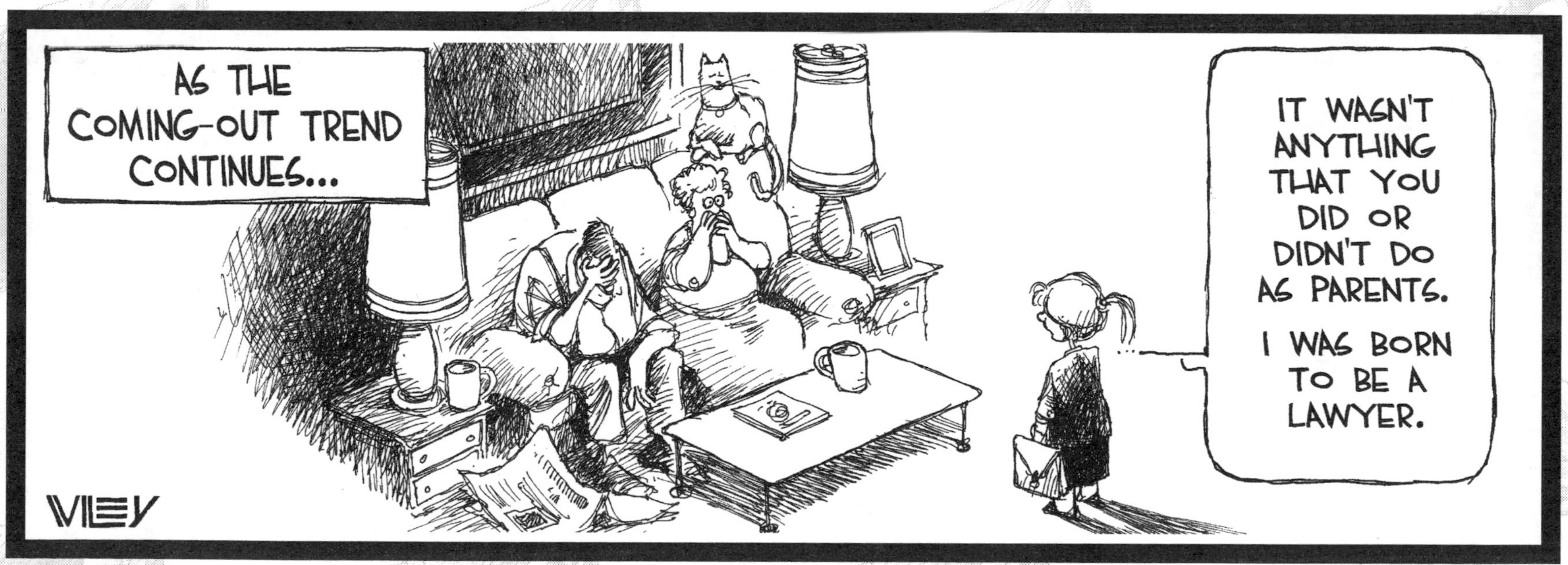
AS THE COMING-OUT TREND CONTINUES...
IT WASN'T ANYTHING THAT YOU DID OR DIDN'T DO AS PARENTS.
I WAS BORN TO BE A LAWYER.
VILEY

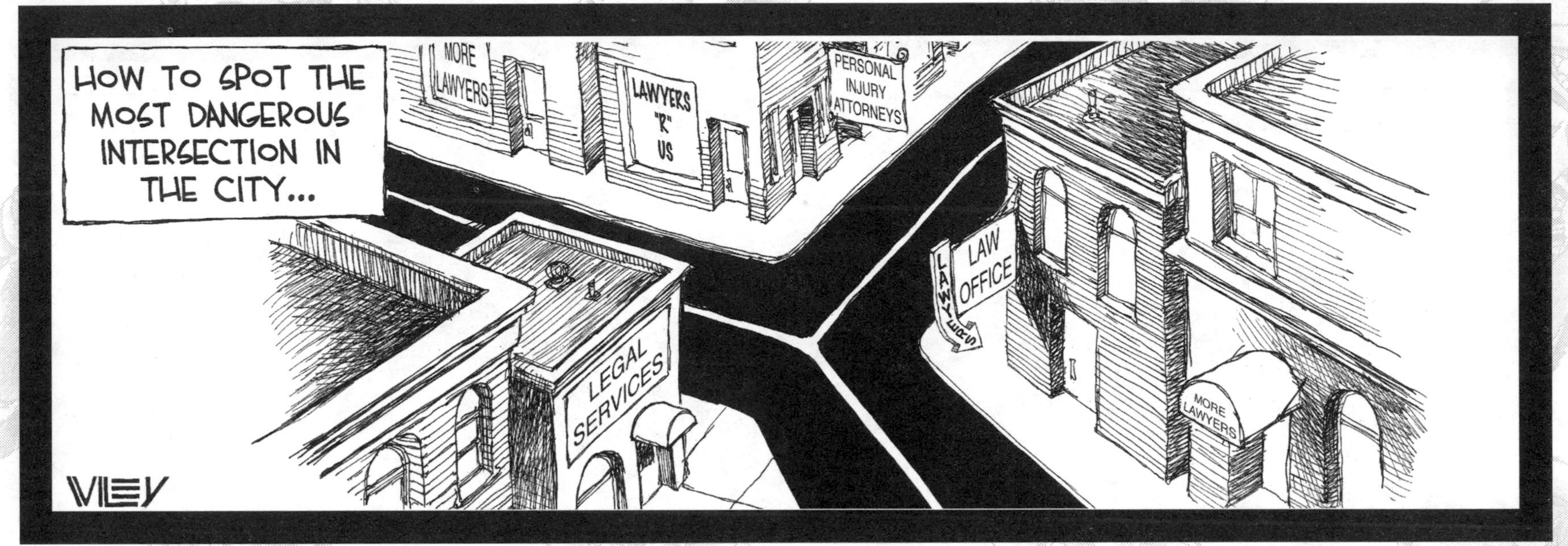
HOW TO SPOT THE MOST DANGEROUS INTERSECTION IN THE CITY...
MORE LAWYERS
LAWYERS "R" US
PERSONAL INJURY ATTORNEYS
LAW OFFICE
LAWYERS
LEGAL SERVICES
MORE LAWYERS
VILEY

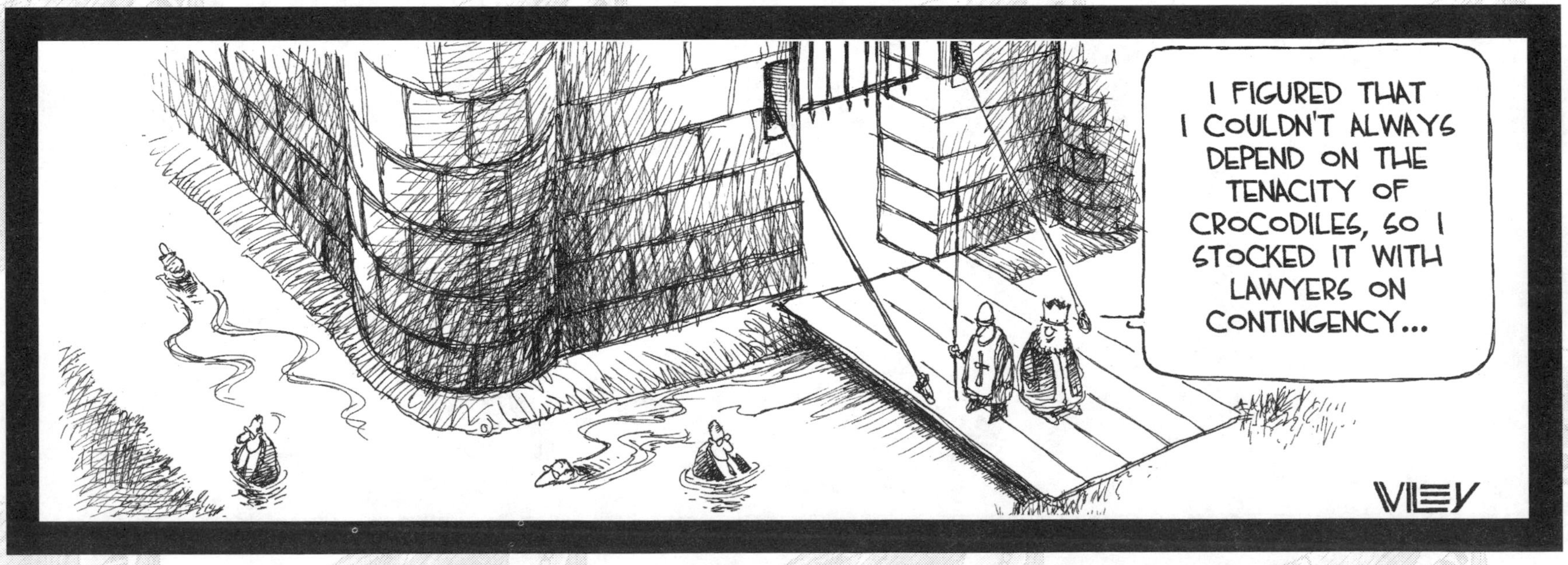
I FIGURED THAT I COULDN'T ALWAYS DEPEND ON THE TENACITY OF CROCODILES, SO I STOCKED IT WITH LAWYERS ON CONTINGENCY...
VILEY

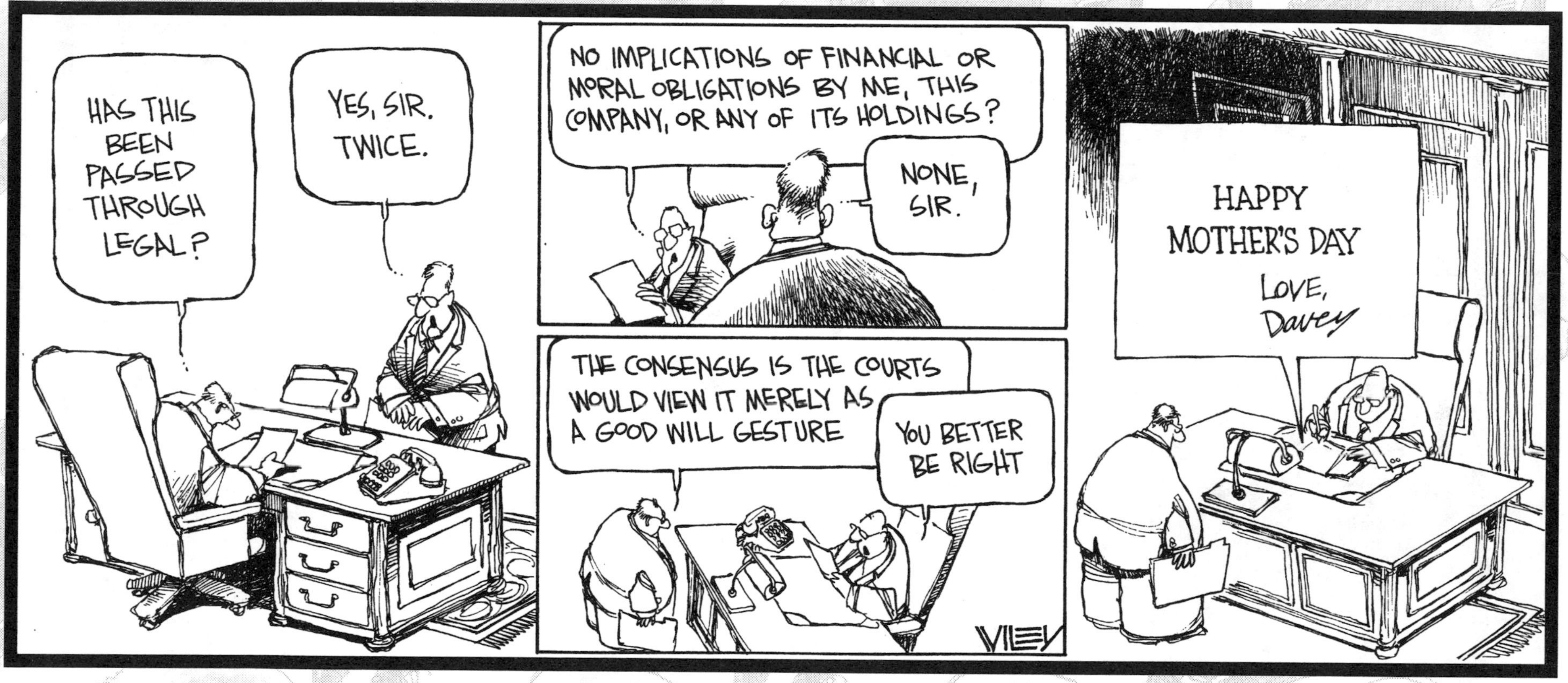
HAS THIS BEEN PASSED THROUGH LEGAL?
YES, SIR. TWICE.
NO IMPLICATIONS OF FINANCIAL OR MORAL OBLIGATIONS BY ME, THIS COMPANY, OR ANY OF ITS HOLDINGS?
NONE, SIR.
THE CONSENSUS IS THE COURTS WOULD VIEW IT MERELY AS A GOOD WILL GESTURE
YOU BETTER BE RIGHT
HAPPY MOTHER'S DAY
LOVE, Davey
WILEY

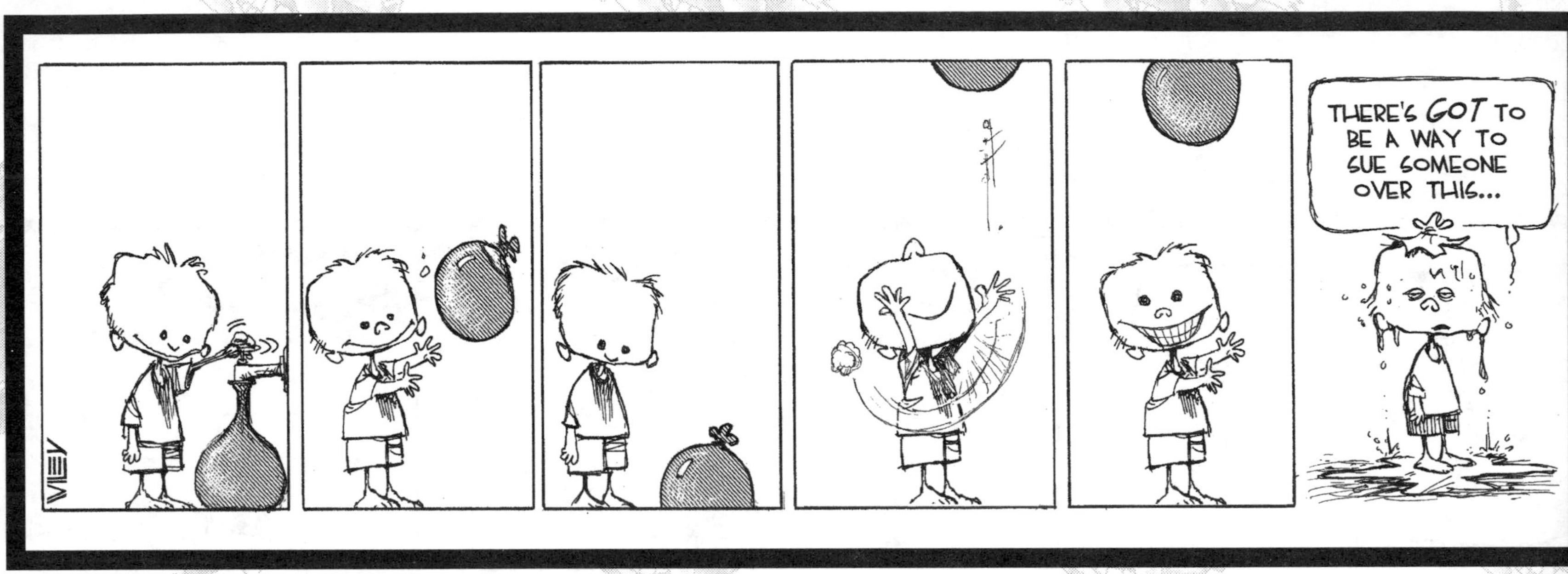
WILEY
THERE'S GOT TO BE A WAY TO SUE SOMEONE OVER THIS...

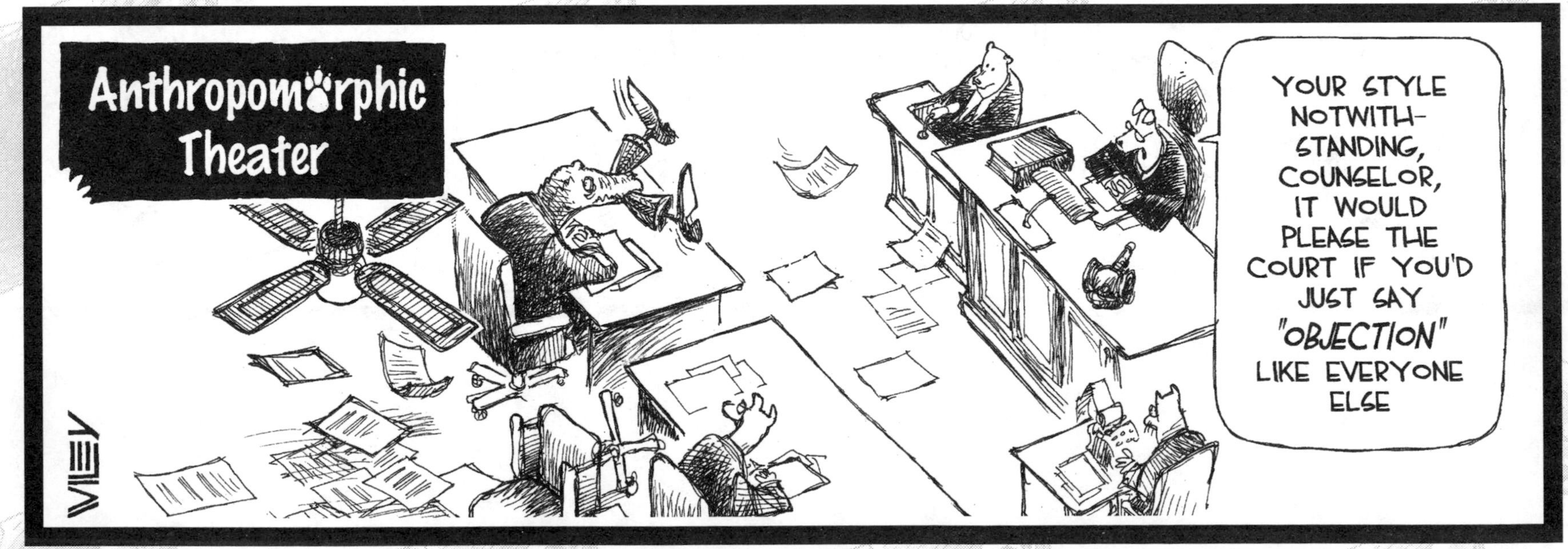
Anthropomorphic Theater
WILEY
YOUR STYLE NOTWITH-STANDING, COUNSELOR, IT WOULD PLEASE THE COURT IF YOU'D JUST SAY "OBJECTION" LIKE EVERYONE ELSE

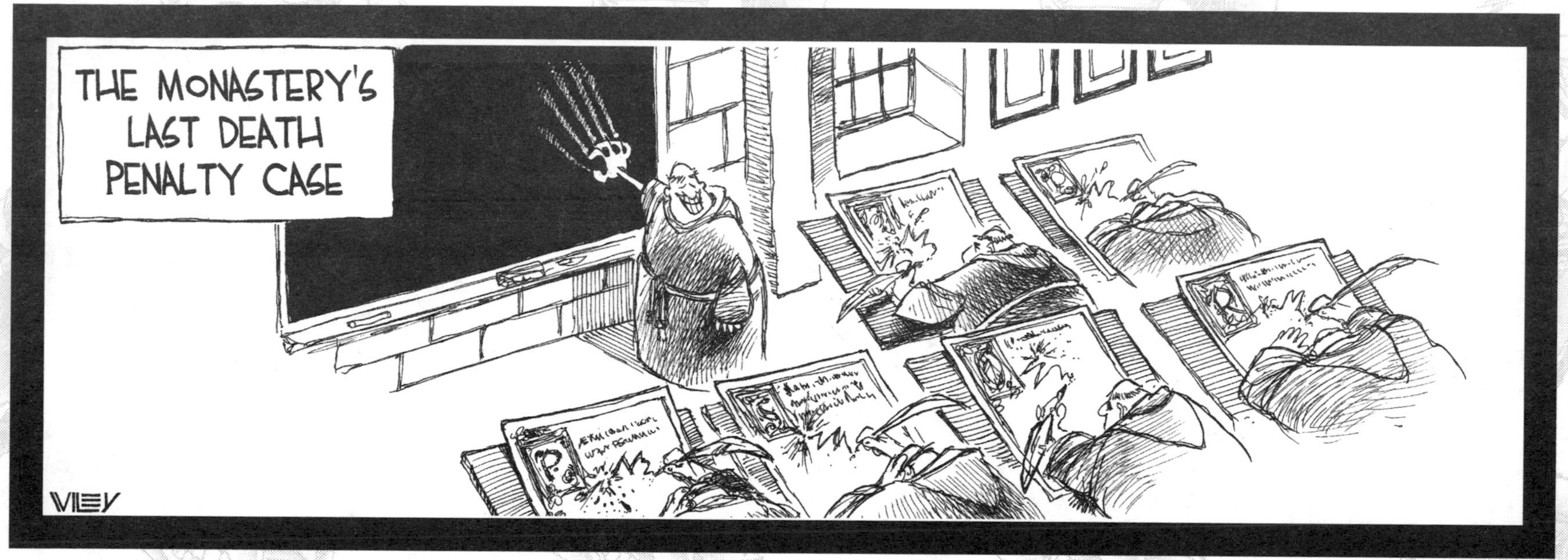
THE MONASTERY'S LAST DEATH PENALTY CASE
WILEY

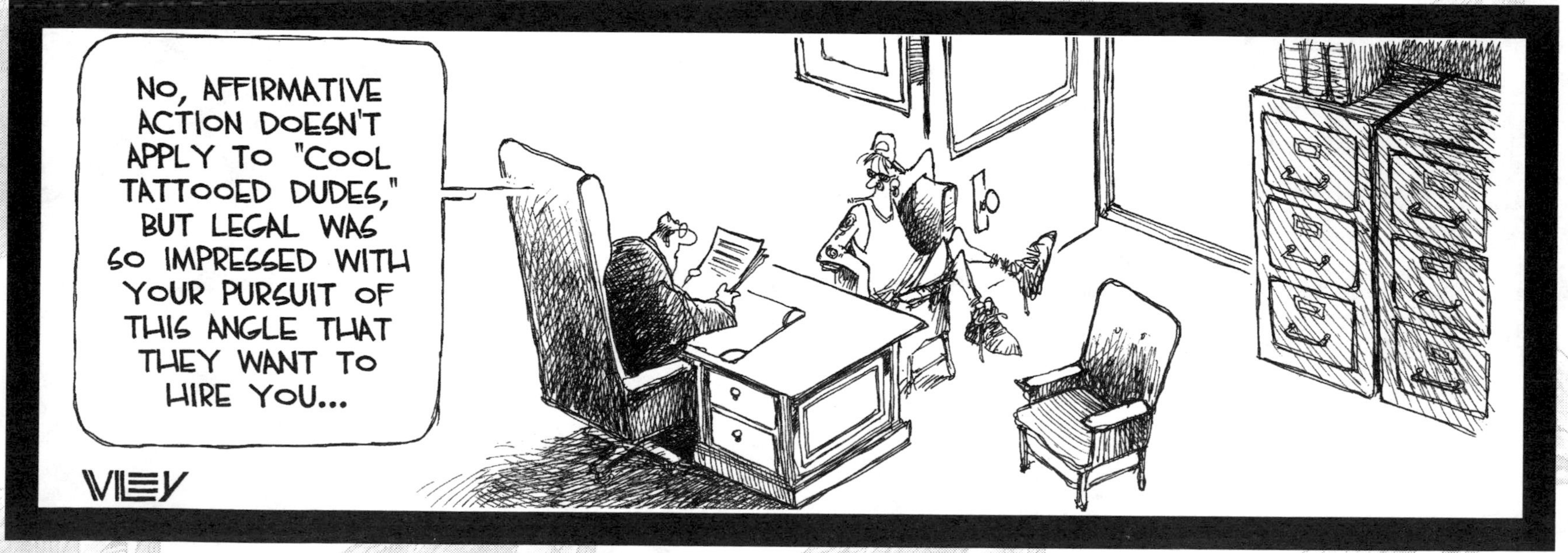
NO, AFFIRMATIVE ACTION DOESN'T APPLY TO "COOL TATTOOED DUDES," BUT LEGAL WAS SO IMPRESSED WITH YOUR PURSUIT OF THIS ANGLE THAT THEY WANT TO HIRE YOU...
WILEY

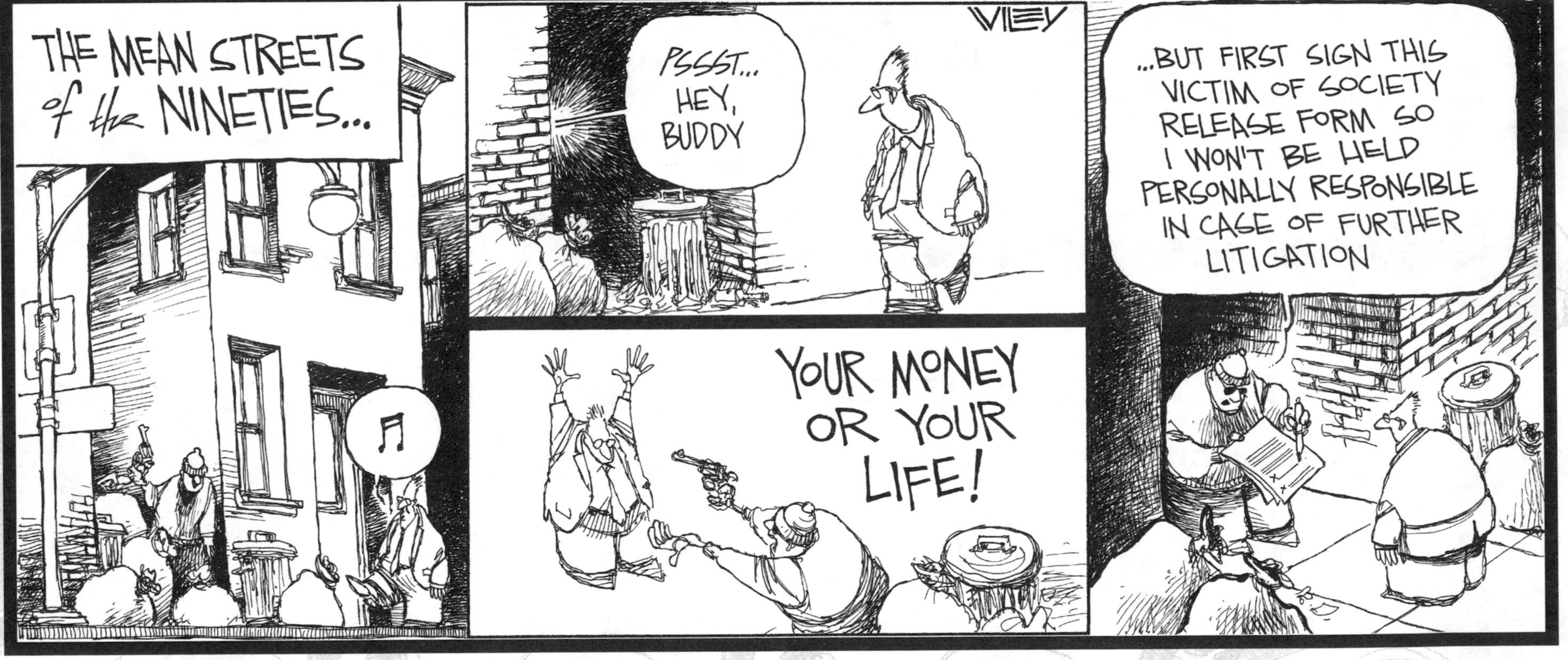
THE MEAN STREETS of the NINETIES...
WILEY
PSSST... HEY, BUDDY
YOUR MONEY OR YOUR LIFE!
...BUT FIRST SIGN THIS VICTIM OF SOCIETY RELEASE FORM SO I WON'T BE HELD PERSONALLY RESPONSIBLE IN CASE OF FURTHER LITIGATION

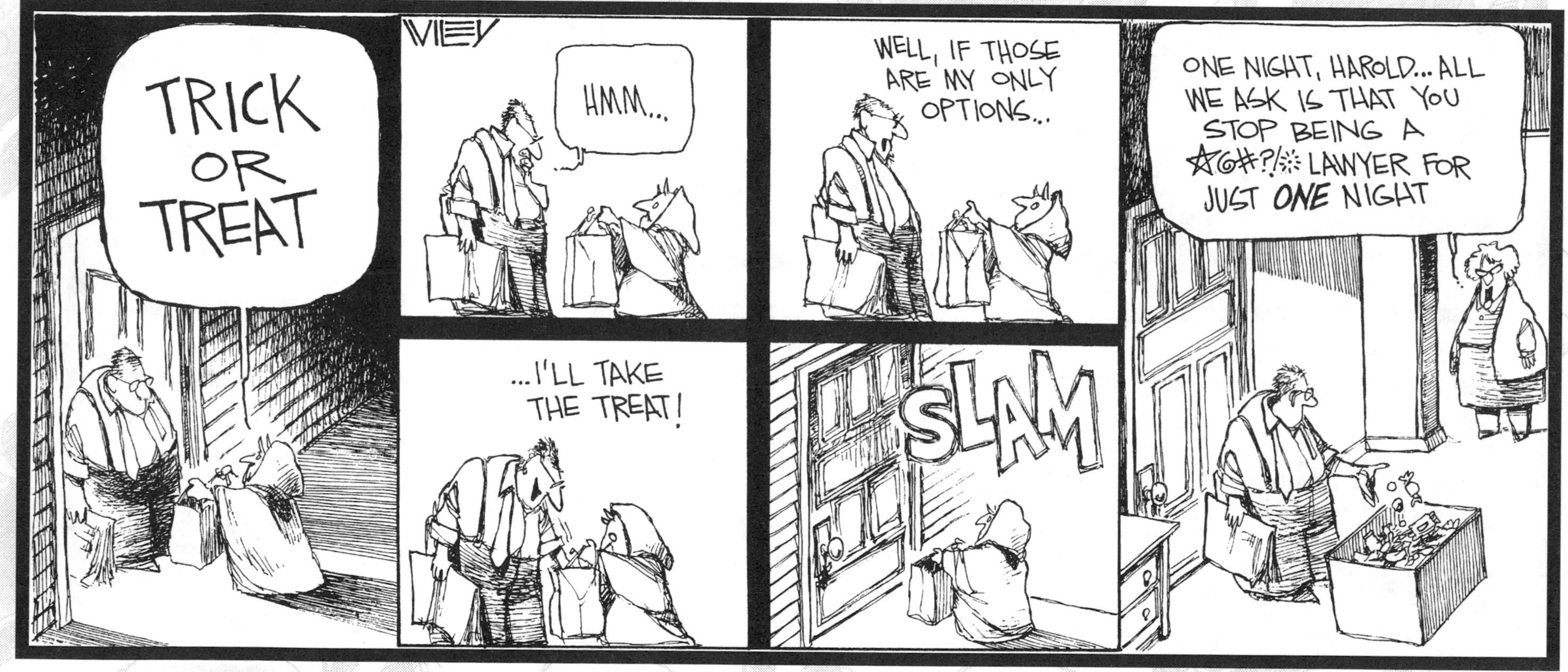
TRICK OR TREAT
HMM...
WELL, IF THOSE ARE MY ONLY OPTIONS...
...I'LL TAKE THE TREAT!
SLAM
ONE NIGHT, HAROLD... ALL WE ASK IS THAT YOU STOP BEING A ☆@#?/☼ LAWYER FOR JUST ONE NIGHT

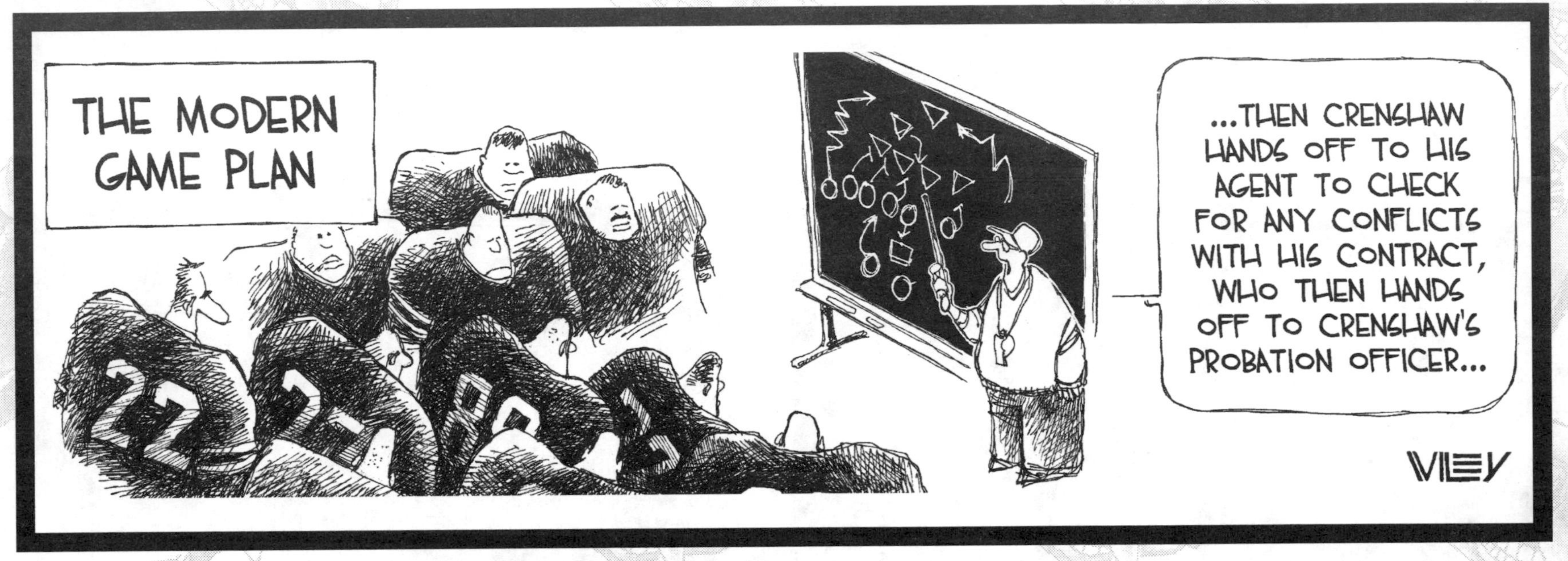
THE MODERN GAME PLAN
...THEN CRENSHAW HANDS OFF TO HIS AGENT TO CHECK FOR ANY CONFLICTS WITH HIS CONTRACT, WHO THEN HANDS OFF TO CRENSHAW'S PROBATION OFFICER...
22
WILEY

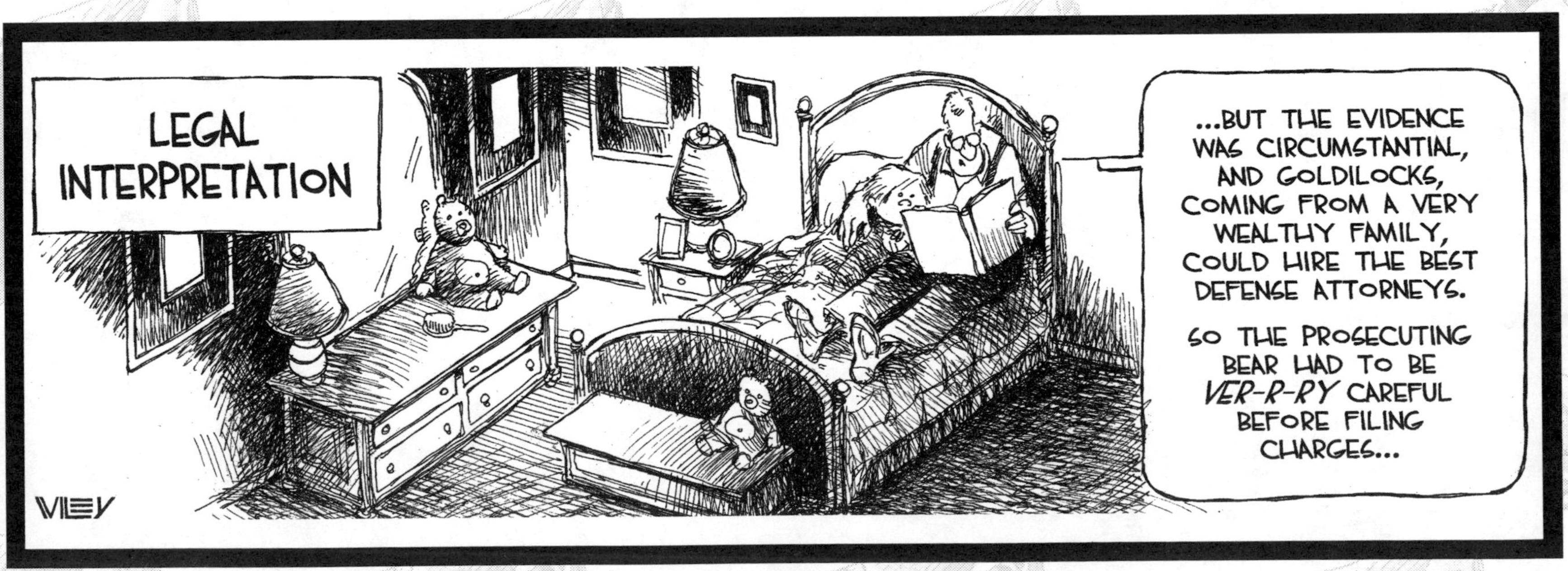
LEGAL INTERPRETATION
...BUT THE EVIDENCE WAS CIRCUMSTANTIAL, AND GOLDILOCKS, COMING FROM A VERY WEALTHY FAMILY, COULD HIRE THE BEST DEFENSE ATTORNEYS.
SO THE PROSECUTING BEAR HAD TO BE *VER-R-RY* CAREFUL BEFORE FILING CHARGES...
WILEY

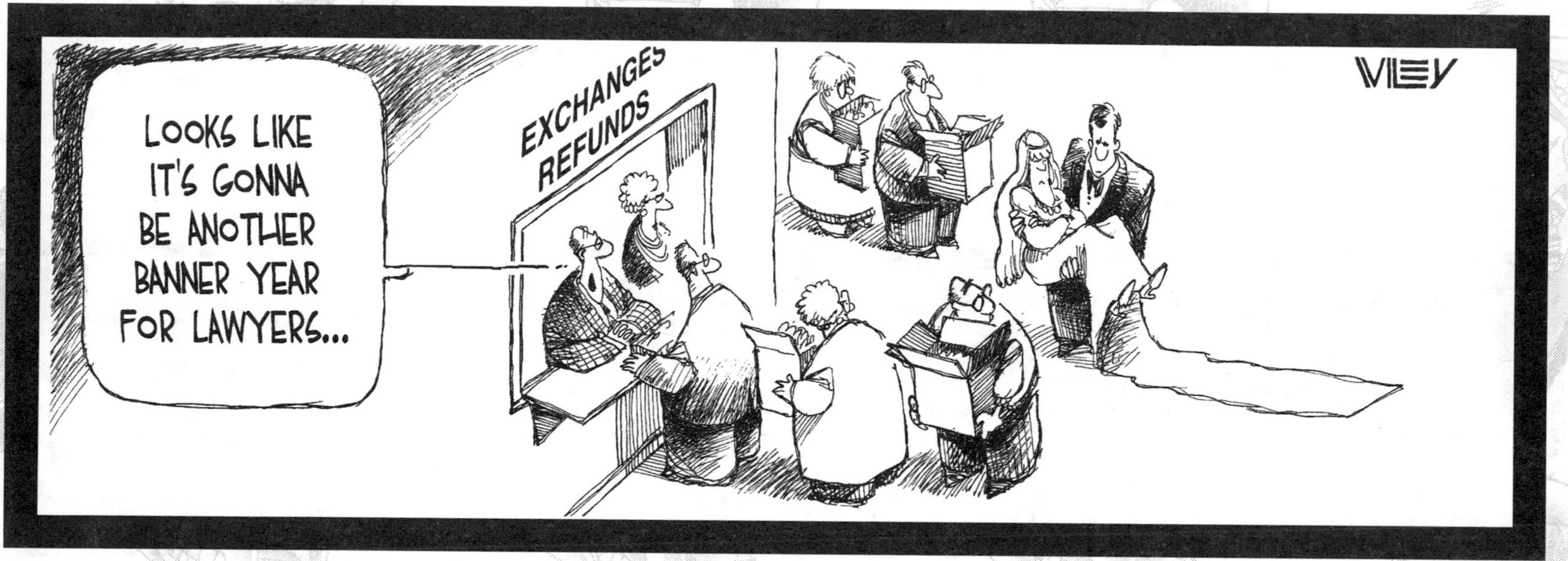
VILEY
EXCHANGES
REFUNDS
LOOKS LIKE IT'S GONNA BE ANOTHER BANNER YEAR FOR LAWYERS...

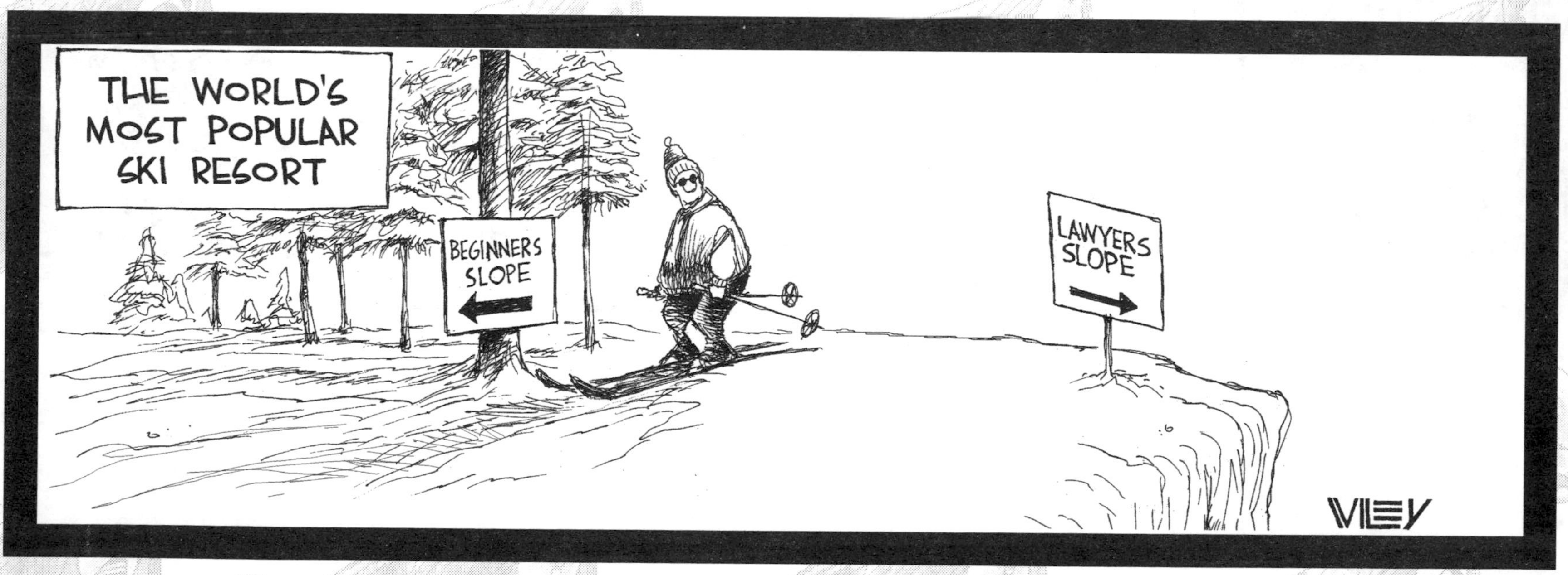
THE WORLD'S MOST POPULAR SKI RESORT
BEGINNERS SLOPE
LAWYERS SLOPE
VILEY

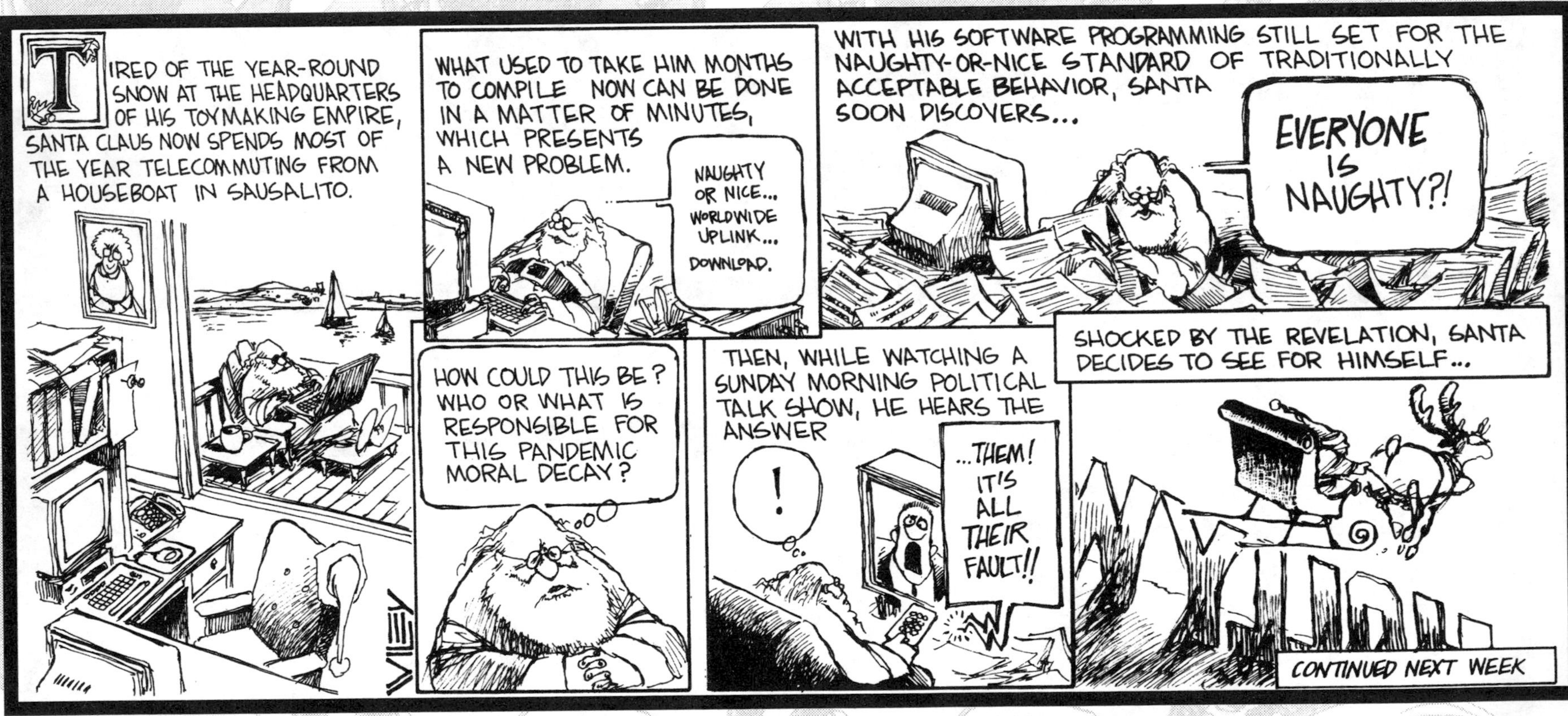
TIRED OF THE YEAR-ROUND SNOW AT THE HEADQUARTERS OF HIS TOYMAKING EMPIRE, SANTA CLAUS NOW SPENDS MOST OF THE YEAR TELECOMMUTING FROM A HOUSEBOAT IN SAUSALITO.
WHAT USED TO TAKE HIM MONTHS TO COMPILE NOW CAN BE DONE IN A MATTER OF MINUTES, WHICH PRESENTS A NEW PROBLEM.
NAUGHTY OR NICE... WORLDWIDE UPLINK... DOWNLOAD.
WITH HIS SOFTWARE PROGRAMMING STILL SET FOR THE NAUGHTY-OR-NICE STANDARD OF TRADITIONALLY ACCEPTABLE BEHAVIOR, SANTA SOON DISCOVERS...
EVERYONE IS NAUGHTY?!
HOW COULD THIS BE? WHO OR WHAT IS RESPONSIBLE FOR THIS PANDEMIC MORAL DECAY?
THEN, WHILE WATCHING A SUNDAY MORNING POLITICAL TALK SHOW, HE HEARS THE ANSWER
!
...THEM! IT'S ALL THEIR FAULT!!
SHOCKED BY THE REVELATION, SANTA DECIDES TO SEE FOR HIMSELF...
CONTINUED NEXT WEEK

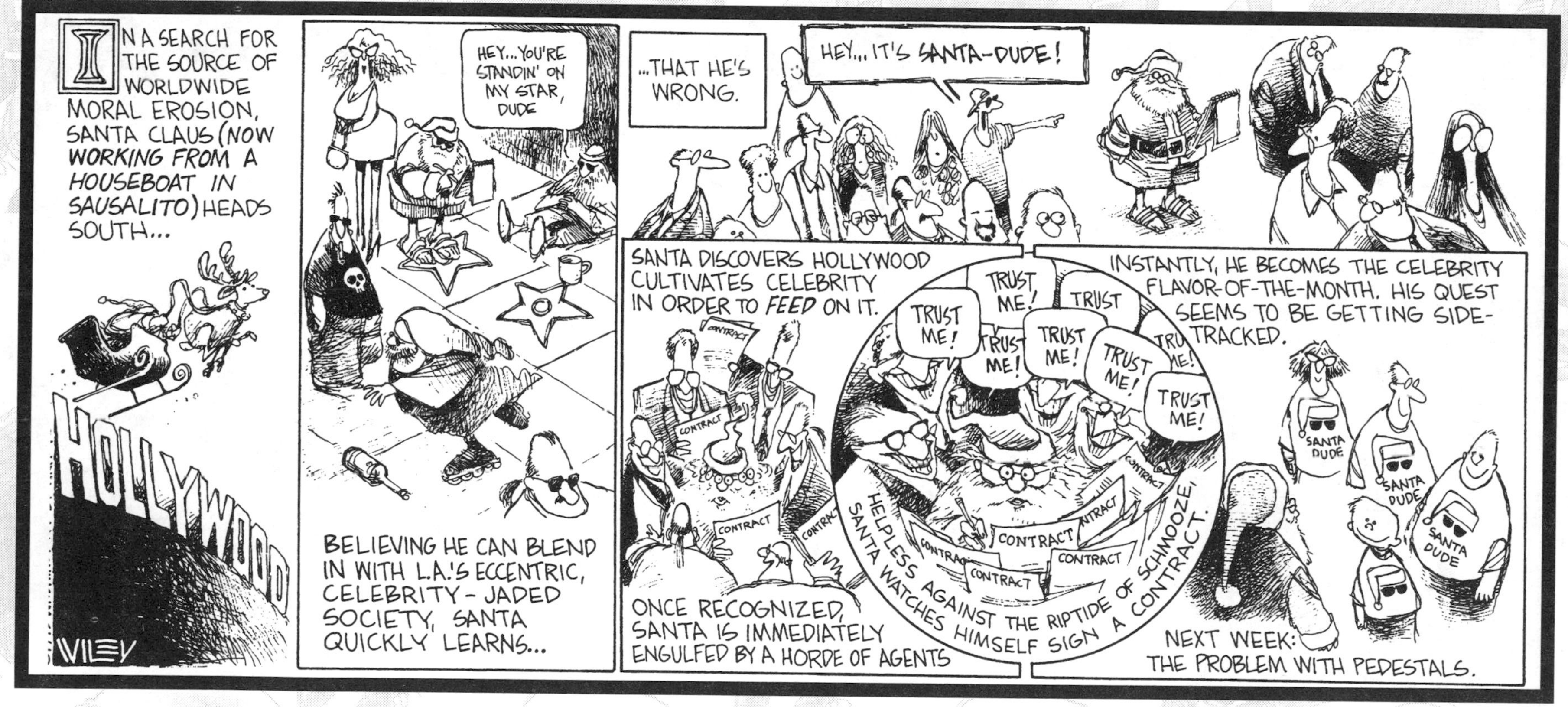
IN A SEARCH FOR THE SOURCE OF WORLDWIDE MORAL EROSION, SANTA CLAUS (NOW WORKING FROM A HOUSEBOAT IN SAUSALITO) HEADS SOUTH...
HOLLYWOOD
WILEY
HEY... YOU'RE STANDIN' ON MY STAR, DUDE
BELIEVING HE CAN BLEND IN WITH L.A.'S ECCENTRIC, CELEBRITY-JADED SOCIETY, SANTA QUICKLY LEARNS...
...THAT HE'S WRONG.
HEY... IT'S SANTA-DUDE!
SANTA DISCOVERS HOLLYWOOD CULTIVATES CELEBRITY IN ORDER TO FEED ON IT.
CONTRACT
ONCE RECOGNIZED, SANTA IS IMMEDIATELY ENGULFED BY A HORDE OF AGENTS
TRUST ME!
TRUST ME!
TRUST ME!
TRUST ME!
TRUST ME!
TRUST ME!
HELPLESS AGAINST THE RIPTIDE OF SCHMOOZE, SANTA WATCHES HIMSELF SIGN A CONTRACT.
INSTANTLY, HE BECOMES THE CELEBRITY FLAVOR-OF-THE-MONTH. HIS QUEST SEEMS TO BE GETTING SIDE-TRACKED.
SANTA DUDE
SANTA DUDE
SANTA DUDE
NEXT WEEK: THE PROBLEM WITH PEDESTALS.

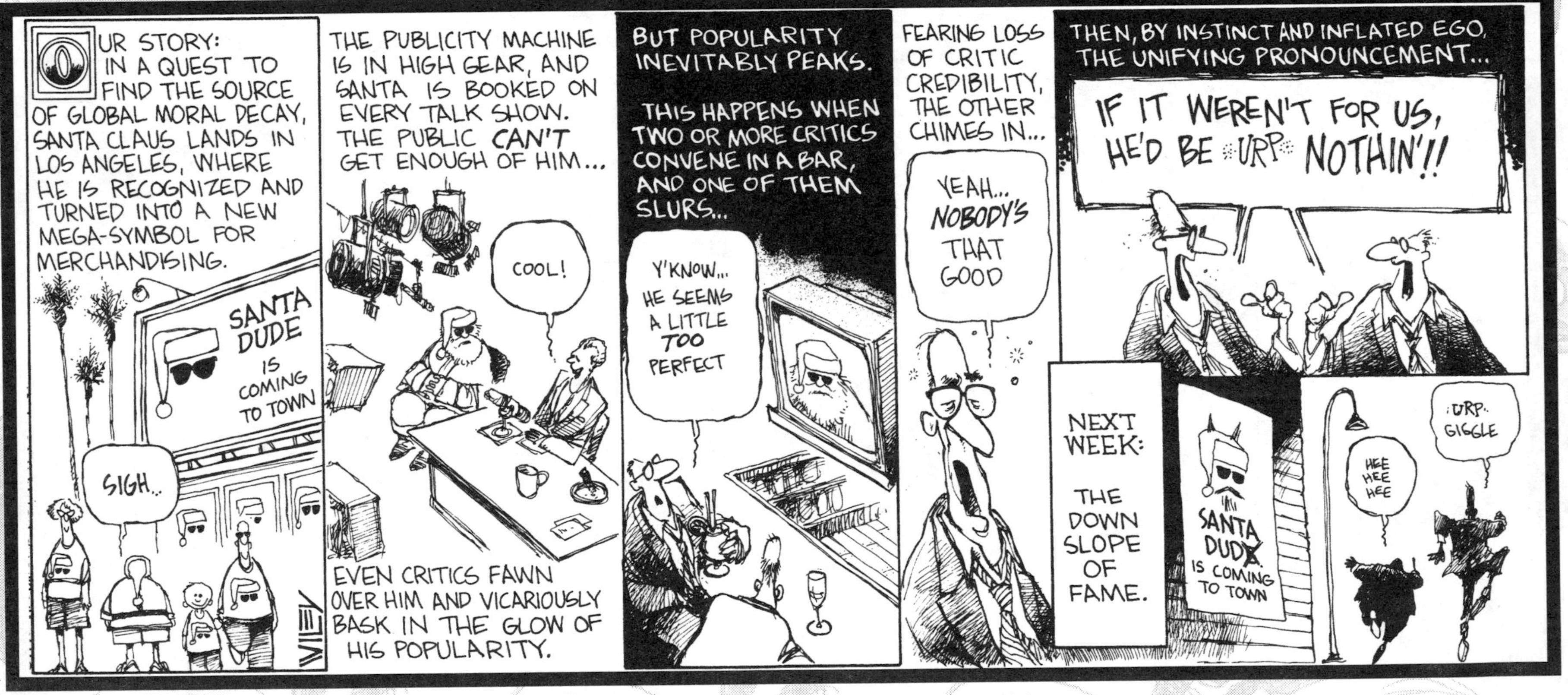
OUR STORY:
IN A QUEST TO FIND THE SOURCE OF GLOBAL MORAL DECAY, SANTA CLAUS LANDS IN LOS ANGELES, WHERE HE IS RECOGNIZED AND TURNED INTO A NEW MEGA-SYMBOL FOR MERCHANDISING.
SANTA DUDE IS COMING TO TOWN
SIGH...
WILEY
THE PUBLICITY MACHINE IS IN HIGH GEAR, AND SANTA IS BOOKED ON EVERY TALK SHOW. THE PUBLIC CAN'T GET ENOUGH OF HIM...
COOL!
EVEN CRITICS FAWN OVER HIM AND VICARIOUSLY BASK IN THE GLOW OF HIS POPULARITY.
BUT POPULARITY INEVITABLY PEAKS.
THIS HAPPENS WHEN TWO OR MORE CRITICS CONVENE IN A BAR, AND ONE OF THEM SLURS...
Y'KNOW... HE SEEMS A LITTLE TOO PERFECT
FEARING LOSS OF CRITIC CREDIBILITY, THE OTHER CHIMES IN...
YEAH... NOBODY'S THAT GOOD
THEN, BY INSTINCT AND INFLATED EGO, THE UNIFYING PRONOUNCEMENT...
IF IT WEREN'T FOR US, HE'D BE URP NOTHIN'!!
NEXT WEEK: THE DOWN SLOPE OF FAME.
SANTA DUDE IS COMING TO TOWN
HEE HEE HEE
URP GIGGLE

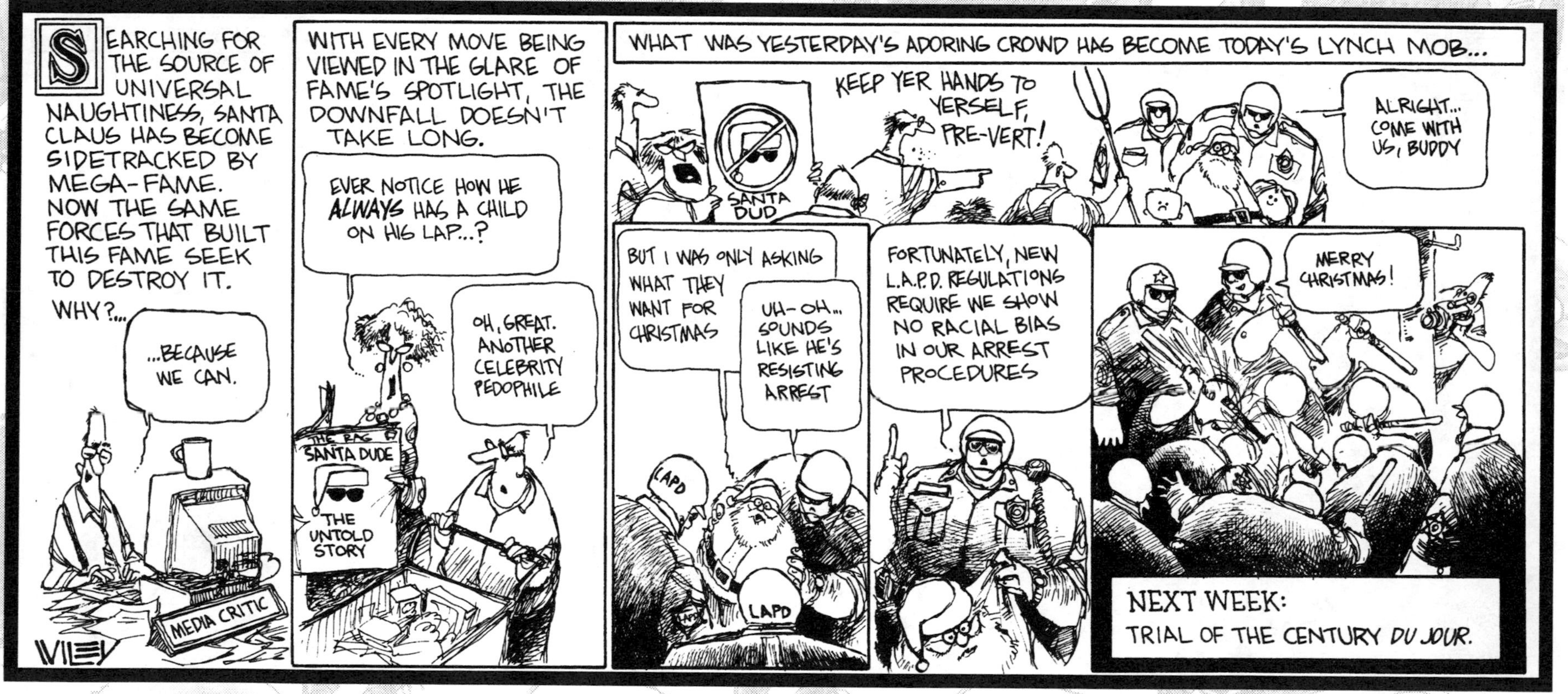
SEARCHING FOR THE SOURCE OF UNIVERSAL NAUGHTINESS, SANTA CLAUS HAS BECOME SIDETRACKED BY MEGA-FAME. NOW THE SAME FORCES THAT BUILT THIS FAME SEEK TO DESTROY IT.
WHY?...
...BECAUSE WE CAN.
MEDIA CRITIC
WILEY
WITH EVERY MOVE BEING VIEWED IN THE GLARE OF FAME'S SPOTLIGHT, THE DOWNFALL DOESN'T TAKE LONG.
EVER NOTICE HOW HE ALWAYS HAS A CHILD ON HIS LAP...?
THE RAG
SANTA DUDE
THE UNTOLD STORY
OH, GREAT. ANOTHER CELEBRITY PEDOPHILE
WHAT WAS YESTERDAY'S ADORING CROWD HAS BECOME TODAY'S LYNCH MOB...
SANTA DUD
KEEP YER HANDS TO YERSELF, PRE-VERT!
ALRIGHT... COME WITH US, BUDDY
BUT I WAS ONLY ASKING WHAT THEY WANT FOR CHRISTMAS
UH-OH... SOUNDS LIKE HE'S RESISTING ARREST
LAPD
LAPD
FORTUNATELY, NEW L.A.P.D. REGULATIONS REQUIRE WE SHOW NO RACIAL BIAS IN OUR ARREST PROCEDURES
MERRY CHRISTMAS!
NEXT WEEK:
TRIAL OF THE CENTURY DU JOUR.

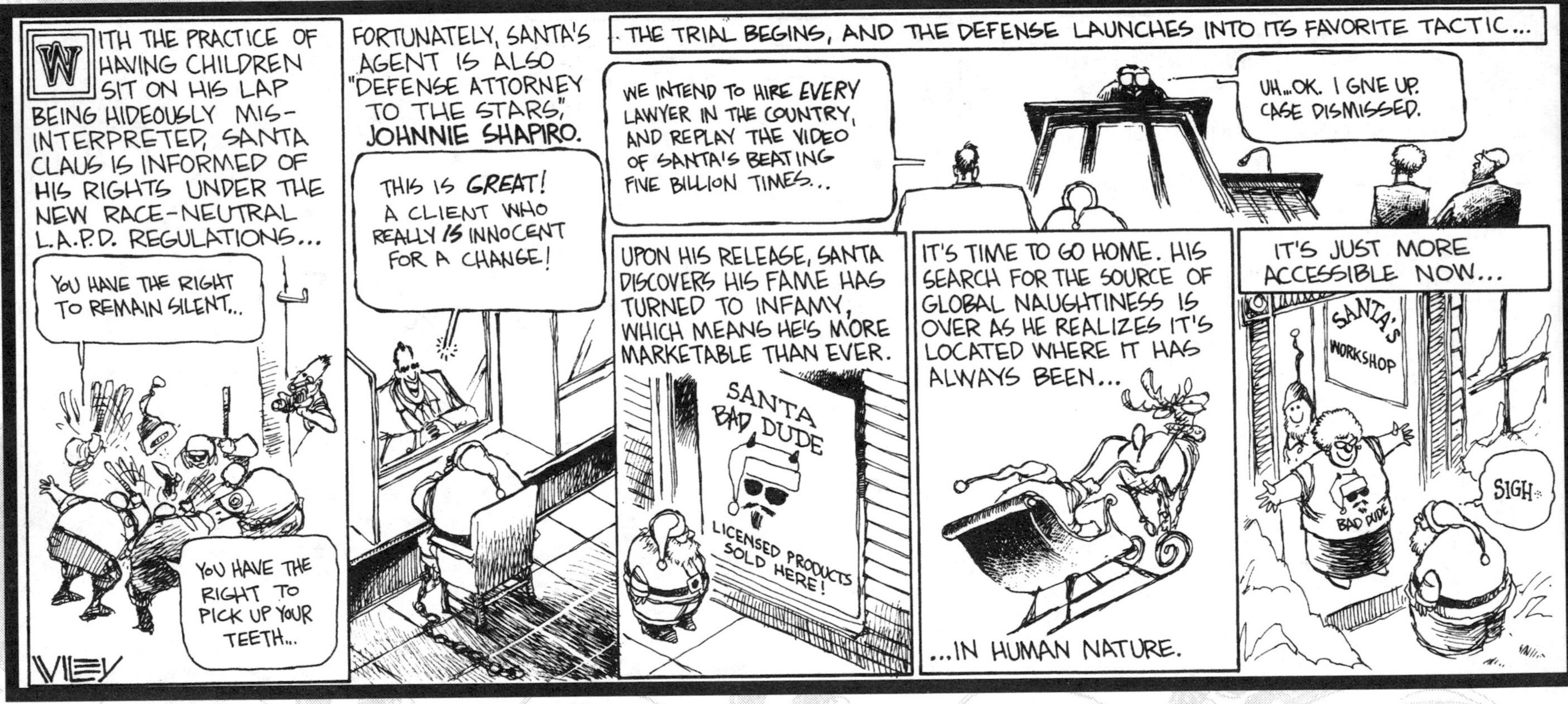
WITH THE PRACTICE OF HAVING CHILDREN SIT ON HIS LAP BEING HIDEOUSLY MIS-INTERPRETED, SANTA CLAUS IS INFORMED OF HIS RIGHTS UNDER THE NEW RACE-NEUTRAL L.A.P.D. REGULATIONS...
YOU HAVE THE RIGHT TO REMAIN SILENT...
YOU HAVE THE RIGHT TO PICK UP YOUR TEETH...
WILEY
FORTUNATELY, SANTA'S AGENT IS ALSO "DEFENSE ATTORNEY TO THE STARS," JOHNNIE SHAPIRO.
THIS IS GREAT! A CLIENT WHO REALLY IS INNOCENT FOR A CHANGE!
THE TRIAL BEGINS, AND THE DEFENSE LAUNCHES INTO ITS FAVORITE TACTIC...
WE INTEND TO HIRE EVERY LAWYER IN THE COUNTRY, AND REPLAY THE VIDEO OF SANTA'S BEATING FIVE BILLION TIMES...
UH...OK. I GIVE UP. CASE DISMISSED.
UPON HIS RELEASE, SANTA DISCOVERS HIS FAME HAS TURNED TO INFAMY, WHICH MEANS HE'S MORE MARKETABLE THAN EVER.
SANTA BAD DUDE
LICENSED PRODUCTS SOLD HERE!
IT'S TIME TO GO HOME. HIS SEARCH FOR THE SOURCE OF GLOBAL NAUGHTINESS IS OVER AS HE REALIZES IT'S LOCATED WHERE IT HAS ALWAYS BEEN...
...IN HUMAN NATURE.
IT'S JUST MORE ACCESSIBLE NOW...
SANTA'S WORKSHOP
BAD DUDE
SIGH

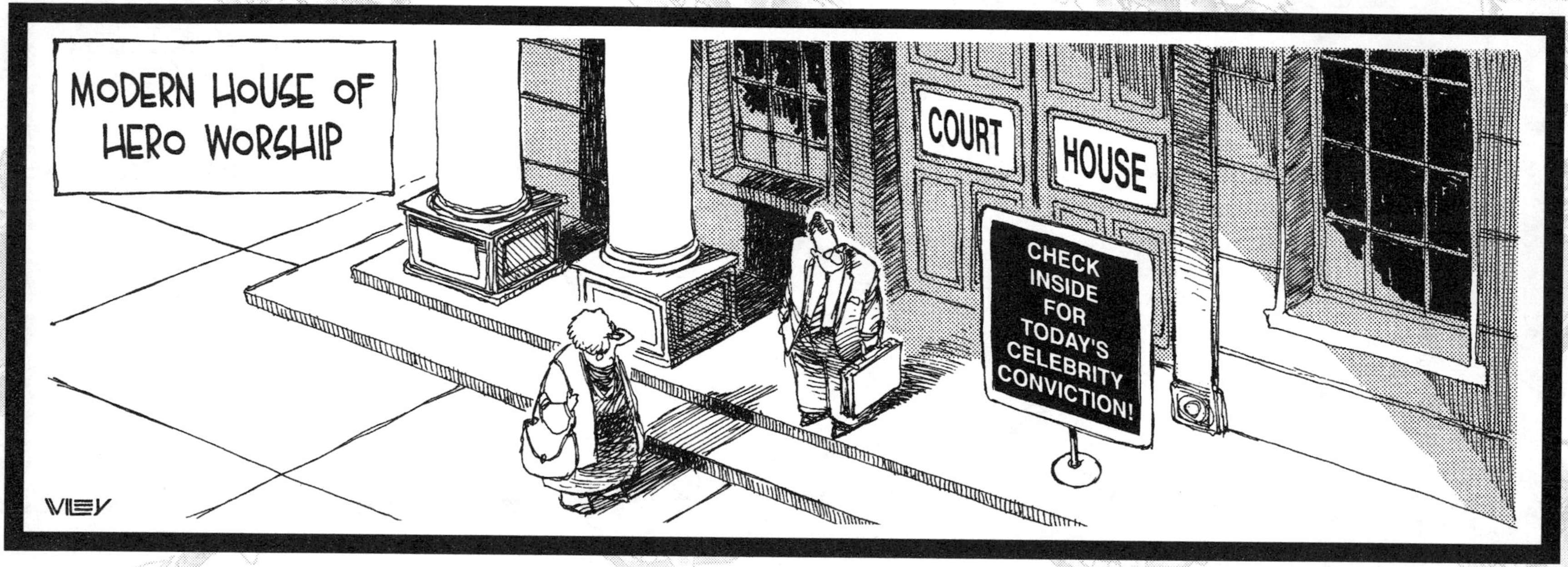
MODERN HOUSE OF HERO WORSHIP
COURT
HOUSE
CHECK INSIDE FOR TODAY'S CELEBRITY CONVICTION!
VILEY

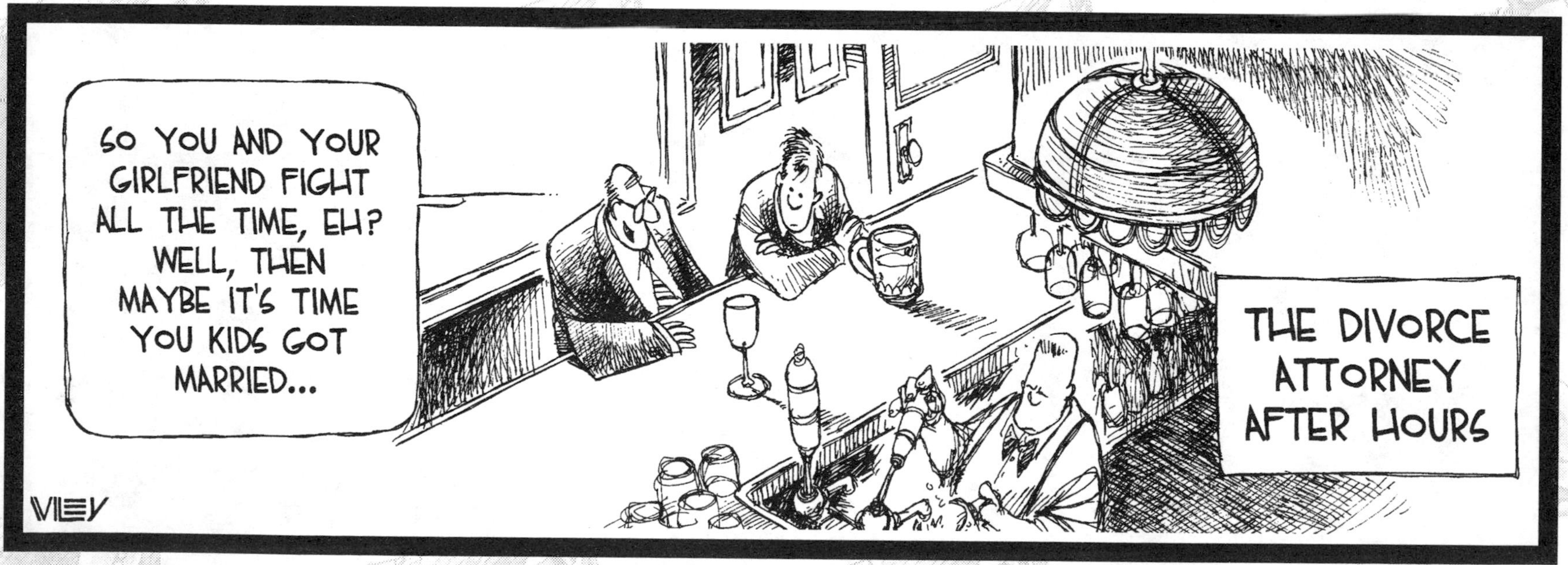
SO YOU AND YOUR GIRLFRIEND FIGHT ALL THE TIME, EH? WELL, THEN MAYBE IT'S TIME YOU KIDS GOT MARRIED...
THE DIVORCE ATTORNEY AFTER HOURS
VILEY

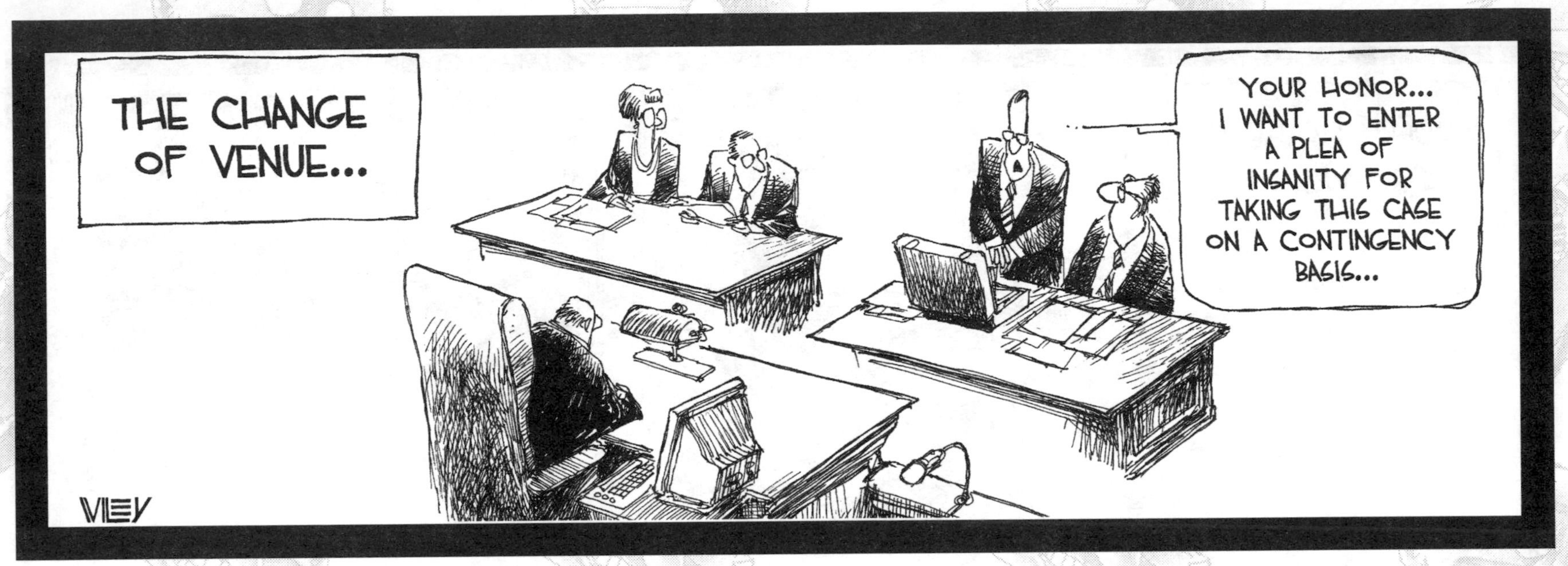
THE CHANGE OF VENUE...
YOUR HONOR... I WANT TO ENTER A PLEA OF INSANITY FOR TAKING THIS CASE ON A CONTINGENCY BASIS...
WILEY

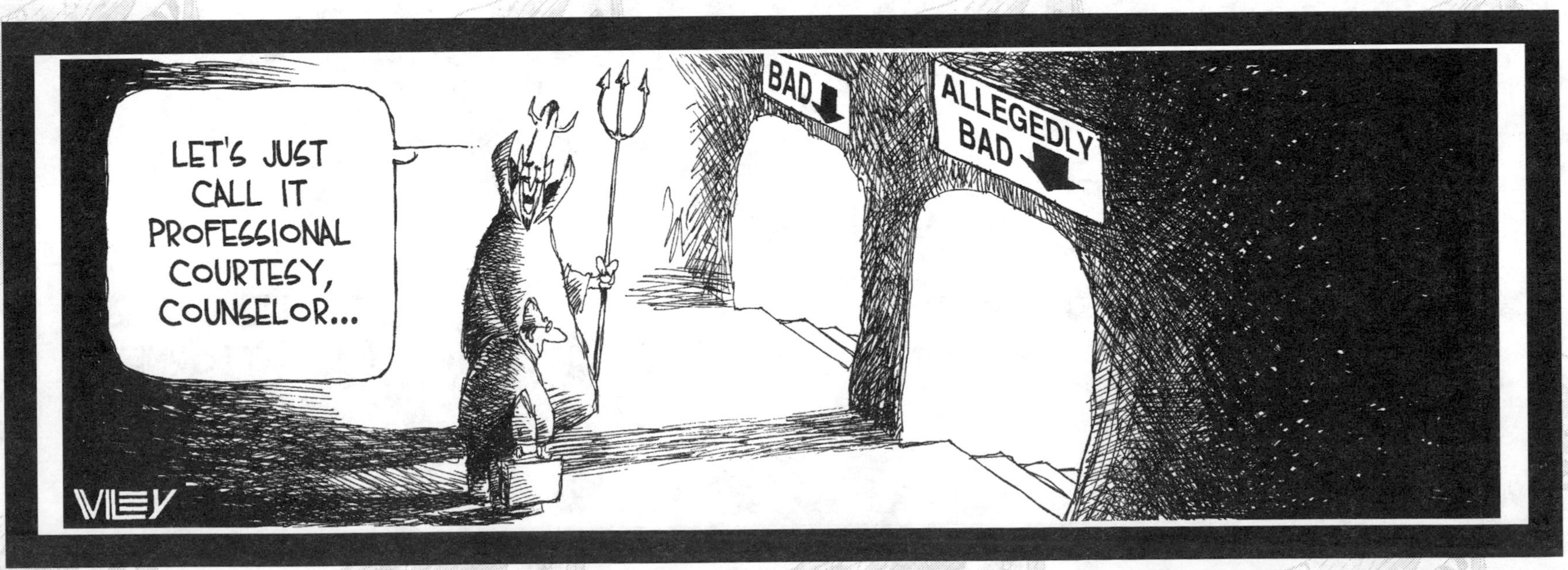
LET'S JUST CALL IT PROFESSIONAL COURTESY, COUNSELOR...
BAD
ALLEGEDLY BAD
WILEY

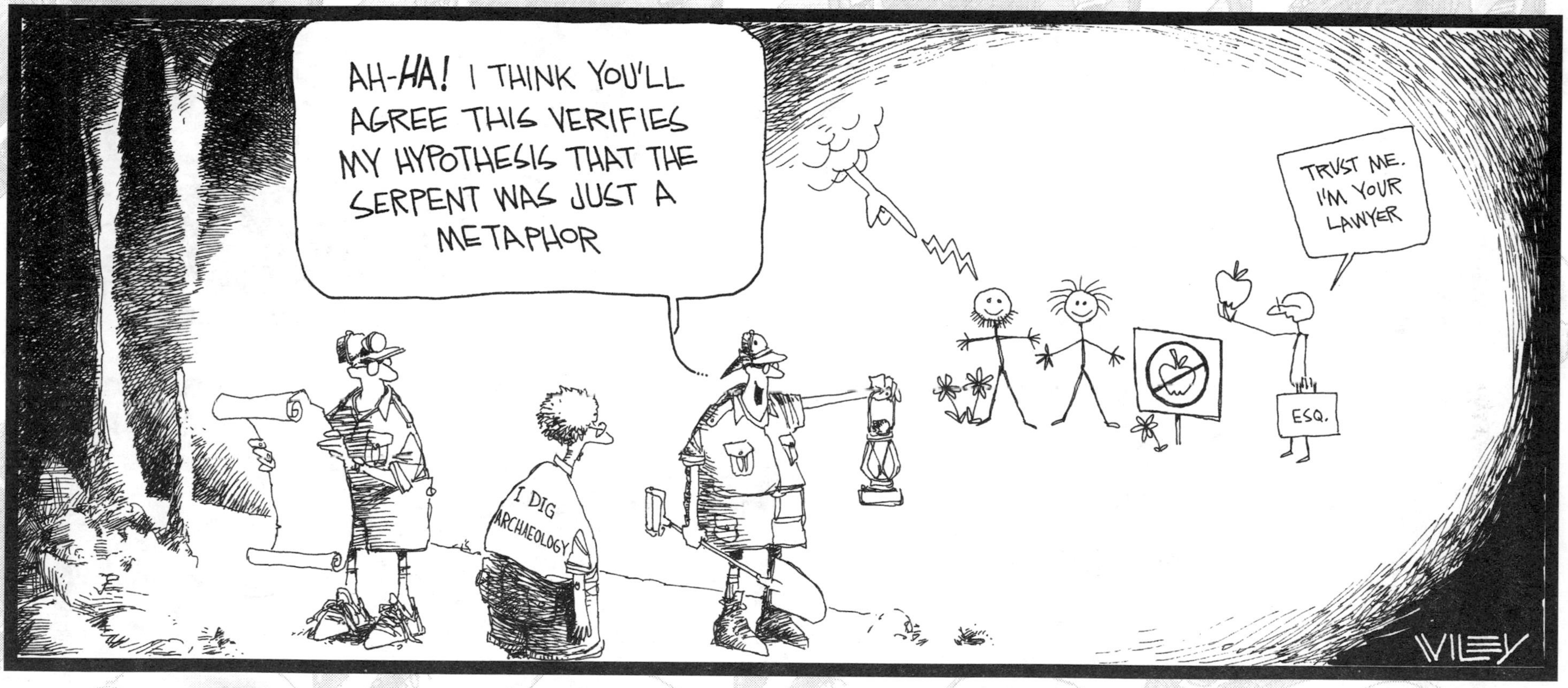
AH-HA! I THINK YOU'LL AGREE THIS VERIFIES MY HYPOTHESIS THAT THE SERPENT WAS JUST A METAPHOR
TRUST ME. I'M YOUR LAWYER
ESQ.
I DIG ARCHAEOLOGY
WILEY

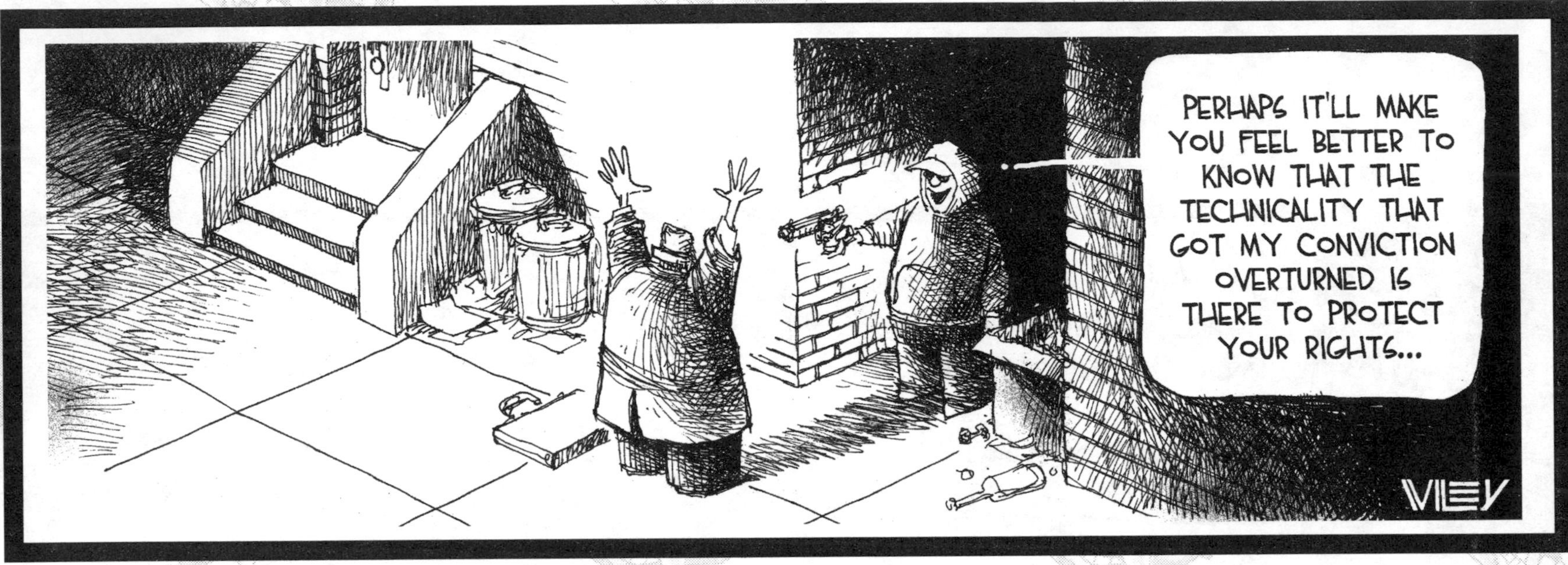
PERHAPS IT'LL MAKE YOU FEEL BETTER TO KNOW THAT THE TECHNICALITY THAT GOT MY CONVICTION OVERTURNED IS THERE TO PROTECT YOUR RIGHTS...
VILEY

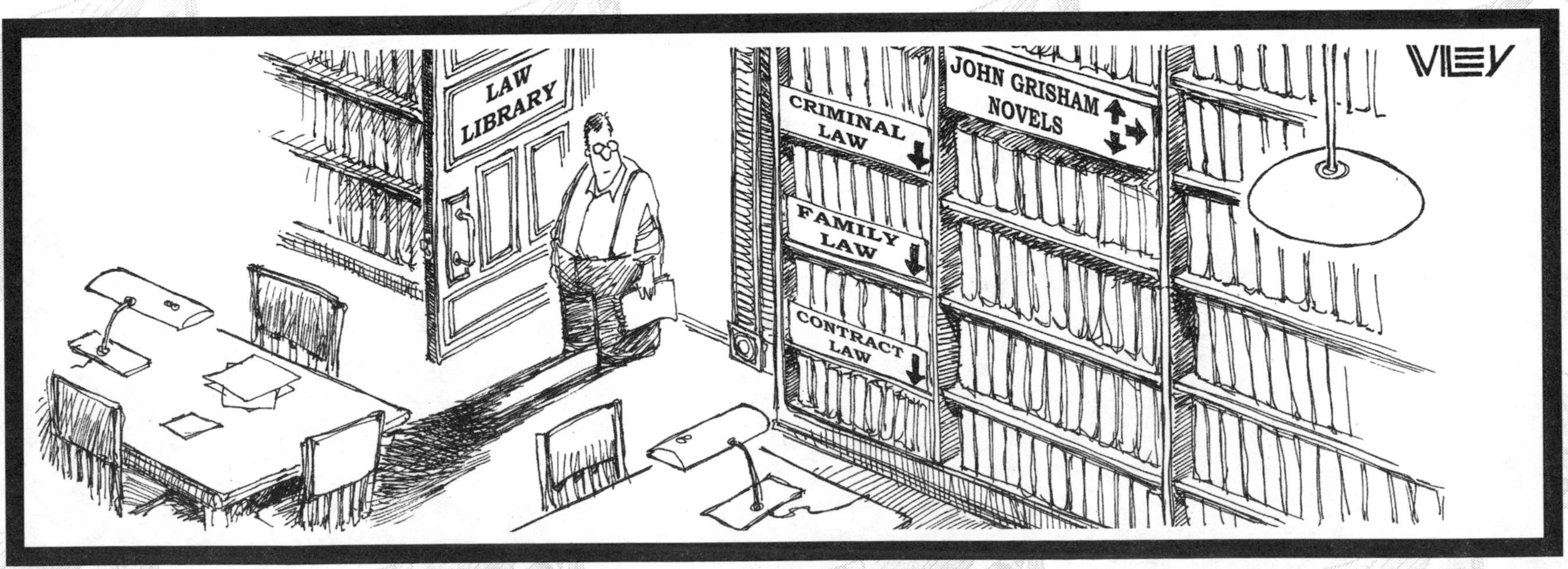
VILEY
LAW LIBRARY
JOHN GRISHAM NOVELS
CRIMINAL LAW
FAMILY LAW
CONTRACT LAW

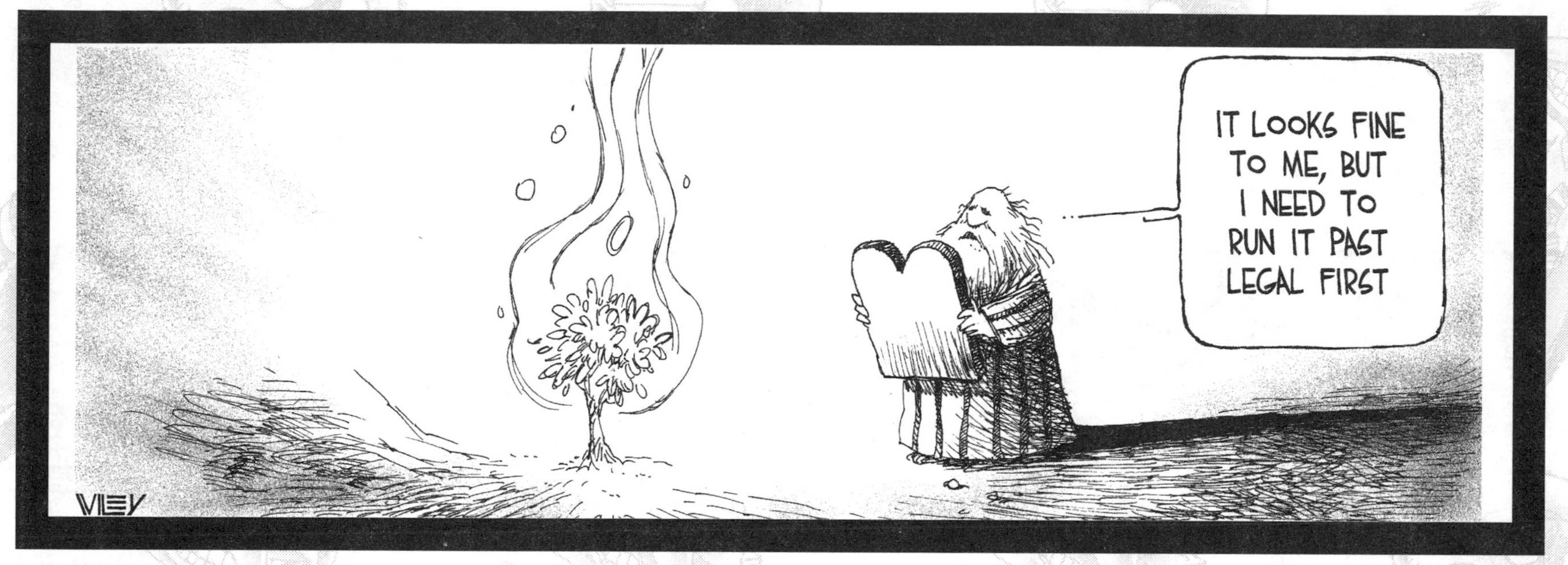
IT LOOKS FINE TO ME, BUT I NEED TO RUN IT PAST LEGAL FIRST
WILEY

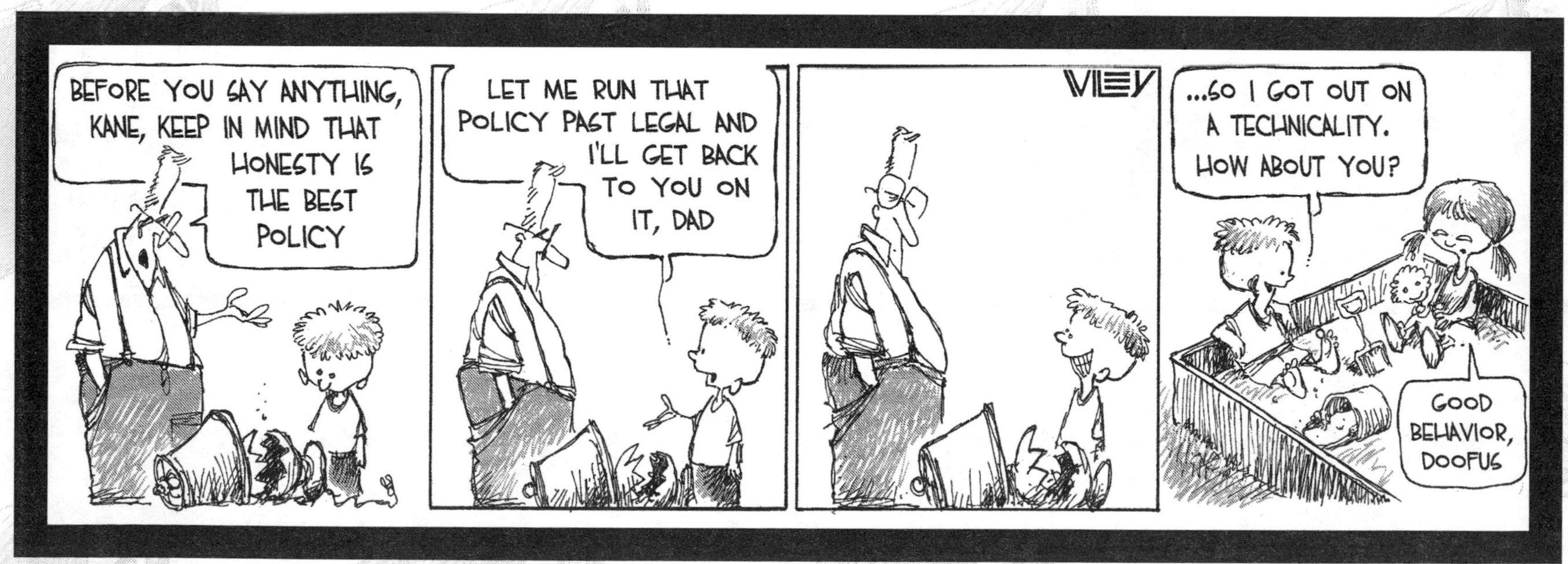
BEFORE YOU SAY ANYTHING, KANE, KEEP IN MIND THAT HONESTY IS THE BEST POLICY
LET ME RUN THAT POLICY PAST LEGAL AND I'LL GET BACK TO YOU ON IT, DAD
WILEY
...SO I GOT OUT ON A TECHNICALITY. HOW ABOUT YOU?
GOOD BEHAVIOR, DOOFUS

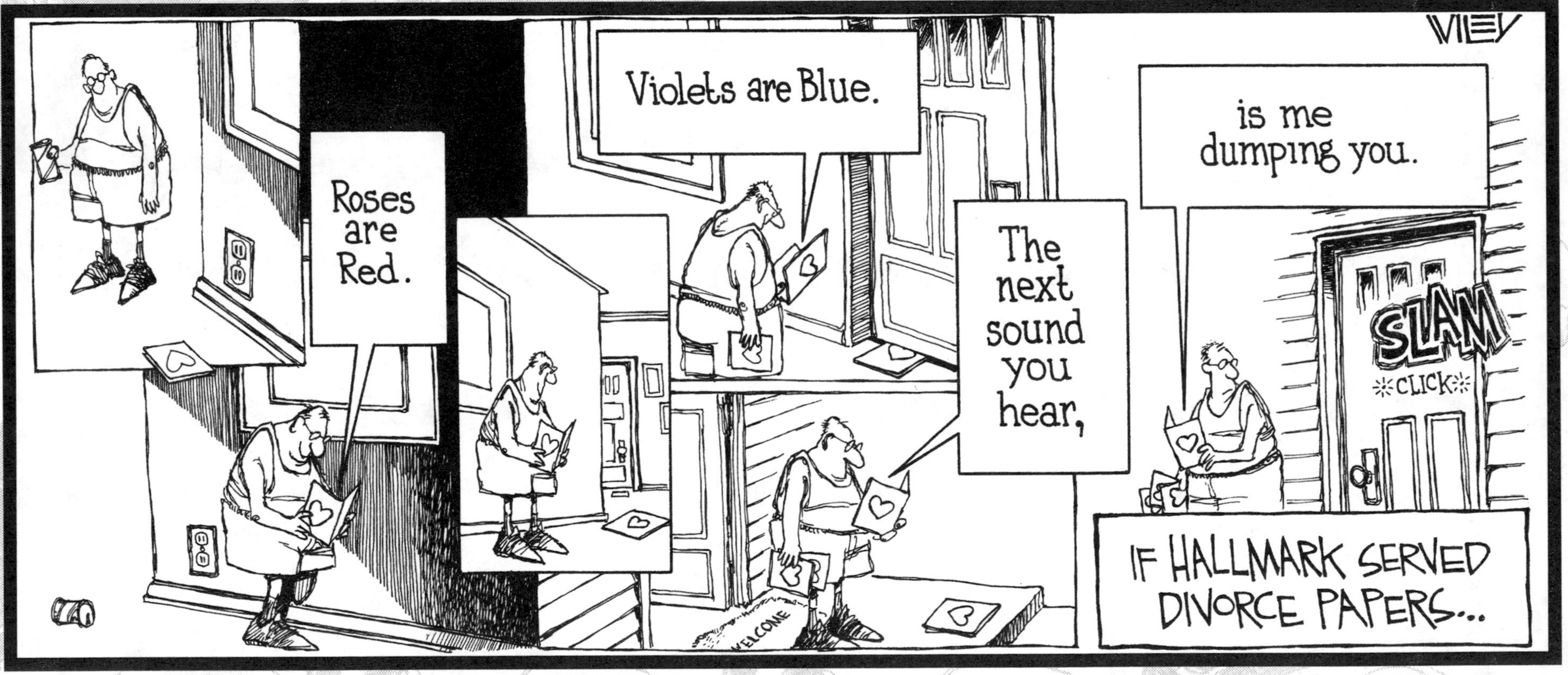
WILEY
Roses are Red.
Violets are Blue.
The next sound you hear,
is me dumping you.
SLAM
CLICK
WELCOME
IF HALLMARK SERVED DIVORCE PAPERS...

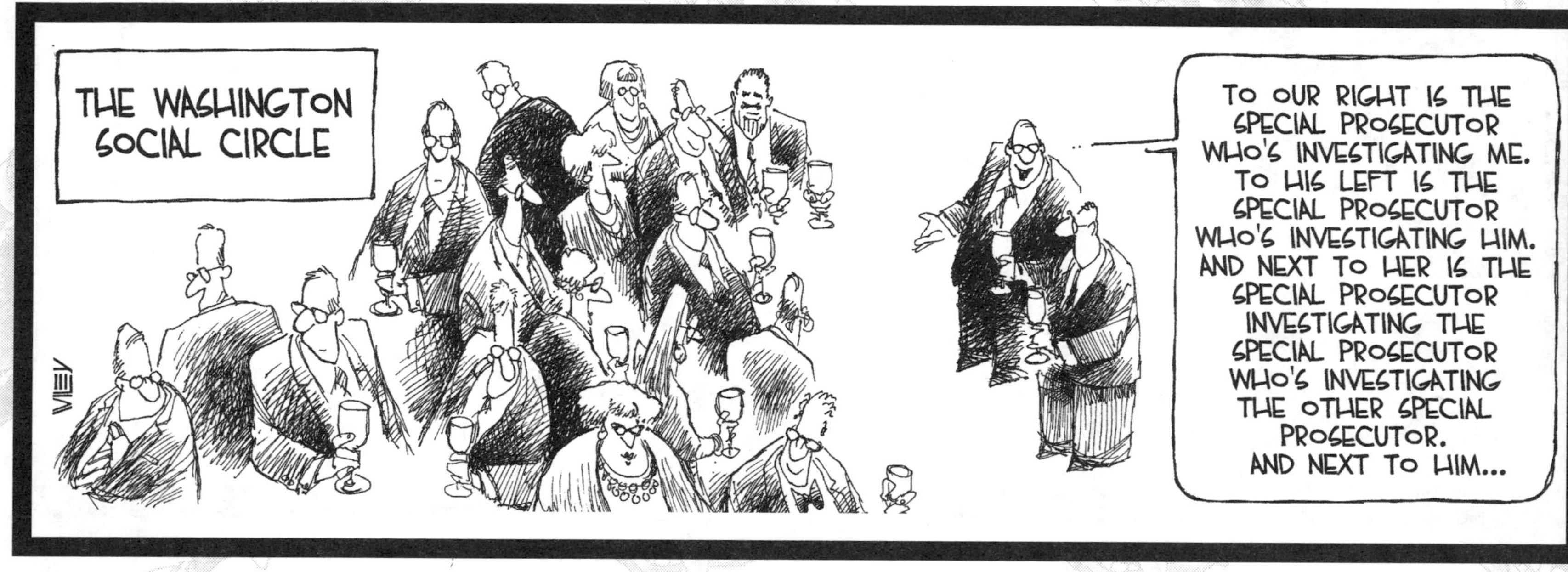
THE WASHINGTON SOCIAL CIRCLE
TO OUR RIGHT IS THE SPECIAL PROSECUTOR WHO'S INVESTIGATING ME. TO HIS LEFT IS THE SPECIAL PROSECUTOR WHO'S INVESTIGATING HIM. AND NEXT TO HER IS THE SPECIAL PROSECUTOR INVESTIGATING THE SPECIAL PROSECUTOR WHO'S INVESTIGATING THE OTHER SPECIAL PROSECUTOR. AND NEXT TO HIM...

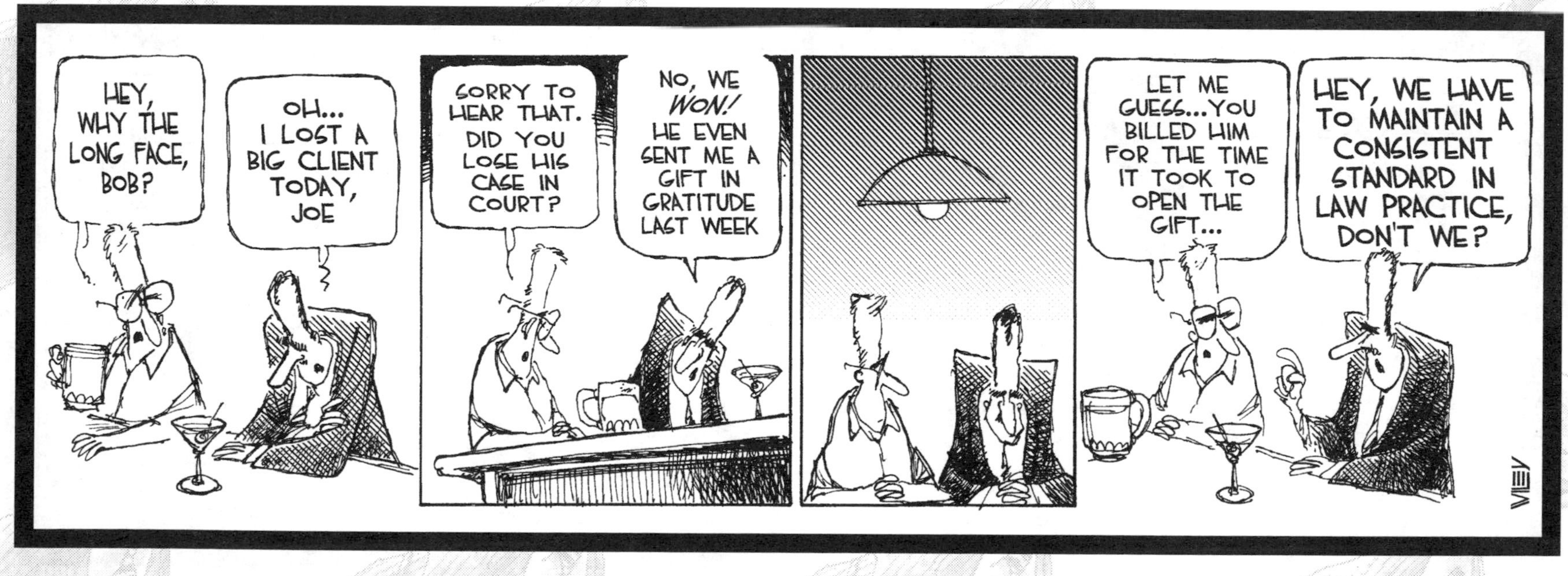
HEY, WHY THE LONG FACE, BOB?
OH... I LOST A BIG CLIENT TODAY, JOE
SORRY TO HEAR THAT. DID YOU LOSE HIS CASE IN COURT?
NO, WE *WON!* HE EVEN SENT ME A GIFT IN GRATITUDE LAST WEEK
LET ME GUESS...YOU BILLED HIM FOR THE TIME IT TOOK TO OPEN THE GIFT...
HEY, WE HAVE TO MAINTAIN A CONSISTENT STANDARD IN LAW PRACTICE, DON'T WE?

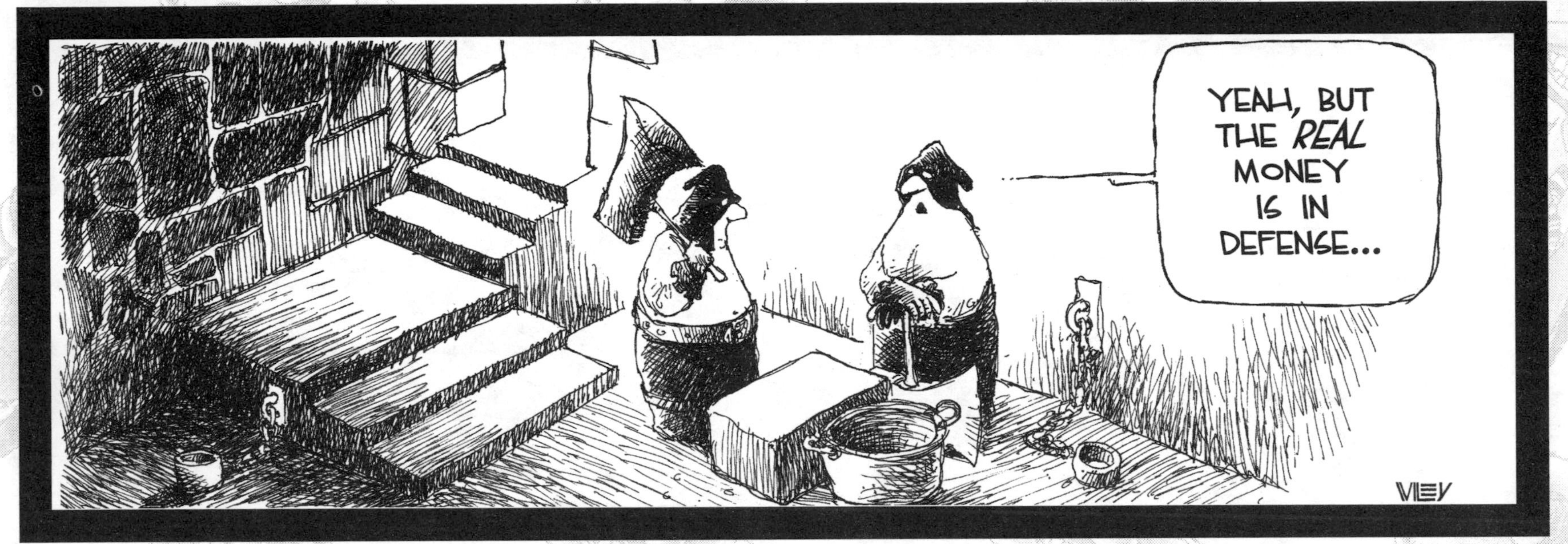
YEAH, BUT THE *REAL* MONEY IS IN DEFENSE...
VILEY

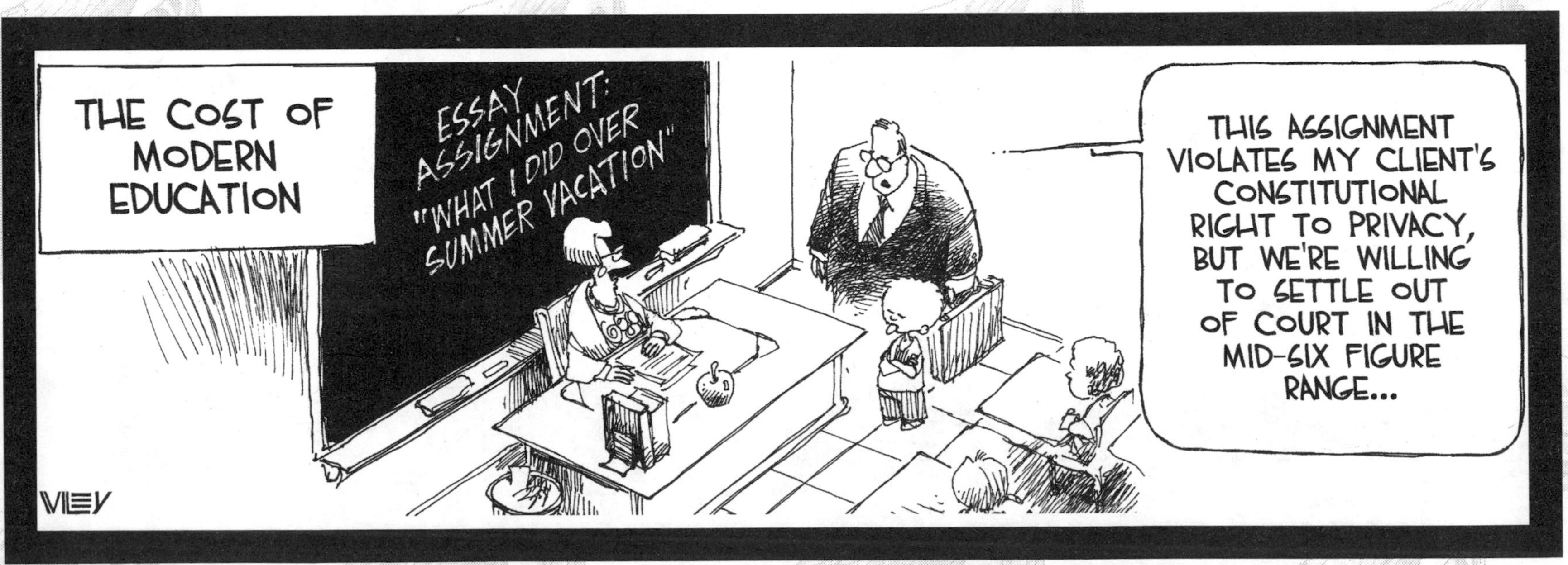
THE COST OF MODERN EDUCATION
ESSAY ASSIGNMENT: "WHAT I DID OVER SUMMER VACATION"
THIS ASSIGNMENT VIOLATES MY CLIENT'S CONSTITUTIONAL RIGHT TO PRIVACY, BUT WE'RE WILLING TO SETTLE OUT OF COURT IN THE MID-SIX FIGURE RANGE...
VILEY

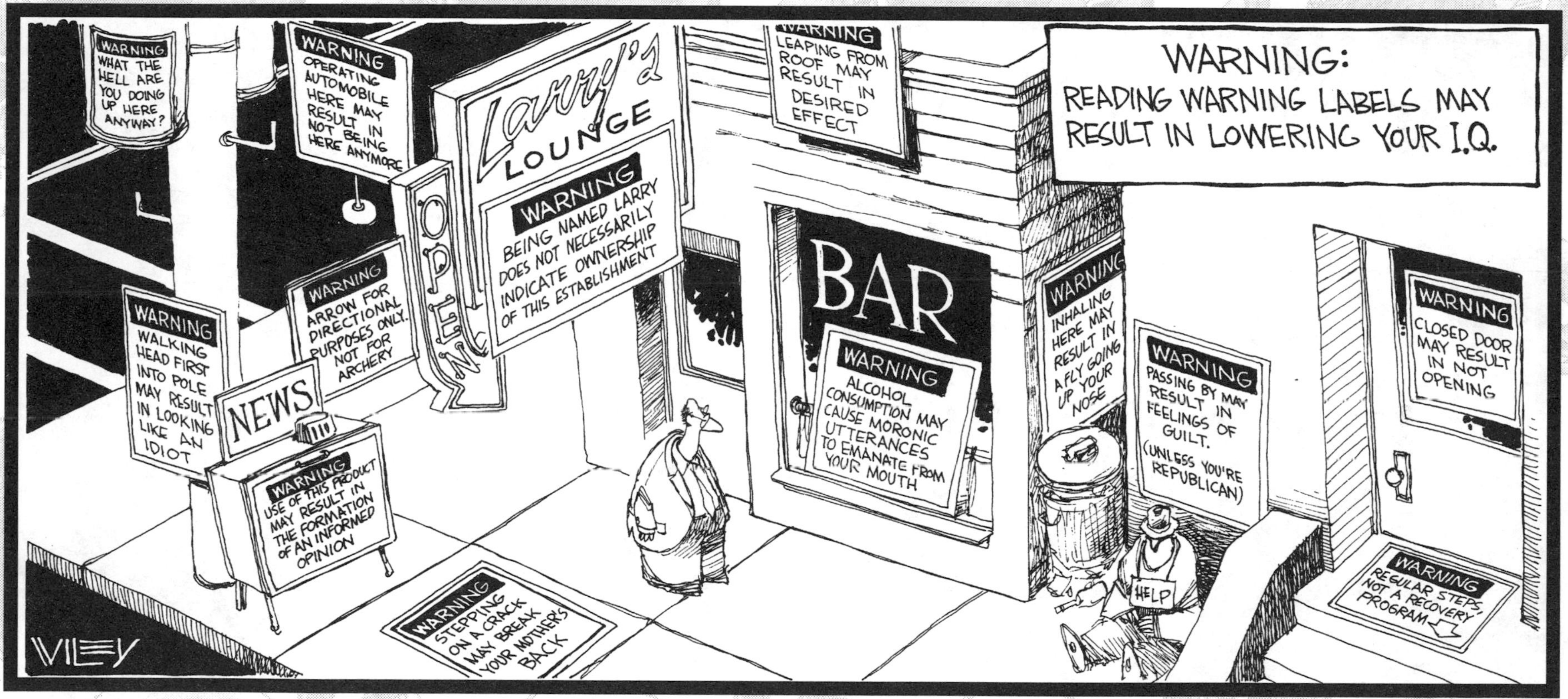
WARNING:
READING WARNING LABELS MAY RESULT IN LOWERING YOUR I.Q.
WARNING WHAT THE HELL ARE YOU DOING UP HERE ANYWAY?
WARNING OPERATING AUTOMOBILE HERE MAY RESULT IN NOT BEING HERE ANYMORE
Larry's LOUNGE
WARNING BEING NAMED LARRY DOES NOT NECESSARILY INDICATE OWNERSHIP OF THIS ESTABLISHMENT
OPEN
WARNING ARROW FOR DIRECTIONAL PURPOSES ONLY. NOT FOR ARCHERY
WARNING WALKING HEAD FIRST INTO POLE MAY RESULT IN LOOKING LIKE AN IDIOT
NEWS
WARNING USE OF THIS PRODUCT MAY RESULT IN THE FORMATION OF AN INFORMED OPINION
WARNING LEAPING FROM ROOF MAY RESULT IN DESIRED EFFECT
BAR
WARNING ALCOHOL CONSUMPTION MAY CAUSE MORONIC UTTERANCES TO EMANATE FROM YOUR MOUTH
WARNING INHALING HERE MAY RESULT IN A FLY GOING UP YOUR NOSE
WARNING PASSING BY MAY RESULT IN FEELINGS OF GUILT. (UNLESS YOU'RE REPUBLICAN)
HELP
WARNING CLOSED DOOR MAY RESULT IN NOT OPENING
WARNING REGULAR STEPS, NOT A RECOVERY PROGRAM
WARNING STEPPING ON A CRACK MAY BREAK YOUR MOTHER'S BACK
WILEY

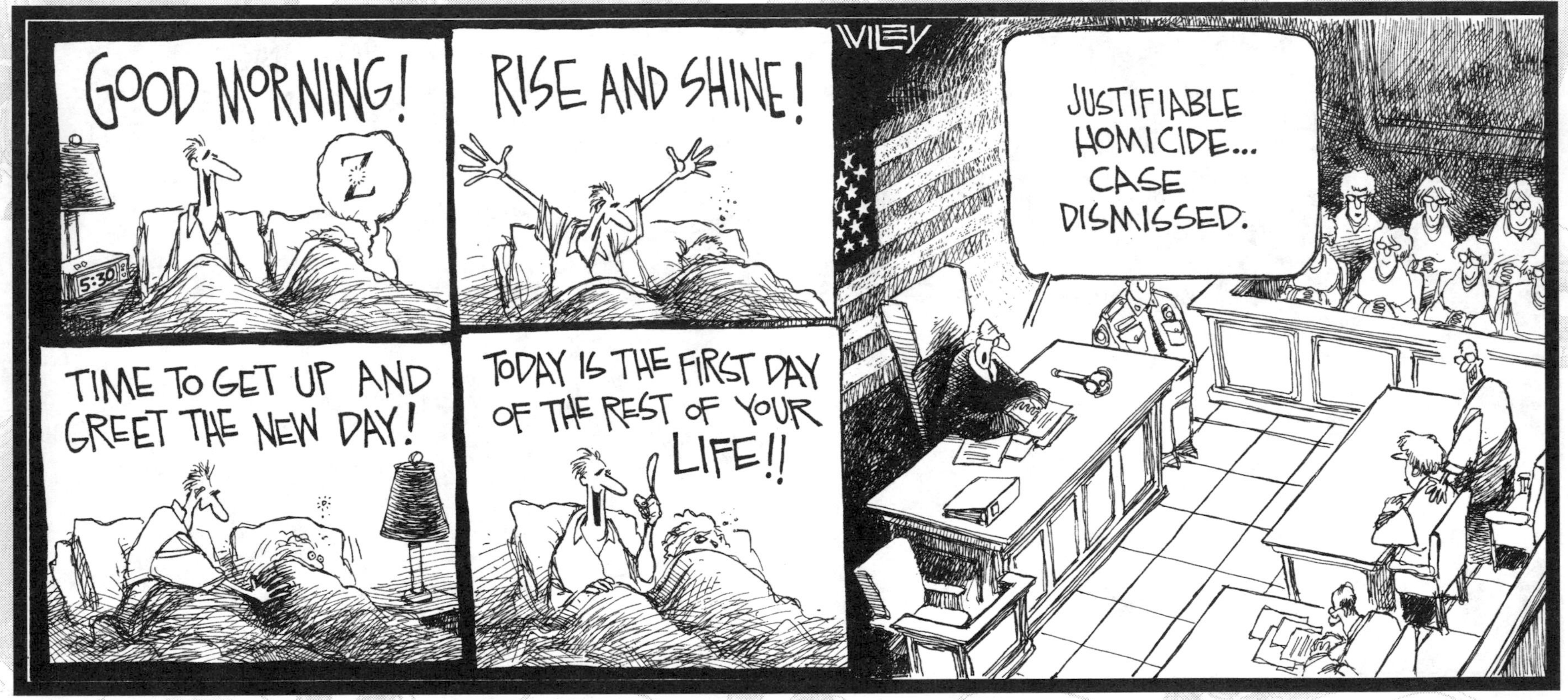
GOOD MORNING!
5:30
Z
RISE AND SHINE!
TIME TO GET UP AND GREET THE NEW DAY!
TODAY IS THE FIRST DAY OF THE REST OF YOUR LIFE!!
WILEY
JUSTIFIABLE HOMICIDE... CASE DISMISSED.

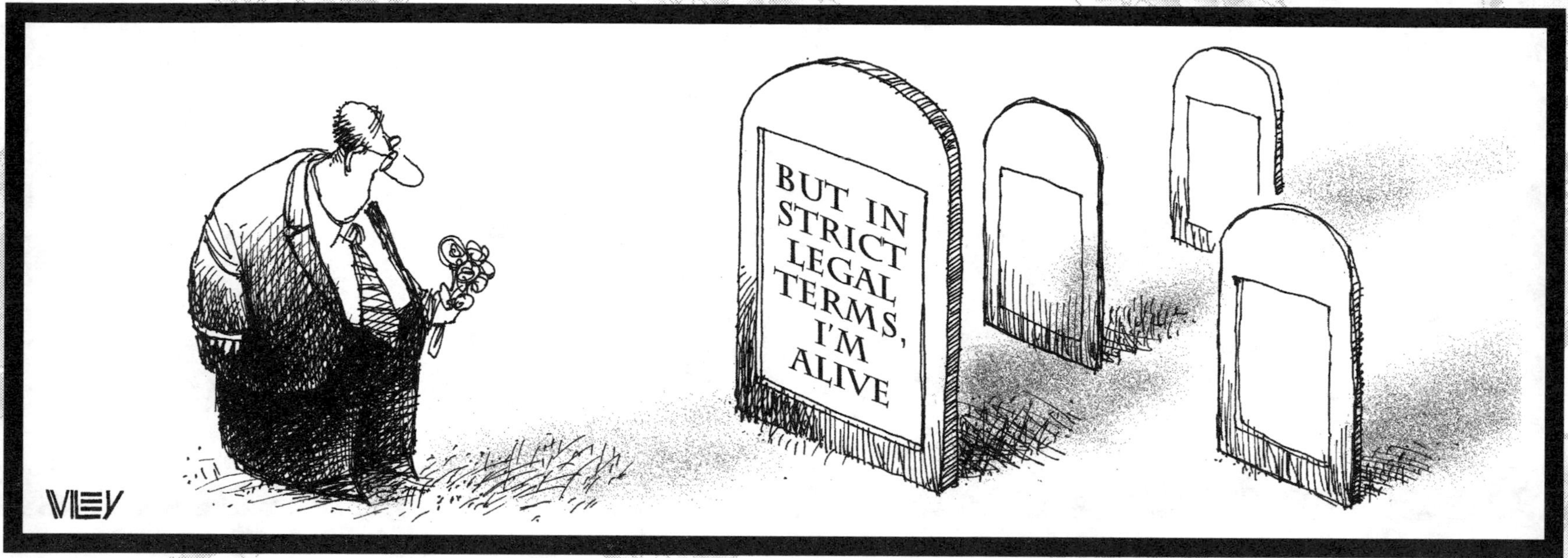
BUT IN STRICT LEGAL TERMS, I'M ALIVE
WILEY

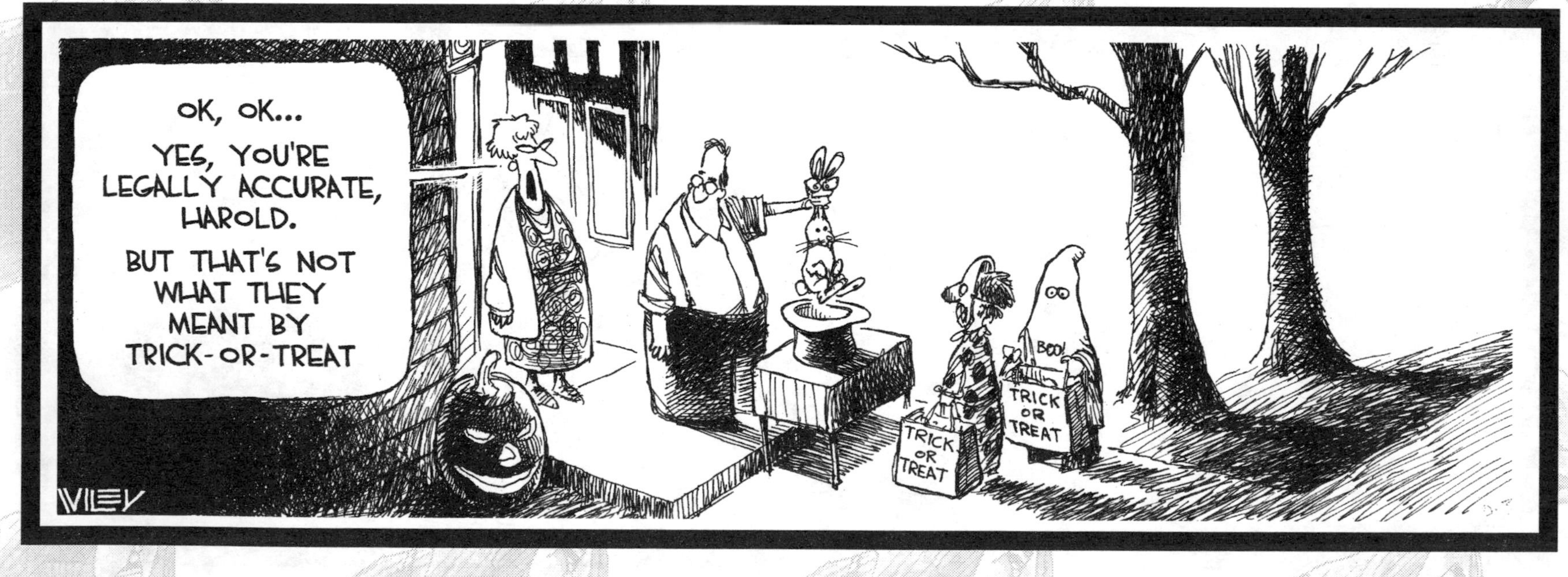
OK, OK...
YES, YOU'RE LEGALLY ACCURATE, HAROLD.
BUT THAT'S NOT WHAT THEY MEANT BY TRICK-OR-TREAT
BOO!
TRICK OR TREAT
TRICK OR TREAT
WILEY

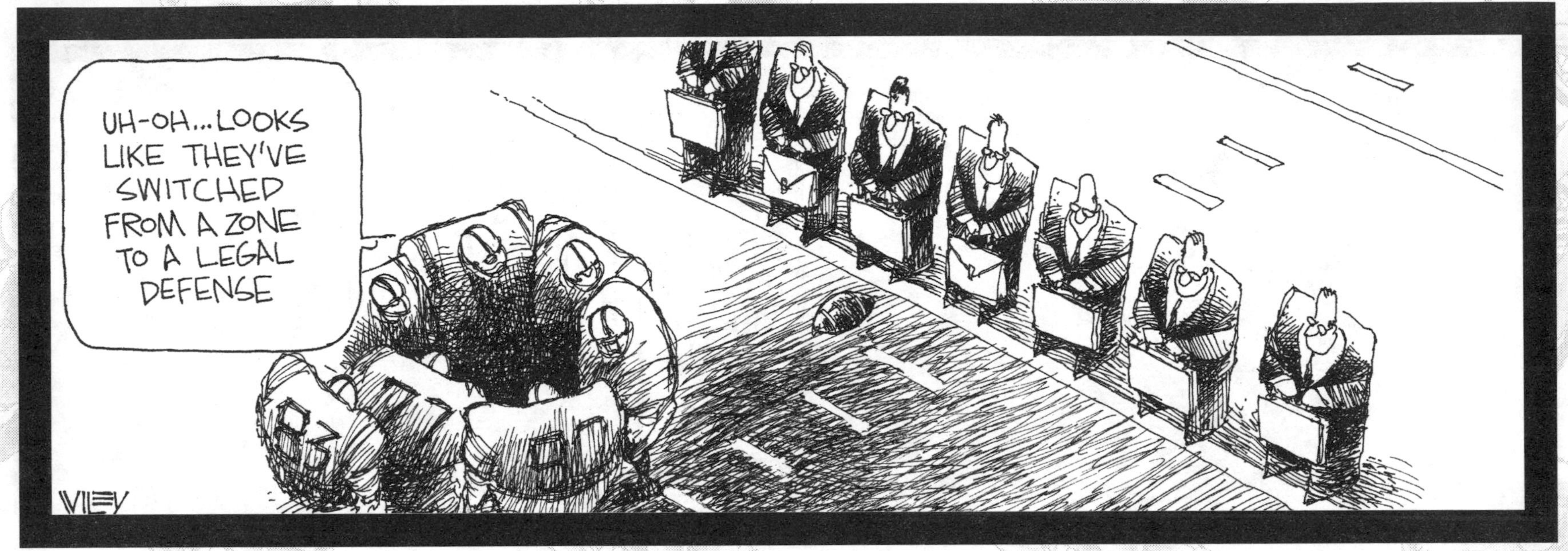
UH-OH...LOOKS LIKE THEY'VE SWITCHED FROM A ZONE TO A LEGAL DEFENSE
VILEY

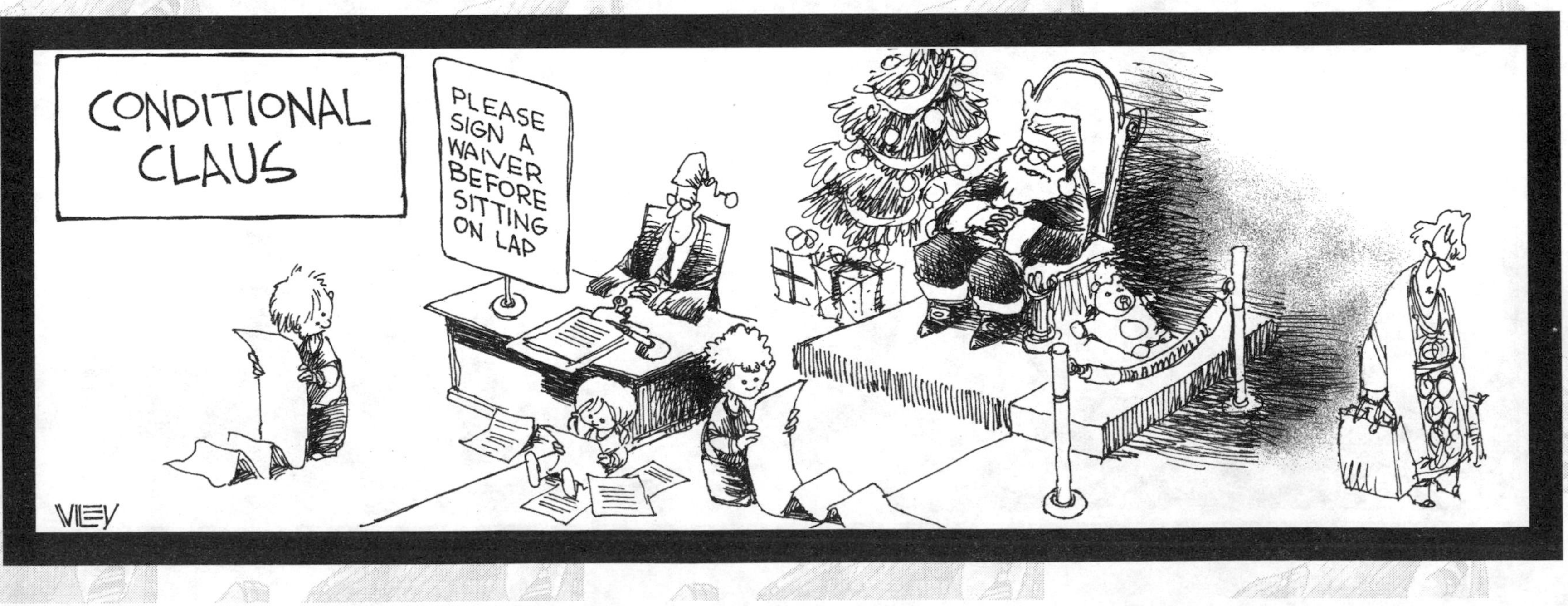
CONDITIONAL CLAUS
PLEASE SIGN A WAIVER BEFORE SITTING ON LAP
VILEY

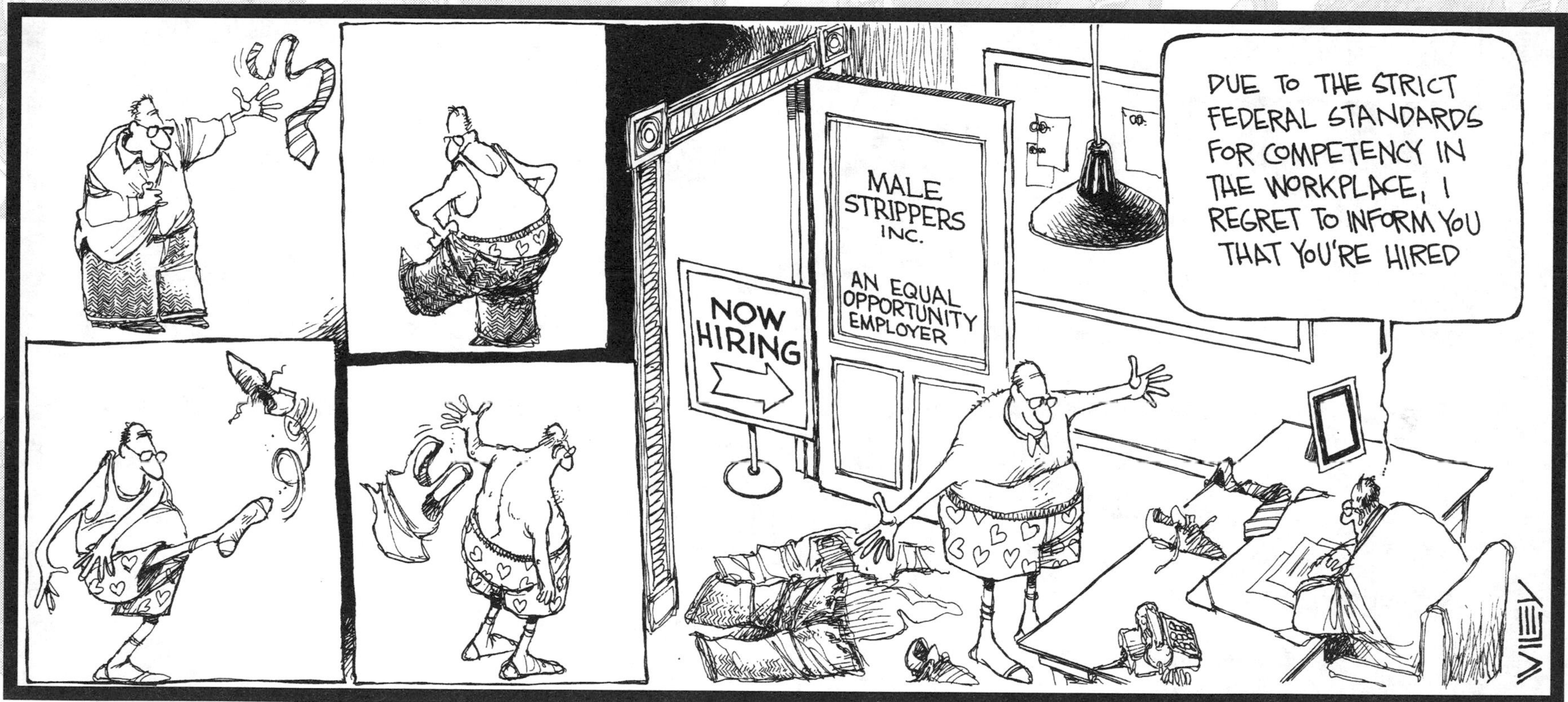
MALE
STRIPPERS
INC.
AN EQUAL
OPPORTUNITY
EMPLOYER
NOW
HIRING
DUE TO THE STRICT FEDERAL STANDARDS FOR COMPETENCY IN THE WORKPLACE, I REGRET TO INFORM YOU THAT YOU'RE HIRED
WILEY

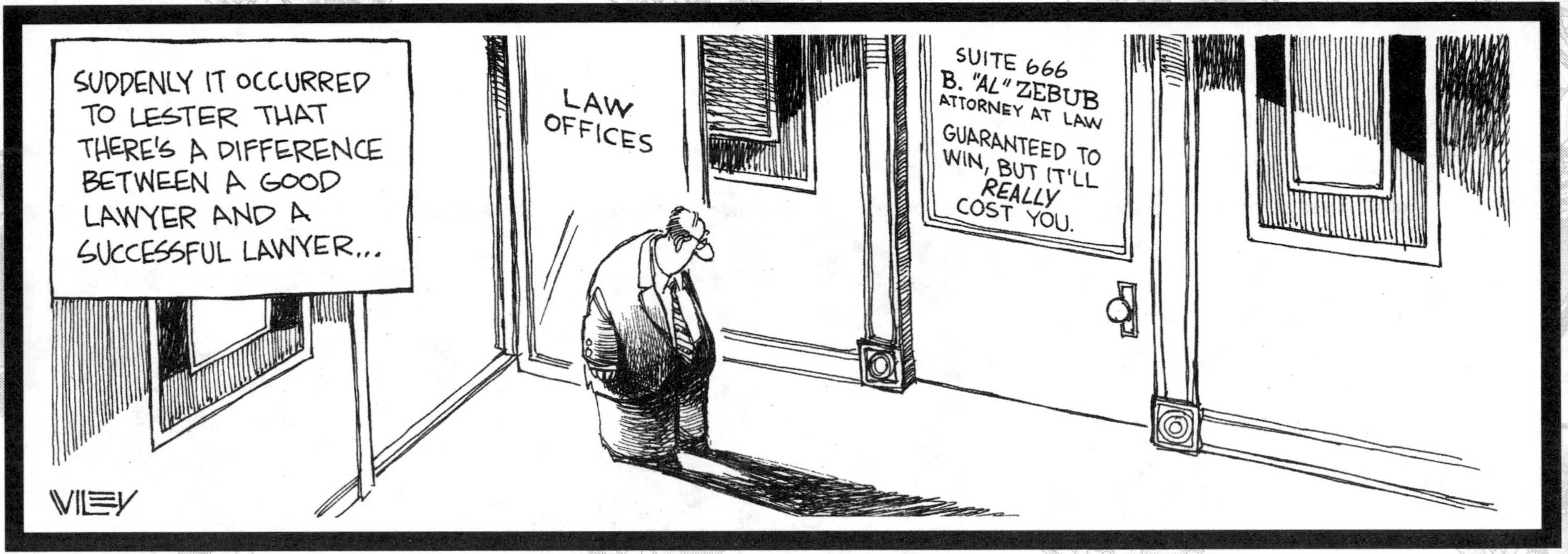
SUDDENLY IT OCCURRED TO LESTER THAT THERE'S A DIFFERENCE BETWEEN A GOOD LAWYER AND A SUCCESSFUL LAWYER...
LAW OFFICES
SUITE 666
B. "AL" ZEBUB
ATTORNEY AT LAW
GUARANTEED TO WIN, BUT IT'LL REALLY COST YOU.
WILEY

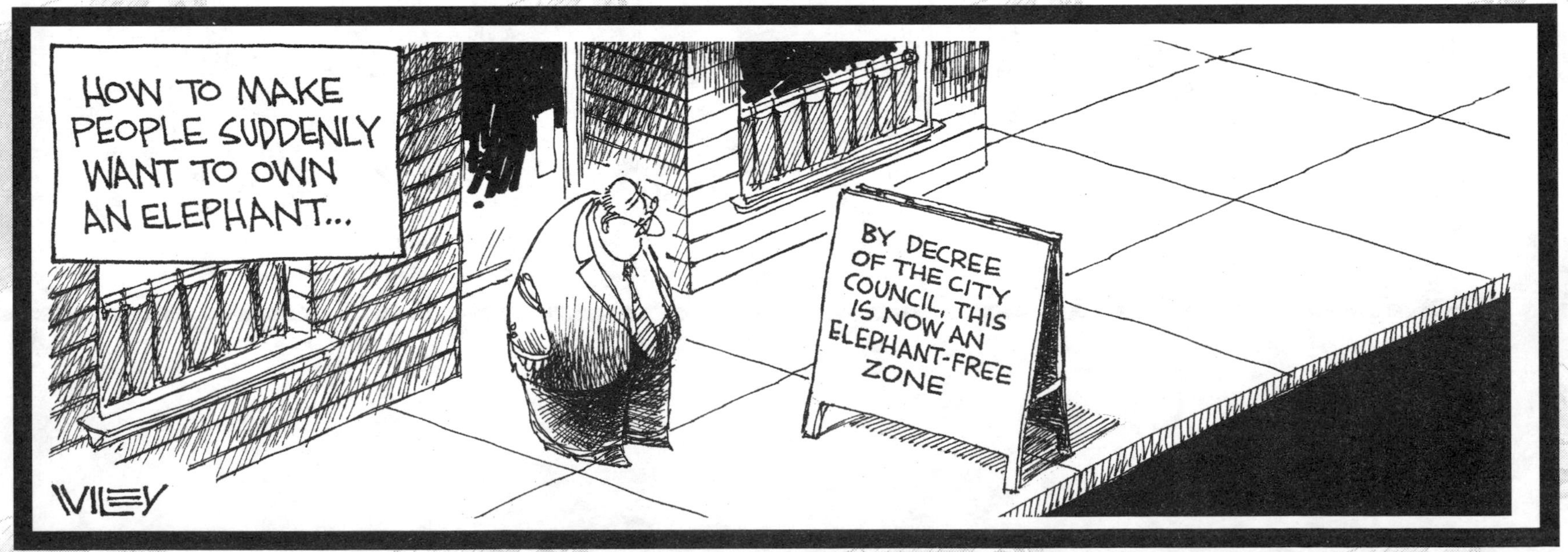
HOW TO MAKE PEOPLE SUDDENLY WANT TO OWN AN ELEPHANT...
BY DECREE OF THE CITY COUNCIL, THIS IS NOW AN ELEPHANT-FREE ZONE
WILEY

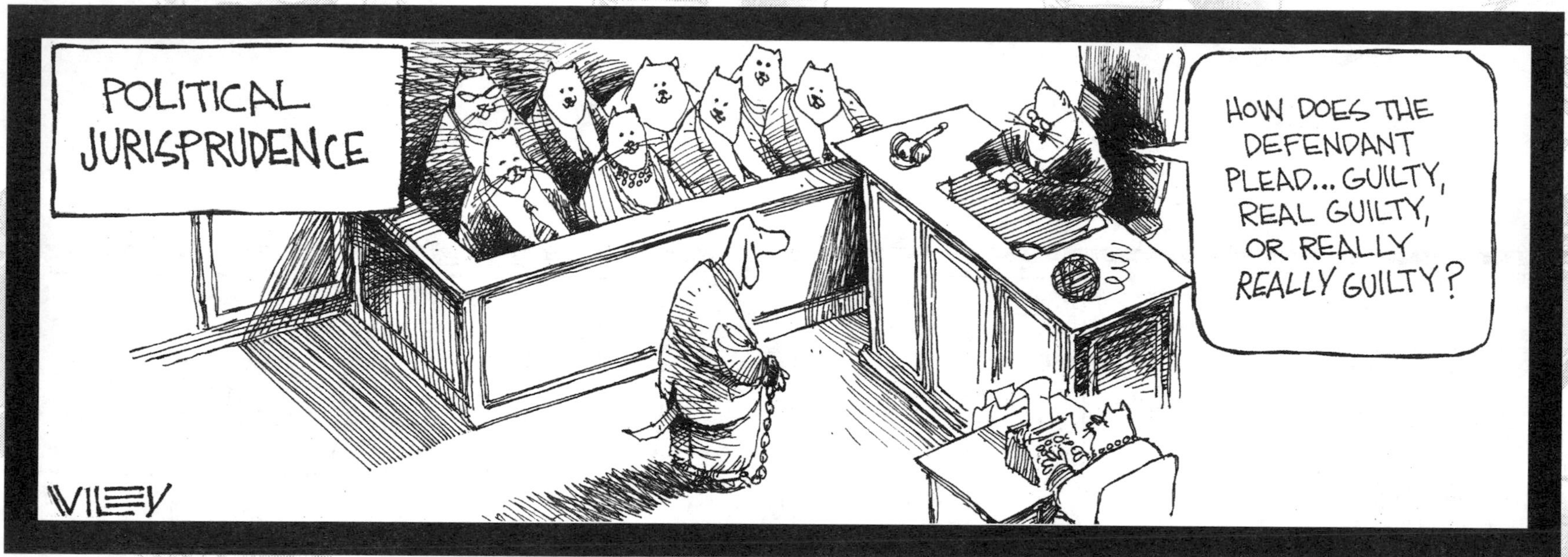
POLITICAL JURISPRUDENCE
HOW DOES THE DEFENDANT PLEAD... GUILTY, REAL GUILTY, OR REALLY REALLY GUILTY?
WILEY

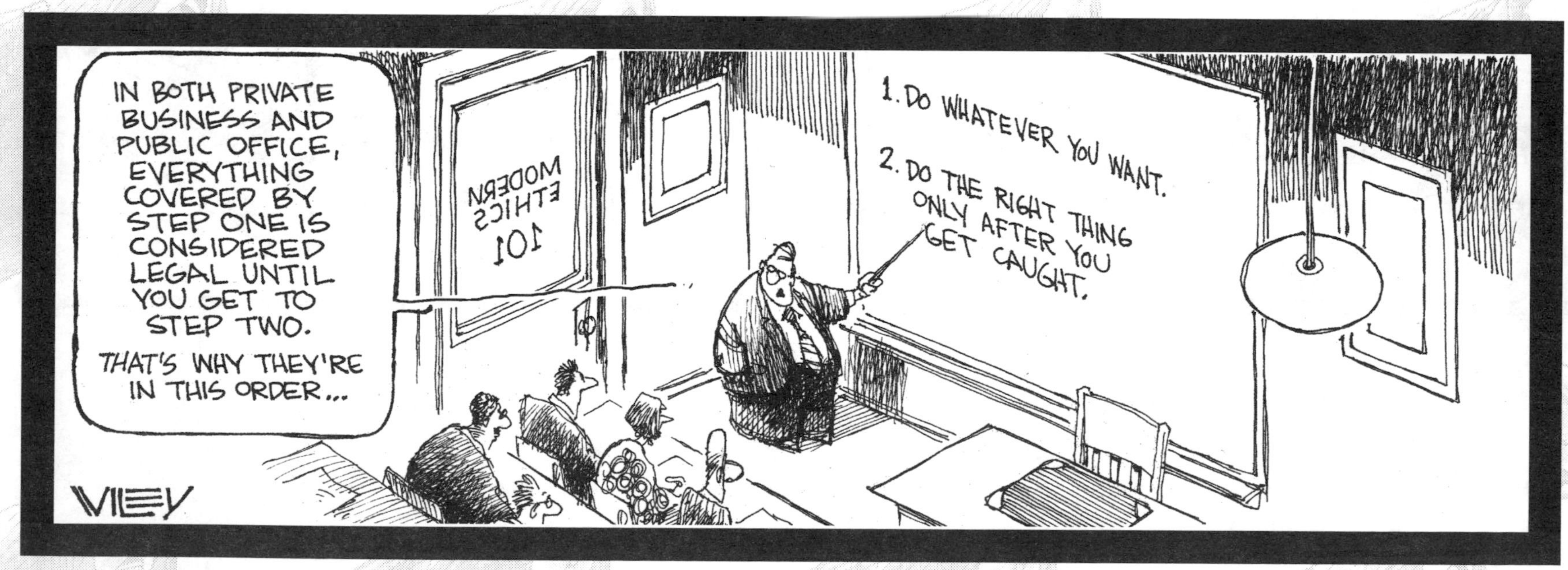
IN BOTH PRIVATE BUSINESS AND PUBLIC OFFICE, EVERYTHING COVERED BY STEP ONE IS CONSIDERED LEGAL UNTIL YOU GET TO STEP TWO.
THAT'S WHY THEY'RE IN THIS ORDER...
MODERN ETHICS 101
1. DO WHATEVER YOU WANT.
2. DO THE RIGHT THING ONLY AFTER YOU GET CAUGHT.
WILEY

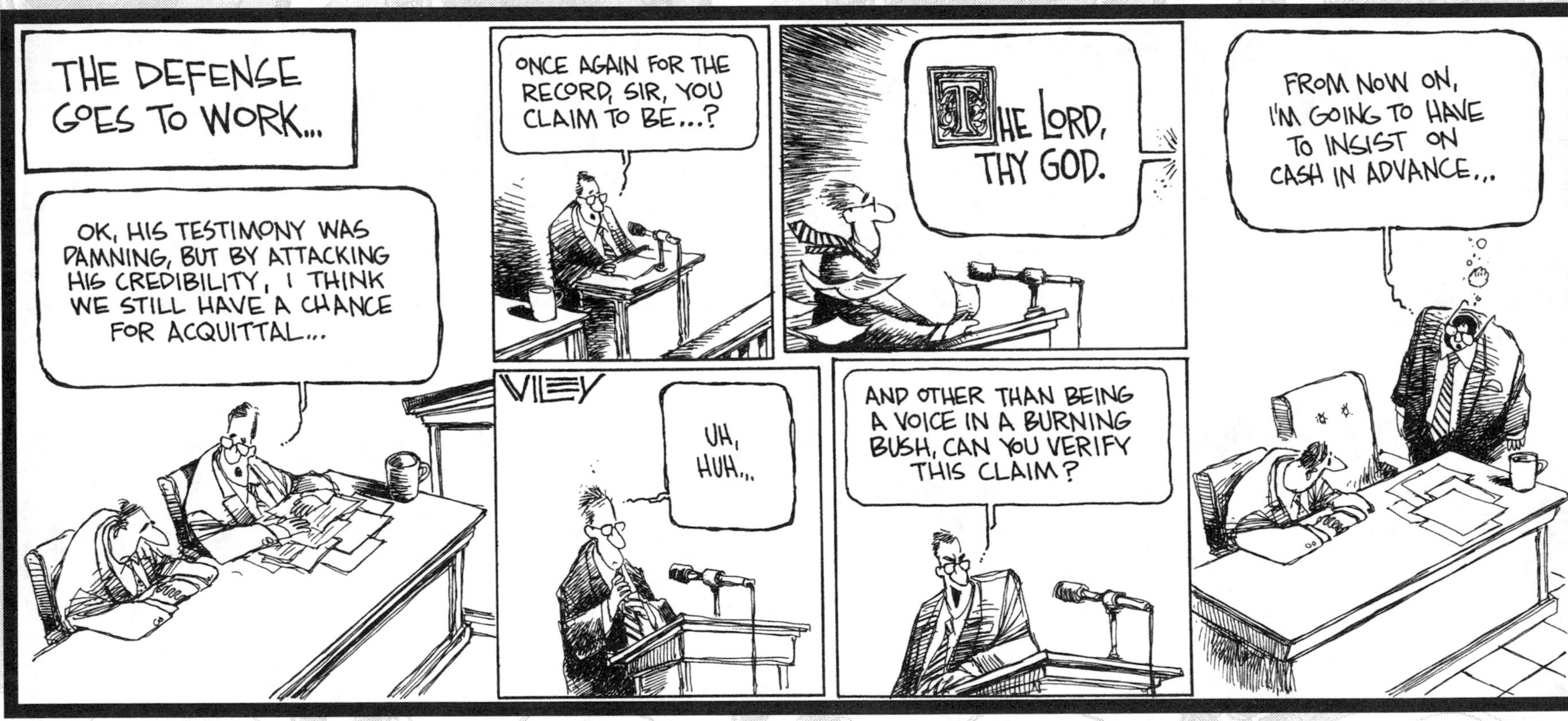
THE DEFENSE GOES TO WORK...
OK, HIS TESTIMONY WAS DAMNING, BUT BY ATTACKING HIS CREDIBILITY, I THINK WE STILL HAVE A CHANCE FOR ACQUITTAL...
ONCE AGAIN FOR THE RECORD, SIR, YOU CLAIM TO BE...?
THE LORD, THY GOD.
VILEY
UH, HUH...
AND OTHER THAN BEING A VOICE IN A BURNING BUSH, CAN YOU VERIFY THIS CLAIM?
FROM NOW ON, I'M GOING TO HAVE TO INSIST ON CASH IN ADVANCE...

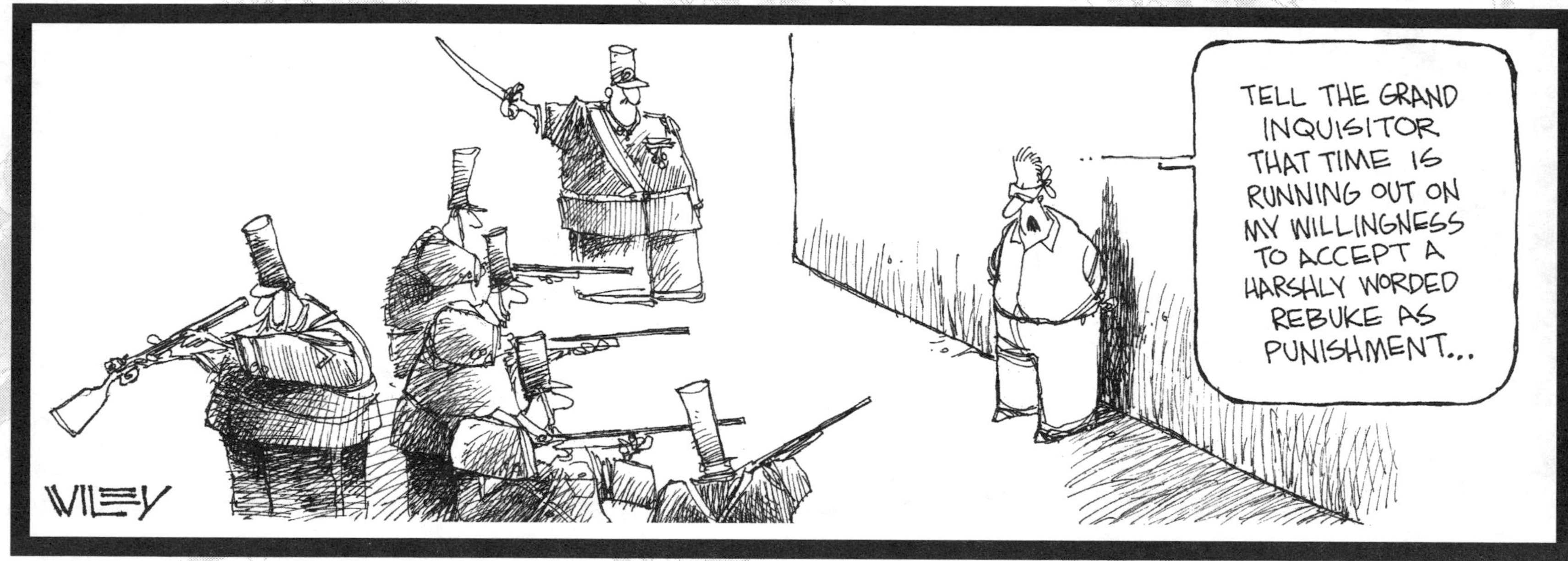
WILEY
TELL THE GRAND INQUISITOR THAT TIME IS RUNNING OUT ON MY WILLINGNESS TO ACCEPT A HARSHLY WORDED REBUKE AS PUNISHMENT...

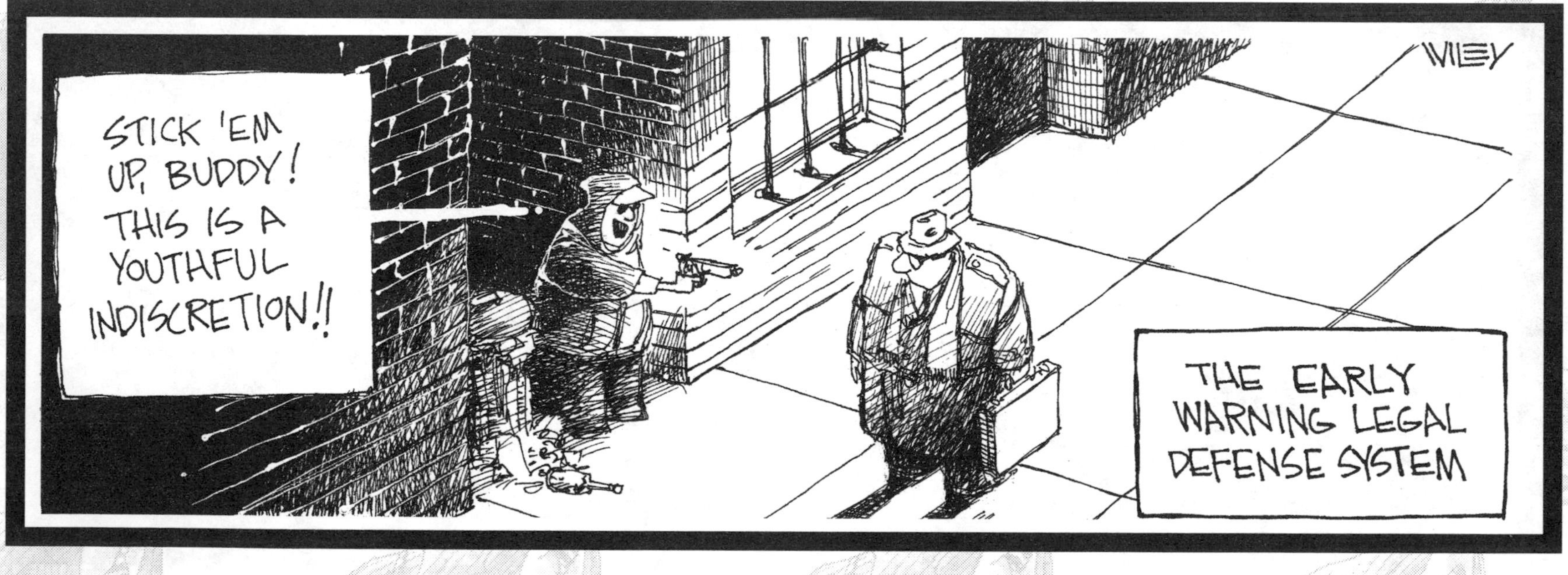
WILEY
STICK 'EM UP, BUDDY! THIS IS A YOUTHFUL INDISCRETION!!
THE EARLY WARNING LEGAL DEFENSE SYSTEM

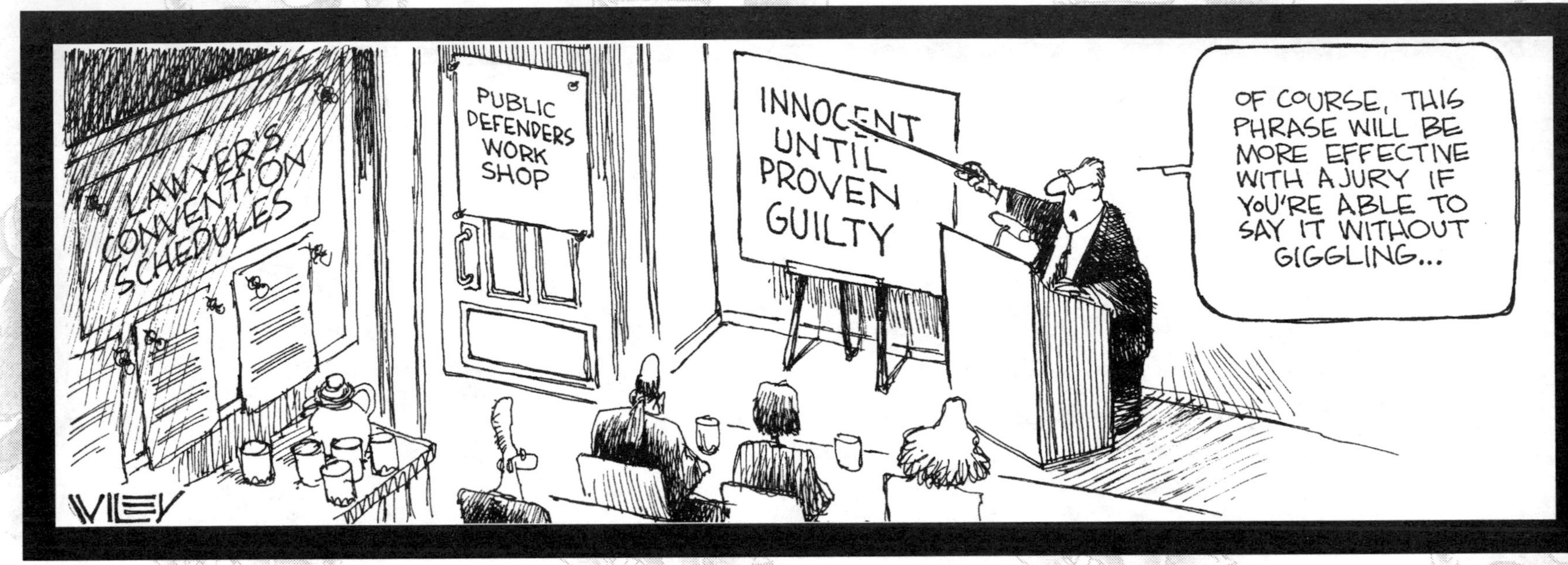
LAWYER'S CONVENTION SCHEDULES
PUBLIC DEFENDERS WORK SHOP
INNOCENT UNTIL PROVEN GUILTY
OF COURSE, THIS PHRASE WILL BE MORE EFFECTIVE WITH A JURY IF YOU'RE ABLE TO SAY IT WITHOUT GIGGLING...
WILEY

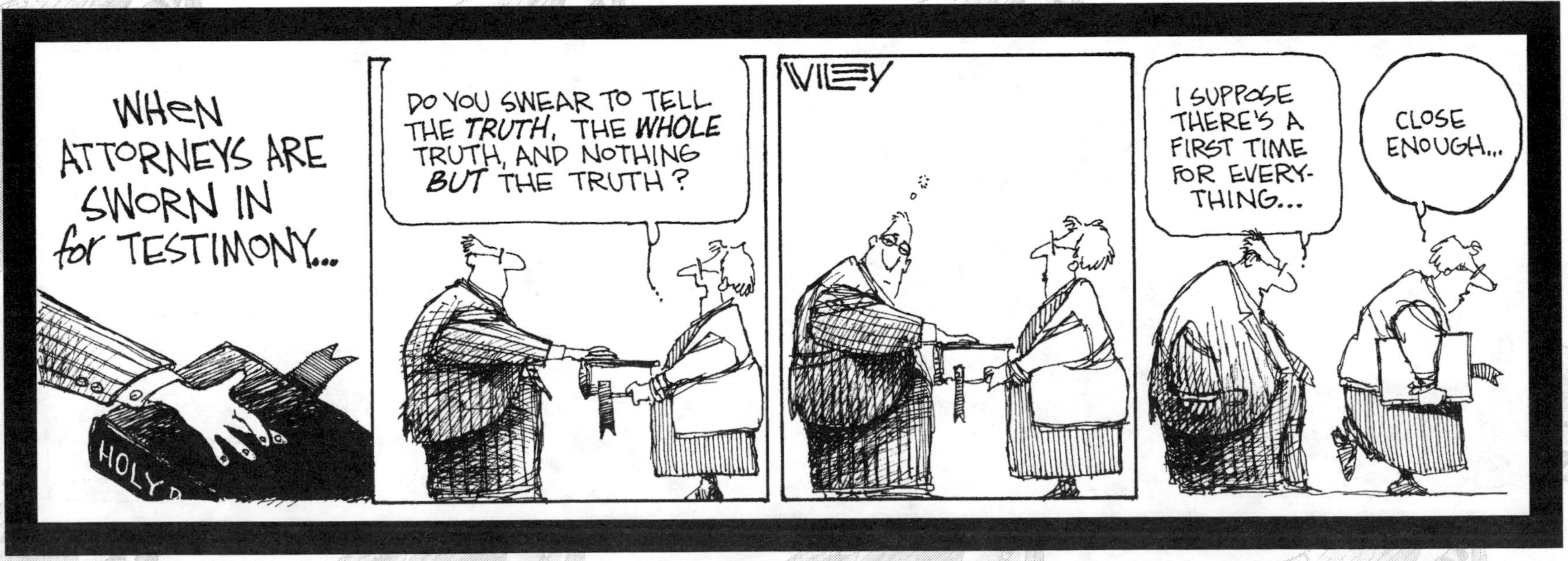
WHEN ATTORNEYS ARE SWORN IN for TESTIMONY...
HOLY
DO YOU SWEAR TO TELL THE *TRUTH*, THE *WHOLE* TRUTH, AND NOTHING *BUT* THE TRUTH?
WILEY
I SUPPOSE THERE'S A FIRST TIME FOR EVERY-THING...
CLOSE ENOUGH...

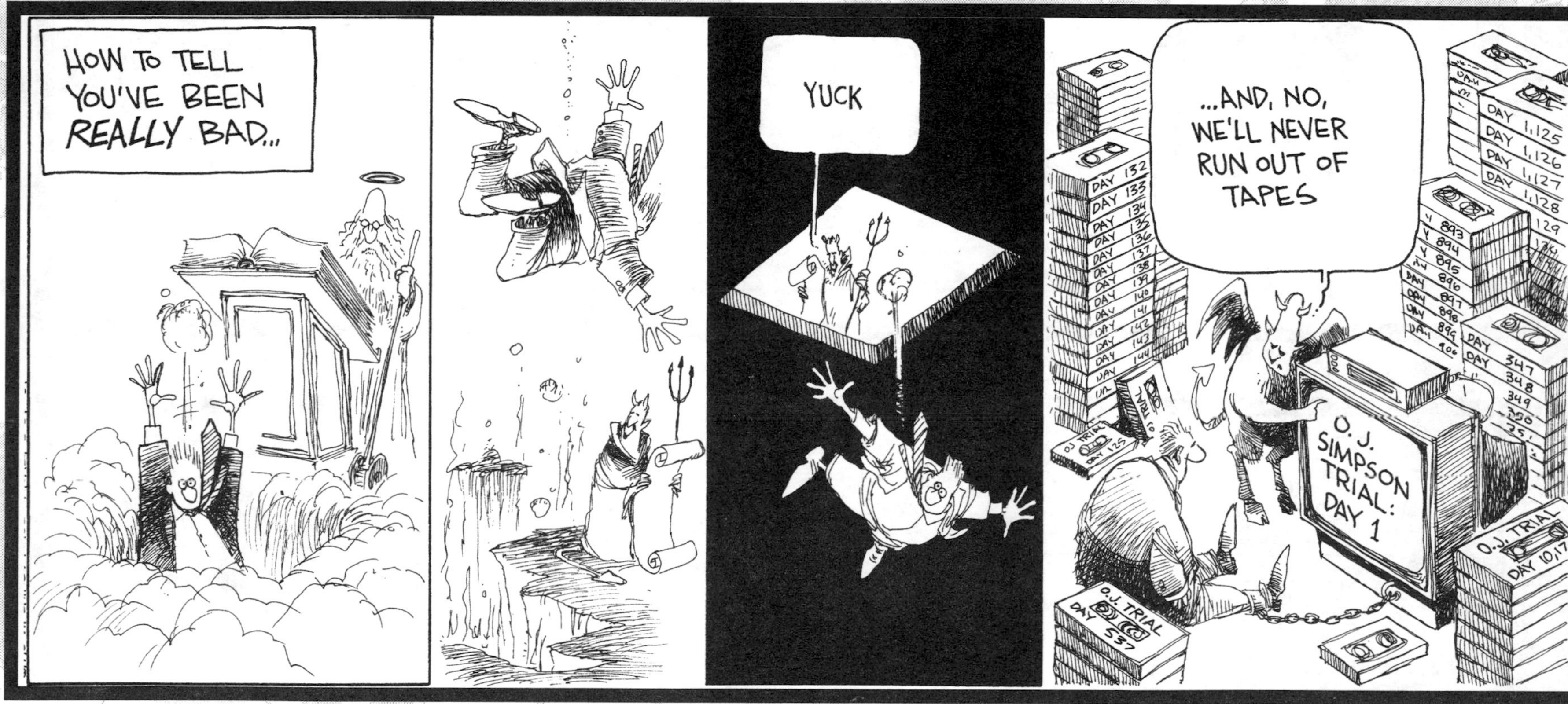

HOW TO TELL YOU'VE BEEN *REALLY* BAD...
YUCK
...AND, NO, WE'LL NEVER RUN OUT OF TAPES
O.J. SIMPSON TRIAL: DAY 1
O.J. TRIAL DAY 537

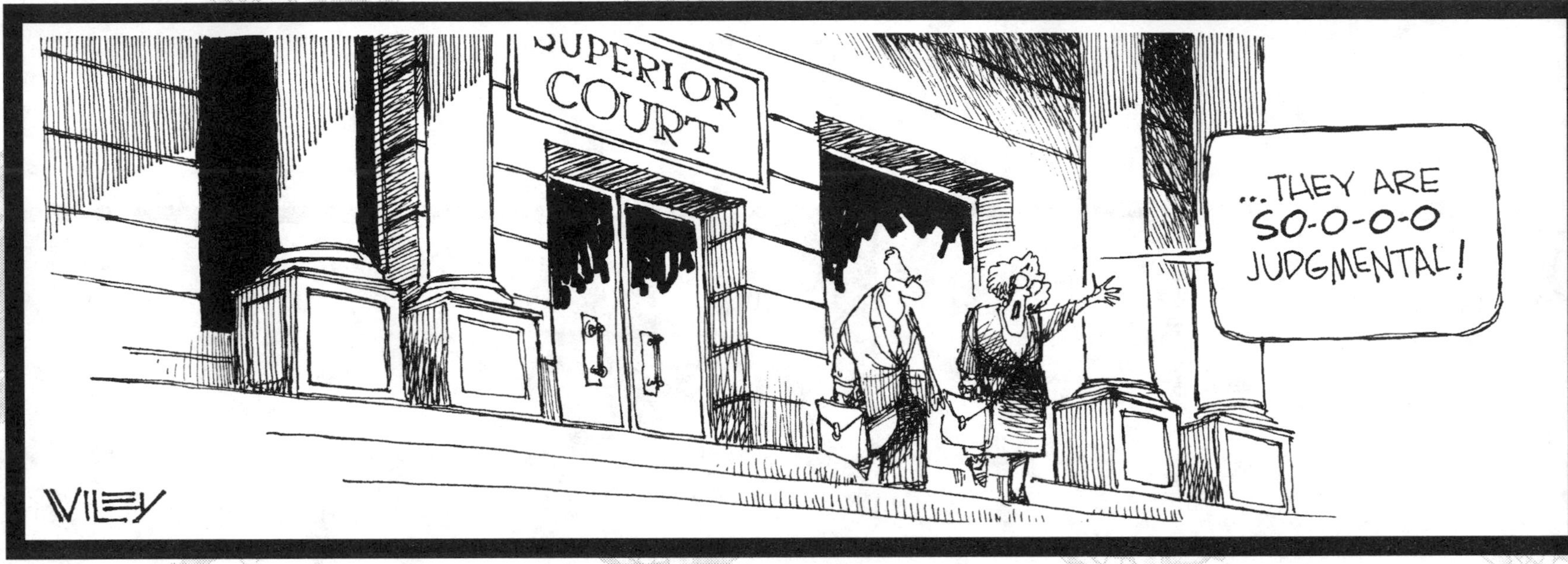
SUPERIOR COURT
...THEY ARE SO-O-O-O JUDGMENTAL!
WILEY

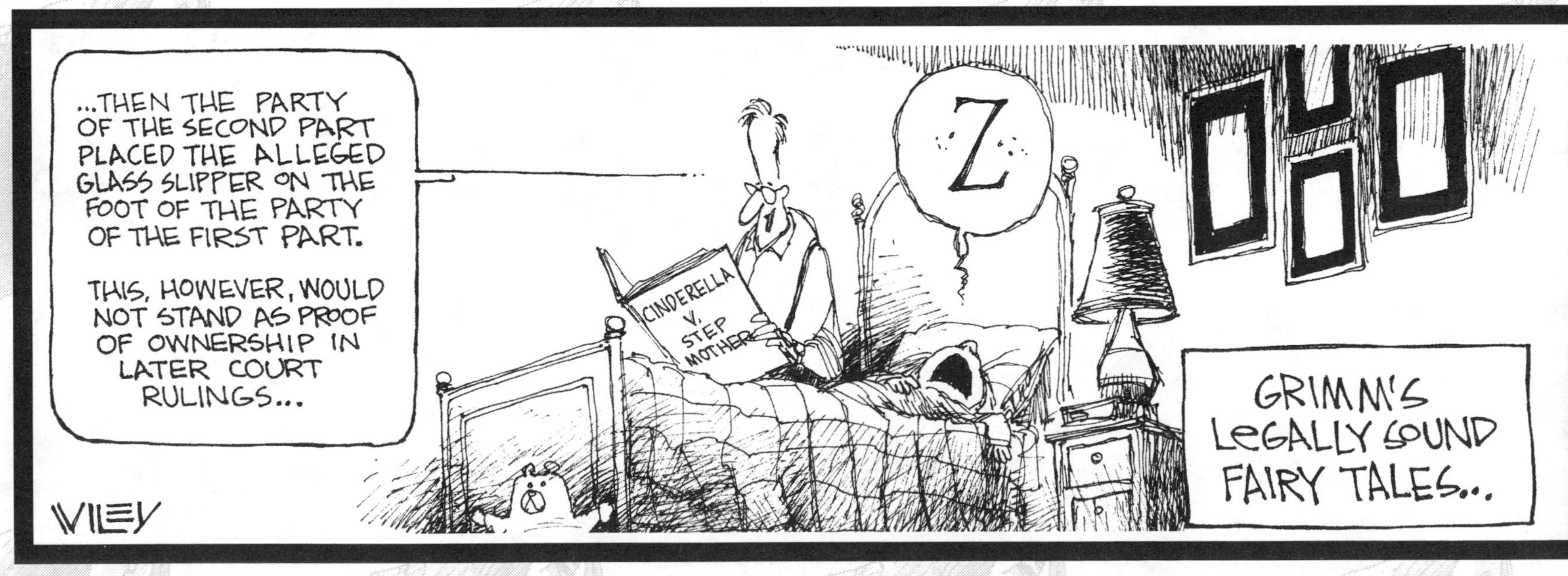
...THEN THE PARTY OF THE SECOND PART PLACED THE ALLEGED GLASS SLIPPER ON THE FOOT OF THE PARTY OF THE FIRST PART.
THIS, HOWEVER, WOULD NOT STAND AS PROOF OF OWNERSHIP IN LATER COURT RULINGS...
Z
CINDERELLA V. STEP MOTHER
GRIMM'S LEGALLY SOUND FAIRY TALES...
WILEY

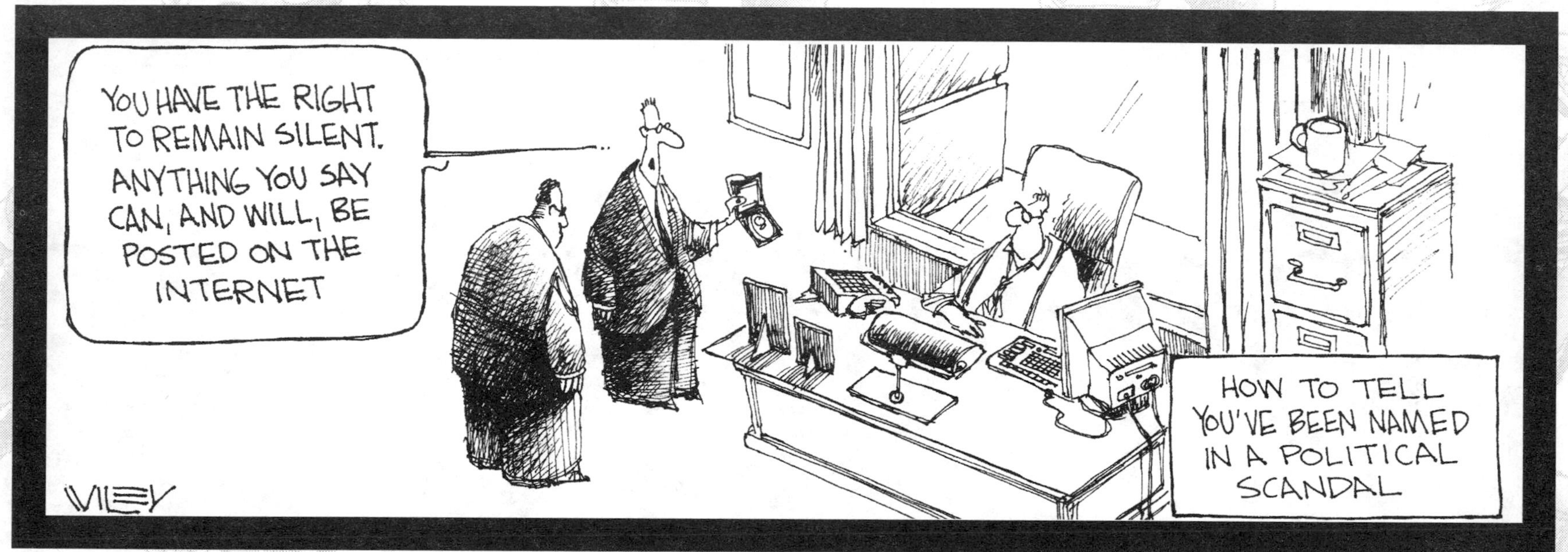
YOU HAVE THE RIGHT TO REMAIN SILENT. ANYTHING YOU SAY CAN, AND WILL, BE POSTED ON THE INTERNET
HOW TO TELL YOU'VE BEEN NAMED IN A POLITICAL SCANDAL
WILEY

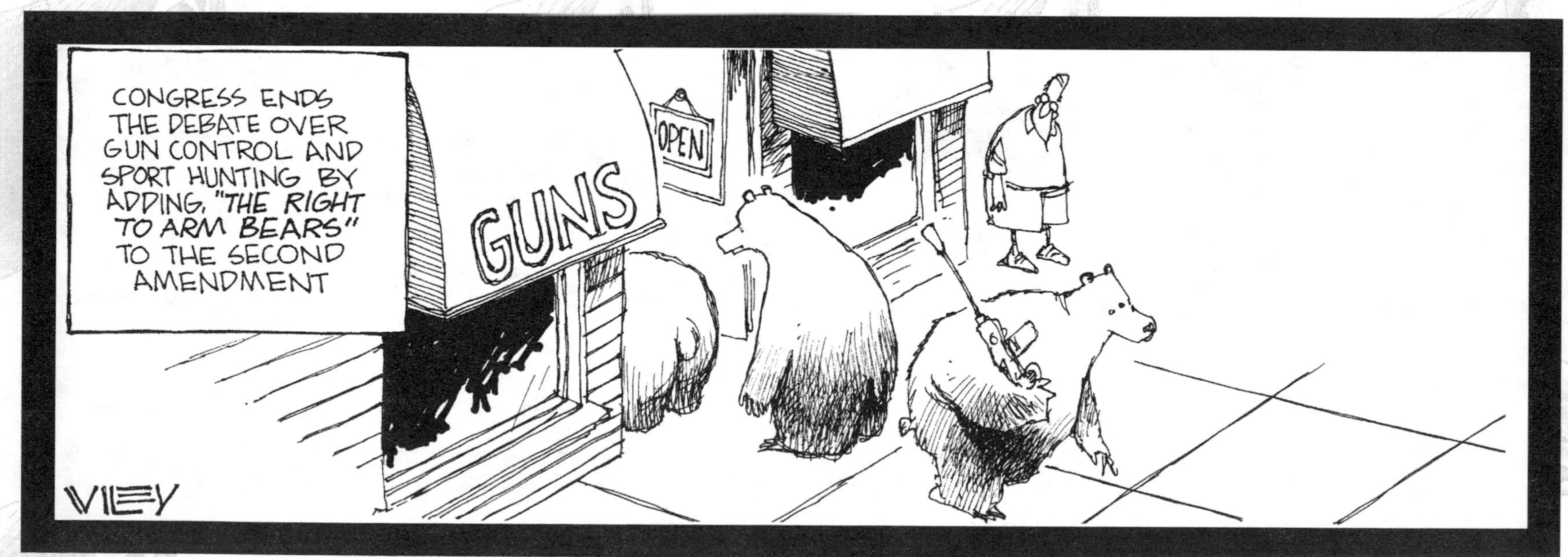
CONGRESS ENDS THE DEBATE OVER GUN CONTROL AND SPORT HUNTING BY ADDING, *"THE RIGHT TO ARM BEARS"* TO THE SECOND AMENDMENT
GUNS
OPEN
WILEY

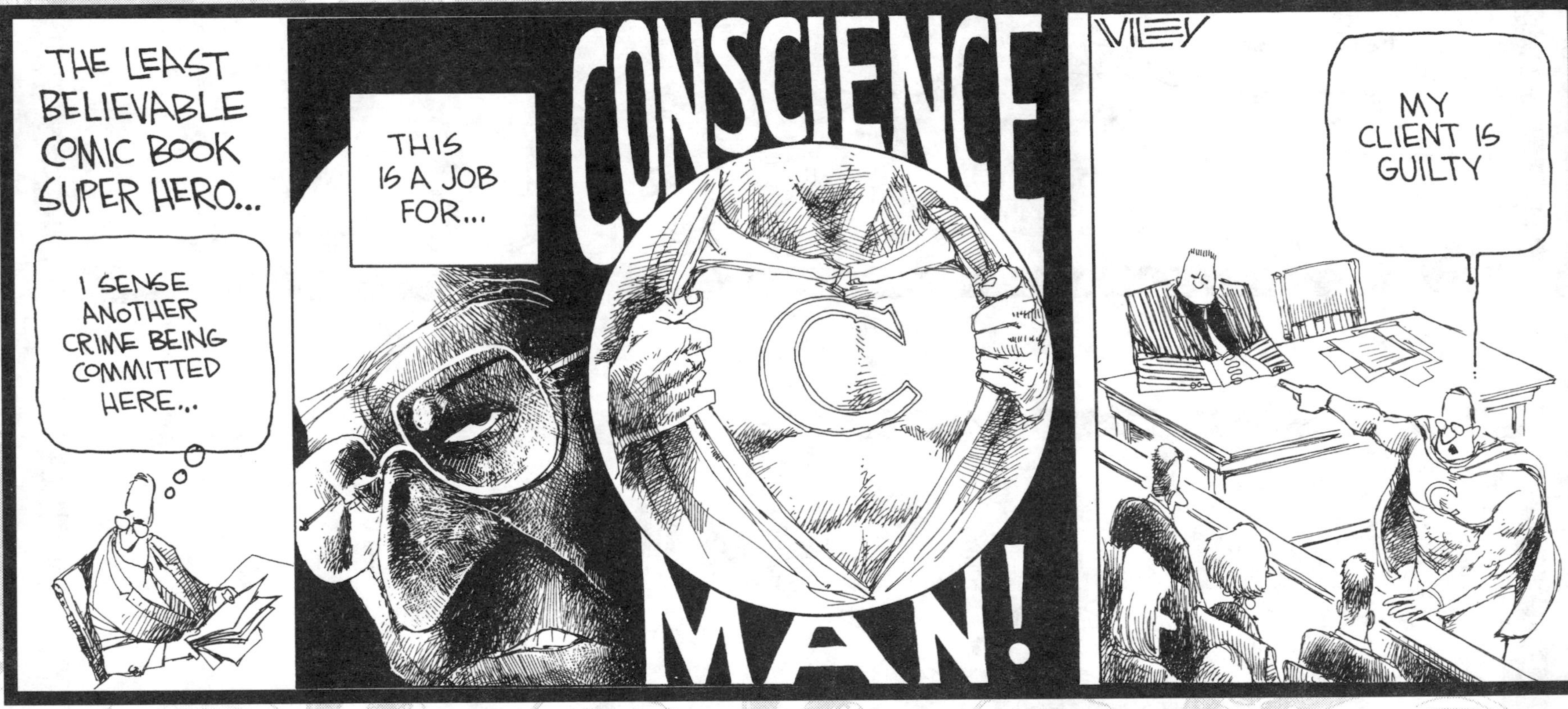
THE LEAST BELIEVABLE COMIC BOOK SUPER HERO...
I SENSE ANOTHER CRIME BEING COMMITTED HERE...
THIS IS A JOB FOR...
CONSCIENCE MAN!
MY CLIENT IS GUILTY

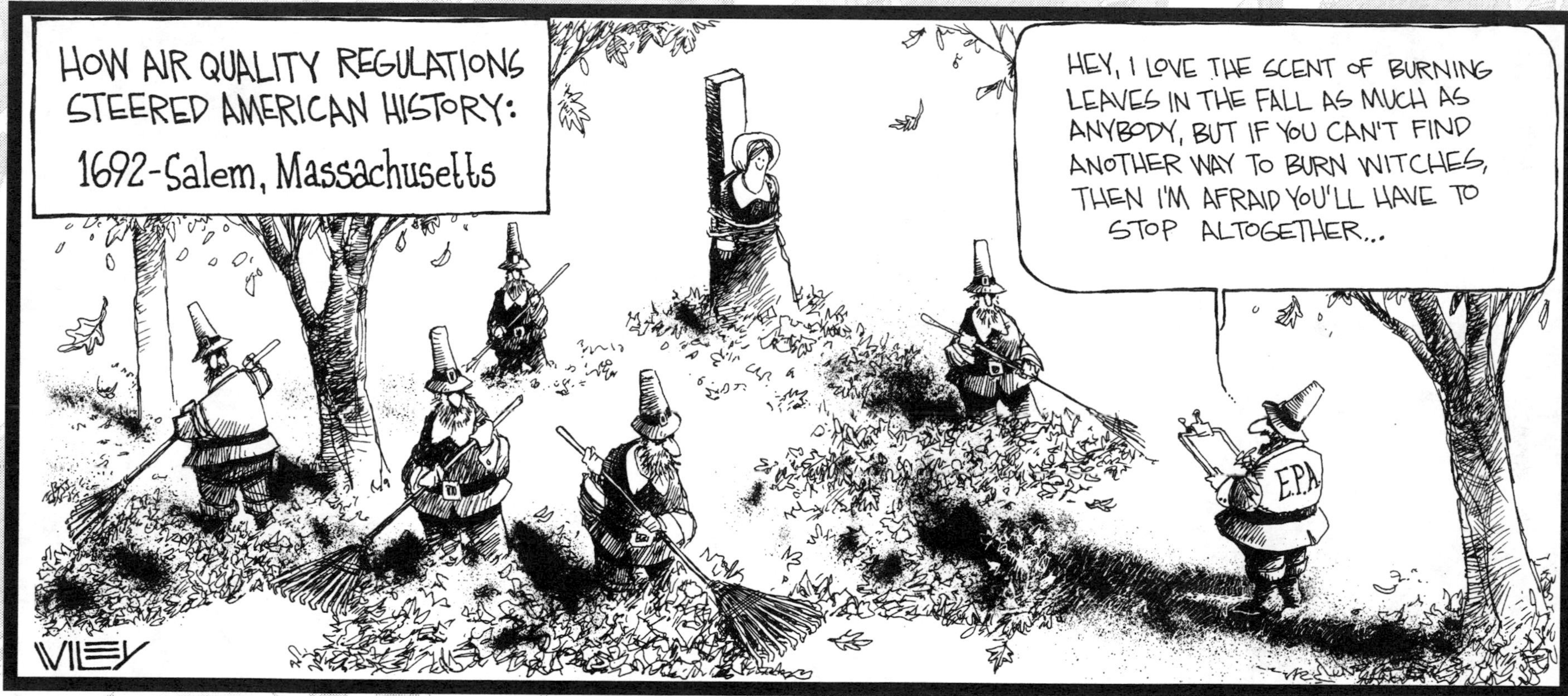
HOW AIR QUALITY REGULATIONS STEERED AMERICAN HISTORY:
1692-Salem, Massachusetts
HEY, I LOVE THE SCENT OF BURNING LEAVES IN THE FALL AS MUCH AS ANYBODY, BUT IF YOU CAN'T FIND ANOTHER WAY TO BURN WITCHES, THEN I'M AFRAID YOU'LL HAVE TO STOP ALTOGETHER...
E.P.A.
WILEY

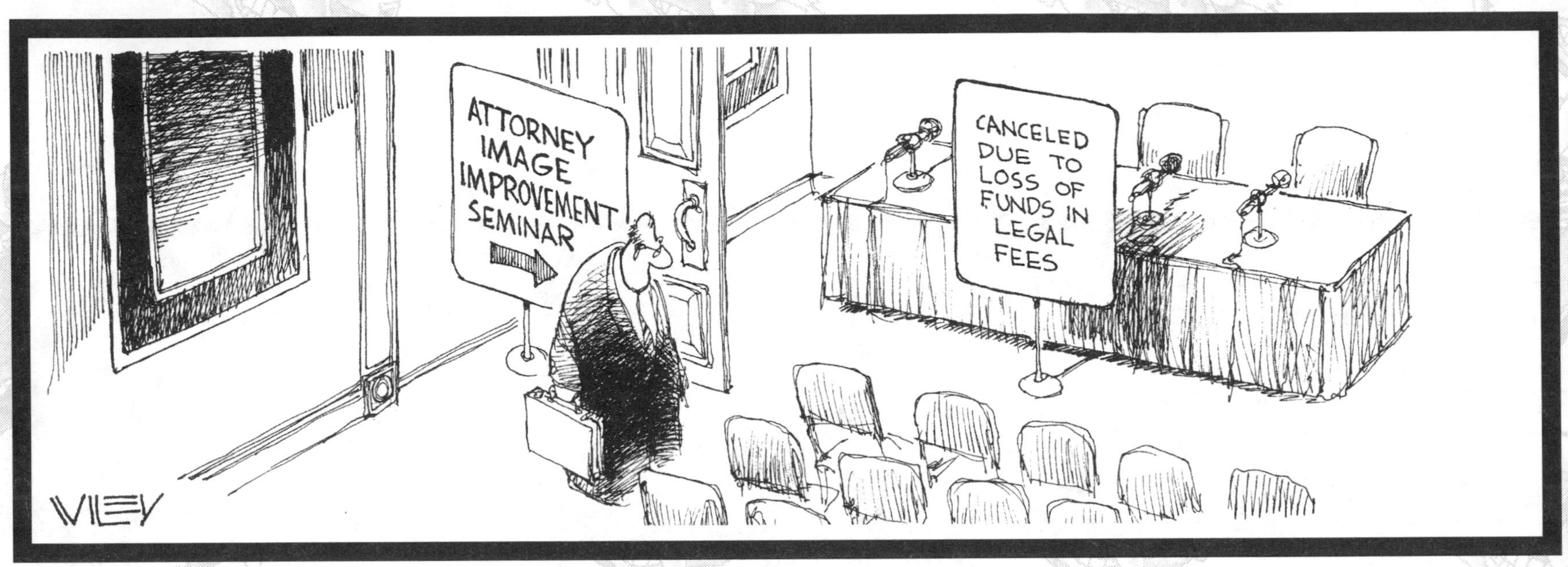
ATTORNEY IMAGE IMPROVEMENT SEMINAR
CANCELED DUE TO LOSS OF FUNDS IN LEGAL FEES
WILEY

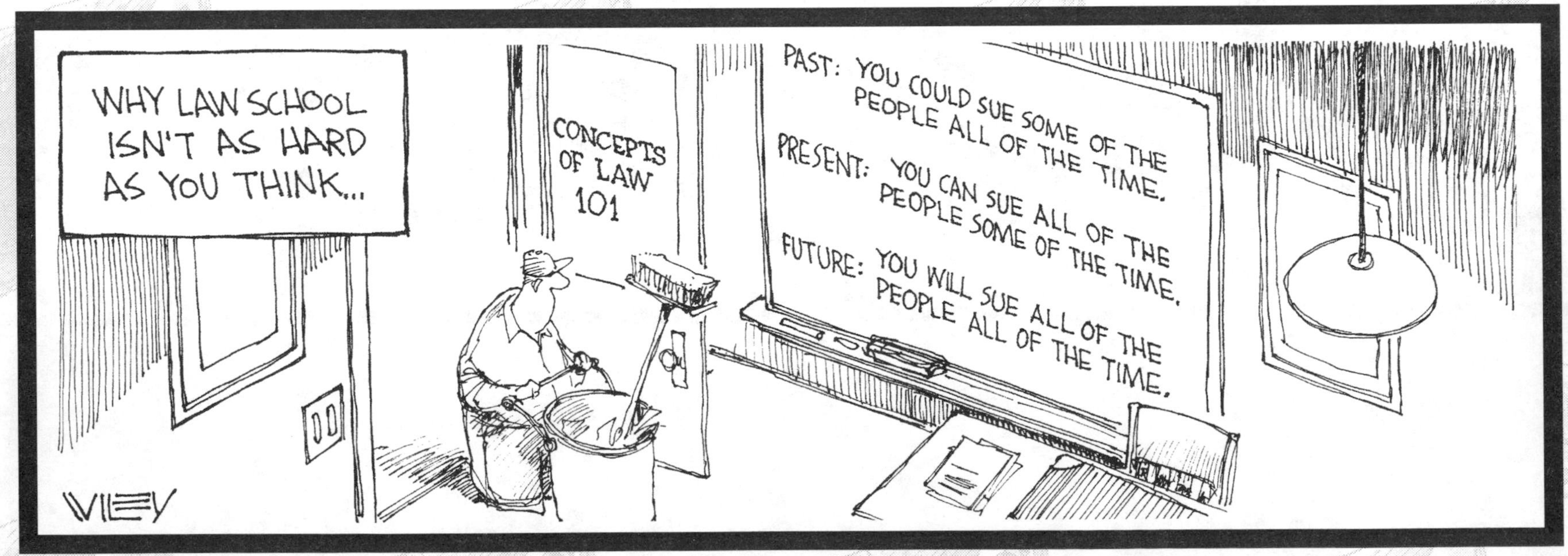
WHY LAW SCHOOL ISN'T AS HARD AS YOU THINK...
CONCEPTS OF LAW 101
PAST: YOU COULD SUE SOME OF THE PEOPLE ALL OF THE TIME.
PRESENT: YOU CAN SUE ALL OF THE PEOPLE SOME OF THE TIME.
FUTURE: YOU WILL SUE ALL OF THE PEOPLE ALL OF THE TIME.
WILEY

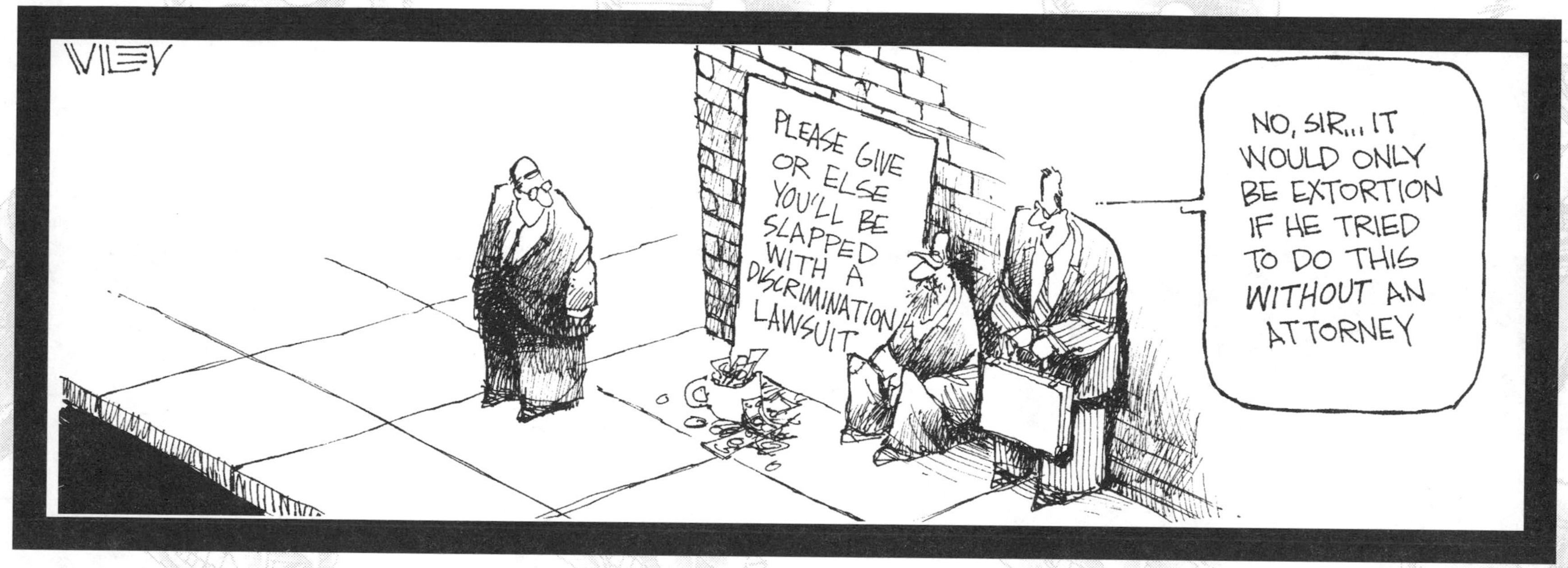
WILEY
PLEASE GIVE OR ELSE YOU'LL BE SLAPPED WITH A DISCRIMINATION LAWSUIT
NO, SIR... IT WOULD ONLY BE EXTORTION IF HE TRIED TO DO THIS WITHOUT AN ATTORNEY

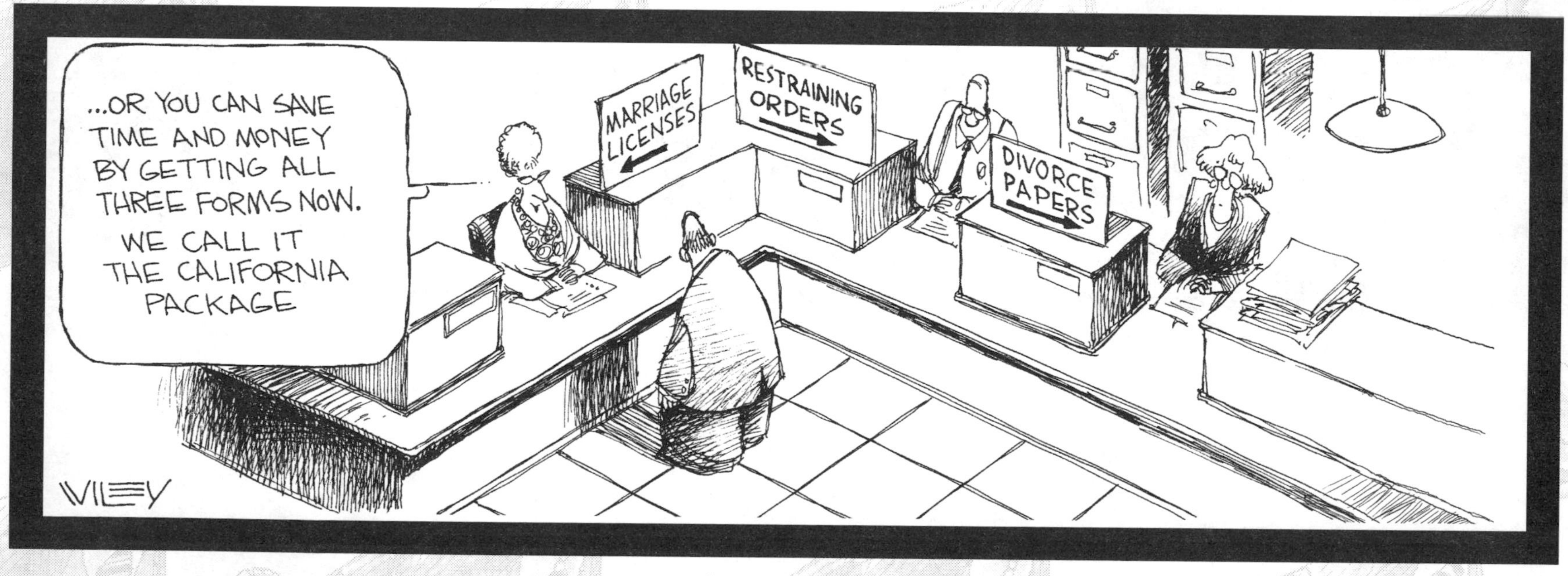
...OR YOU CAN SAVE TIME AND MONEY BY GETTING ALL THREE FORMS NOW. WE CALL IT THE CALIFORNIA PACKAGE
MARRIAGE LICENSES
RESTRAINING ORDERS
DIVORCE PAPERS
WILEY

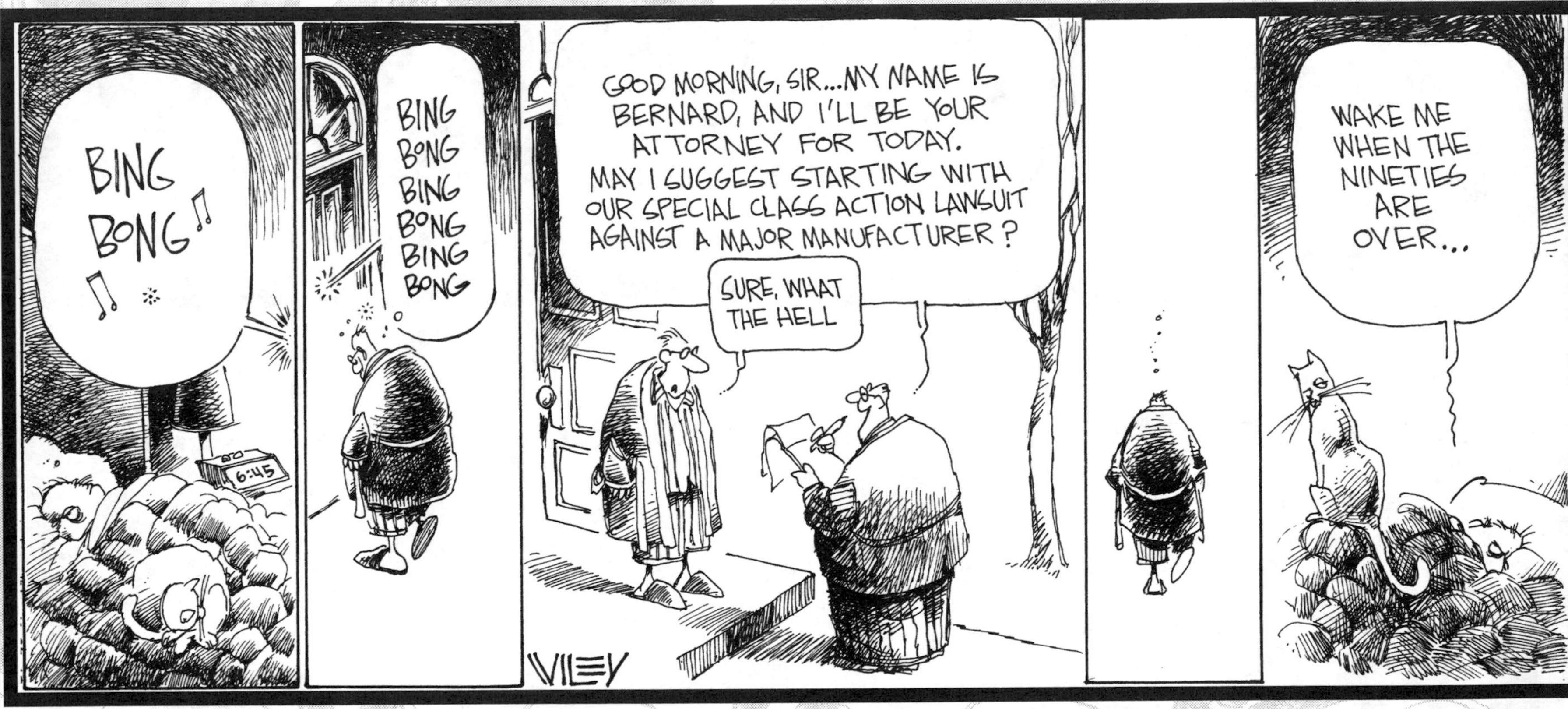
BING BONG
6:45
BING BONG BING BONG BING BONG
GOOD MORNING, SIR...MY NAME IS BERNARD, AND I'LL BE YOUR ATTORNEY FOR TODAY. MAY I SUGGEST STARTING WITH OUR SPECIAL CLASS ACTION LAWSUIT AGAINST A MAJOR MANUFACTURER?
SURE, WHAT THE HELL
WILEY
WAKE ME WHEN THE NINETIES ARE OVER...

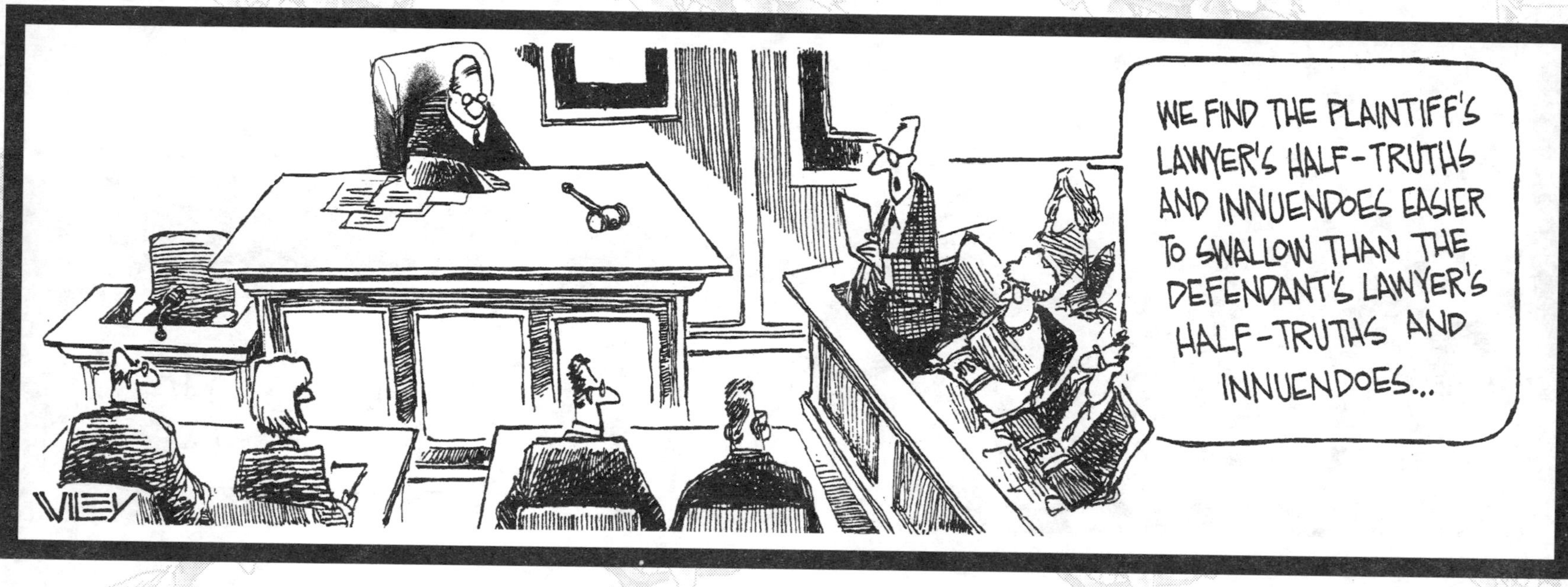
WE FIND THE PLAINTIFF'S LAWYER'S HALF-TRUTHS AND INNUENDOES EASIER TO SWALLOW THAN THE DEFENDANT'S LAWYER'S HALF-TRUTHS AND INNUENDOES...
WILEY

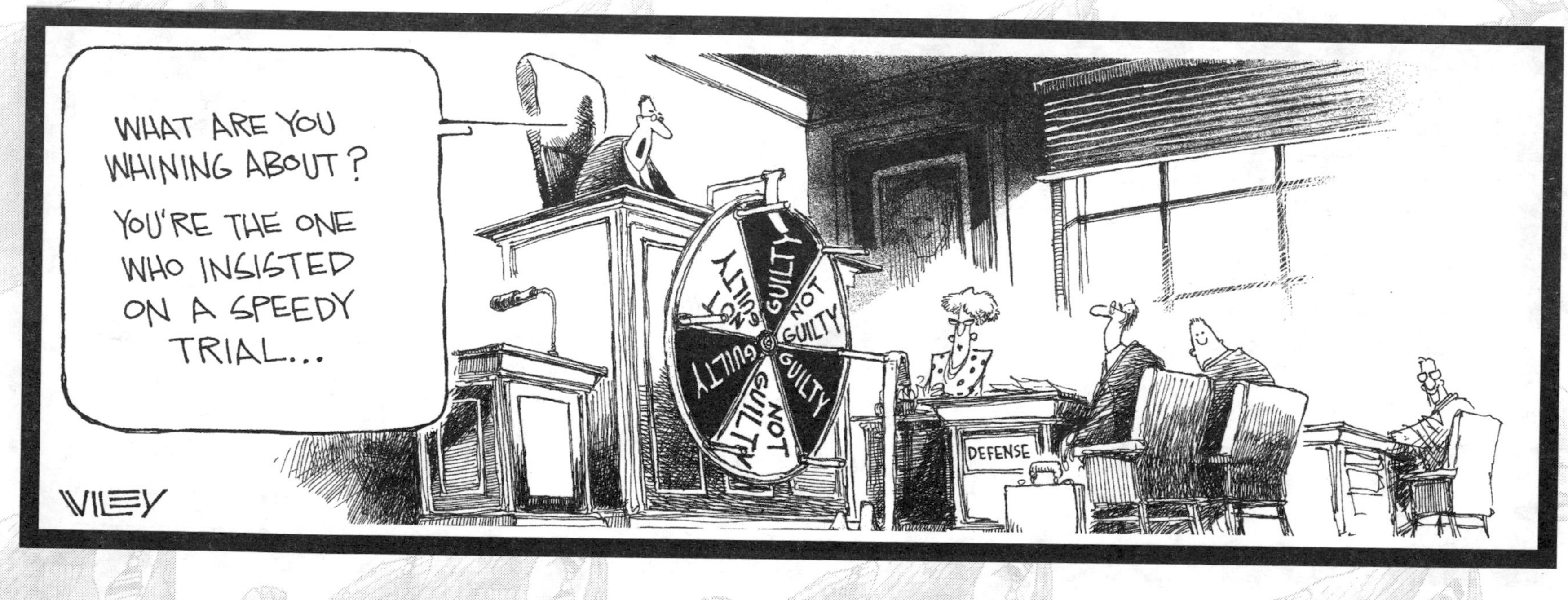
WHAT ARE YOU WHINING ABOUT? YOU'RE THE ONE WHO INSISTED ON A SPEEDY TRIAL...
GUILTY
NOT GUILTY
GUILTY
NOT GUILTY
GUILTY
NOT GUILTY
DEFENSE
WILEY

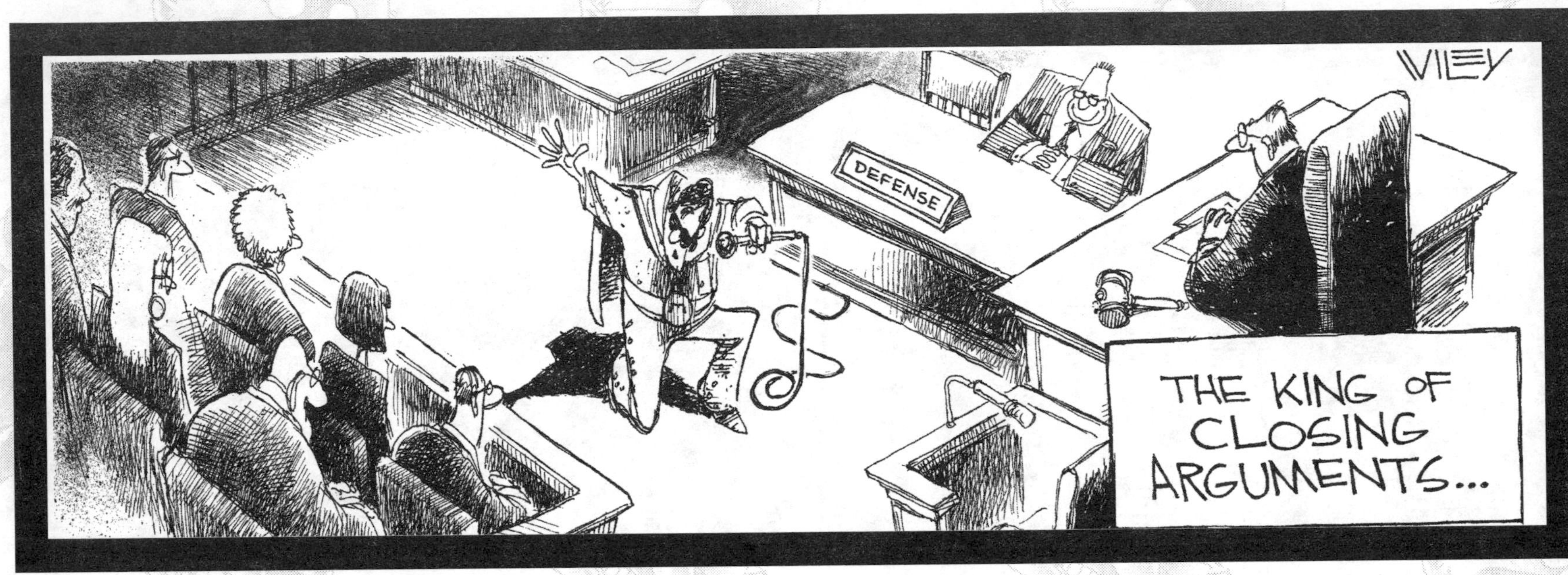
DEFENSE
THE KING OF CLOSING ARGUMENTS...

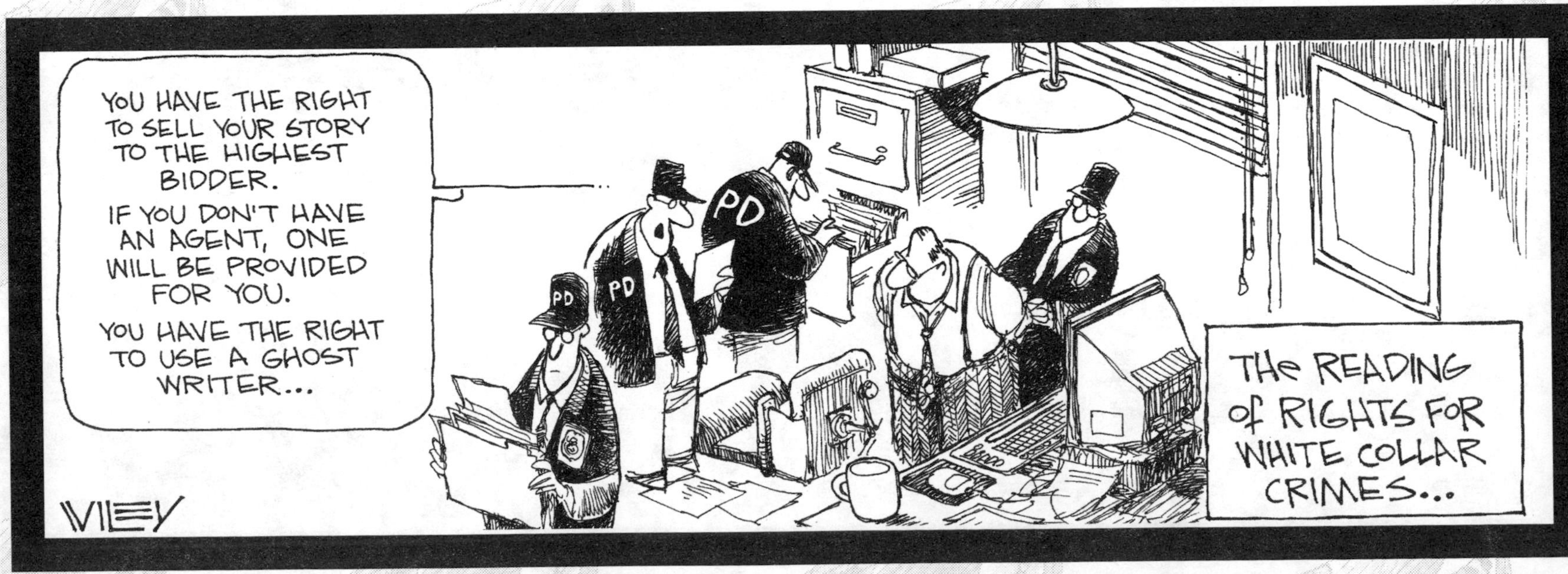
YOU HAVE THE RIGHT TO SELL YOUR STORY TO THE HIGHEST BIDDER.
IF YOU DON'T HAVE AN AGENT, ONE WILL BE PROVIDED FOR YOU.
YOU HAVE THE RIGHT TO USE A GHOST WRITER...
PD
PD
PD
PD
The READING of RIGHTS FOR WHITE COLLAR CRIMES...

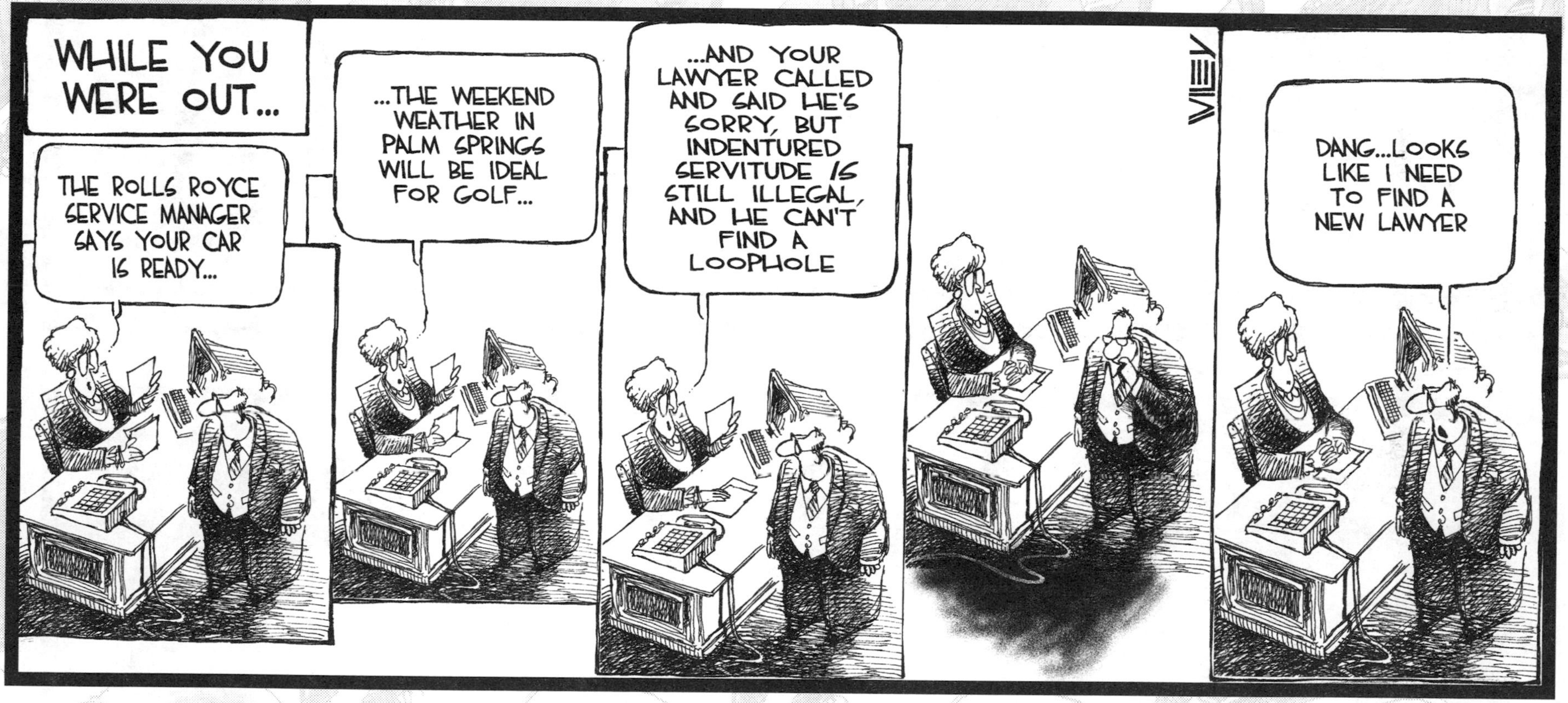
WHILE YOU WERE OUT...
THE ROLLS ROYCE SERVICE MANAGER SAYS YOUR CAR IS READY...
...THE WEEKEND WEATHER IN PALM SPRINGS WILL BE IDEAL FOR GOLF...
...AND YOUR LAWYER CALLED AND SAID HE'S SORRY, BUT INDENTURED SERVITUDE IS STILL ILLEGAL, AND HE CAN'T FIND A LOOPHOLE
WILEY
DANG...LOOKS LIKE I NEED TO FIND A NEW LAWYER

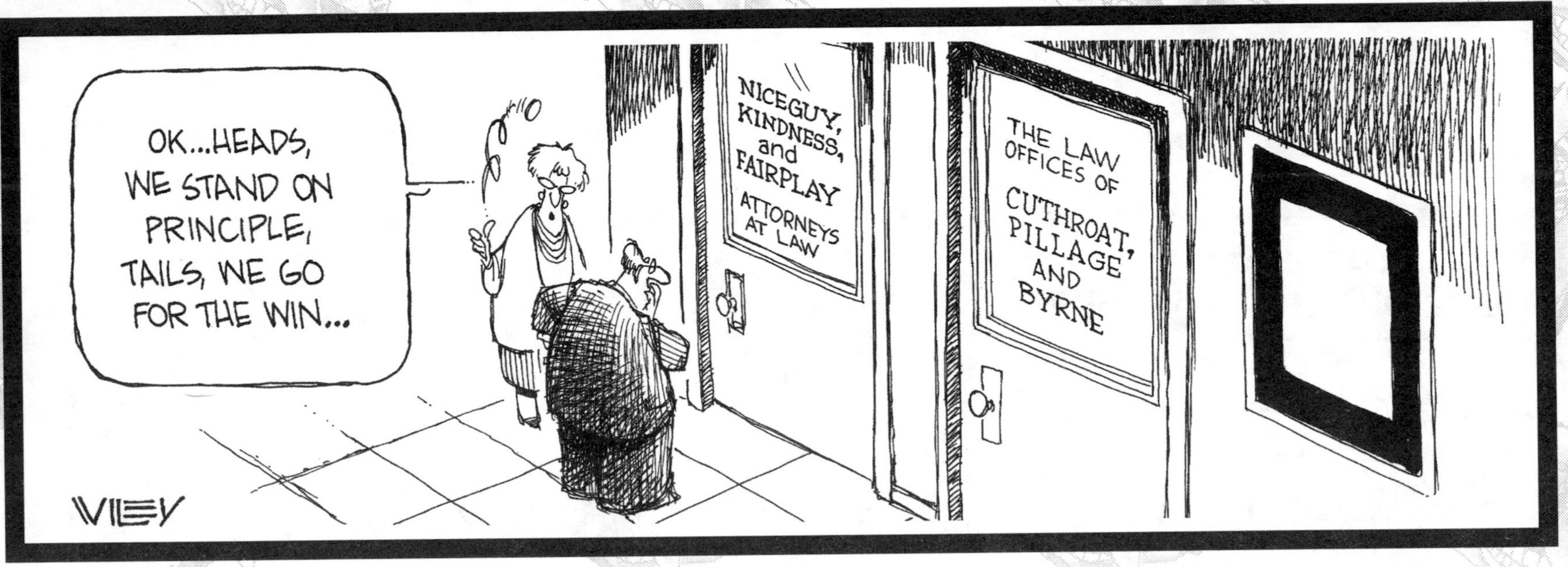
OK...HEADS, WE STAND ON PRINCIPLE, TAILS, WE GO FOR THE WIN...
NICEGUY, KINDNESS, and FAIRPLAY
ATTORNEYS AT LAW
THE LAW OFFICES OF
CUTHROAT, PILLAGE AND BYRNE
WILEY

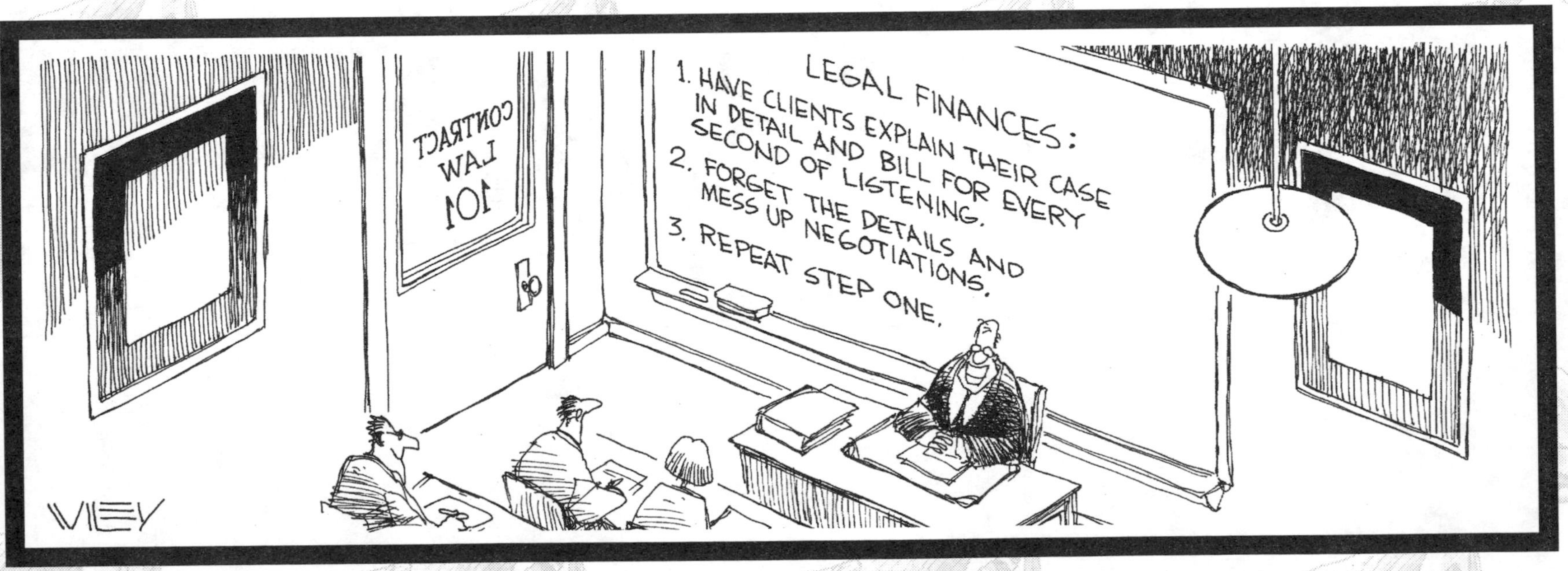
CONTRACT LAW 101
LEGAL FINANCES:
1. HAVE CLIENTS EXPLAIN THEIR CASE IN DETAIL AND BILL FOR EVERY SECOND OF LISTENING.
2. FORGET THE DETAILS AND MESS UP NEGOTIATIONS.
3. REPEAT STEP ONE.
WILEY

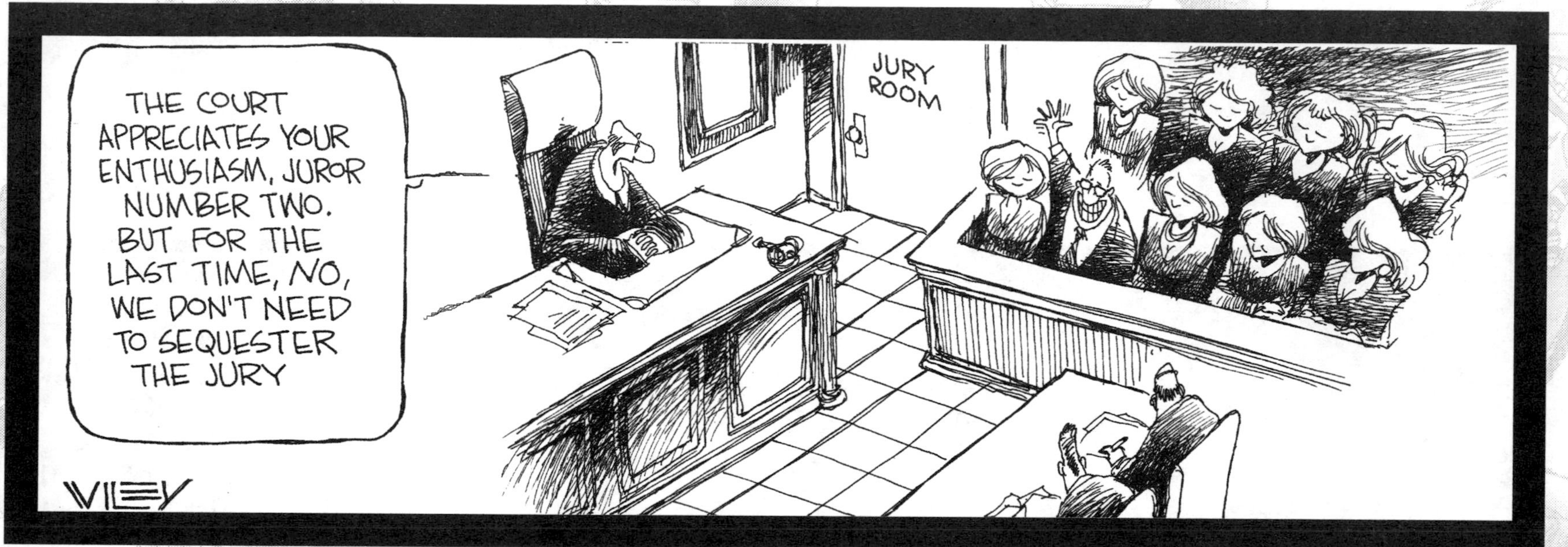
THE COURT APPRECIATES YOUR ENTHUSIASM, JUROR NUMBER TWO. BUT FOR THE LAST TIME, NO, WE DON'T NEED TO SEQUESTER THE JURY
JURY ROOM
WILEY

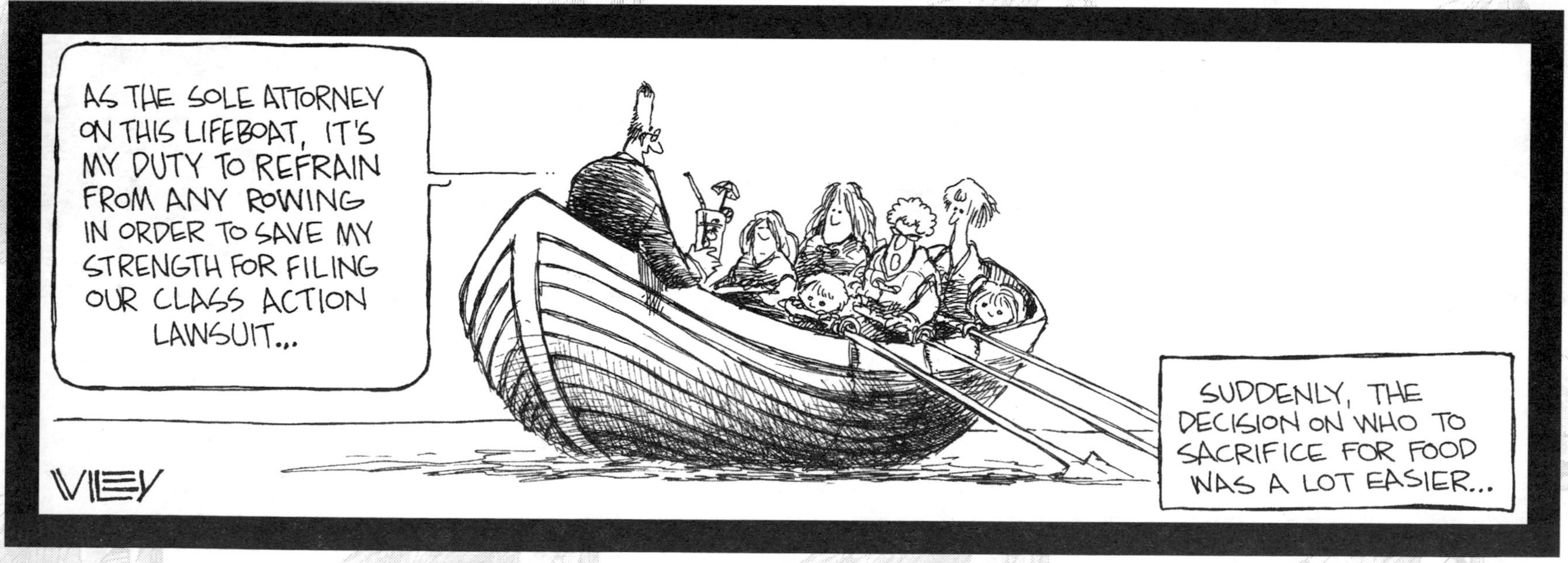
AS THE SOLE ATTORNEY ON THIS LIFEBOAT, IT'S MY DUTY TO REFRAIN FROM ANY ROWING IN ORDER TO SAVE MY STRENGTH FOR FILING OUR CLASS ACTION LAWSUIT...
SUDDENLY, THE DECISION ON WHO TO SACRIFICE FOR FOOD WAS A LOT EASIER...
WILEY

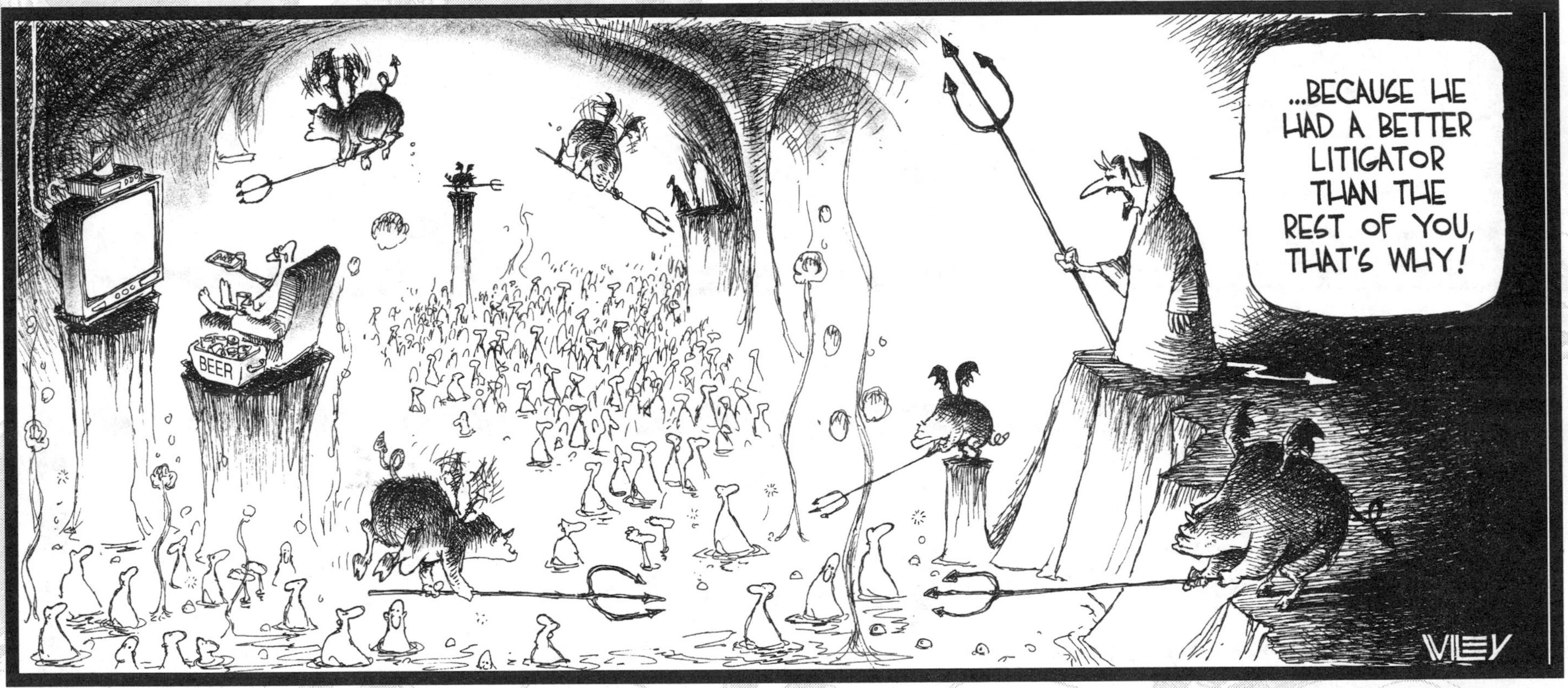
...BECAUSE HE HAD A BETTER LITIGATOR THAN THE REST OF YOU, THAT'S WHY!
BEER
WILEY

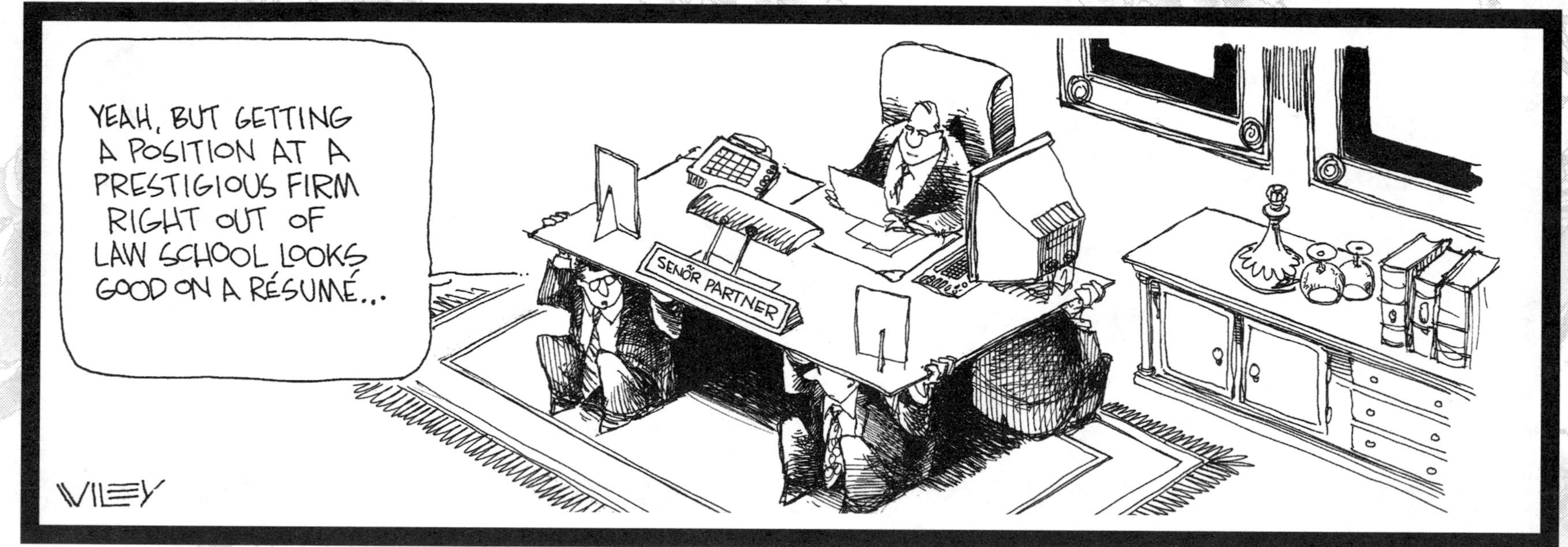
YEAH, BUT GETTING A POSITION AT A PRESTIGIOUS FIRM RIGHT OUT OF LAW SCHOOL LOOKS GOOD ON A RÉSUMÉ...
SEÑOR PARTNER
WILEY

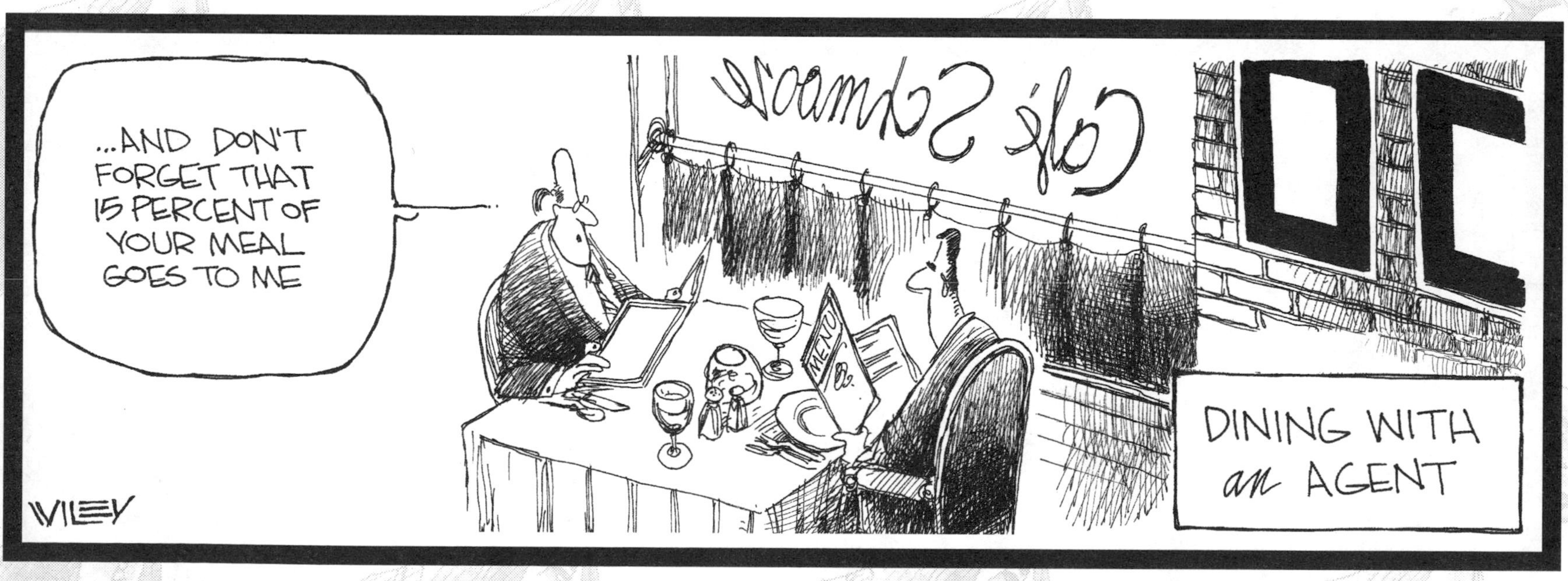
...AND DON'T FORGET THAT 15 PERCENT OF YOUR MEAL GOES TO ME
MENU
DINING WITH an AGENT
WILEY

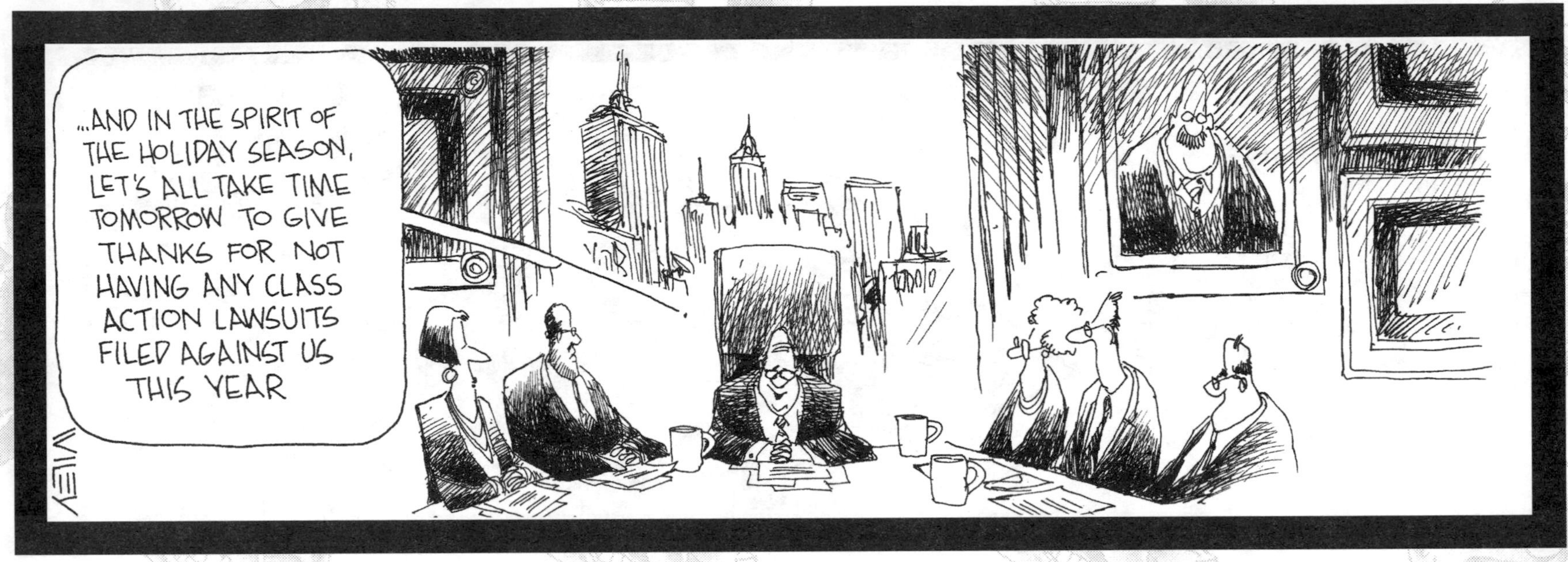
...AND IN THE SPIRIT OF THE HOLIDAY SEASON, LET'S ALL TAKE TIME TOMORROW TO GIVE THANKS FOR NOT HAVING ANY CLASS ACTION LAWSUITS FILED AGAINST US THIS YEAR
WILEY

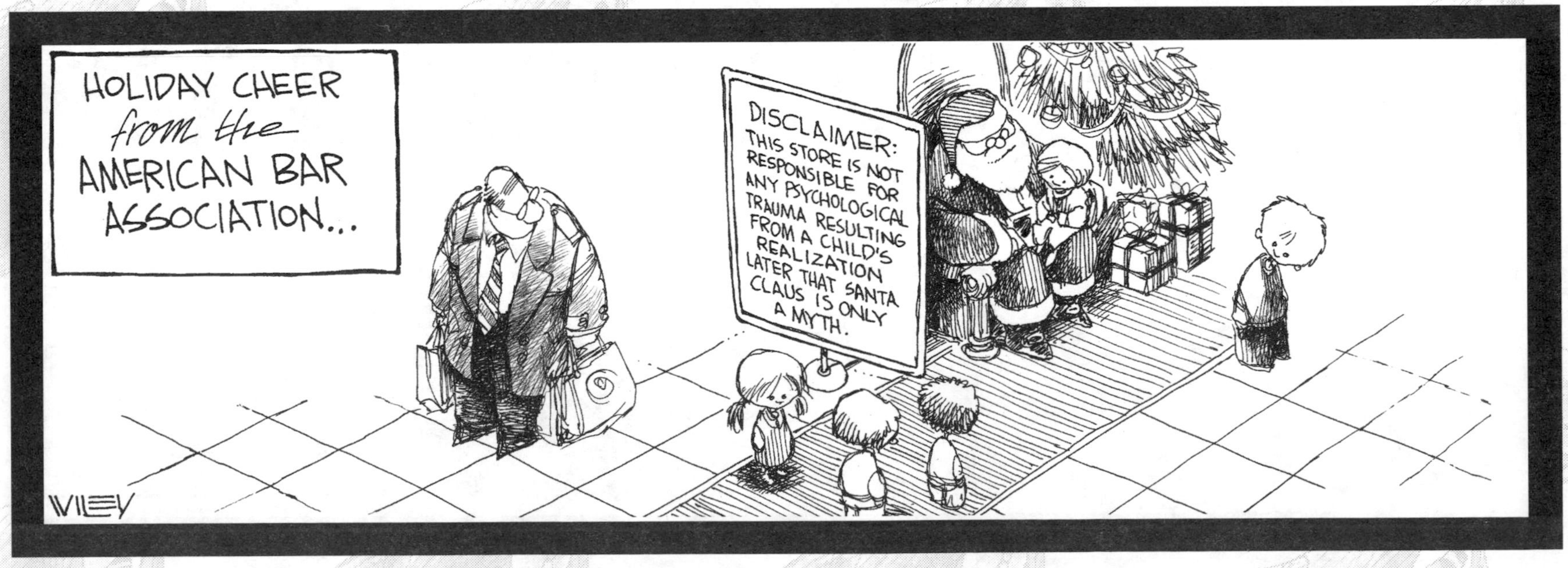
HOLIDAY CHEER from the AMERICAN BAR ASSOCIATION...
DISCLAIMER: THIS STORE IS NOT RESPONSIBLE FOR ANY PSYCHOLOGICAL TRAUMA RESULTING FROM A CHILD'S REALIZATION LATER THAT SANTA CLAUS IS ONLY A MYTH.
WILEY

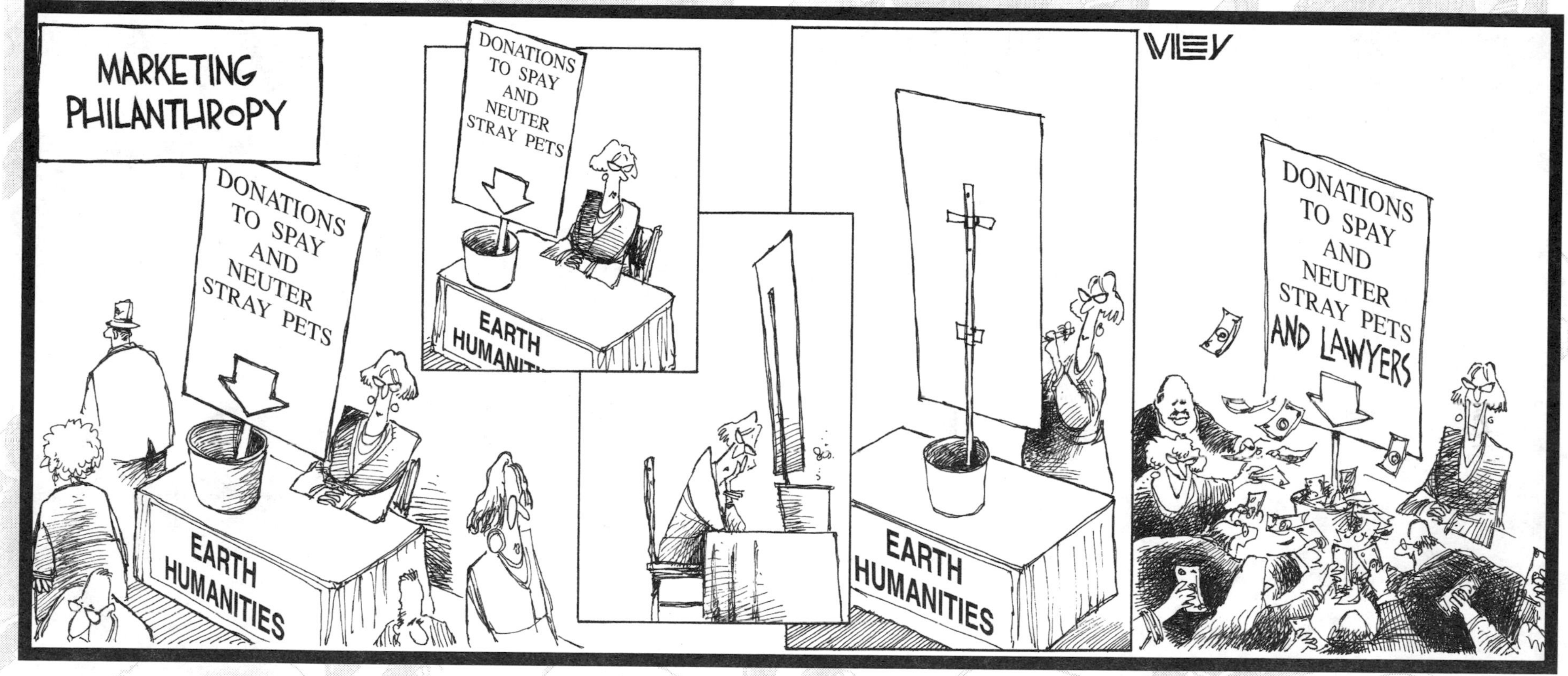
MARKETING PHILANTHROPY
DONATIONS TO SPAY AND NEUTER STRAY PETS
EARTH HUMANITIES
DONATIONS TO SPAY AND NEUTER STRAY PETS
EARTH HUMANITIES
EARTH HUMANITIES
DONATIONS TO SPAY AND NEUTER STRAY PETS AND LAWYERS

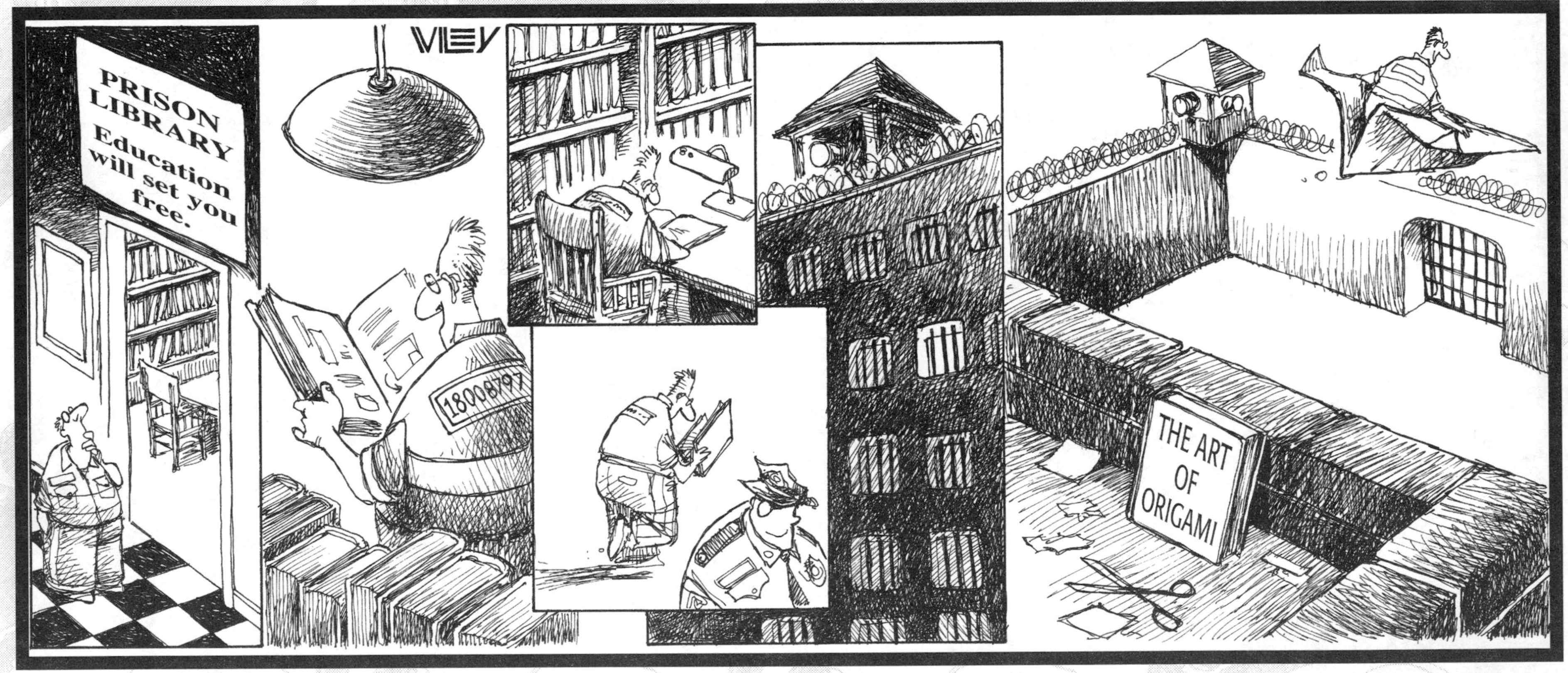
PRISON LIBRARY
Education will set you free.
WILEY
18008797
THE ART OF ORIGAMI

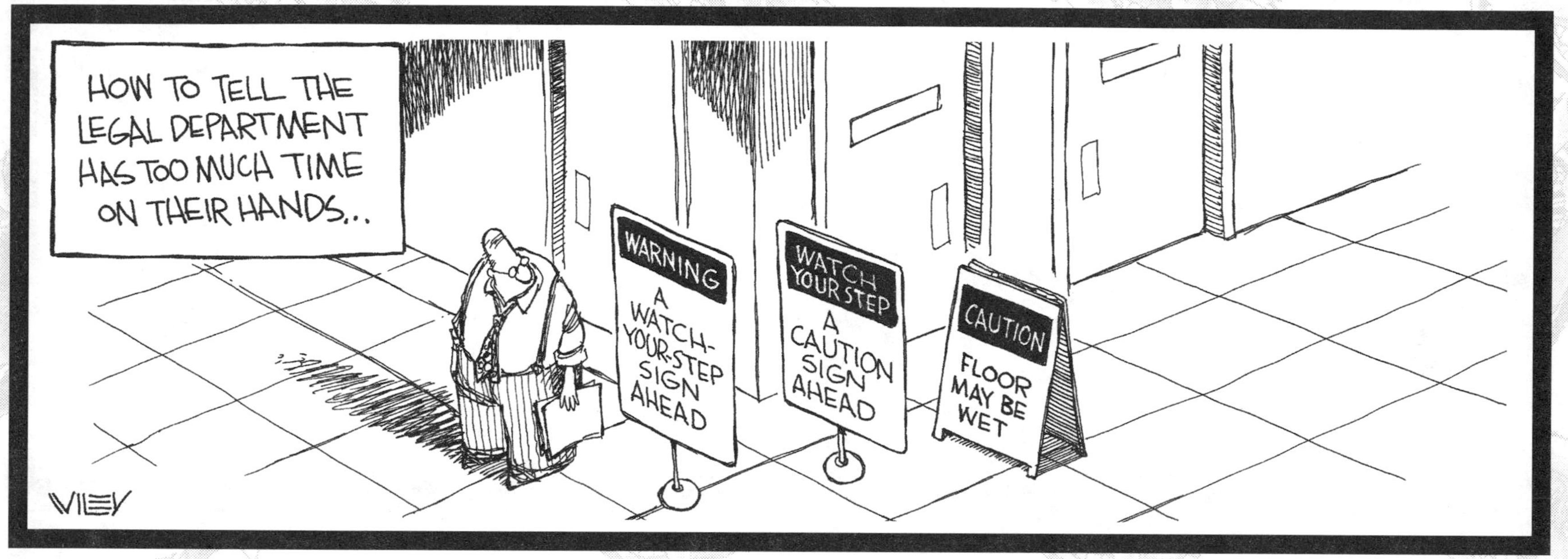
HOW TO TELL THE LEGAL DEPARTMENT HAS TOO MUCH TIME ON THEIR HANDS...
WARNING
A WATCH-YOUR-STEP SIGN AHEAD
WATCH YOUR STEP
A CAUTION SIGN AHEAD
CAUTION
FLOOR MAY BE WET
WILEY

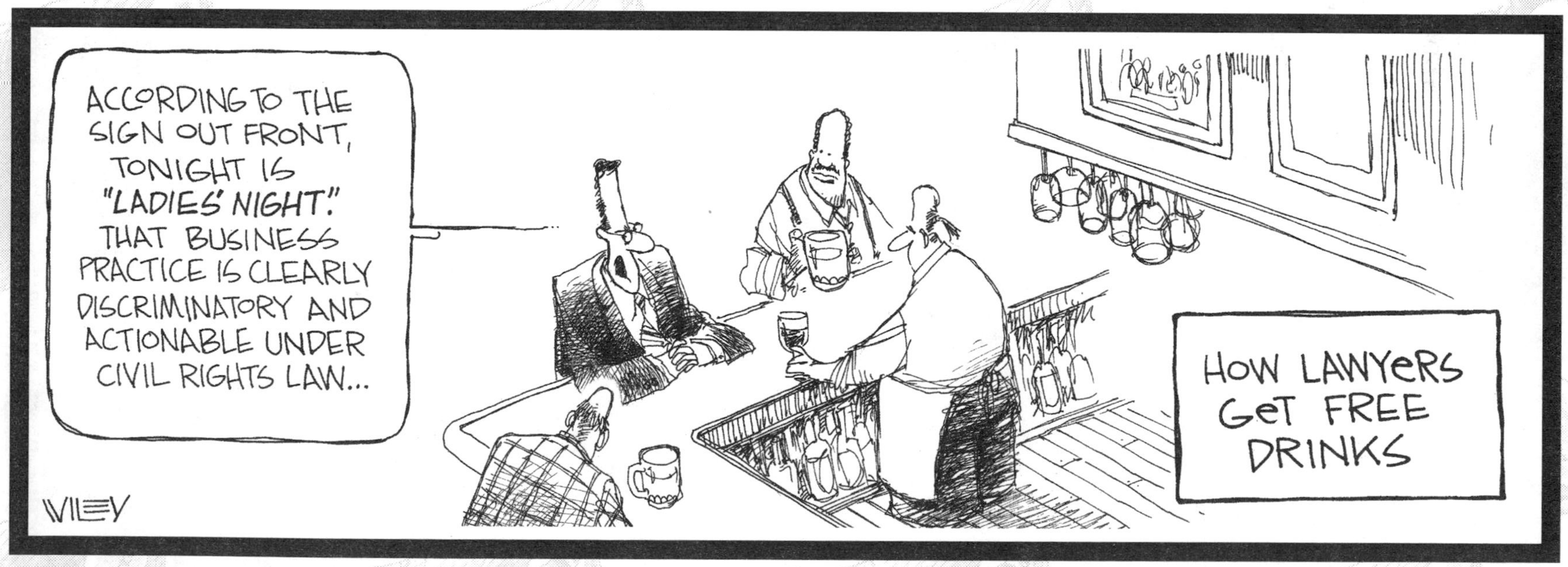
ACCORDING TO THE SIGN OUT FRONT, TONIGHT IS "LADIES' NIGHT." THAT BUSINESS PRACTICE IS CLEARLY DISCRIMINATORY AND ACTIONABLE UNDER CIVIL RIGHTS LAW...
HOW LAWYERS GET FREE DRINKS
WILEY

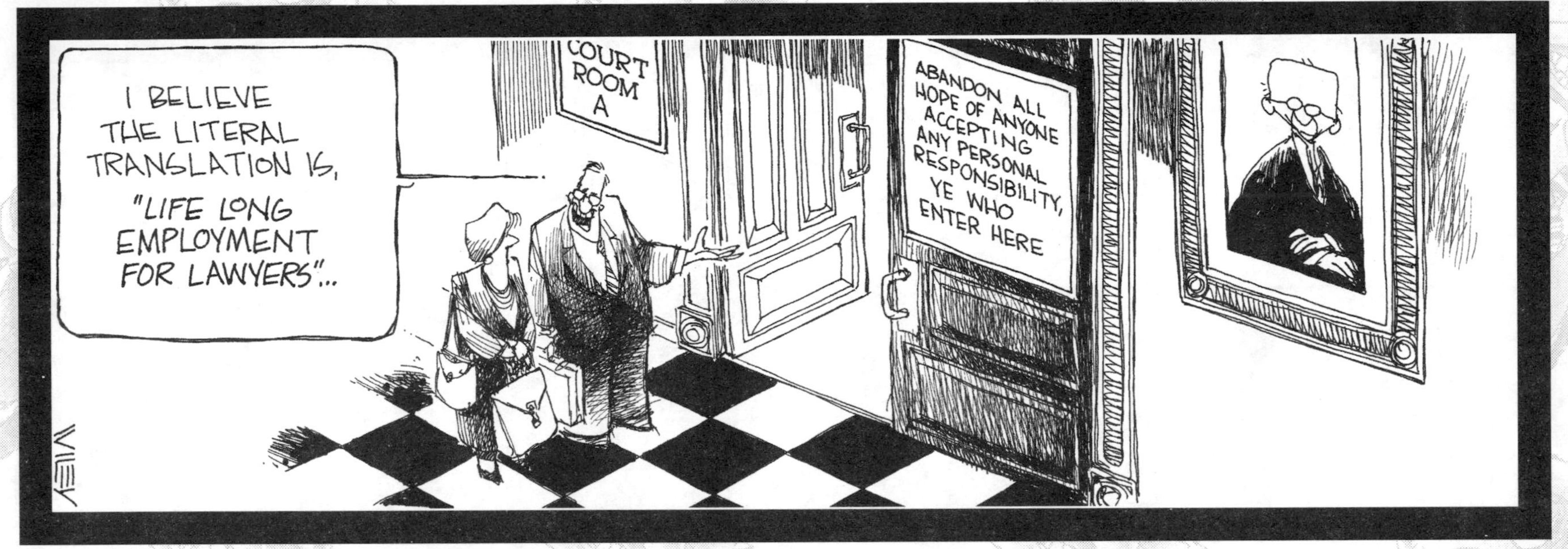
I BELIEVE THE LITERAL TRANSLATION IS, "LIFE LONG EMPLOYMENT FOR LAWYERS"...
COURT ROOM A
ABANDON ALL HOPE OF ANYONE ACCEPTING ANY PERSONAL RESPONSIBILITY, YE WHO ENTER HERE
WILEY

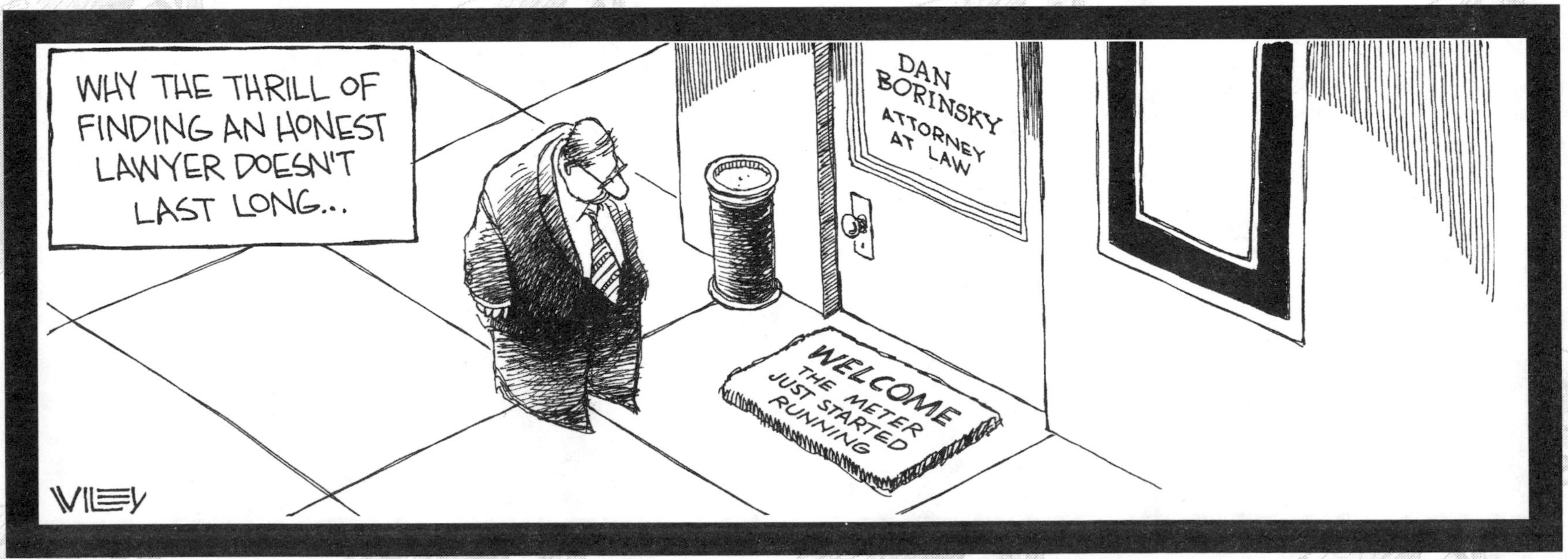
WHY THE THRILL OF FINDING AN HONEST LAWYER DOESN'T LAST LONG...
DAN BORINSKY
ATTORNEY AT LAW
WELCOME
THE METER JUST STARTED RUNNING
WILEY

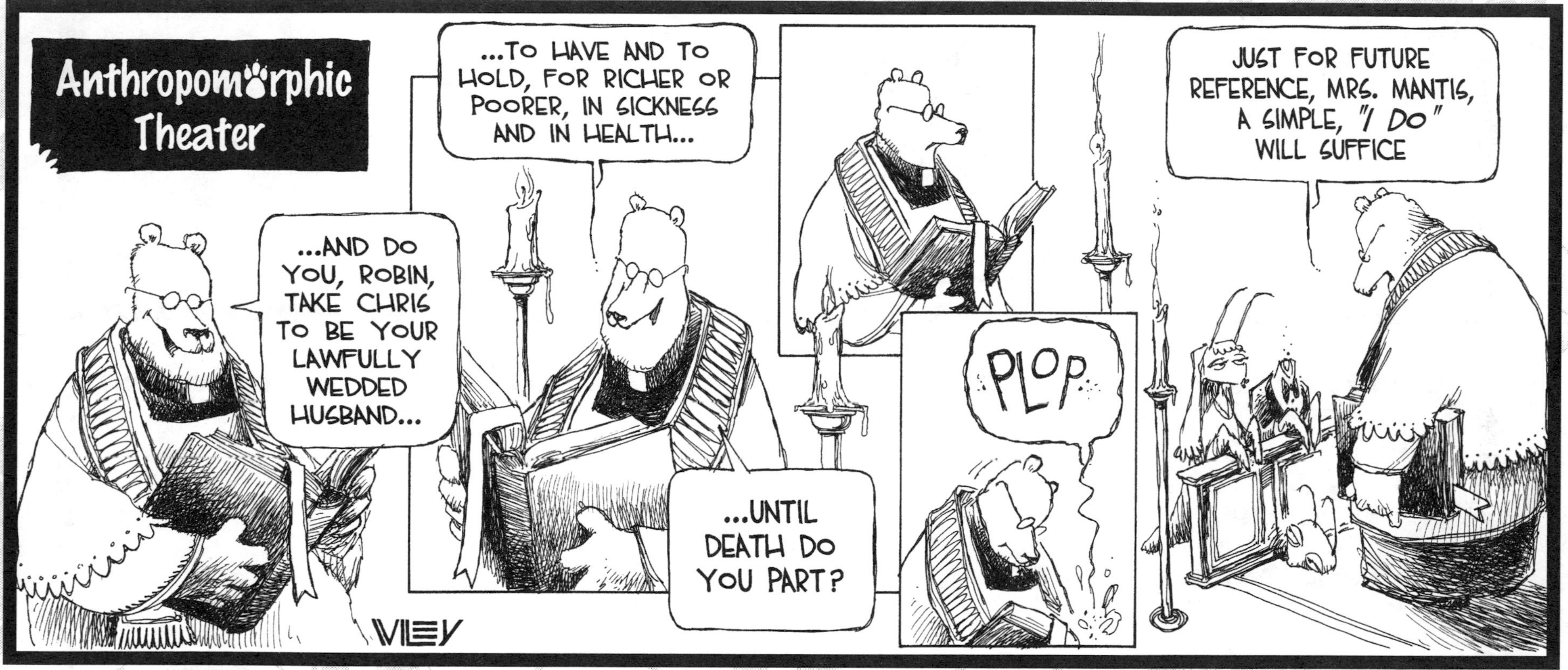
Anthropomorphic Theater
...AND DO YOU, ROBIN, TAKE CHRIS TO BE YOUR LAWFULLY WEDDED HUSBAND...
...TO HAVE AND TO HOLD, FOR RICHER OR POORER, IN SICKNESS AND IN HEALTH...
...UNTIL DEATH DO YOU PART?
PLOP
JUST FOR FUTURE REFERENCE, MRS. MANTIS, A SIMPLE, "I DO" WILL SUFFICE
VILEY

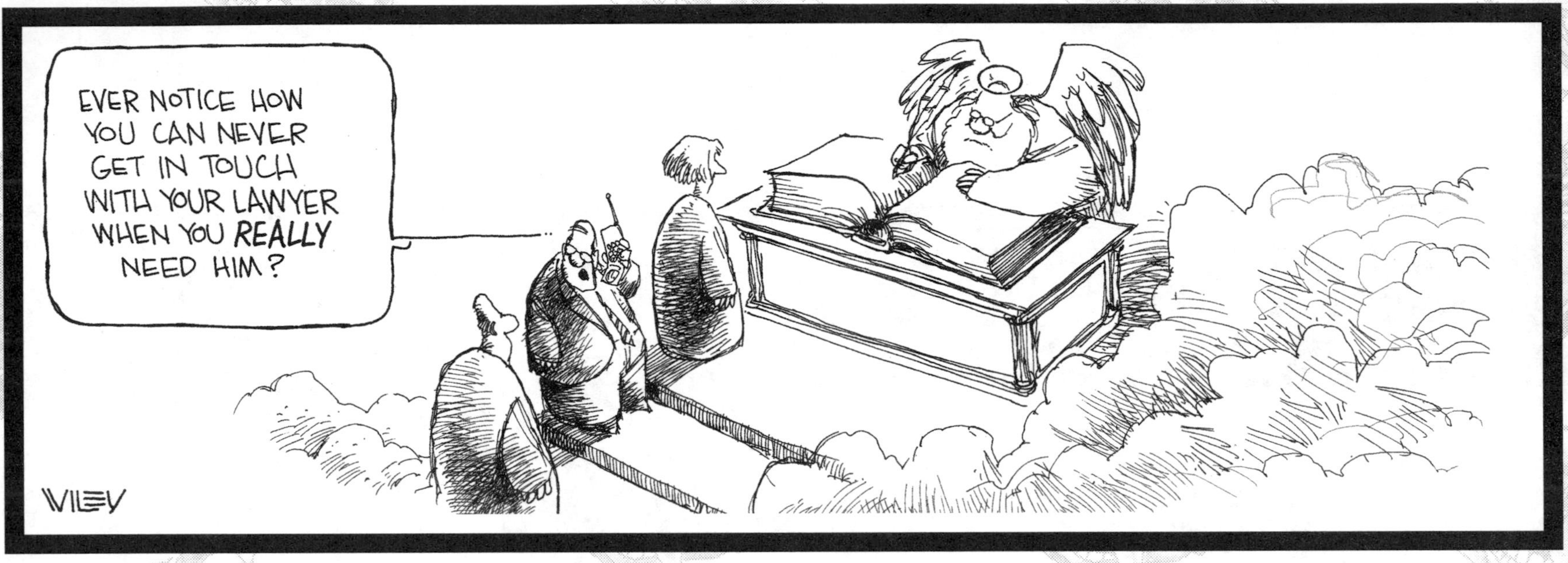
EVER NOTICE HOW YOU CAN NEVER GET IN TOUCH WITH YOUR LAWYER WHEN YOU REALLY NEED HIM?
WILEY

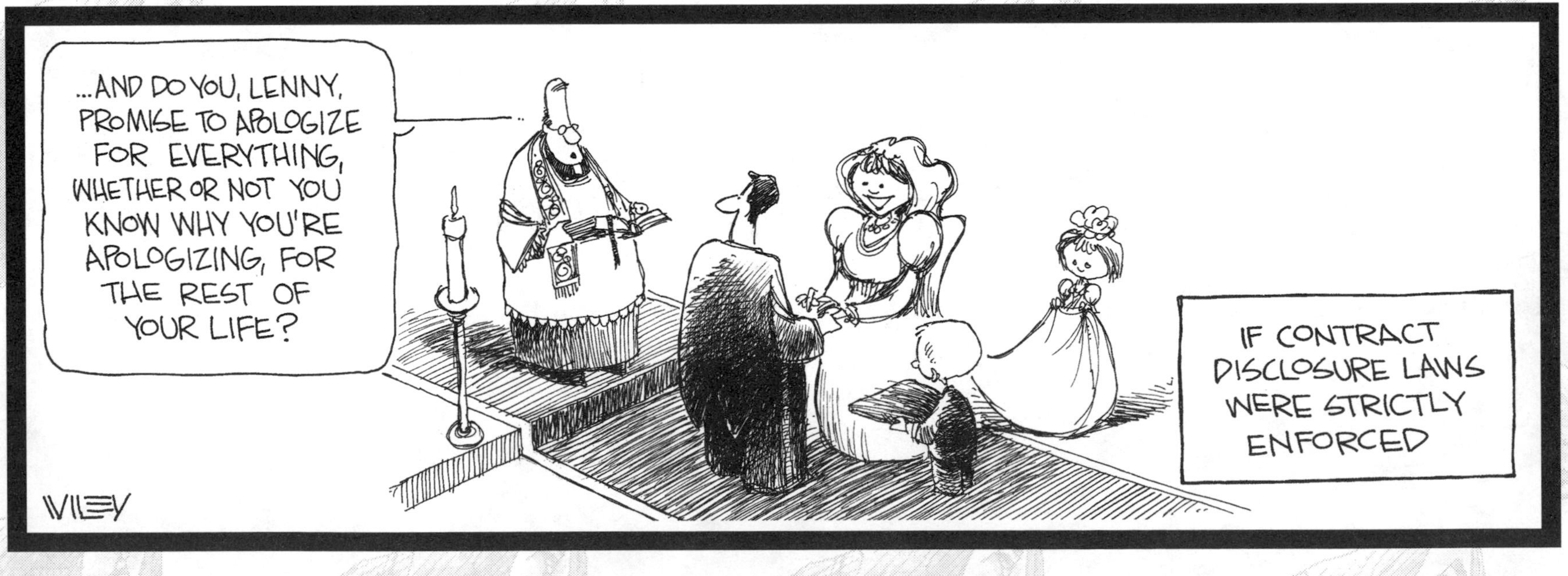
...AND DO YOU, LENNY, PROMISE TO APOLOGIZE FOR EVERYTHING, WHETHER OR NOT YOU KNOW WHY YOU'RE APOLOGIZING, FOR THE REST OF YOUR LIFE?
IF CONTRACT DISCLOSURE LAWS WERE STRICTLY ENFORCED
WILEY

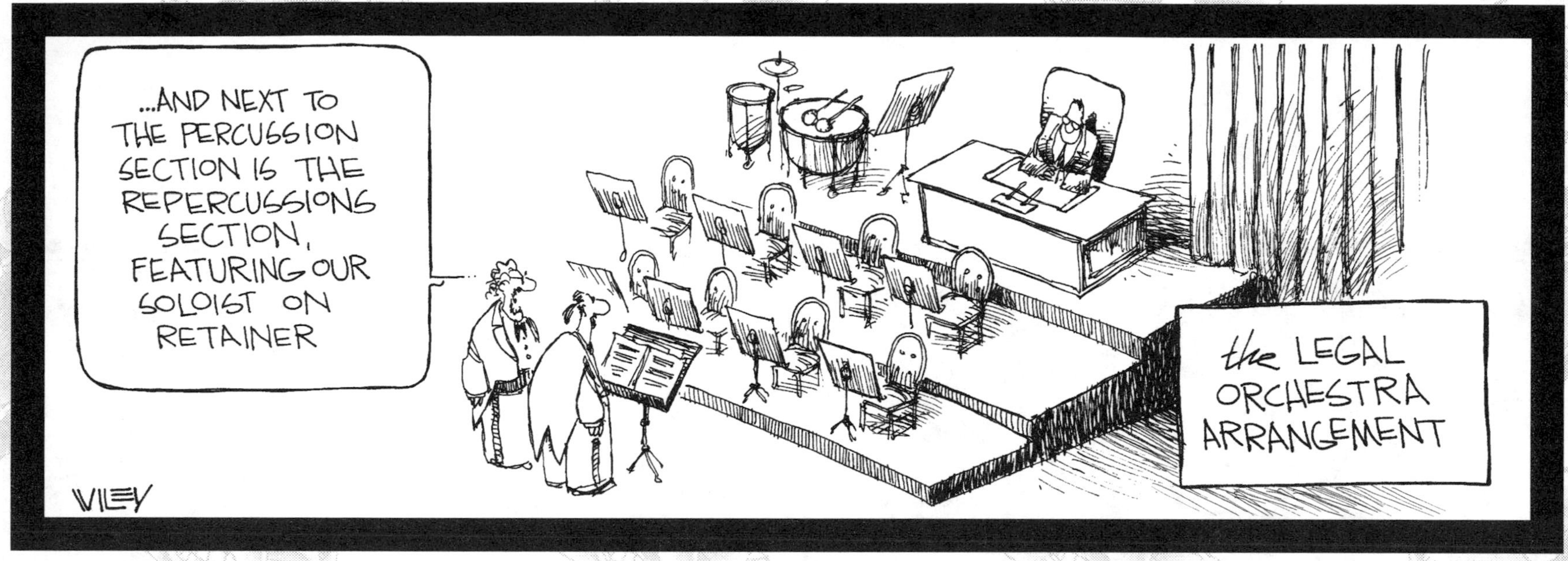
...AND NEXT TO THE PERCUSSION SECTION IS THE REPERCUSSIONS SECTION, FEATURING OUR SOLOIST ON RETAINER
the LEGAL ORCHESTRA ARRANGEMENT
WILEY

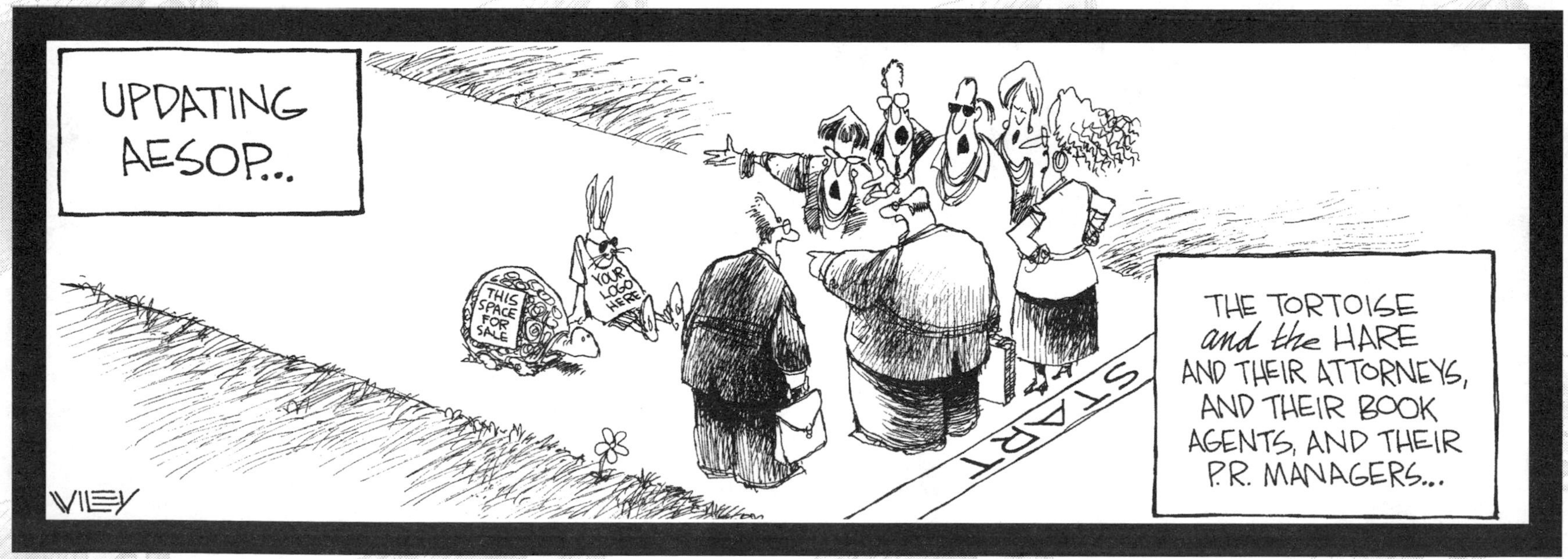
UPDATING AESOP...
THIS SPACE FOR SALE
YOUR LOGO HERE
START
THE TORTOISE and the HARE AND THEIR ATTORNEYS, AND THEIR BOOK AGENTS, AND THEIR P.R. MANAGERS...
WILEY

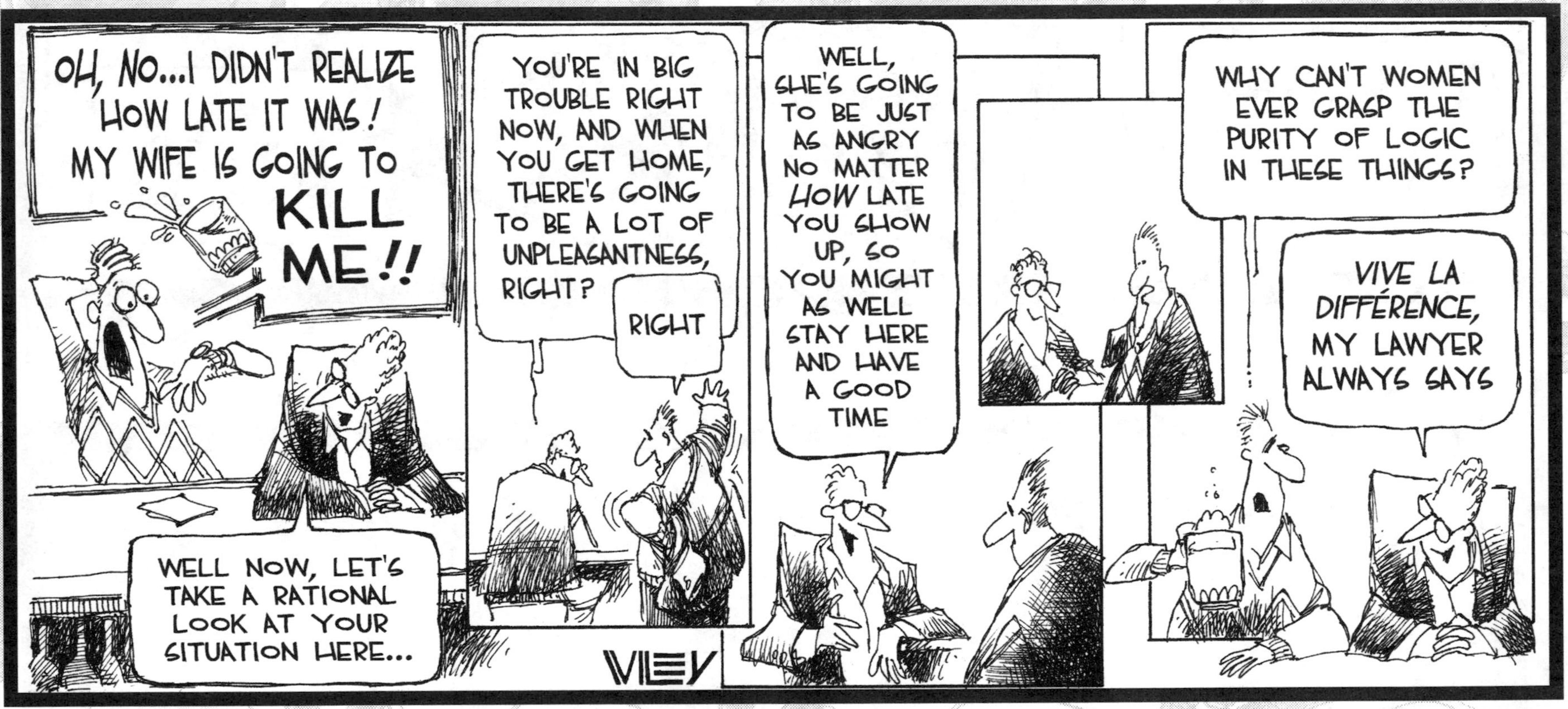
OH, NO...I DIDN'T REALIZE HOW LATE IT WAS! MY WIFE IS GOING TO KILL ME!!
WELL NOW, LET'S TAKE A RATIONAL LOOK AT YOUR SITUATION HERE...
YOU'RE IN BIG TROUBLE RIGHT NOW, AND WHEN YOU GET HOME, THERE'S GOING TO BE A LOT OF UNPLEASANTNESS, RIGHT?
RIGHT
WILEY
WELL, SHE'S GOING TO BE JUST AS ANGRY NO MATTER *HOW* LATE YOU SHOW UP, SO YOU MIGHT AS WELL STAY HERE AND HAVE A GOOD TIME
WHY CAN'T WOMEN EVER GRASP THE PURITY OF LOGIC IN THESE THINGS?
VIVE LA DIFFÉRENCE, MY LAWYER ALWAYS SAYS

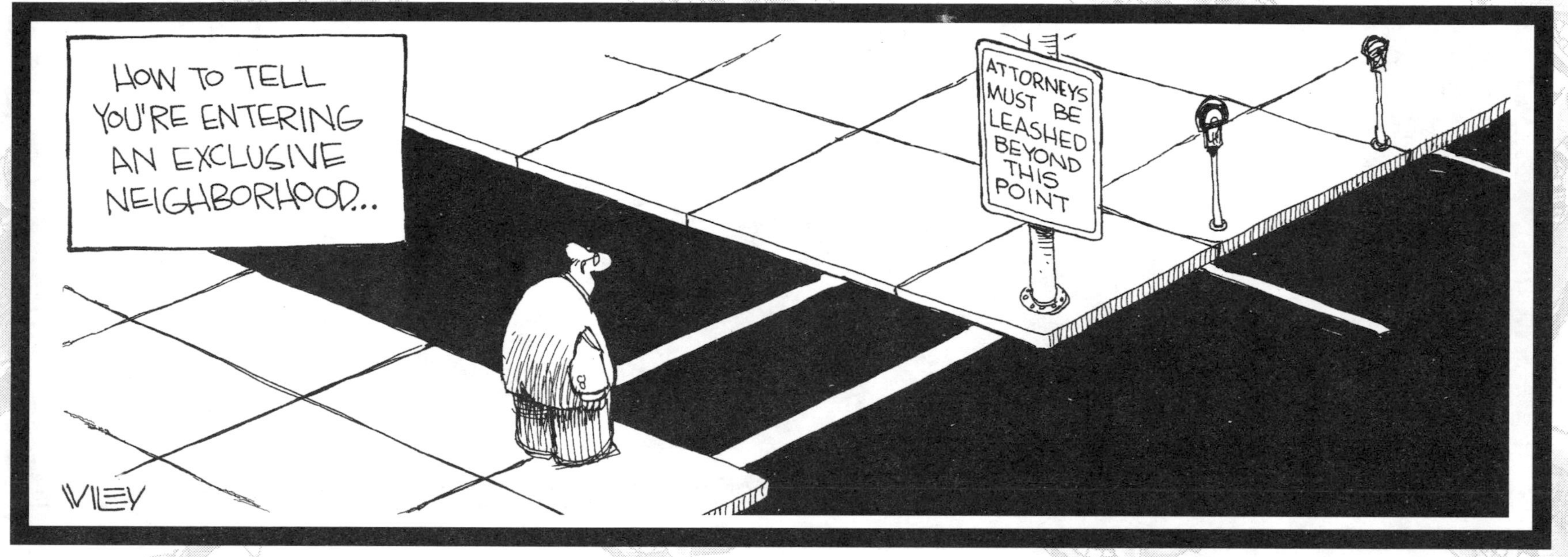
HOW TO TELL YOU'RE ENTERING AN EXCLUSIVE NEIGHBORHOOD...
ATTORNEYS MUST BE LEASHED BEYOND THIS POINT
WILEY

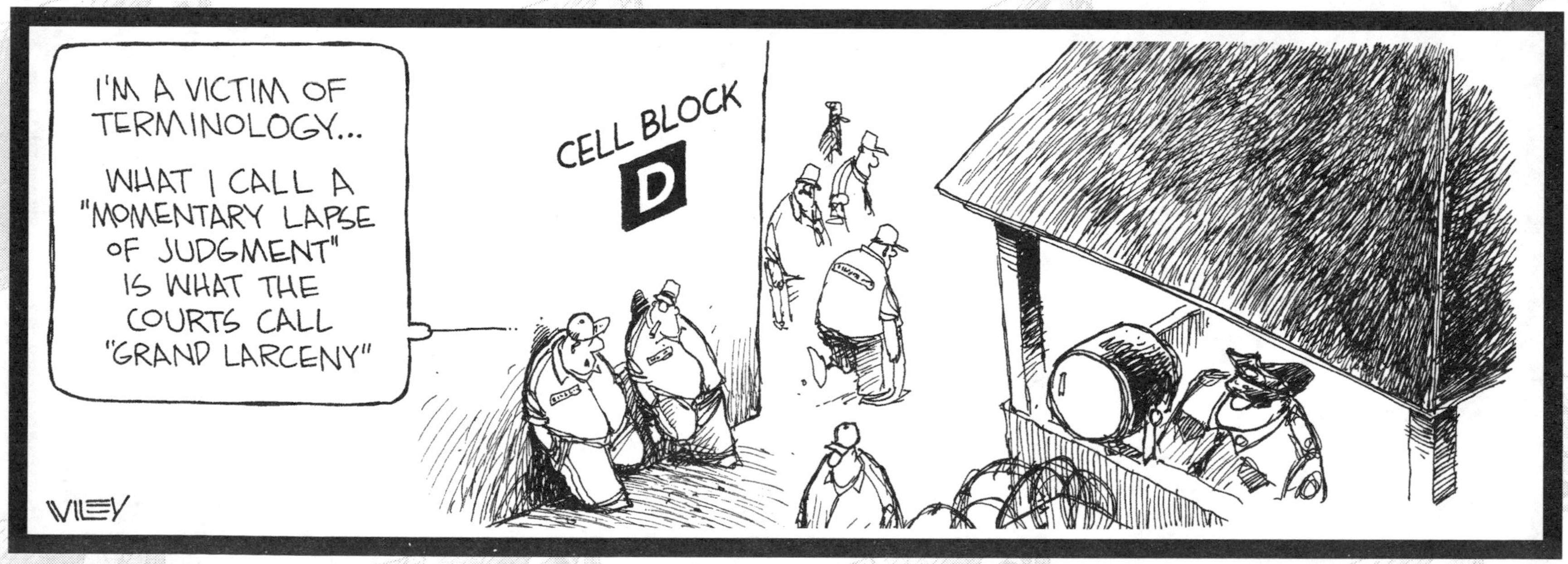
I'M A VICTIM OF TERMINOLOGY...
WHAT I CALL A "MOMENTARY LAPSE OF JUDGMENT" IS WHAT THE COURTS CALL "GRAND LARCENY"
CELL BLOCK D
WILEY

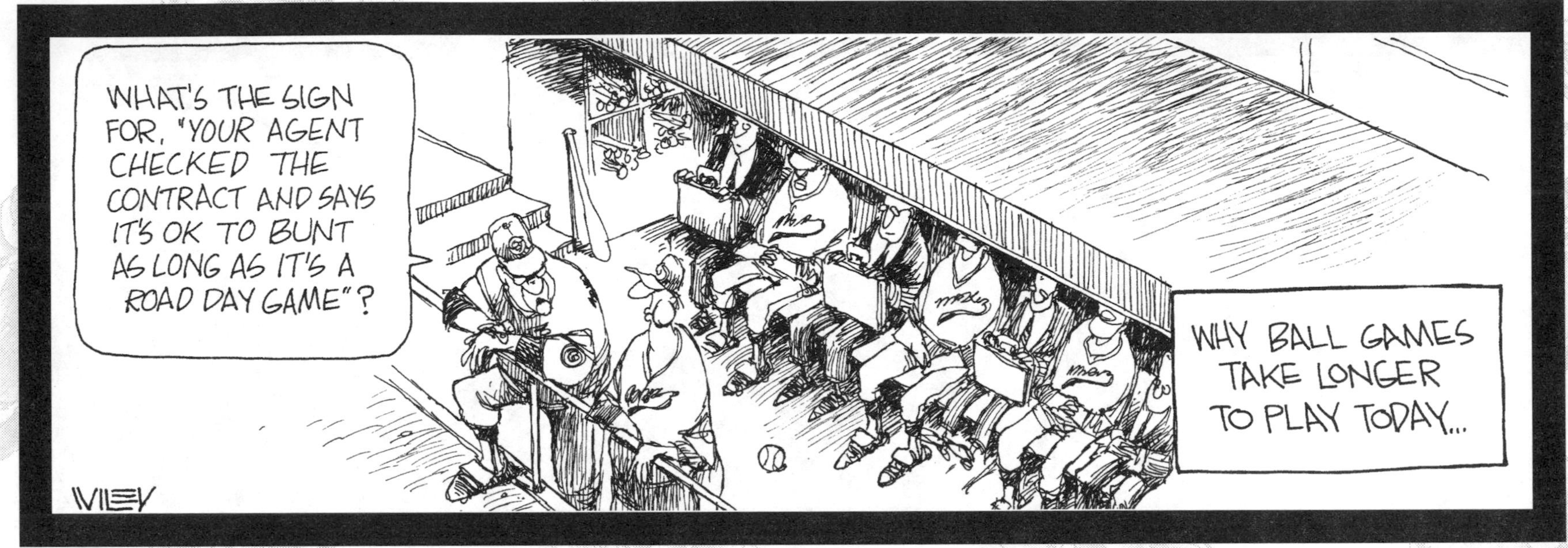
WHAT'S THE SIGN FOR, "YOUR AGENT CHECKED THE CONTRACT AND SAYS IT'S OK TO BUNT AS LONG AS IT'S A ROAD DAY GAME"?
WHY BALL GAMES TAKE LONGER TO PLAY TODAY...
WILEY

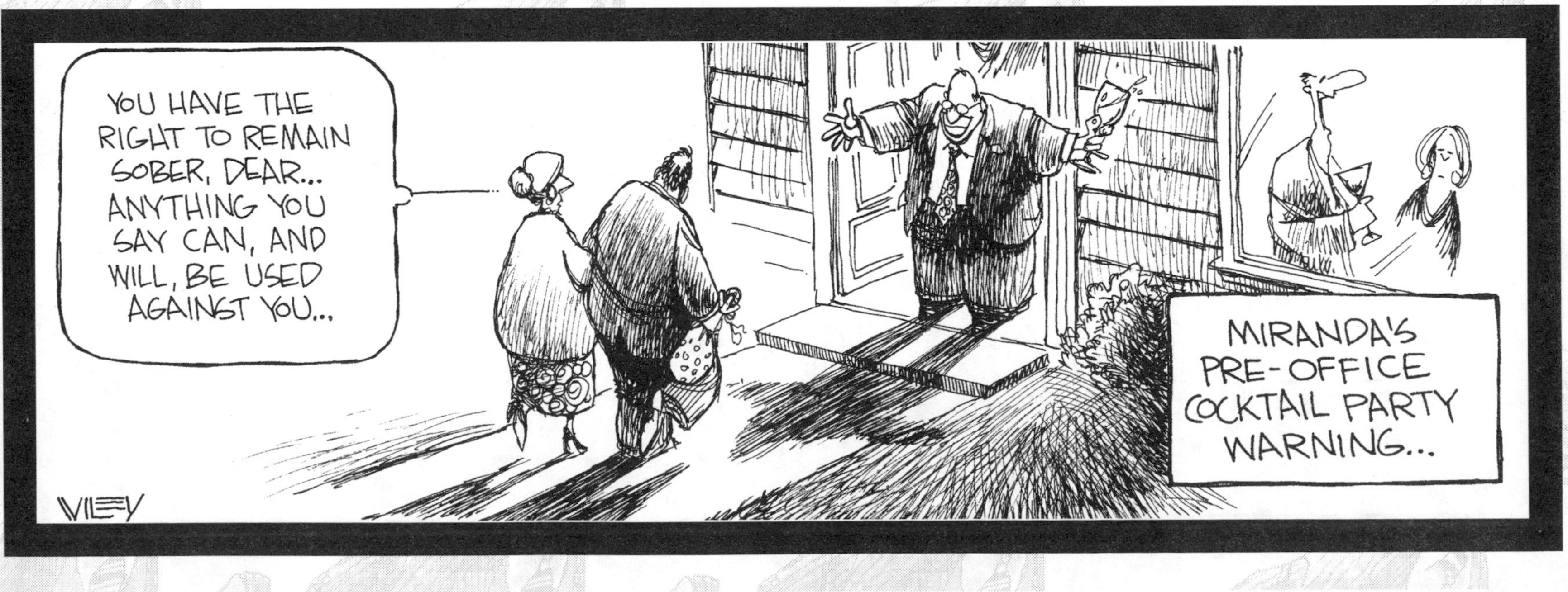
YOU HAVE THE RIGHT TO REMAIN SOBER, DEAR... ANYTHING YOU SAY CAN, AND WILL, BE USED AGAINST YOU...
MIRANDA'S PRE-OFFICE COCKTAIL PARTY WARNING...
WILEY

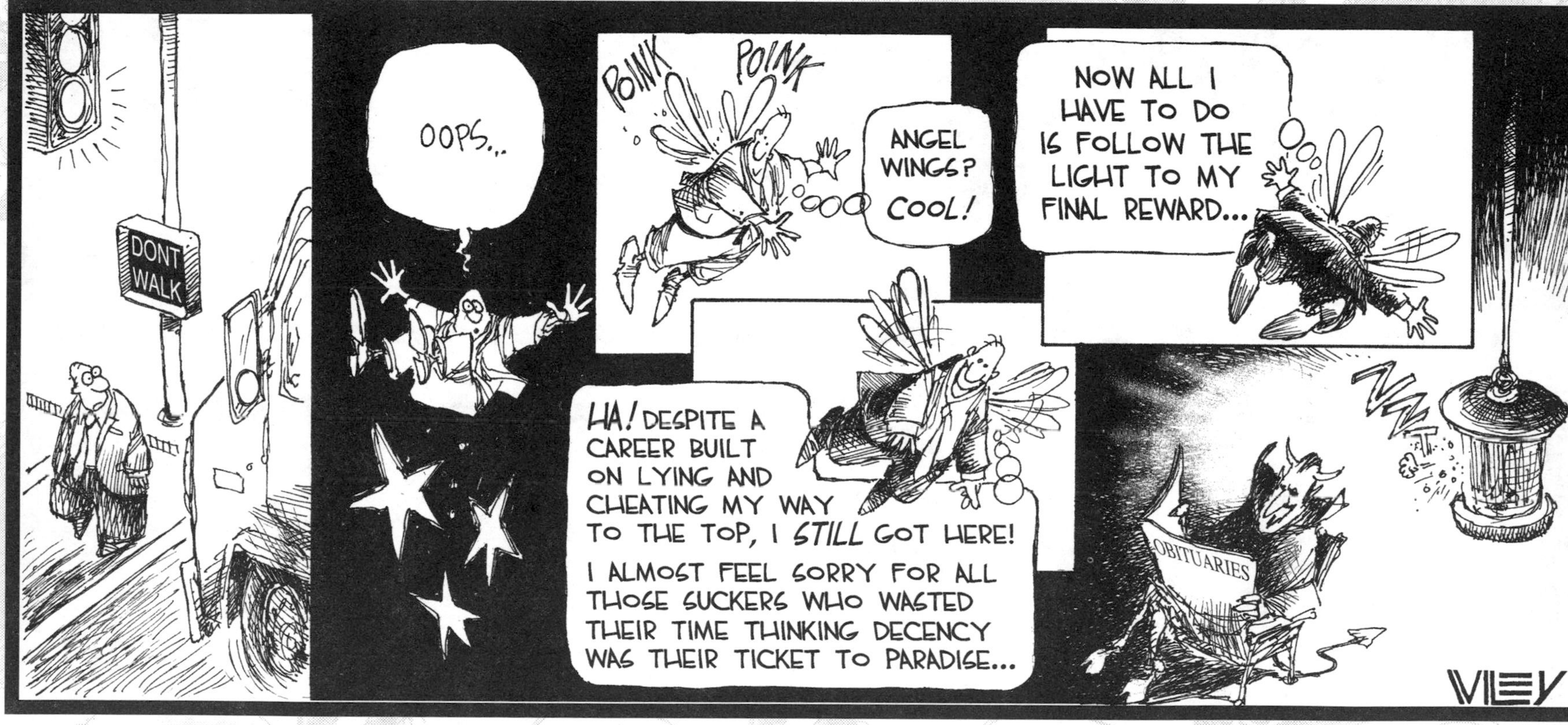
DONT WALK
OOPS...
POINK POINK
ANGEL WINGS? COOL!
HA! DESPITE A CAREER BUILT ON LYING AND CHEATING MY WAY TO THE TOP, I STILL GOT HERE!
I ALMOST FEEL SORRY FOR ALL THOSE SUCKERS WHO WASTED THEIR TIME THINKING DECENCY WAS THEIR TICKET TO PARADISE...
NOW ALL I HAVE TO DO IS FOLLOW THE LIGHT TO MY FINAL REWARD...
ZZZT
OBITUARIES

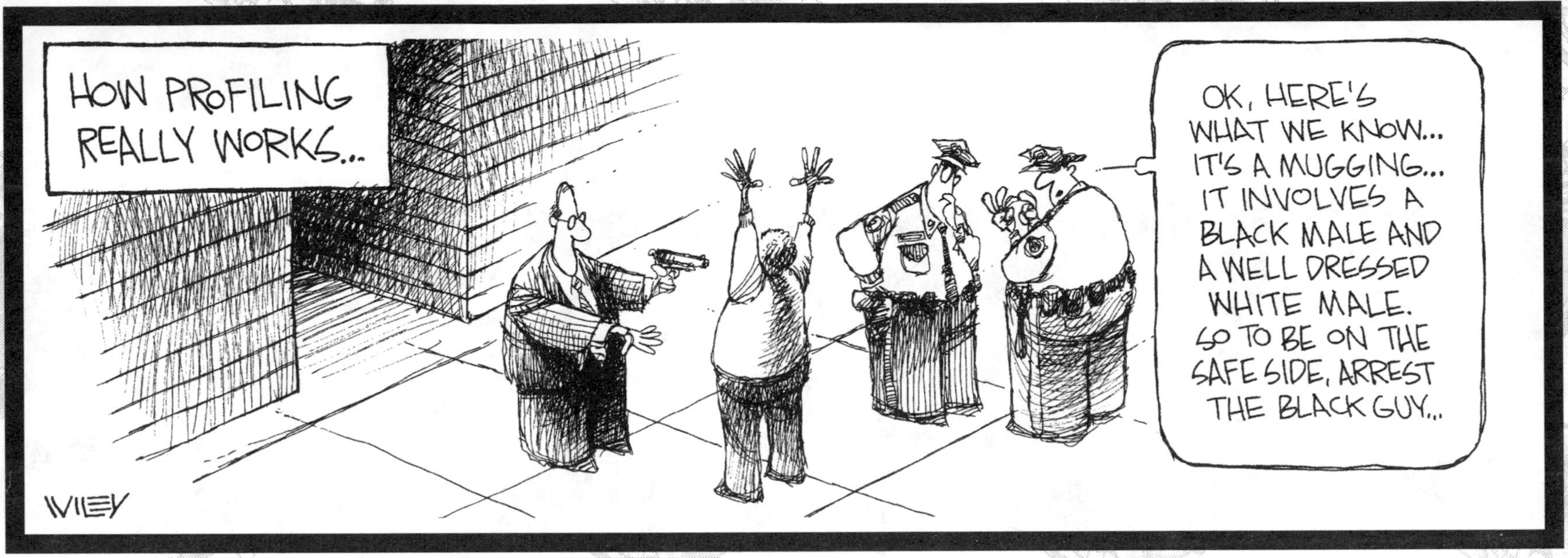
HOW PROFILING REALLY WORKS...
OK, HERE'S WHAT WE KNOW... IT'S A MUGGING... IT INVOLVES A BLACK MALE AND A WELL DRESSED WHITE MALE. SO TO BE ON THE SAFE SIDE, ARREST THE BLACK GUY...
WILEY

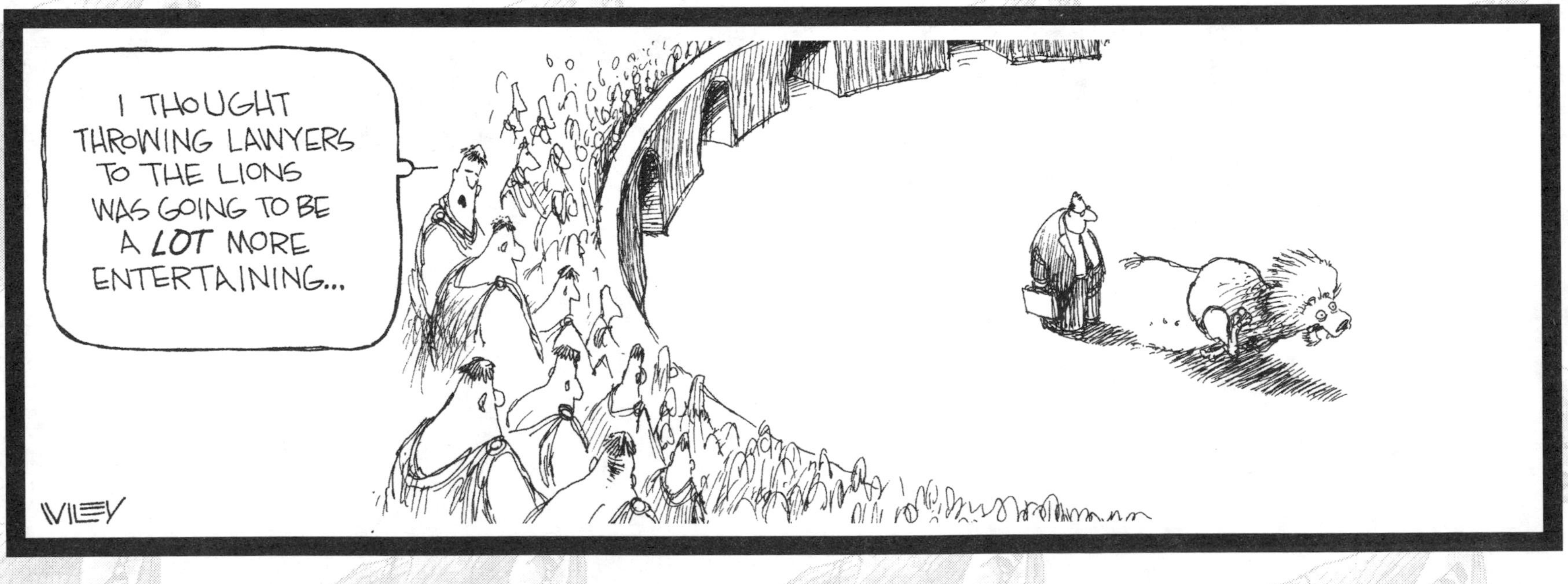
I THOUGHT THROWING LAWYERS TO THE LIONS WAS GOING TO BE A *LOT* MORE ENTERTAINING...
WILEY

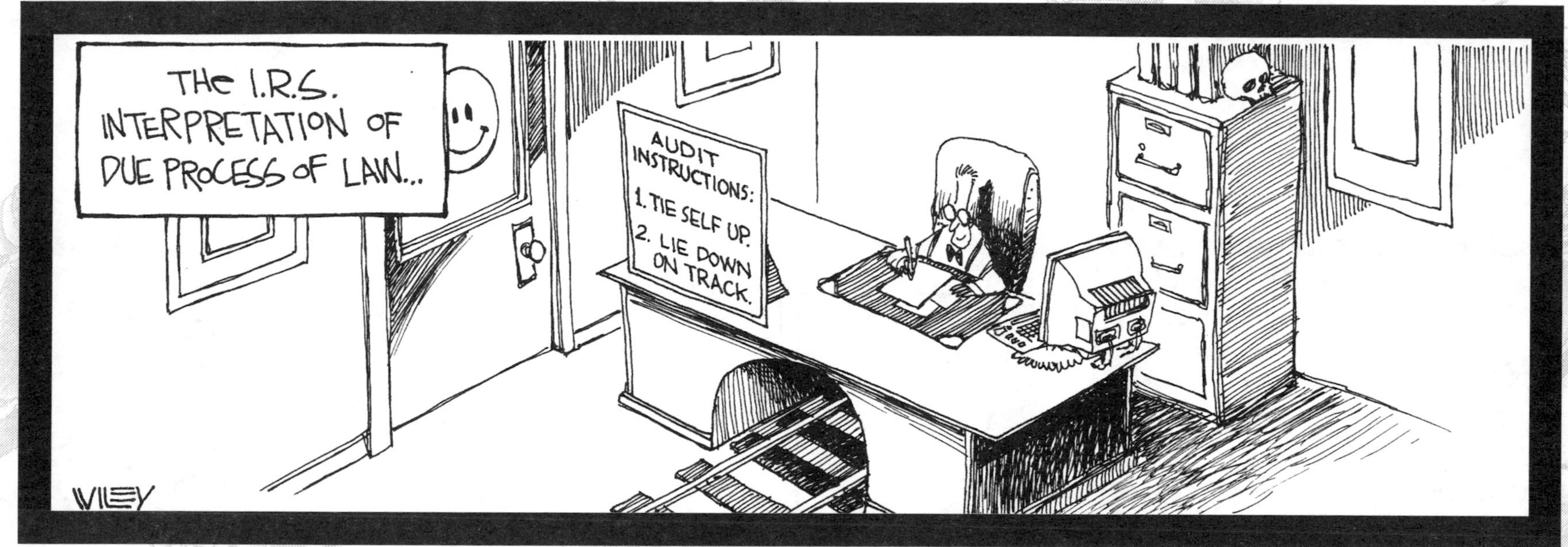
The I.R.S. INTERPRETATION OF DUE PROCESS OF LAW...
AUDIT INSTRUCTIONS:
1. TIE SELF UP.
2. LIE DOWN ON TRACK.
WILEY

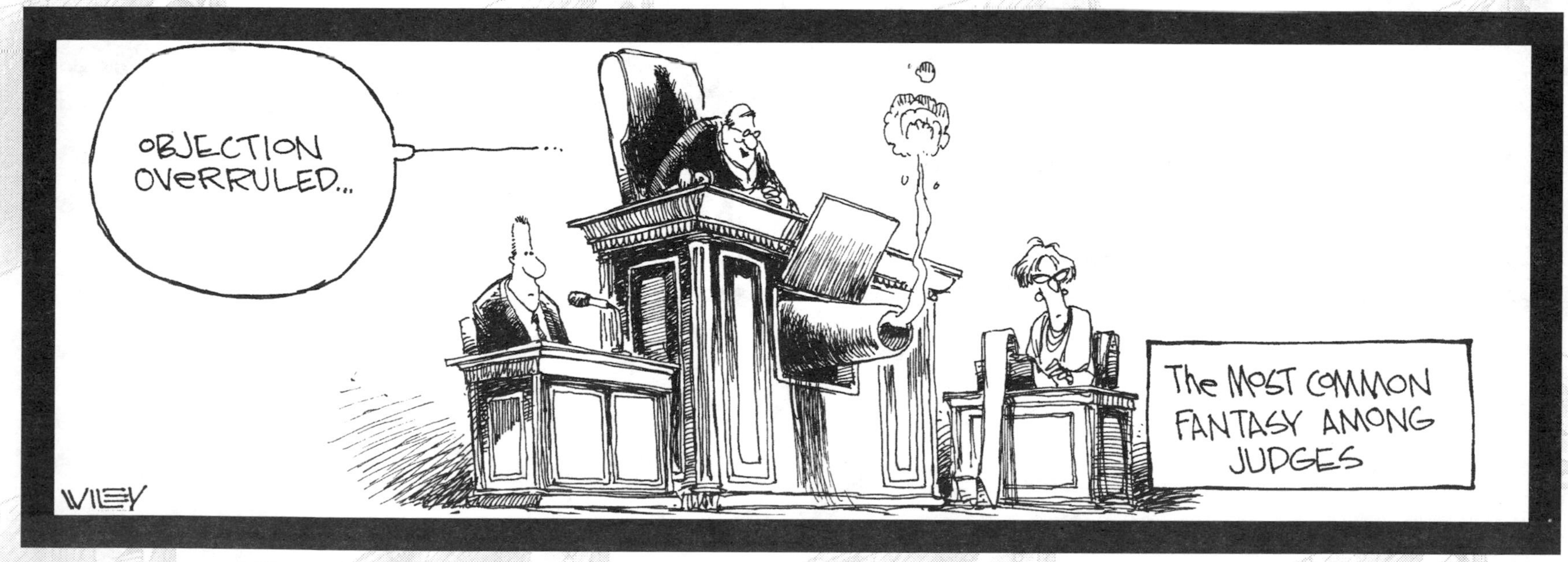
OBJECTION OVERRULED...
The MOST COMMON FANTASY AMONG JUDGES
WILEY

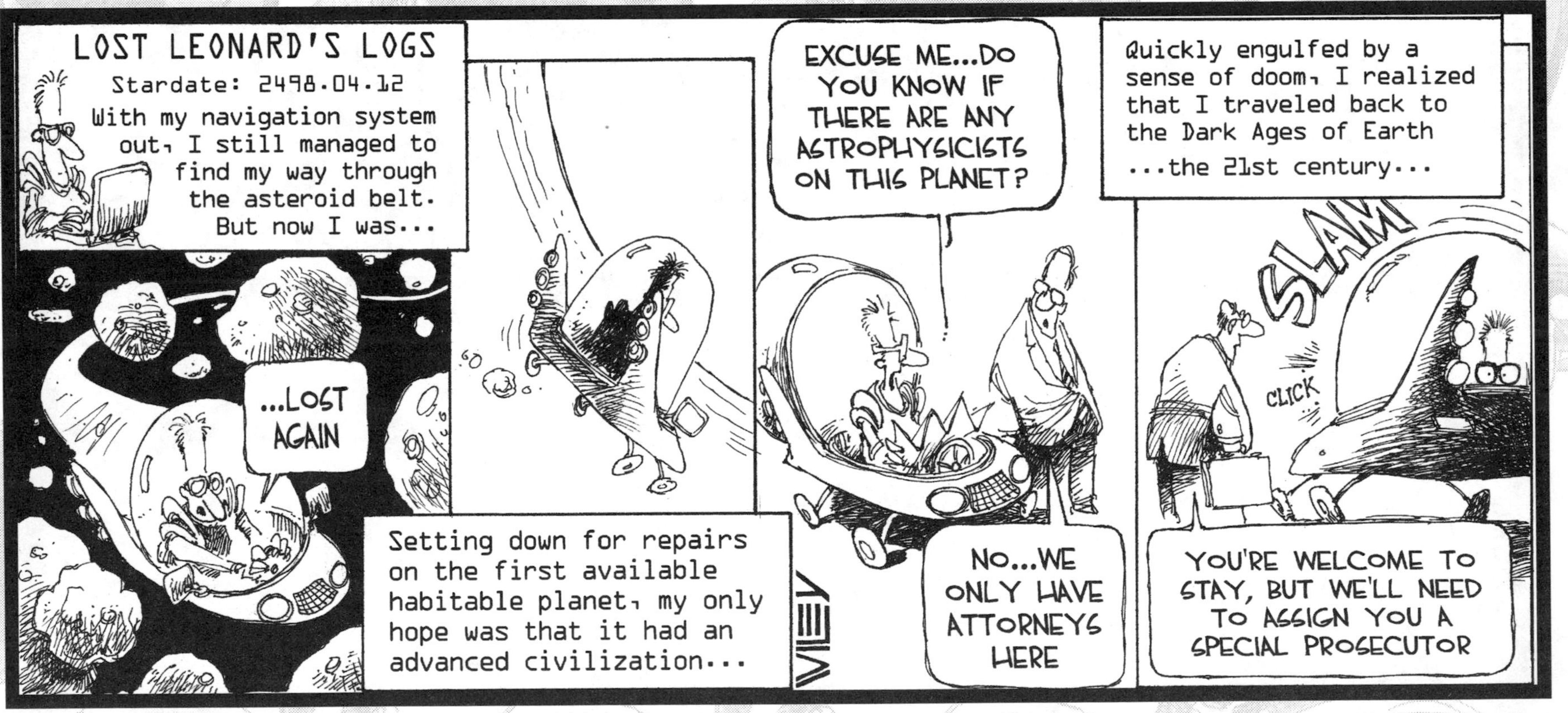
LOST LEONARD'S LOGS
Stardate: 2498.04.12
With my navigation system out, I still managed to find my way through the asteroid belt. But now I was...
...LOST AGAIN
Setting down for repairs on the first available habitable planet, my only hope was that it had an advanced civilization...
EXCUSE ME...DO YOU KNOW IF THERE ARE ANY ASTROPHYSICISTS ON THIS PLANET?
NO...WE ONLY HAVE ATTORNEYS HERE
Quickly engulfed by a sense of doom, I realized that I traveled back to the Dark Ages of Earth
...the 21st century...
SLAM
CLICK
YOU'RE WELCOME TO STAY, BUT WE'LL NEED TO ASSIGN YOU A SPECIAL PROSECUTOR

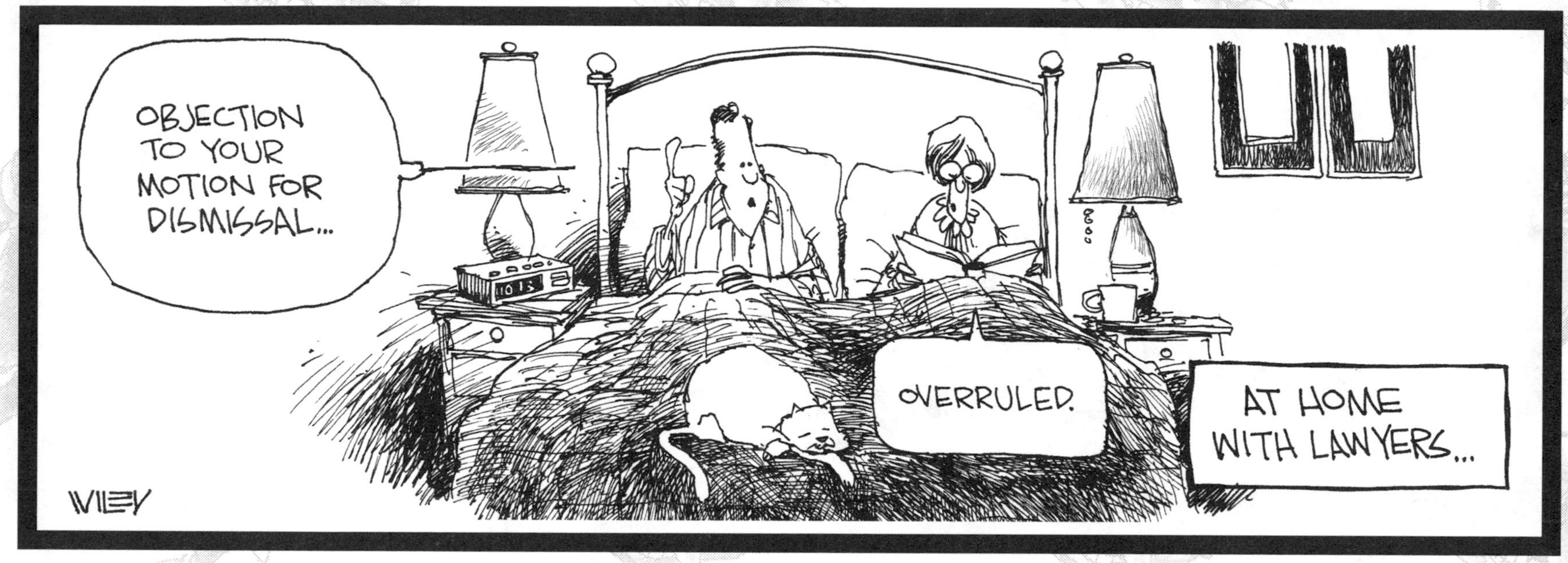
OBJECTION TO YOUR MOTION FOR DISMISSAL...
OVERRULED.
AT HOME WITH LAWYERS...
WILEY

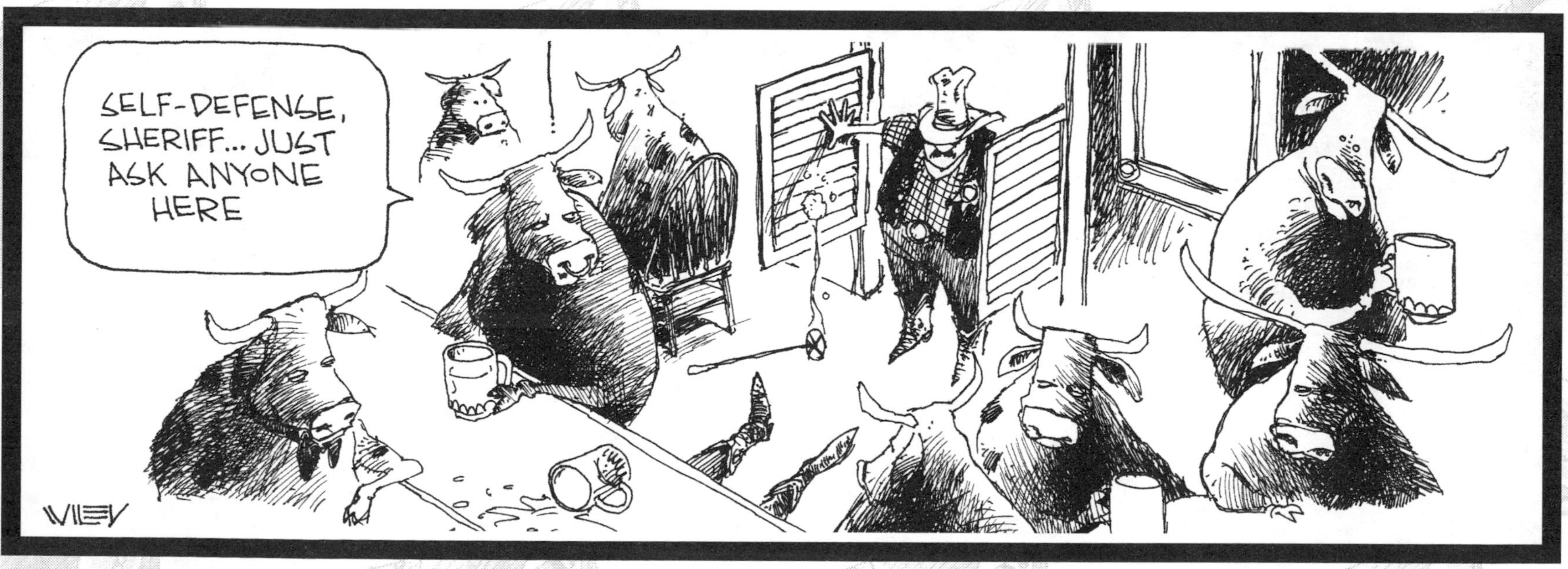
SELF-DEFENSE, SHERIFF... JUST ASK ANYONE HERE
WILEY

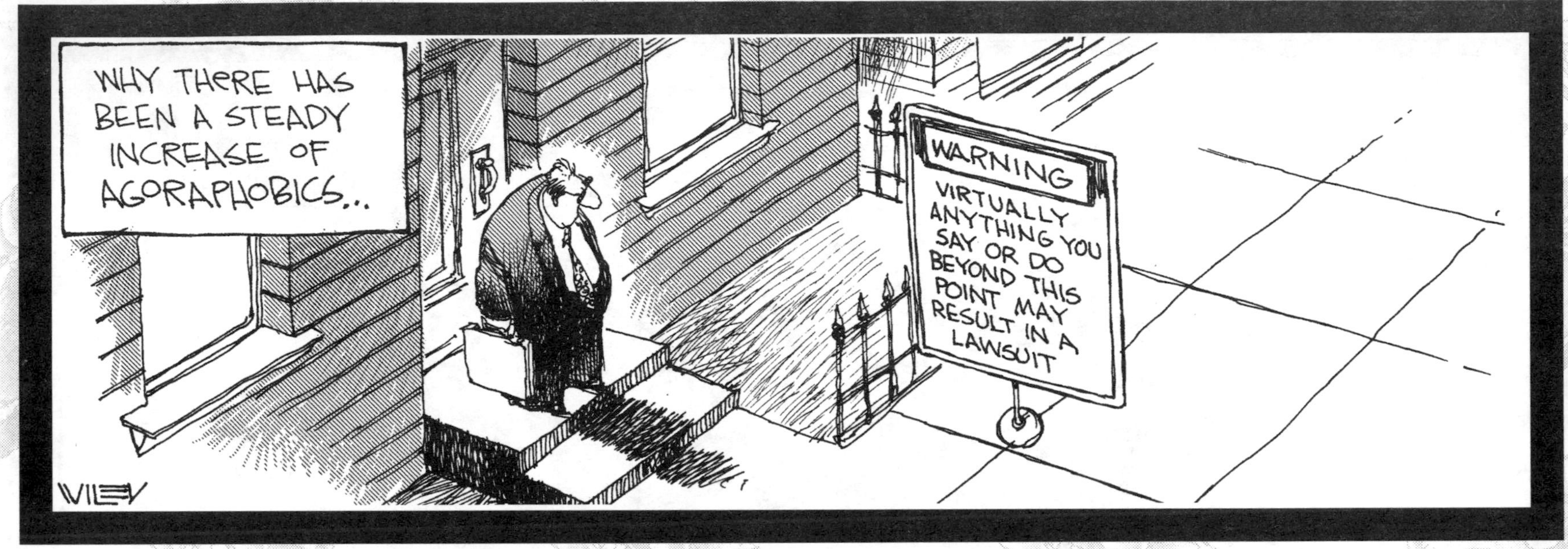
WHY THERE HAS BEEN A STEADY INCREASE OF AGORAPHOBICS...
WARNING
VIRTUALLY ANYTHING YOU SAY OR DO BEYOND THIS POINT MAY RESULT IN A LAWSUIT
WILEY

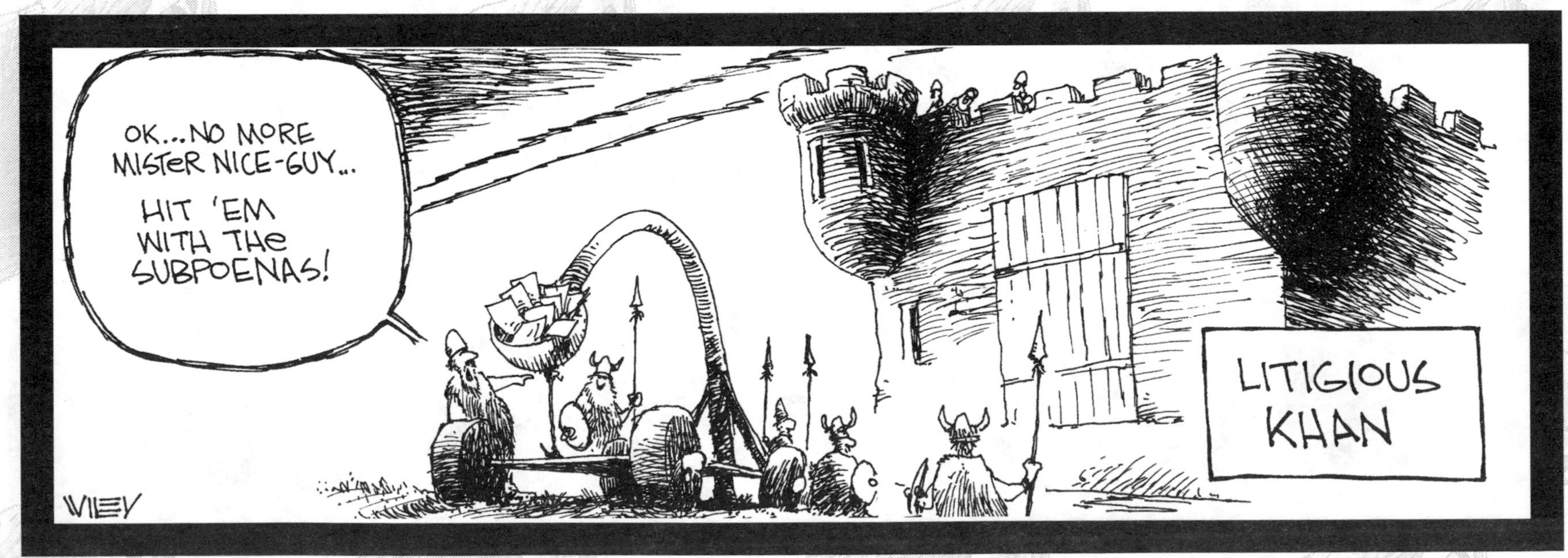
OK...NO MORE MISTER NICE-GUY...
HIT 'EM WITH THE SUBPOENAS!
LITIGIOUS KHAN
WILEY

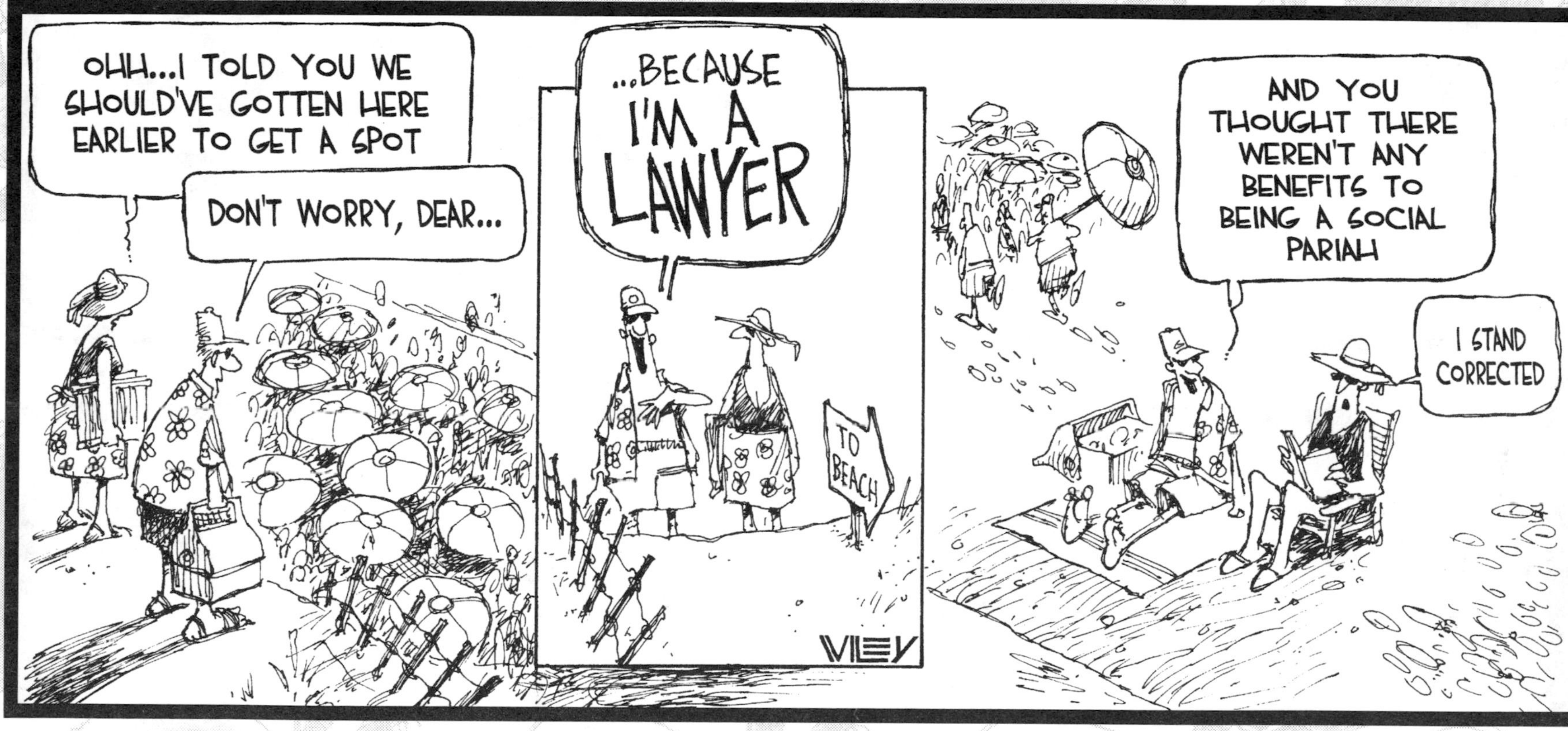
OHH...I TOLD YOU WE SHOULD'VE GOTTEN HERE EARLIER TO GET A SPOT
DON'T WORRY, DEAR...
...BECAUSE I'M A LAWYER
TO BEACH
AND YOU THOUGHT THERE WEREN'T ANY BENEFITS TO BEING A SOCIAL PARIAH
I STAND CORRECTED

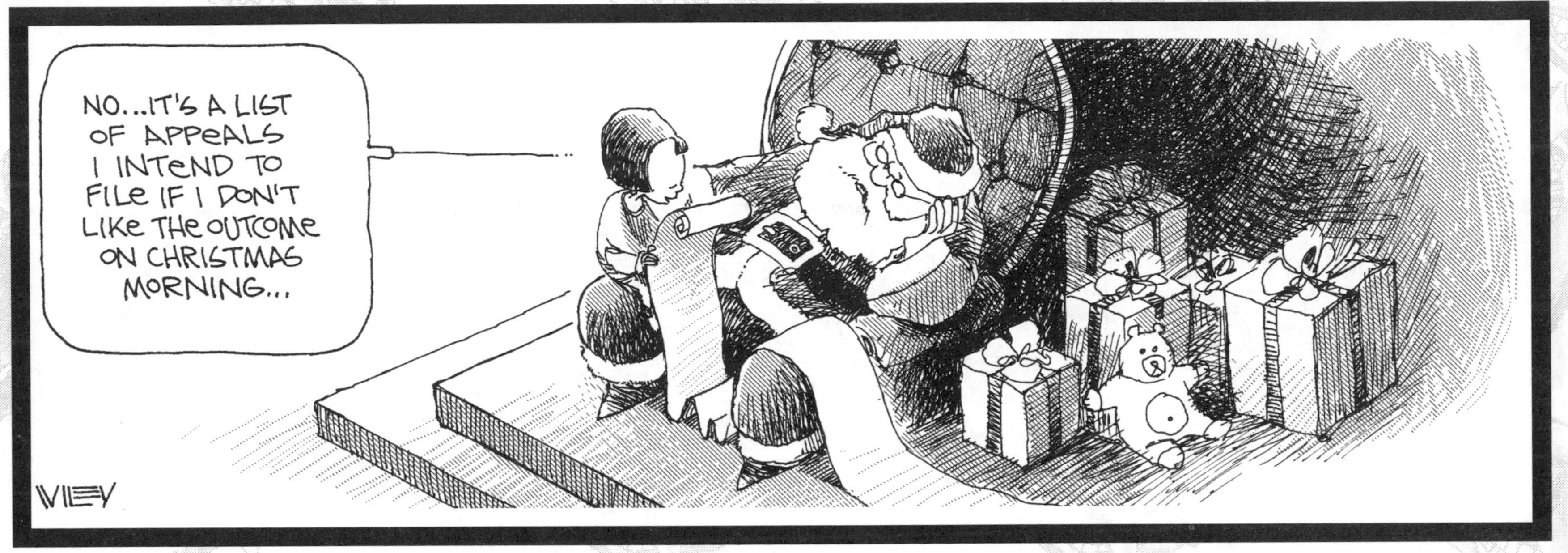
NO...IT'S A LIST OF APPEALS I INTEND TO FILE IF I DON'T LIKE THE OUTCOME ON CHRISTMAS MORNING...

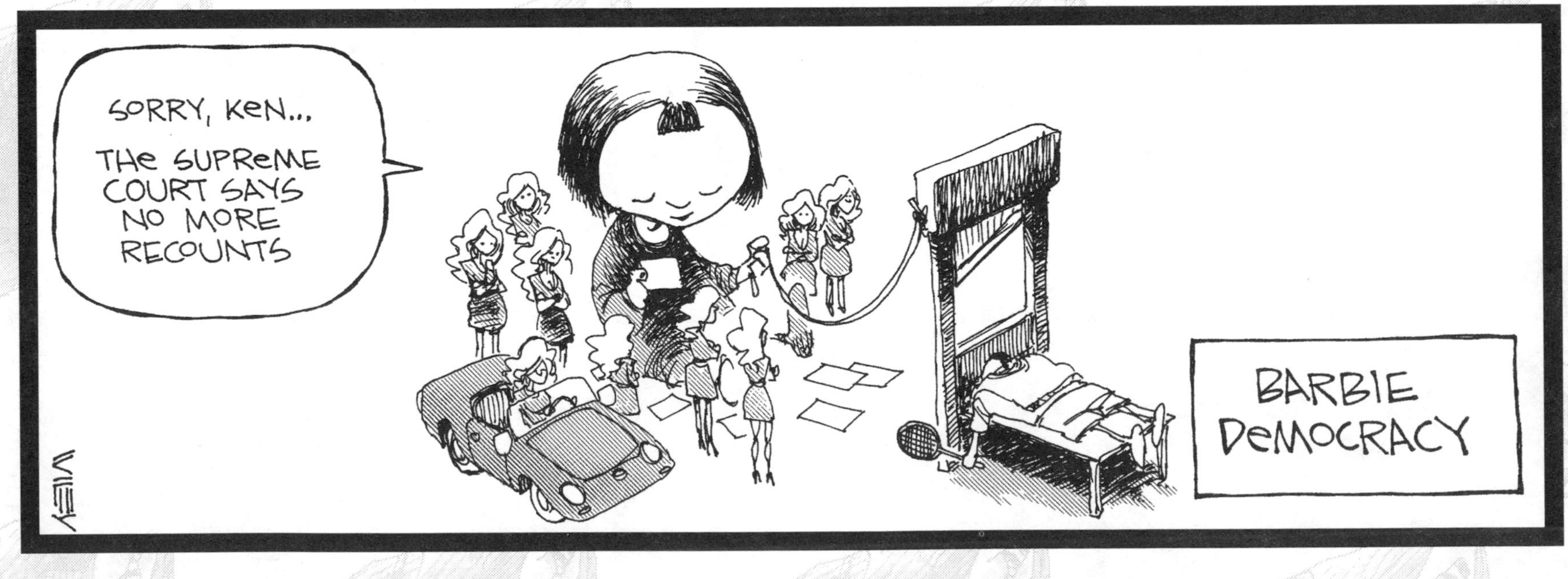
SORRY, KEN...
THE SUPREME COURT SAYS NO MORE RECOUNTS
BARBIE DEMOCRACY

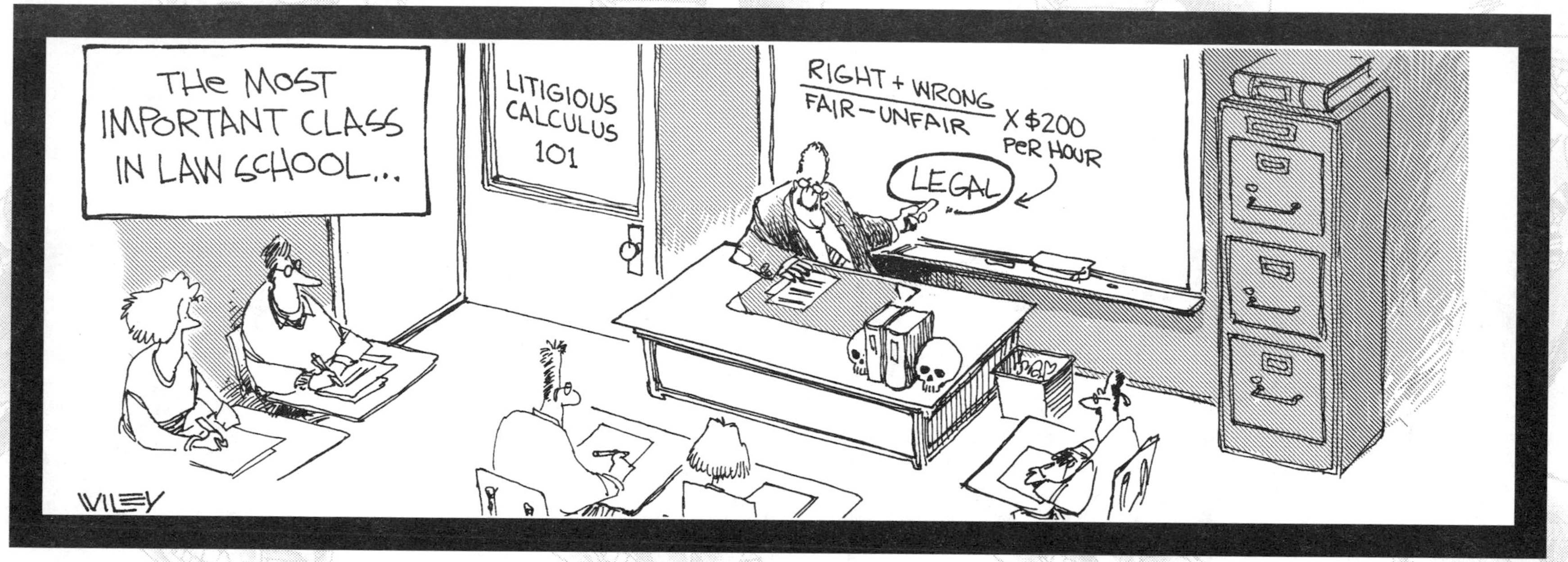
THE MOST IMPORTANT CLASS IN LAW SCHOOL...
LITIGIOUS CALCULUS 101
RIGHT + WRONG
FAIR – UNFAIR
X $200 PER HOUR
LEGAL
WILEY

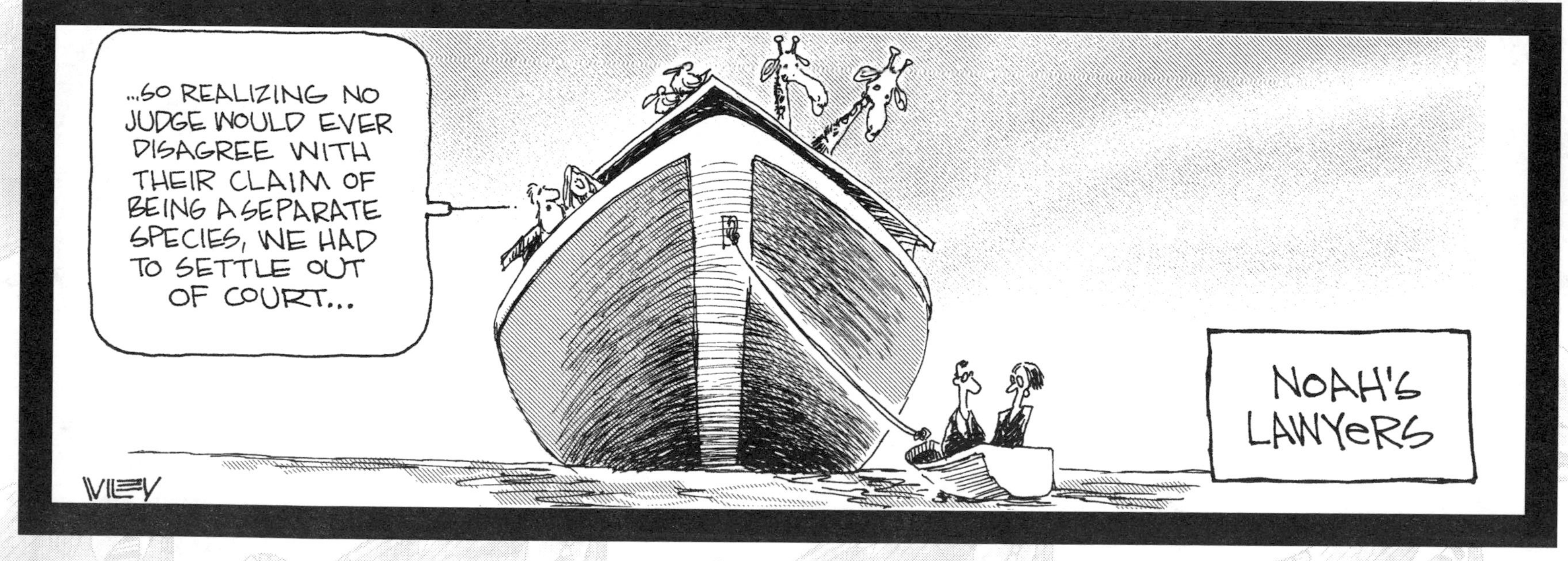
...SO REALIZING NO JUDGE WOULD EVER DISAGREE WITH THEIR CLAIM OF BEING A SEPARATE SPECIES, WE HAD TO SETTLE OUT OF COURT...
NOAH'S LAWYERS
WILEY

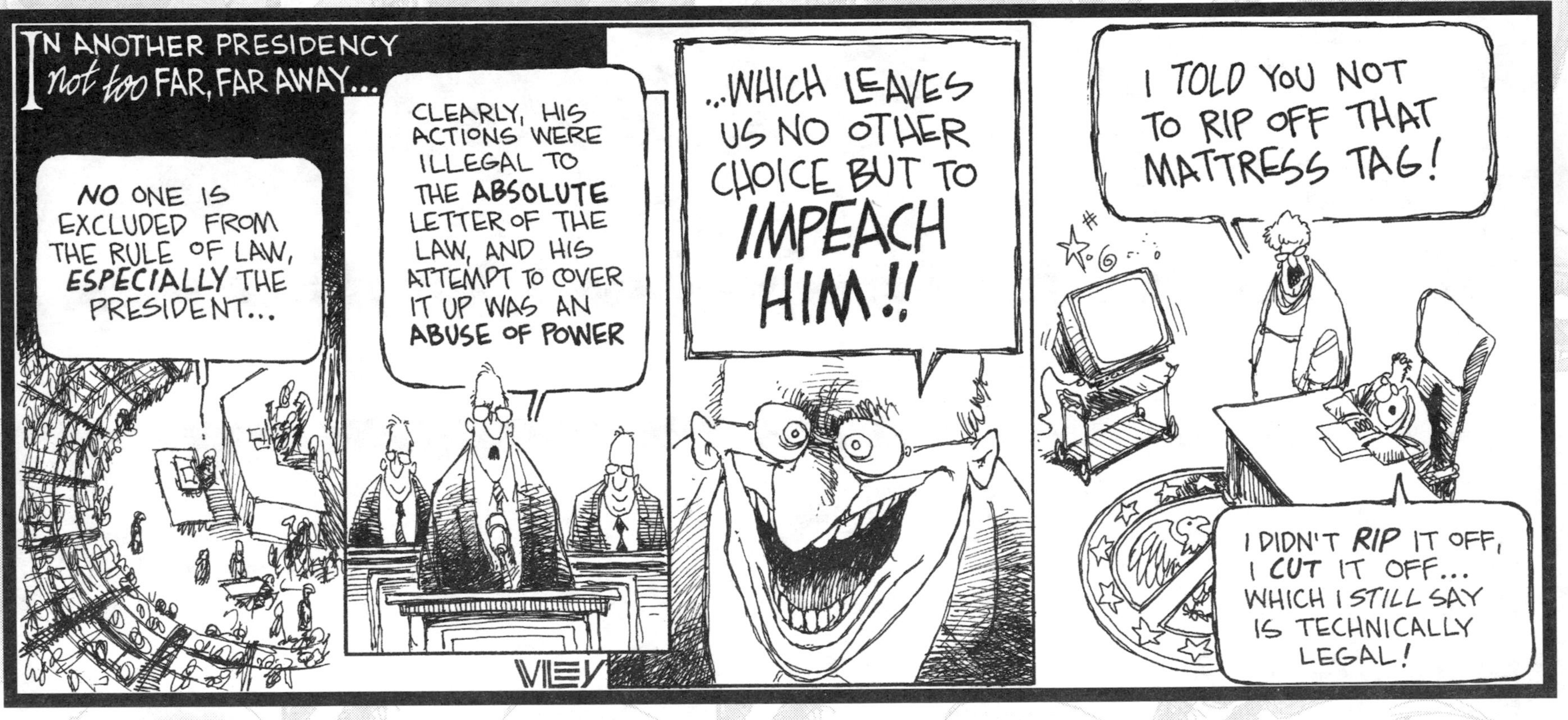
IN ANOTHER PRESIDENCY not too FAR, FAR AWAY...
NO ONE IS EXCLUDED FROM THE RULE OF LAW, ESPECIALLY THE PRESIDENT...
CLEARLY, HIS ACTIONS WERE ILLEGAL TO THE ABSOLUTE LETTER OF THE LAW, AND HIS ATTEMPT TO COVER IT UP WAS AN ABUSE OF POWER
...WHICH LEAVES US NO OTHER CHOICE BUT TO IMPEACH HIM!!
I TOLD YOU NOT TO RIP OFF THAT MATTRESS TAG!
I DIDN'T RIP IT OFF, I CUT IT OFF... WHICH I STILL SAY IS TECHNICALLY LEGAL!

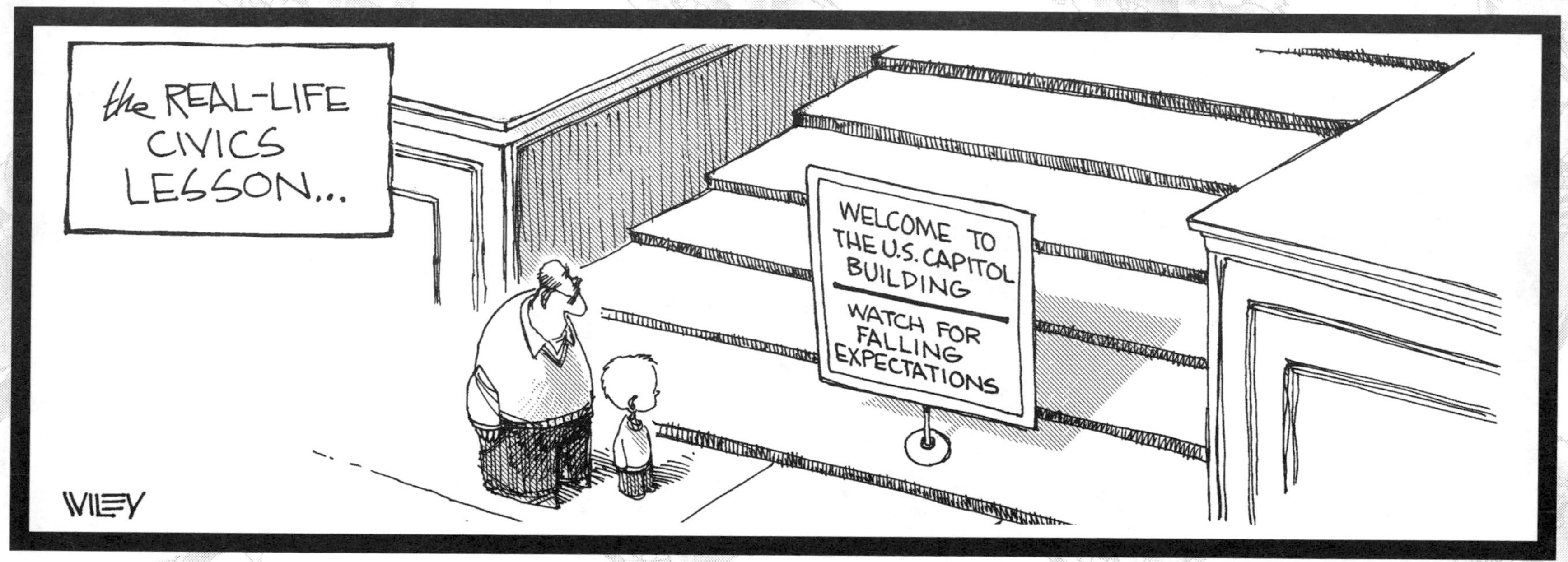
the REAL-LIFE CIVICS LESSON...
WELCOME TO THE U.S. CAPITOL BUILDING
WATCH FOR FALLING EXPECTATIONS
WILEY

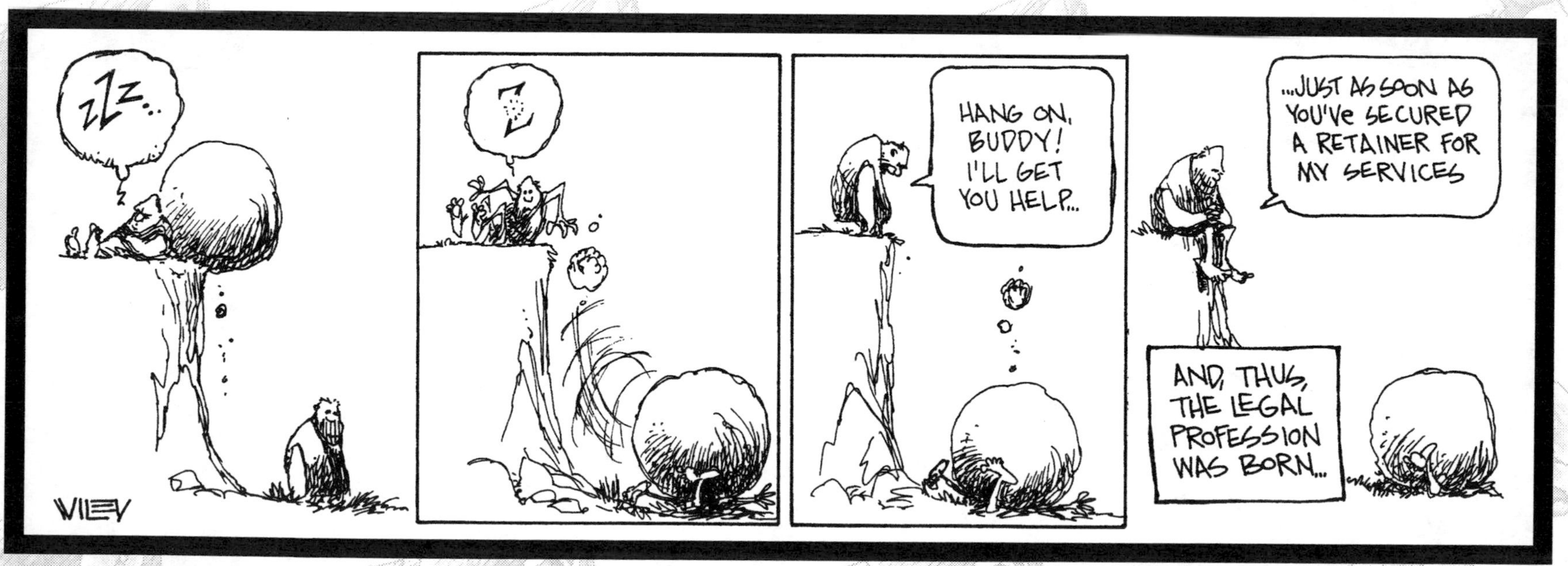
zZz...
Z
HANG ON, BUDDY! I'LL GET YOU HELP...
...JUST AS SOON AS YOU'VE SECURED A RETAINER FOR MY SERVICES
AND, THUS, THE LEGAL PROFESSION WAS BORN...
WILEY

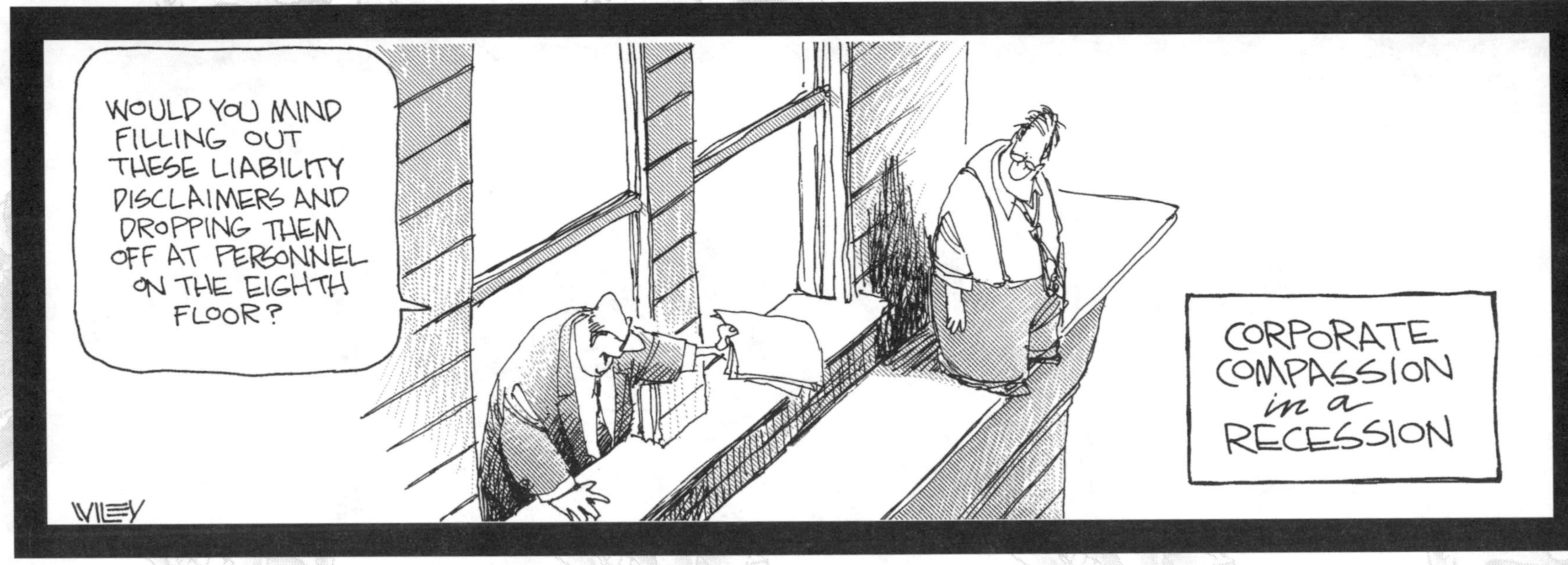
WOULD YOU MIND FILLING OUT THESE LIABILITY DISCLAIMERS AND DROPPING THEM OFF AT PERSONNEL ON THE EIGHTH FLOOR?
CORPORATE COMPASSION in a RECESSION
WILEY

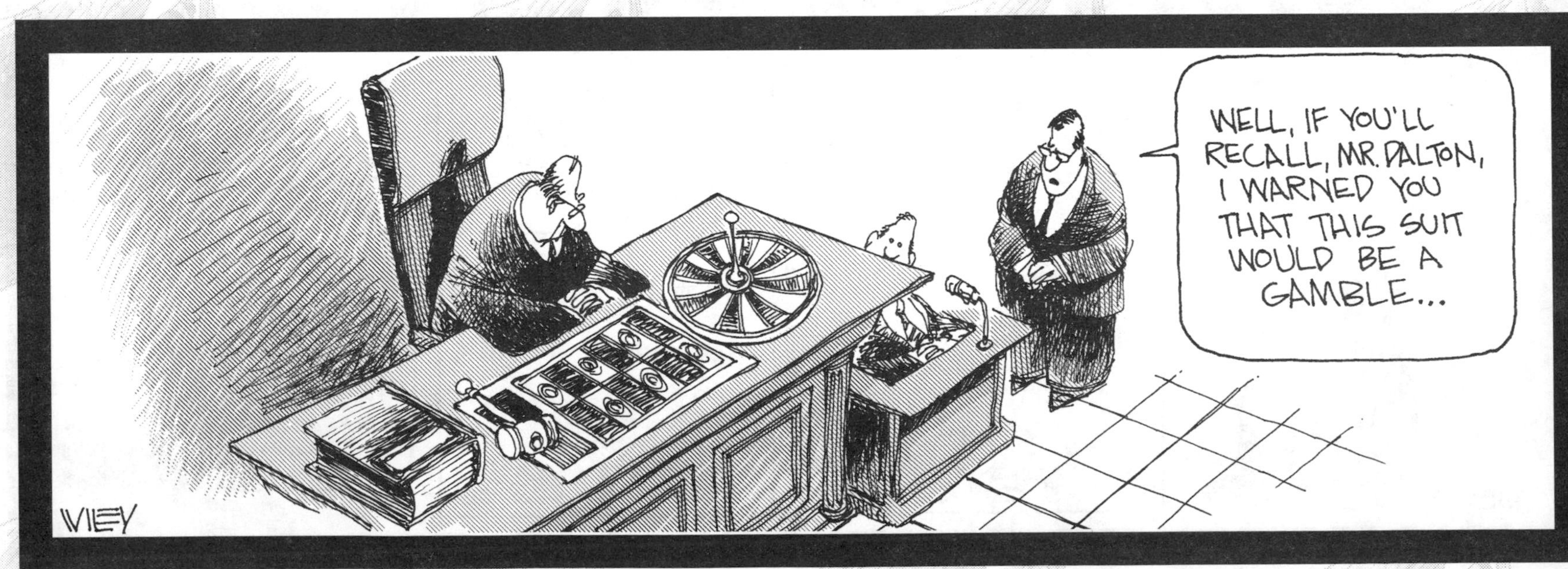
WELL, IF YOU'LL RECALL, MR. DALTON, I WARNED YOU THAT THIS SUIT WOULD BE A GAMBLE...
WILEY

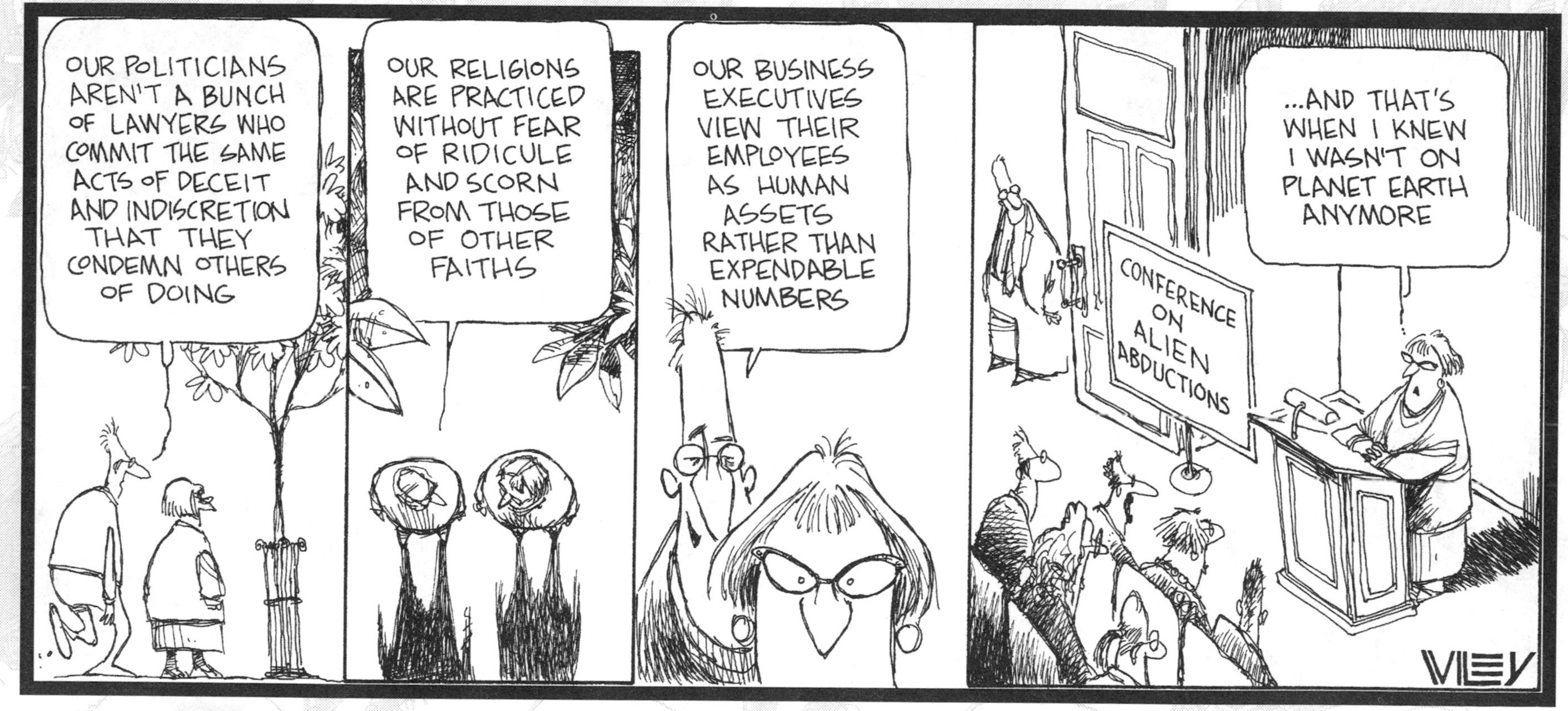
OUR POLITICIANS AREN'T A BUNCH OF LAWYERS WHO COMMIT THE SAME ACTS OF DECEIT AND INDISCRETION THAT THEY CONDEMN OTHERS OF DOING
OUR RELIGIONS ARE PRACTICED WITHOUT FEAR OF RIDICULE AND SCORN FROM THOSE OF OTHER FAITHS
OUR BUSINESS EXECUTIVES VIEW THEIR EMPLOYEES AS HUMAN ASSETS RATHER THAN EXPENDABLE NUMBERS
CONFERENCE ON ALIEN ABDUCTIONS
...AND THAT'S WHEN I KNEW I WASN'T ON PLANET EARTH ANYMORE
WILEY

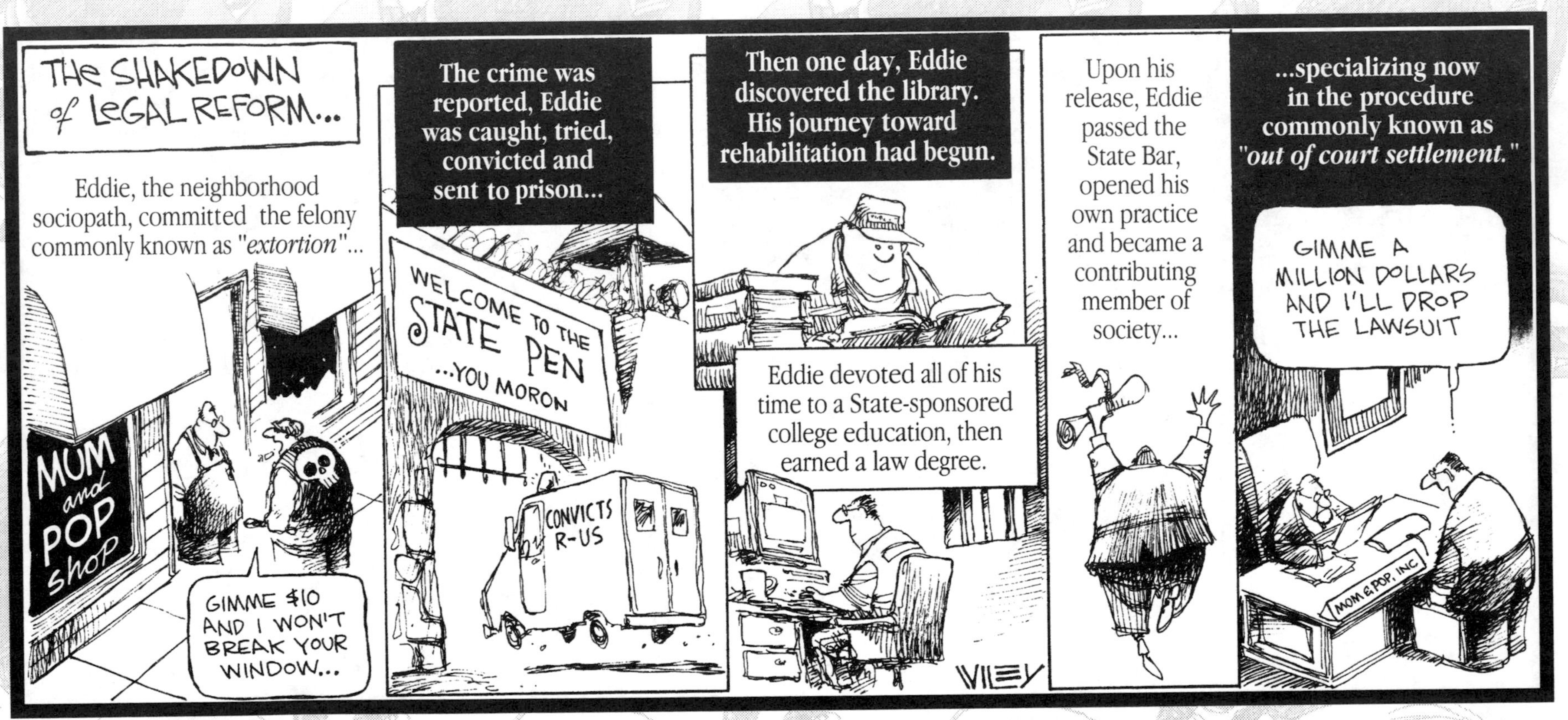

THE SHAKEDOWN of LEGAL REFORM...
Eddie, the neighborhood sociopath, committed the felony commonly known as "*extortion*"...
MUM and POP shop
GIMME $10 AND I WON'T BREAK YOUR WINDOW...
The crime was reported, Eddie was caught, tried, convicted and sent to prison...
WELCOME TO THE STATE PEN ...YOU MORON
CONVICTS R-US
Then one day, Eddie discovered the library. His journey toward rehabilitation had begun.
Eddie devoted all of his time to a State-sponsored college education, then earned a law degree.
WILEY
Upon his release, Eddie passed the State Bar, opened his own practice and became a contributing member of society...
...specializing now in the procedure commonly known as "*out of court settlement.*"
GIMME A MILLION DOLLARS AND I'LL DROP THE LAWSUIT
MOM & POP, INC.

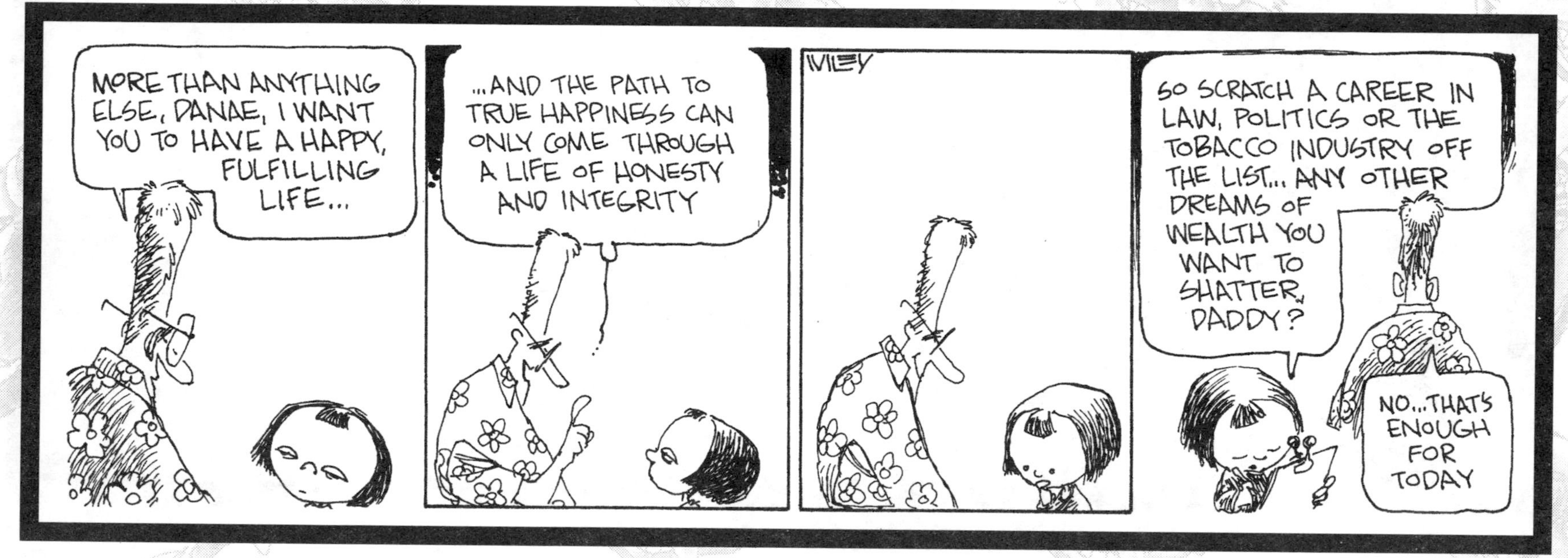
MORE THAN ANYTHING ELSE, DANAE, I WANT YOU TO HAVE A HAPPY, FULFILLING LIFE...
...AND THE PATH TO TRUE HAPPINESS CAN ONLY COME THROUGH A LIFE OF HONESTY AND INTEGRITY
WILEY
SO SCRATCH A CAREER IN LAW, POLITICS OR THE TOBACCO INDUSTRY OFF THE LIST... ANY OTHER DREAMS OF WEALTH YOU WANT TO SHATTER, DADDY?
NO...THAT'S ENOUGH FOR TODAY

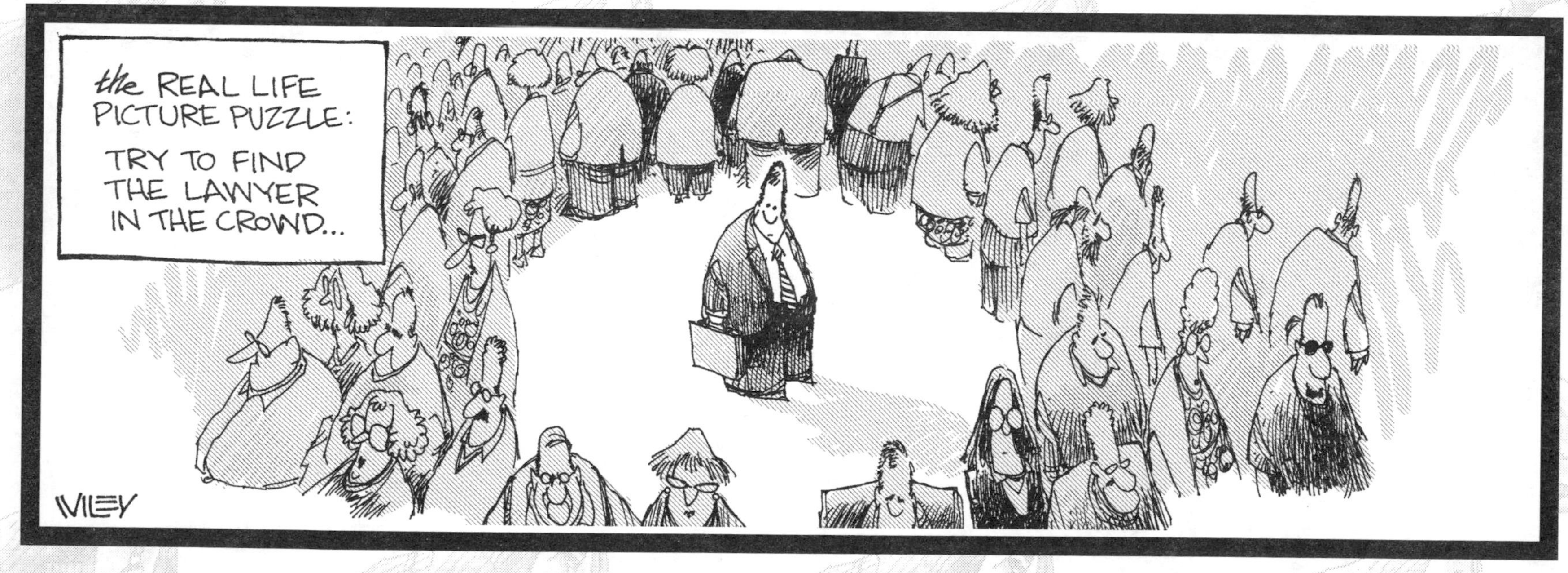
the REAL LIFE PICTURE PUZZLE:
TRY TO FIND THE LAWYER IN THE CROWD...
WILEY

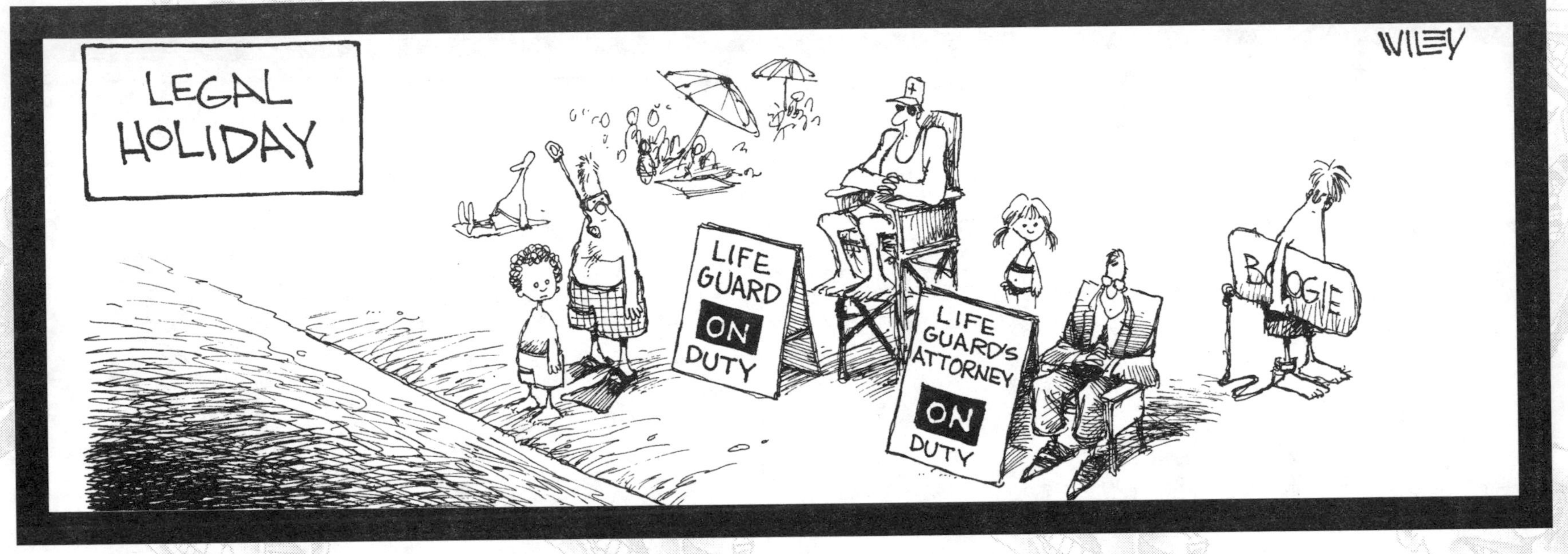
WILEY
LEGAL HOLIDAY
LIFE GUARD ON DUTY
LIFE GUARD'S ATTORNEY ON DUTY

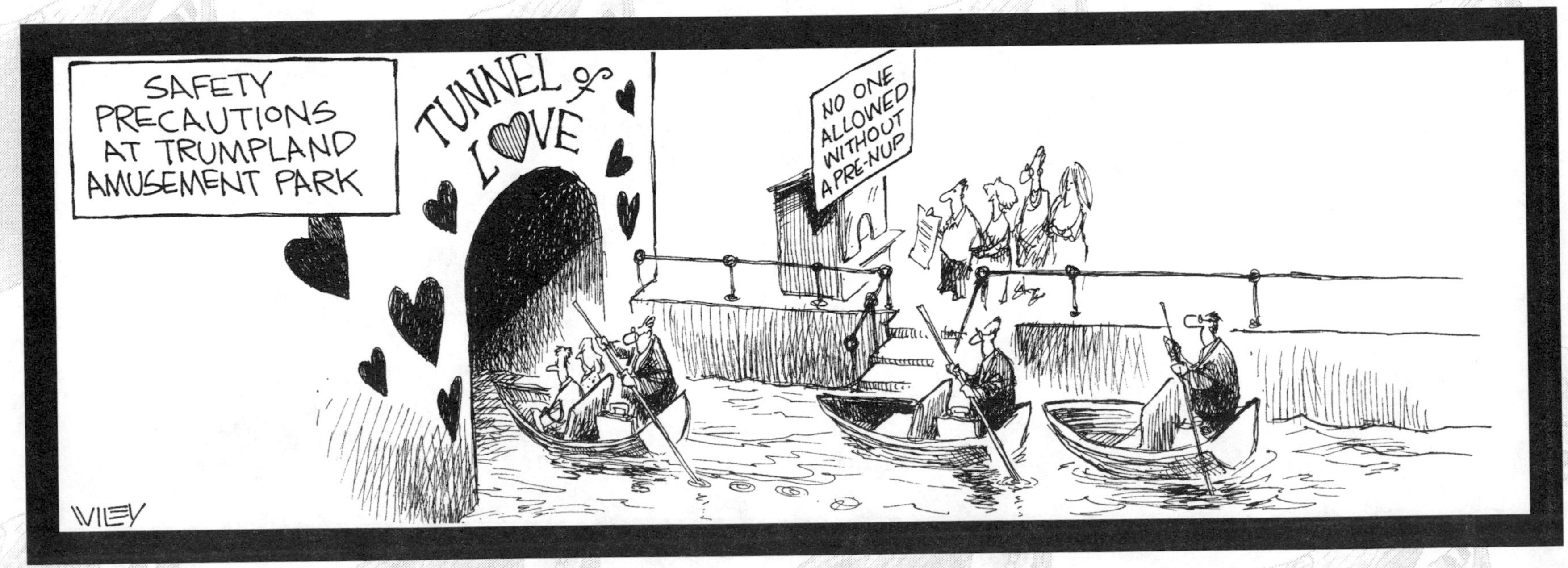
SAFETY PRECAUTIONS AT TRUMPLAND AMUSEMENT PARK
TUNNEL of LOVE
NO ONE ALLOWED WITHOUT A PRE-NUP
WILEY

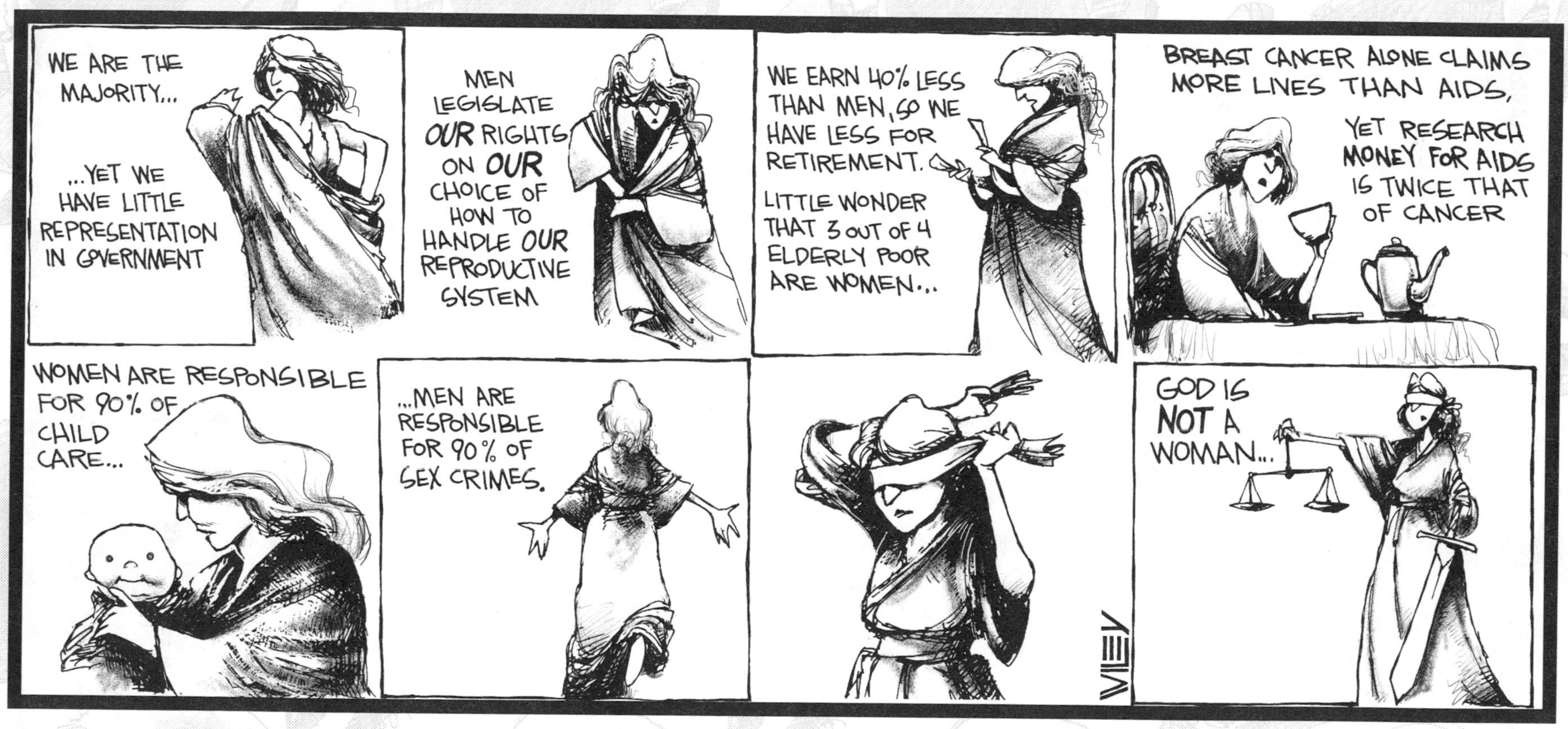
WE ARE THE MAJORITY...
...YET WE HAVE LITTLE REPRESENTATION IN GOVERNMENT
MEN LEGISLATE OUR RIGHTS ON OUR CHOICE OF HOW TO HANDLE OUR REPRODUCTIVE SYSTEM
WE EARN 40% LESS THAN MEN, SO WE HAVE LESS FOR RETIREMENT.
LITTLE WONDER THAT 3 OUT OF 4 ELDERLY POOR ARE WOMEN...
BREAST CANCER ALONE CLAIMS MORE LIVES THAN AIDS,
YET RESEARCH MONEY FOR AIDS IS TWICE THAT OF CANCER
WOMEN ARE RESPONSIBLE FOR 90% OF CHILD CARE...
...MEN ARE RESPONSIBLE FOR 90% OF SEX CRIMES.
VIEV
GOD IS NOT A WOMAN...

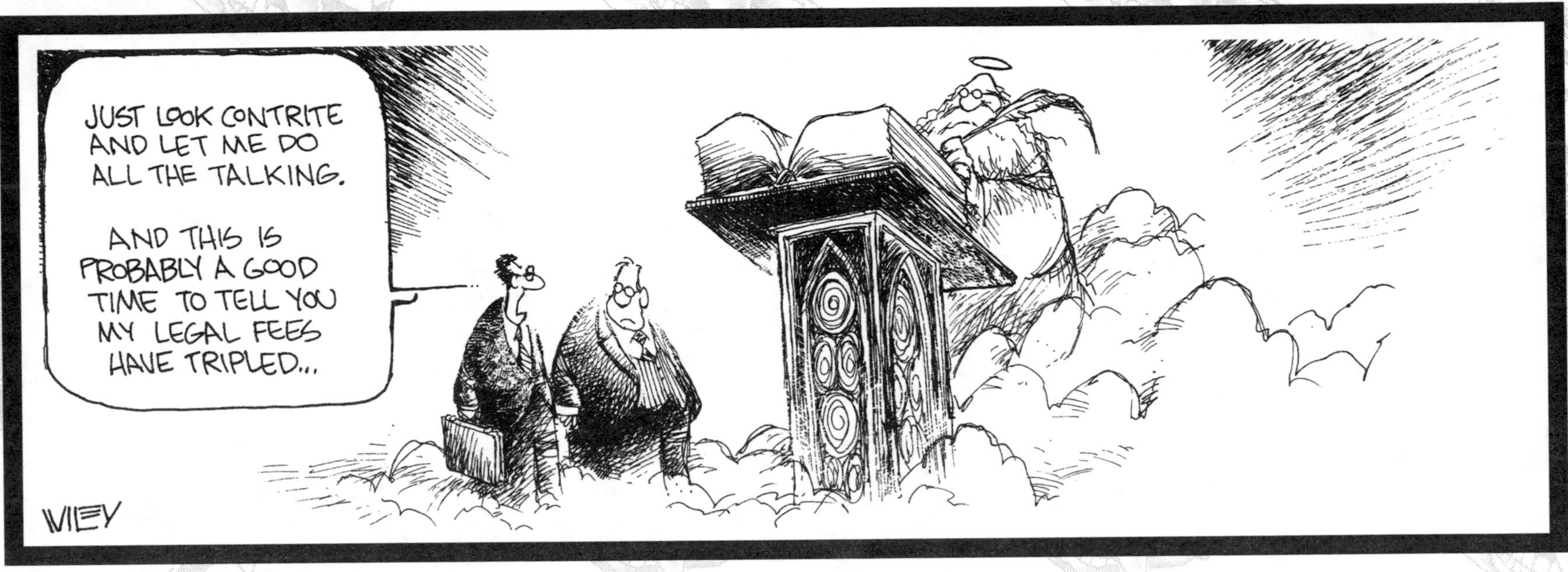
JUST LOOK CONTRITE AND LET ME DO ALL THE TALKING.
AND THIS IS PROBABLY A GOOD TIME TO TELL YOU MY LEGAL FEES HAVE TRIPLED...
WILEY

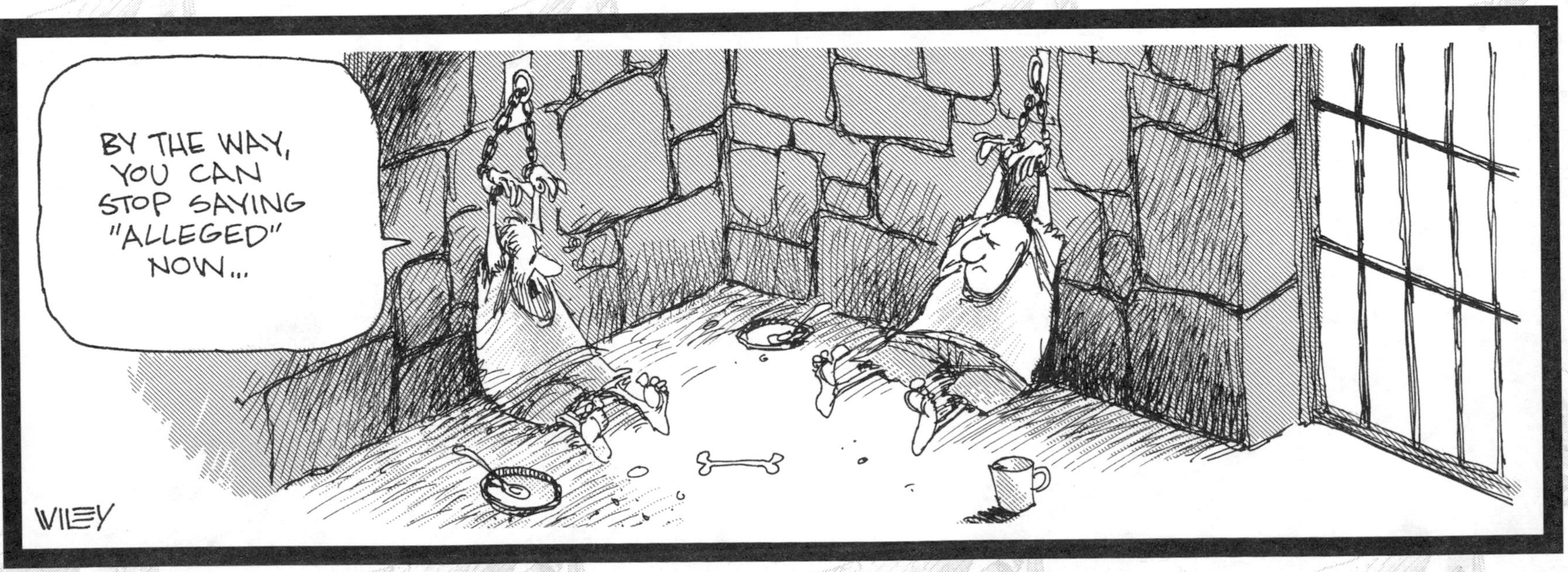
BY THE WAY, YOU CAN STOP SAYING "ALLEGED" NOW...
WILEY

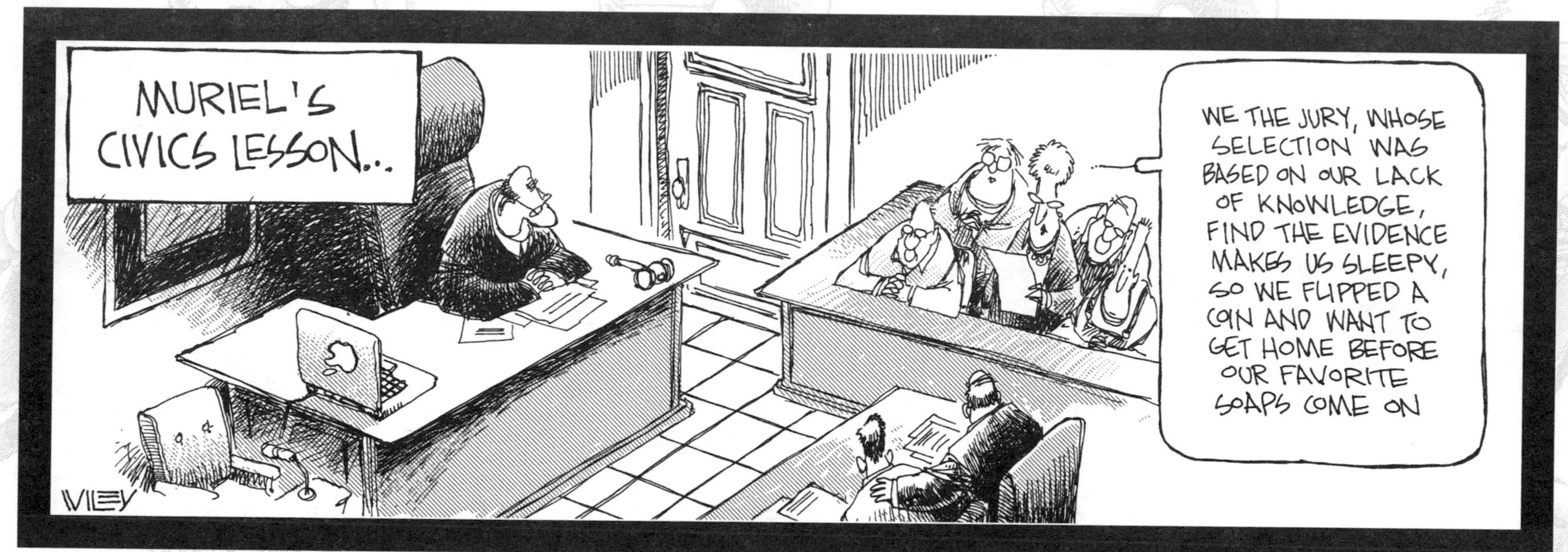
MURIEL'S CIVICS LESSON...
WE THE JURY, WHOSE SELECTION WAS BASED ON OUR LACK OF KNOWLEDGE, FIND THE EVIDENCE MAKES US SLEEPY, SO WE FLIPPED A COIN AND WANT TO GET HOME BEFORE OUR FAVORITE SOAPS COME ON
WILEY

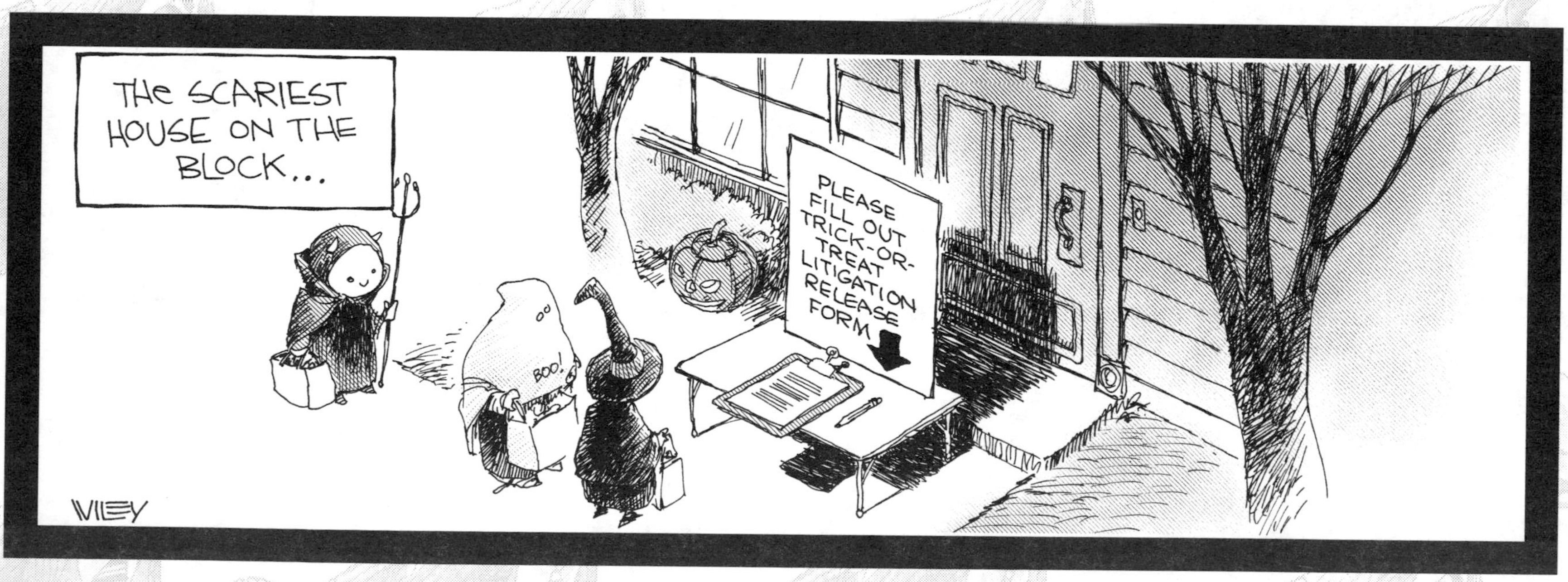
THE SCARIEST HOUSE ON THE BLOCK...
PLEASE FILL OUT TRICK-OR-TREAT LITIGATION RELEASE FORM
BOO!
WILEY

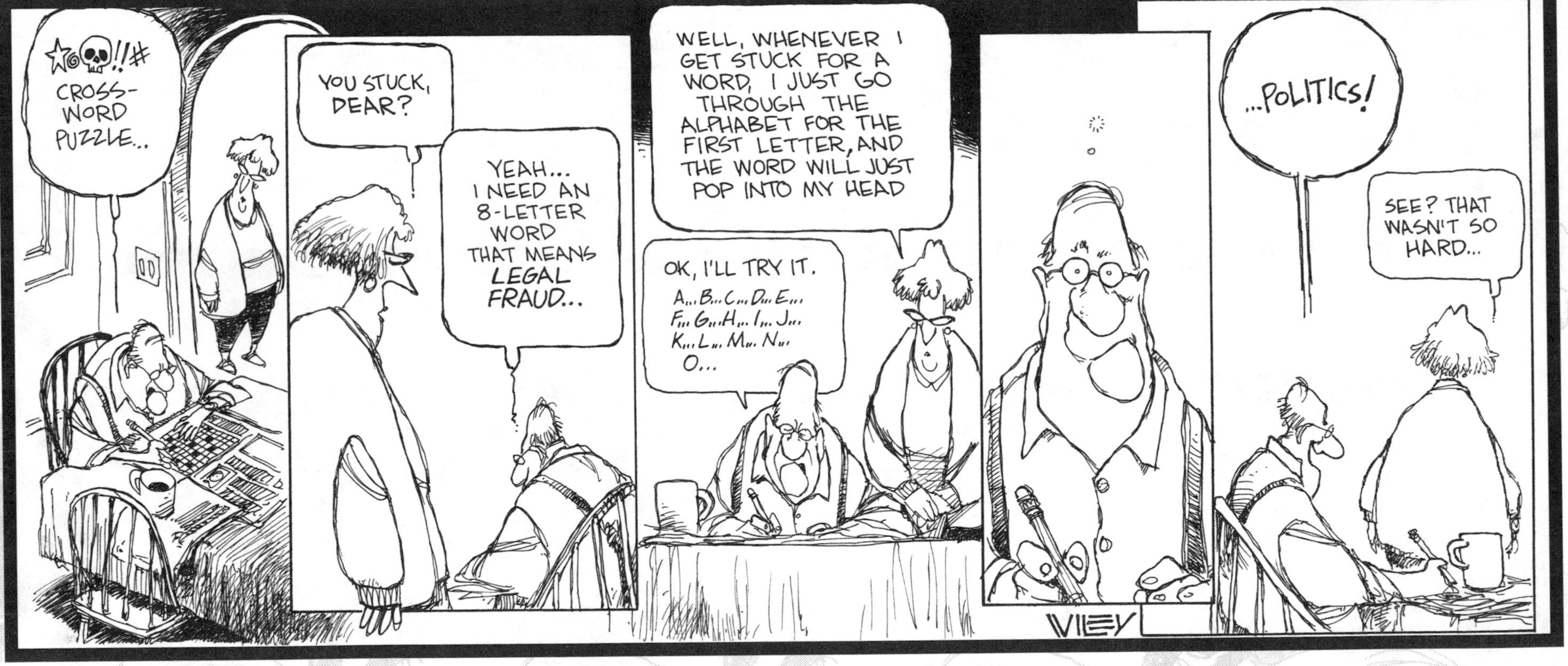
CROSS-WORD PUZZLE...
YOU STUCK, DEAR?
YEAH... I NEED AN 8-LETTER WORD THAT MEANS LEGAL FRAUD...
WELL, WHENEVER I GET STUCK FOR A WORD, I JUST GO THROUGH THE ALPHABET FOR THE FIRST LETTER, AND THE WORD WILL JUST POP INTO MY HEAD
OK, I'LL TRY IT.
A... B... C... D... E... F... G... H... I... J... K... L... M... N... O...
...POLITICS!
SEE? THAT WASN'T SO HARD...
WILEY